SURVIVAL!

DON ROUGEUX

authorHOUSE

AuthorHouse™
1663 Liberty Drive
Bloomington, IN 47403
www.authorhouse.com
Phone: 1 (800) 839-8640

Published by AuthorHouse 01/19/2018

ISBN: 978-1-5462-2113-5 (sc)
ISBN: 978-1-5462-2112-8 (e)

Introduction

In 1977 a number of circumstances led me to find and visit the village of 'Rougeux' in France, the original home of our family from ancient days. This discovery triggered the research and revelation of much of the story of their emigration to Frenchville, Pennsylvania that was compiled into the book titled 'The Long Journey' and still available on Amazon.

Subsequent work into their story revealed a great deal of interesting events many centuries before their decision to leave their homeland, and is, in effect, the story behind the story. This is what this book, 'Survival' is about.

More than two thousand years ago a tribe of invaders from the East decided to remain in a beautiful little fertile valley in the northeastern corner of France and form a settlement they named, in the Gaulic tongue, "Robiac." Gradually, after well over than a thousand years of numerous foreign conquers and languages, the name evolved into its current spelling: 'Rougeux'. The place they chose to establish themselves is known as the Valley of the Amance (River) in what is now known as the Champagne or Haute Marne region of Burgundy about 100 miles west of the Rhine River, 300 miles east of Paris and 40 miles north of Dijon.

In the process of researching the material for 'The Long Journey', I had the very great fortune to connect with a wonderfully cooperative professor living in Pierrefaites, one of the nearby villages of Rougeux. His name is Francois Joffrain. Our debt to him is immeasurable. He voluntarily found numerous invaluable ancient documents and the work of Abbots Mulson and Briffaut. Their work, as well as others, form the basis of this book.

In 'The Long Journey' were translated excerpts from an old book written in 17th century French by Abbot Mulson of Pierrefaites in 1898, titled 'History of the Valley of Pierrefaites'. James Rougeux (1929-2014), a French scholar and cousin, graciously translated this for me. At that time Francois had also sent me 125 pages of a book, written in 1891 by Abbot Briffaut, an earlier abbot at Pierrefaite, titled, 'History of the Valley of the Amance'. Much of Briffaut's work was based on ancient documents written in the archaic Old French, known as the 'langue d'oil,' an archaic language spoken in northern France from about the 8th to the 14th centuries. Jim and I found it impossible to translate the archaic because so many words were incomprehensible and not included in the most extensive French dictionaries available. And so I reluctantly put it on the shelf.

Fortunately, a few years later I met an old friend, John A. Sayers, whom I had not seen since his return from the WWII China Theater of Operations in 1946. John, a Frenchville native raised in a French-speaking family and a 30-year retired Marine Gunnery Sergeant with major battle experience on several islands including Iwo Jima, China Theater, Korean and Vietnam, listened closely to my tale about the 'The Long Journey' and the problem with translation of the Old French material. Immediately reaching to his bookshelf he removed an obviously old French dictionary previously acquired for fifty cents at a yard sale years before.

Leather bound and printed in 1801, it was fragile, somewhat tatttered, and its browned leaves contained numerous pressed flowers, some faded pencil notations and an initial datied 1842. John's gift remained on my bookshelf during years of procrastination until his death prompted me to tackle the translation of this 52,983 word monster. After six weeks of intense concentration the last page was finally reached. In the process I found approximately 75 words not even in this old dictionary but the meaning of about half of those, when fitted into the context, became possible to decipher.

History books are normally written about the activities and events surrounding kings and people of power, constituting less than five percent of the population. Unlike Abbot Mulson's book which focused on the genealogy of the ancient ruling classes, Abbot Briffaut's work focused on the remaining ninety-five percent—those who were slaughtered, starved, dislocated, enslaved, impoverished, and otherwise endured the burden of the foibles and mad decisions of those few aristocratats at the top.

This ancient material, likely the first translation from its archaic French, opens a tiny and unique window for us to see the local impact of the weather, national politics and numerous outside forces ruling the daily life of our ancestors through 1800 years of recorded history. This unique and contemporary documentation of life in those times preserves for us the brutalities and vicissitudes endlessly encountered by our forefathers who managed to survive in this beautiful but blood-soaked and constantly harassed little valley.

Abbot Briffaut's work awakens a sense of gratitude and thankfulness to our Creator who blessed our ancestors with ample fortitude and courage to make the painful decision to uproot from their homeland, never again to see or speak to friends and relatives. Determined to begin a new life for themselves and their descendants they plunged into a life-threatening expedition to an unknown and very primitive land.

FRANCOIS AND MARIE CLAIRE JOFFRAIN 2016
OWNED BY AUTHOR

The unintended but indispensable consequence of their eons of pain and travails have led to the monumental blessings that we, the beneficiaries living in this wonderful country called The United States of America, enjoy today.

I have followed the general structure and scheme of Abbot Briffaut's work, but have freely taken liberties when the wording just got too obscure or repetitious or even contrary to known facts in a couple of cases. A few references to events totally extraneous to the Valley of the Amance have been also been omitted. The entire history is thoroughly complicated by endless war, turmoil, plagues, misinformation, political and personal agendas of the many competing powers, and by Abbot Briffaut's assumption that the reader commonly knew of the characters involved and many of the long lost bits of common knowledge of the time.

In many cases I have introduced background information of characters or events. (All such information is in reduced font) Brevity of background research was necessary to maintain focus and to avoid the generally confusing and frequently far too complex nuances involved. Also, some of the information of Abbot Briffaut's history been combined or relocated so that a specific story line is more or less continuous rather than scattered in various disconnected chapters, therefore deviance from the structure of the old text is not too uncommon.

In the supplementary sections titled, **'Supplements from Abbot Mulson and others',** there are numerous other bits of information from Abbot Mulson and others, some very similar to Abbot Briffaut's and others with a different or expanded point of view.

The village of 'Rougeux' is used as the center of the universe and where notes indicate approximate miles and direction, it is referring to miles from Rougeux and the compass heading.

Numerous photos of some of the surrounding villages and Rougeux are included. An updated geanology of the Rougeux line from 1614 until approximately 1960 is appended including the family tree of those who remained in France and numerous others whose relationship not currently discovered.

It is not swift but it is fascinating reading.

Don Rougeux
10605 Stonebreaker Rd
Louisville, KY 40291
December 2017

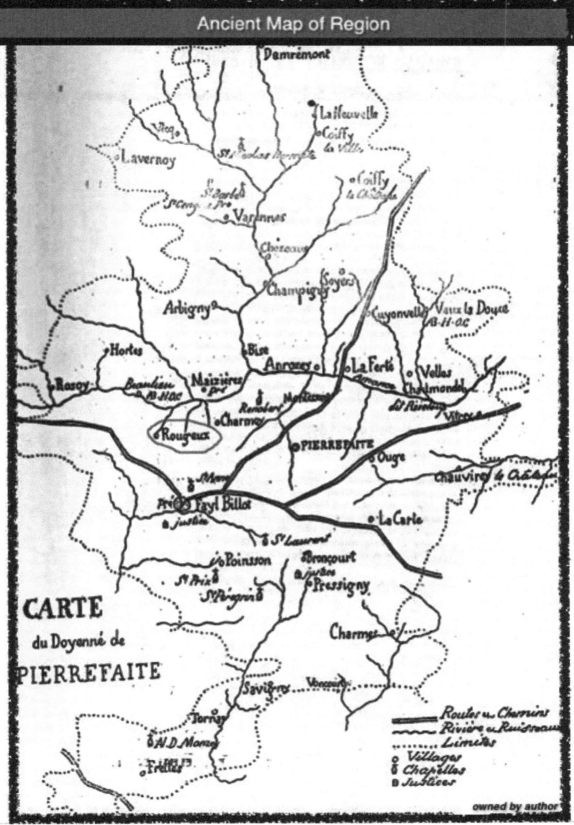

Ancient Map of Region

CARTE
du Doyenné de
PIERREFAITE

owned by author

3

dant des fondateurs du prieuré de Varennes, dont la garde lui avait été confiée, trouva mauvais que les religieux ne considérassent point sa protection comme suffisante. D'ailleurs il craignait de voir diminuer son autorité et son influence. Il réclama vivement près de l'évêque, du comte et même du roi. Vis-à-vis des moines, il n'épargna ni menaces ni promesses ; il leur abandonna même douze deniers qu'il levait sur chaque feu de Coiffy (1247). Les débats durèrent dix ans ; mais il ne put rien obtenir.

Usant de l'autorisation épiscopale, l'abbé Christophe céda, en son nom et en celui du couvent, au comte Thibaut, la moitié de tous les droits qu'il avait à Coiffy et à Vicq, en hommes, femmes, cens, terrages, forêts, etc., etc. [1].

3. Cet acte d'association, daté du mois de juillet 1250, « en donnant au comte de Champagne la garde du prieuré de Varennes et de ses dépendances, entraînait naturellement la construction d'un château pouvant protéger les religieux et au besoin être pour eux un refuge assuré. Aussi fut-il bientôt question d'une forteresse couronnant la montagne de Coiffy et dominant tout le pays aux environs. »

« Alors le mécontentement de Jean de Choiseul ne connut plus de bornes ; il déclara s'opposer formellement à l'exécution de ce projet [2]. » Il chercha des alliés pour faire la guerre au comte. Mais la mort de celui-ci (10 juillet 1253) arrêta les hostilités. Sa veuve, Marguerite, mère et tutrice du jeune Thibaut V, et Jean convinrent de soumettre leur contestation à l'arbitrage de Guy, évêque de Langres, et de Jean, comte de Bourgogne, seigneur de Salins. Il fut décidé d'un commun accord que les villages de Vicq et de Coiffy demeureraient à ladite reine, à son fils et à leurs héritiers, lesquels pourraient faire en ces lieux forteresse, qu'ils tiendraient de l'évêque [3].

1. Le texte de ce traité est imprimé dans l'Histoire de Vicq, et reproduit dans les Chasteau et citadelle de Coiffy, où nous avons puisé plusieurs des documents de ce chapitre.

2. Les Chasteau et citadelle de Coiffy, p. 83.

3. Vicq a-t-il été fortifié, soit aux temps gallo-romains, soit sous les comtes de Champagne ? L'histoire ne nous l'apprend pas. Mais l'auteur des Chasteau et citadelle de Coiffy a commis une erreur en disant, p. 21, que la montagne de Coiffy était appelée, à l'époque romaine, Regalis ou regius mons, et qu'on en a la preuve dans le registre des hommages faits à Thibaut V de 1256-1270, sous le n° 612, où on lit : Feoda regalis montis vel Cufei quod idem est (Hist. des comtes de Champagne, par d'Arbois de Jubainville), puis à la table, placée à la fin du registre (n° 707), Regalis mons. — Il s'agit de la montagne de Vicq, maintenant couverte de bois, nommée vulgairement Régemont, et, par corruption, Rougemont.

CHAPTER I
PREHISTORIC

TOPOGRAPHY

The Upper Marne region is traversed from NorthEast to SouthWest by a chain of mountains that rise repeatedly but gently and have many naturally running streams of water. It is called the Plateau of Langres.

Beginning at the Vosges Mountains, the Plateau passes at Fresnoy, Sauylxures, Ranconnieres, Orbigny-au-Mont, Montlandon, Saint-Vallier, Noidant-Chalenoy, Bourg, Perrogney, Aujeures, Vaillant, Lamargelle, and penetrates into the Cote-d'Or.

At the bottom edges of that long line of mountains (The Vosges) are prolonged promontories of foothills of various distances.

In the districts that we are going to describe to you, the altitude varies generally from 1000 to 1300 feet. Close to Coiffy-le-Haut (11 miles N), the height rises to 1300 feet; at the SouthWest of Damremont, 1400 feet; and between the village and woods of Trou-aux-Chals, 1500 feet, the highest elevation.

The plateau of Langres sends water in three directions: North to the ocean via the Meuse; to the Manche (English Channel) via the Marne and the Aube; and to the Mediterranean via a number of rivers, all tributaries of the Saone. The principal rivers are the Apance, the Amance, the Saolou and the Vigeanne. The one whose path crosses the district of Pierrefaites Eastward is the Amance.

The Amance gathers a great number of wild and tumbling streams and passes through these villages: on the right side of the map, Ranconnieres, Andilly, Plesnoy, Celsoy, Chaudenay, Rougeux, Charmoy Pierrefaites; and on the left (and North side), Damremont, Laneuvelle, Coiffy, Soyers, Guyonvelle, Vaux-la-Douce. Flowing down somewhat to the South, the Amance swings to the East. After having crossed Vicq (12 miles N) it passes the hill of Chezeaux, (7 miles NE) Champigny, Bize, Anrosey, Pissseloup (9 miles E), and exits the department and drains into the Saone at Jussey (19 miles E) It waters the beautiful prairies and forms a fertile valley.

The hills are covered with vines and belts of forests. One reason for the narrowness of the river bed is that it is subject to flooding that is far from being dangerous to the end of autumn and during the winter but quite dangerous to the harvests of April to September 1.

Other than the Amance and its effluents, we have the Ougeotte, who gets its name from Ouge 2. It flows near Chauviery at the Soane; the Rigotte, that comes near La Rochelle, leading to Charmes but sinks underneath Houzette, and Farincourt. Though its source is at Pressigny, the Vannon loses itself into a hole at Tornay (9 miles S) These two streams, after a course underground for many kilometers, manage to resurface at Fouvent (Fons Vennae)(13 miles S); finally close to Fayl (2 miles S), and gushes up close to the farm of Louvieres. They water Fayl-Billot, Bussieres, Belmont, then join the River Saolon 3.

Narrow to the East past the diocese of Besancon, (60 miles SE) to the North by the deanery of Is; to the West opposite Moge (25 miles W); to the South past Fouvent, (18 miles S) our territory has been formed into an irregular oval. To the North and to the South it extends from the Damremont to Frettes; to the East and West it goes from Rosey to Bentecourt. Its surface is thirty-seven to thirty-eight thousand hectares. It comprises parts of the cantons of Varennes,-- Fayl-Billot, La Frete, Bourbonne, and Vitrey. One can count forty centers of population--thirty-four can be appropriated to Haute-Marne. Here are their names in alphabetical order: Anrosey, Arbigny, Beaulieu, Broncourt, Bize, Champigny-sous-Varennes, Charmoy, Chezeaux, Coiffy-le-Bas, Coiffy-le-Haut, Damremont, Fayl-Billot, Frettes, Guyonvelle, Hortes, La Ferte, Laneuvelle, Lavernoy, Maizieres, Montesson, Pierrefaites, Rosoy, Rougeux, Savigny, Soyers, Tornay, Varnness, Vaux-La-Douce, Velles, Vicq, and Voncourt. The six others that complete the list of Haute-Saone are: Bentcourt, Charmes-Saint-Valbert, Chauviery-le-Chatel, La Quarte, Ouge, and Vitrey.

1. Hippolyte Chauchard was the dredger of the Amance. The dredging was done in 1858, 1868, at a cost of 170,892 fr. The State supplied a grant of 36,000 fr. The balance was divided among the interested communities with the money to pay their share for their properties who bordered the river.

2. The Celtic; Oug, stream, according to Ch. Longchamp.

3. The Saolon is called Saulon in the Haute-Marne; the Salon, in the Haute-Saone. It's regrettable; but we can believe its the same river.

Supplements from Abbot Mulson and others

The history of France dates back many thousands of years with evidence that Homo sapiens lived there around 40,000 BC

Toward 1,000 BC the Celts arrived from the East, bringing druids, warriors and craftsmen to share the land with the inhabitants. The area included the lands later known as Belgium and Switzerland.

At that time, the language used was Celtic, related to modern Breton, Gaelic or Welsh.

The country now known as France was first known as Gaul, (or Gallia), a territory conquered in 51 BC by Julius Caesar in the Gallic Wars.

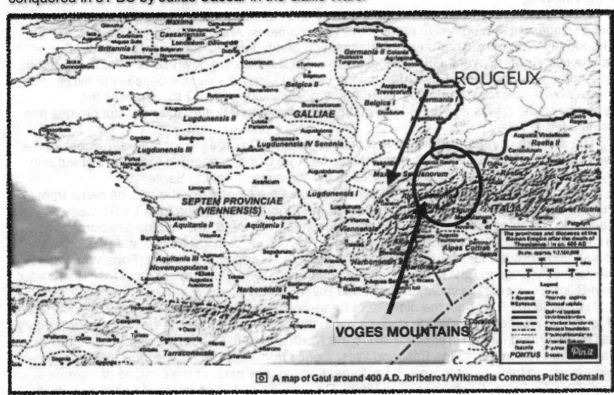

A map of Gaul around 400 A.D. Jbribeiro1/Wikimedia Commons Public Domain

"Throughout Gaul" Cæsar stated, *"there are only two classes of men who are of any real consequence - Druids and the baronage. The ordinary people count as nothing and are considered almost as slaves."*

The ancient inhabitants, unlike the Sumerians and other ancient cultures, never developed the art of writing.

Little is known of their history or culture during those early centuries. The Romans give us the first written, but sparse, description of their first contacts with those Celtic tribes. They gave the name Gaul to the vast region to the North, encompassing France, Belgium, Austria, Germany, and the Baltic countries. Run-ins with the Celts along their frontier gave the Romans cause for concern.

The first migration into the region of Rougeux, made by the Gadhelic Branch of the Celtic tribes, probably occurred before 500 BC. These Celtic people migrated from lands to the East and North beyond the Rhine (about 100 miles E) and Moselle Rivers. Seeming to confirm this migration date were discoveries of Gaulic graves in the region which contained large bronze beaked flagons of Etruscan manufacture during the period 550 BC to 450 BC, and later imitated by Gaulic craftsmen. Also found in the region of Rougeux were large Etruscan wine jars, and Athenian black and red-figured cups from that period of time. (The Etruscan civilization is the name given to the culture and way of life of a people of ancient Italy whom ancient Romans called *Etrusci* or *Tusci*. Distinguished by its own language, the civilization endured from an unknown prehistoric time prior to the foundation of Rome until its complete assimilation to Ancient Rome)

Survival of these early tribes depended on the presence of game and domesticated animals. It is not thought they were agrarian at the time of their migration but rather, supplemented their diet with wild fruits and leaves.

During this time, parts of these tribes also migrated into Ireland, Scotland, England and into Turkey and the Middle East, possibly giving Galatia its name. We see from the Epistle of St. Paul to the Galatians (Ch.3 v.1) '…that the foolish Galatians, who were so easily bewitched,…' were like the whole of the Gaulic race.

Frequent references in ancient literature, as well as Cæsar and Hirtius, who wrote the eighth book of Cæsar's 'Conquest of Gaul' have portrayed them as fickle, enthusiastic, impulsive, loving change, prone to panic, and fond of glory, while at the same time lively, witty, eloquent, full of good sense and good feeling. Cæsar was not the first ancient author to write about the Gallic temperament. Like his younger contemporaries, the geographer Strabo and the historian Diodorous Siculus, Cæsar drew some of his information about the ethology and habits about the Gauls from the 'Histories of Posidonius,' written in the first half of the first century BC. This history states, *"The Gauls are madly keen about war, brave, and easily outwitted. Because of their frankness and straightforwardness, their sympathies are easily roused to war in support of friends who think themselves wronged"*.

In 390 BC Gallic tribes (Sequanii, Senones, Arverni, Aedui and others) from the region described above, had penetrated into the Roman Empire and had actually sacked Rome and the Northern parts of Italy. They were still receiving payments in Cæsar's time, 300 years later. Another bad scare for the Romans came at the end of the 2nd century, which only ended after additional appeasement was made. These events coupled with the much greater physical size, scorn for comfort, and primitive savagery, (for example, in the case of a call-up for war, the last man to report to duty was tortured and dismembered in front of his comrades) greatly concerned the Romans for centuries.

Greek records of about 600 BC indicate that exports to Gaul up the Rhone Valley were reciprocated by imports of cattle, gold, silver, iron, together with hides, slaves, and hunting dogs. Over time, this contact and commerce with Mediterranean civilizations, in particular the Greeks and Romans, began to mitigate the savage nature of Gallic culture.

The lands of the Treveri, (a Celtic tribe who lived in the vast region NorthEast of Rougeux); the Sequanii, the tribe who lived to the SouthEast between the Soane and Doube Rivers (the tribe to whom our ancestors probably belonged); the Helveti, (the powerful tribe directly South beyond the Doube);

and the Lingon, were all situated between Langres (about 16 miles W of Rougeux) and Dijon (40 miles S)

Facing these lands from the East were the Vosges Mountains in the NorthEast and the Rhine River and the Jura Mountains directly to the East and Southeast. Since ancient times, these mountain ranges have formed a natural frontier and crossroad from the North and East. These same crossroads were the scenes of many battles and territorial disputes between Germanic, Celtic, and numerous smaller tribes. In his book, Cæsar mentions 96 tribes living in Gaul with whom he contested and eventually vanquished during his war.

Cæsar tells us these tribes were already evolving out of the old tribal kingship system into a primitive type of government similar to the Romans, in that the leaders were subject to recall by a governing council. Treaties and promises of friendship already existed between many of the tribes. However, Cæsar reports that these governments were far from stable, and ambitious leaders continually schemed to usurp the council. Many of the larger villages were encompassed by walls made of a combination of dirt and logs and were connected by good roads and bridges.

Even though a form of the Celtic language was still spoken in the 6th century, the Germanic and Latin languages made substantial inroads and gradually developed into what became known as the Romance language. The name of such cities as Paris, Reims, Dijon, and Burgundy are patronymic but few other Celtic words remain in the French language.

German continued to be spoken, more or less, at lEast until sometime beyond the year 812 when the Council of Tours decreed that every priest be able to preach in both the Romance and Teutonic languages.

In the 6th century BC the former Gaul continued to be divided in three parts, as Caesar had described in his book: Gallia Celtica, Belgica and Aquitania. Archaeologically, the Gauls were bearers of the La Tène culture, (La Tène is the term archaeologists use for the later period of the culture and art of the ancient Celts) which extended across all of Gaul, as well as East to Raetia, Noricum, Pannonia and SouthWestern Germania during the 5th to 1st centuries BC.

During the 2nd and 1st centuries BC, Gaul fell under Roman rule: Gallia Cisalpina was conquered in 203 BC and Gallia Narbonensis in 123 BC. Gaul was invaded by the Cimbri and the Teutons after 120 BC, who were in turn defeated by the Romans by 103 BC. Julius Caesar finally subdued the remaining parts of Gaul in his campaigns of 58 to 51 BC. The Franks had been in occupation of most of the territory.

A Visigothic kingdom was later established in the SouthWest region that would become Aquitaine. And in the areas that would become Provence and Languedoc (Southern regions of France) a Gallo-Roman culture continued into the time of Gregory of Tours. (538 AD)

Long before Julius Cæsar captured the region in 50 BC, a Celtic pagan, whose name was the root of the word 'Rougeux,' eventually settled in this region. He was likely head of a canton of a Celtic tribe whose village of crude huts became known by his name.

The name 'Rougeux' changed through conquest and during the centuries of the middle ages when illiteracy was universal, superimposition of various dialects and languages occurred again and again.

Nevertheless the Rougeux name has roots which goes back to pre-Christian tribes, and quoting Abbot Mulson, *"Rougeux is, without doubt, the posterity of ancient invasions."*

Research by the former mayor of Rougeux (M. Jacques Karasz) traced the roots of the name back through the Romans to the Gauls. (This information is taken from notes I wrote during our conversations in 1978 but unfortunately I did not record his sources. Regrettably, to escape prosecution and certain imprisonment for a fatal DUI driving accident (his second), he abandoned his family and disappeared in 1979)

According to his research, 'Robiac' was the ancient, pre-Christian form of the name and 'Regress' was the form used by early Romans. This information was partially confirmed through recent correspondence with our cousin Gerard, (born at the farm 'Moulin Jobard' adjacent to Pierrefaites) who remembers having learned this in his early years. A page from an ancient book

(History of Pierrefaites) dealing with the history of various local villages, including Rougeux, states the Latin spelling of the name during the 13th century was 'Rogeio'.

The Dictionnaire Topographique du département de la Haute-Marne — Par Alphonse Roserot, Paris Imprimerie Nationale, MDCCCCIII— has this to say about the different references to the village of 'Rougeux' (located in the canton of Fayl-Billot):

— Rogeolus, 1198 (Beaulieu)   (Cistercian Monastery 2 miles from Rougeux)
— Ruegol, 1213 (Beaulieu)
— Rojol, 1248 (Beaulieu)
— Roguel, 1255 (Beaulieu)
— Rojol, 1269.
— Roiguel, 1312 (Beaulieu)
— Rougieul, 1379 (Beaulieu)
— Rubeolus, 1451 (Beaulieu)
— Rougeul, 1459 (Beaulieu)
— Rougeux, 1463 (Beaulieu)
— Rougeux, 1700 (Dillon)

In 1379 an unknown author wrote this (From TGF 13th century pg. 670):

In 1027 the name 'Rougeux' was sometimes known as 'Regales';
In 1198, 'Rogol';
In 1248, 'Rougieul';
In 1379, perhaps Rubelllius = Rubelolus.

The form of the spelling by the fourteenth century was 'Rougeux' representing the final change occurring during the 1400 years after Cæsar captured Gaul (50 BC)

The meaning of Rougeux at this date remains unclear. In 1400 an unidentified author made the following comment: *"We have equally remarked that some words such as, amoureux or courageux, are not masculine or femine and are almost exclusively adjectives, rather are pejoratives ('fallacieux, hideux, deserteux, crapeux, grappeux, rippeux, pientureux, rougeux, angoisseux, etc.')*

While there is no dispute of the meaning of the word 'rouge' the additional 'ux' or alternatively 'roug' with 'eux' is an issue unresolved at this time.

Linguists at the University of Louisville, University of Pennsylvania, University of Ottawa and University of Calgary have not been able to offer a solution. However they agree that it is incorrect to consider the name to mean, 'to redden,' or 'red water' and in one opinion, may not even refer to 'red' at all.

Perhaps the name is an ancient pejorative and the root is 'roug' rather than 'rouge'. More research by experts is needed.

Foundation of the villages of Champigny and Laneuvelle can be attributed to the IV century. In the first part of the names Betoncourt, Broncourt, Voncourt, the name of the master of the colony is designated have and the second part of the name described either a rustic house of his exploitation, or recalling the places that the Bourguignons had possessed, or of sharing the land.

Rougeux, Charmes, Charmoy, Fayl, Lavernoy forest of Charmes, were possibly named after the beech and the alders, or designation of cleared woods, but are all, without doubt, the posterity of ancient invasions.

Velles and Guyonvelle, founded by the seigneurs of La Frete and Damremont, rightly were originated during the VII century.

During the VIII century the chateau of Coiffy-le-Haut, gave birth of the village with the same name. Then in the XVI century was founded.

"For the most part," says the Abbot Roussel, *"our villages were constructed during the times of the Gauls and Romans".* (Roma 4 BC-4 AD)

This was the period of time of the beginning of an abbey or of a chateau (Nothing like those of the Medieval Period!)

"We believe," says Abbot Briffaut, "that this assertion is true; there are assurances that our country was inhabited well before the occupation by the Gauls (4BC) It is probable that this favorable time led to creation of more localities. But much is mute during this remote age and it is not possible to classify in order each ancient center of population. Therefore, we will hypothesize our opinion upon whatever is given by the etymologists.

Settled agriculture, by Cæsar's time, was widespread, with corn being a principal crop. (This is an error by Abbot Mulson in his 'History of Pierrefaites', extensively quoted in this material, because it was not until after Columbus returned with the first corn seeds and its rapid spread across the continent that corn became known to Europe)

"Cæsar tells us, in his 'Conquest of the Gauls' that wine grapes were not grown in this region during his time but by 800 the medieval warming period had begun favoring growth of the vine. Prior to this time, wine was imported by boats and wagons across the plains and fetched enormous prices." Cæsar also said: "The Gaul's loved wine so much that they would trade a slave for a jar of wine."

He further commented that: "Most of the common people are groaning under the hand of the powerful and are treated as slaves. They never act on their initiative, have no choice in public affairs, are burdened with debt, crushed with taxation. Husbands have the power of life and death over his wife and children." (An obvious indication that the vast majority of the population could not afford to enjoy wine let alone own a slave. Centuries of inter-tribal warfare had developed them into excellent soldiers as shown by the furious and protracted resistance against the Romans)

When a noble died, his relatives met, and if there was suspicion of foul play the widow was examined in the Roman way (tortured and flogged) just as Roman slaves were treated. If her guilt was established she was consigned to the flames after suffering the most excruciating torments. Everything, including animals, that the dead man owned was consigned to the pyre, and on occasion, even including slaves and retainers known to have been loved by their masters.

For unknown centuries, slavery had been commonly practiced by those in power. Capture by an opposing force meant either execution or slavery. Whole towns were sold into slavery, as in the example of Cæsar's actions after his capture of Atuatuci in 57 BC. There, he had the entire population sold in one lot, and the purchasers' returns showed a count of 53,000 souls. Men who had been captured in warfare were used as slaves in the great iron (iron from mines in the region of Rougeux was used to make sections of the Eiffel Tower) and salt mines of Gaul.

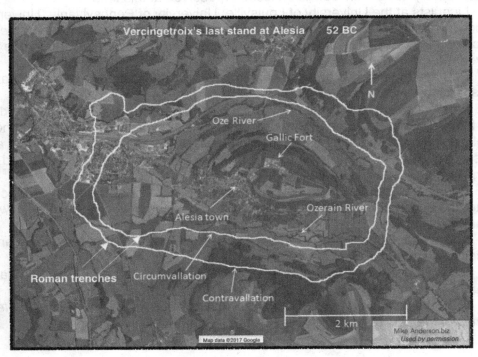

10

The women were used in the normal ways of helpless women. Once enslaved they were seldom freed and soon worked to death.

In 58 BC the Sequanii, (the tribe probably inhabiting Rougeux) whose lands were strategically positioned along the Rhine River Southeast of Rougeux, were unable to stop the waves of Germanic invaders from across the Rhine. Furthermore, they were not powerful enough to prevent the brutal treatment of hostages captured by their traditional and more powerful enemies, the Helveti. They had no recourse but to apply to Cæsar for assistance. Julius Cæsar's reply resulted in the establishment of a permanent Roman garrison at Besancon, (40 miles SE) and subsequent application of the Roman yoke to the entire region.

Myrabella / Wikimedia Commons / CC BY-SA 4.0

Finally, early in 52 BC, after six years of bitter warfare, surging back and forth across the countryside, scorched earth policies on both sides led to famine and repeated victories by Cæsar. In desperation the Sequanii, made common cause with other tribes, many their traditional enemies. After much wrangling, the various tribes agreed to be led by the powerful Avernian chief, Vercingetorix (pronounced Ver-sun-get-rix), whose father had once held suzerainty over all of Gaul. After a series of closely lost and bloody contests, Vercingetorix, in late 52 BC, was forced to make a final stand on a hill top at a place called Alesia (60 miles W) This was a village built upon a hill of minor elevation, thirty miles Northwest of Dijon, and about sixty miles West of Rougeux. The Romans encircled Vercingetorix's army with eighteen miles of trenches lined with pointed logs facing the Gauls. (Circumvallation) Then in order to protect himself from Gaulic attacks from his rear, Cæsar ordered his army to dig another similar trench a few yards further out and lined that trench with similarly pointed logs facing outward. (Contravallation) To further thwart cavalry attacks, Cæsar dug shallower trenches beyond the outer one, and filled them with sharp, fire hardened pointed sticks, concealed under branches and twigs. (Imagine how many trees had to be cut to prepare these 36 miles of fortifications!)

After about a month of fruitless attacks by the Gauls from both sides of these trenches, and failure to resupply the trapped army with provisions, starvation forced their surrender and Vercingetorix was captured. After six years of imprisonment he was displayed as a trophy in Cæsar's triumphal march through Rome and publicly strangled in the Temple of Jupiter Capitolinus.

Cæsar spent his last winter (50 BC) in the area just South of Rougeux and quelled the final vestiges of rebellion. His army of 60,000 ruthlessly pillaged seed stocks and caused a severe famine over a wide region.

When Cæsar was asked to consider the most dangerous events of his life he replied, *"The Gauls (Celtic tribes) were the most dangerous enemies he had ever faced."* This war was estimated by Cæsar to have slain a million tribesmen, women and children, and yielded an equal amount of slaves for Rome. Only Alexander is reputed to have been more brutal to the people he conquered. Through cunning Cæsar had gotten himself appointed governor of Gaul but the Roman Senate, not trusting him, forbade him to operate outside the clearly defined borders of Gaul. Cæsar was ambitious to be emperor and with the capture of Gaul completed, he proceeded South toward Rome with his army, however because their fear of him, the Senate, forbade him to cross the Rubicon River into Italy. The famous saying, 'Crossing the Rubicon' originated from Cæsar's rebellious and irretrievable act of crossing this river into Italy at the Southern edge of Gaul, near the city of Bologna and igniting Civil War. Battles in Italy, Spain, the region East of the Adriatic Sea, Egypt, and Africa during the ensuing three-year uprising led to the death of Pompey and Cæsar's successful claim to the title 'Emperor' of the Roman Empire. All this is recorded in Cæsar's' book, titled 'Conquest of Gaul,' written in 50 BC, and a few years later, 'Cæsar, The Civil War'.

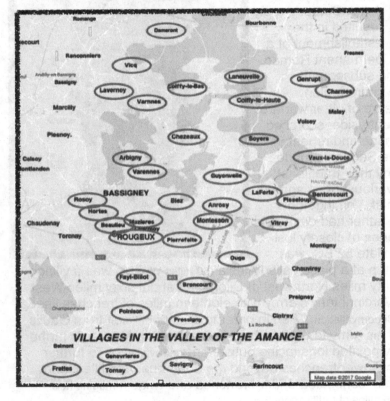

VILLAGES IN THE VALLEY OF THE AMANCE.

Seventy years after Cæsar's conquest, a revolt against the Roman rule in Gaul was centered in the area of Rougeux and according to Tactus Silvus (a Roman general), *"He marched into the land of the Sequanii and laid waste to their territory, completely defeating them"*. However, Rome was taught a lesson by the ferocious resistance and the Gallic captivity somewhat alleviated.

The portion of NE France, that occupies the department of Haute Marne, is exposed to trememblement of the ground. In the environs of Langres and as of Neuilly, research has found records from 1118, 1154, 1155, 1157, 1216, 1233, 1535, 1549, 1682, 1780, 1783, 1810, 1811, and 1820 at Hortes of tremblers that have shaken the region and destroyed buildings.

12

CHAPTER II

TIMES OF THE GALLO-ROMANS

1. VESTIGES OF GAULS ---- 2. MODERN ROMANS ---- 3. WATERS ---- 4. RETRENCHMENTS --- 5. FUNERAL MONUMENTS ---- 6. CURRENCY ---- 7. RESULTS OF THE SEARCH OF VALLEROY ---- 8. PLAGUES

For the first inhabitants of our country, flint was a precious material. It was used as a material for defense as well as for armaments in offensive warfare. It also provided tools for industry and well as for food preparation in the form of knives, scraping, defleshing of animals, lances, daggers, etc. There are deposits of flint at Courtesoult, Pierrecourt, Farincourt and Argilleres. During previous times it had been seriously exploited. We have found workshops existing during this age of stone1. In this epoch we have mined small pieces of flint. One hatchet made of green polished flint was found at Montesson, (7 miles E) one made of 'fibrolithe' and a hatchet of the same material.

(Sillimanite or fibrolite is a brown, pale green, or white glassy silicate mineral that often occurs in long, slender, needlelike crystals frequently found in fibrous aggregates. An aluminum silicate, Al_2OSiO_4, it occurs in high-temperature regionally metamorphosed clay-rich rocks, e.g., schists and gneisses. Sillimanite is found at many localities in France, Madagascar, and the Eastern US)

When we reconnoiter the environs of Langres (15 miles W) we find a number of Roman Roads.

Various others have written and made maps and it is sufficient to review their work. We will add to that work if we feel it is necessary 2.The roadway that M. Pistollet of Saint-Ferjeux titled 'The second way of Langres to the Rhine', following for a while close to the direction of the actual national route of Paris to Belfort, (78 miles SE) it passes at Fayl-Billot (2 miles S) and on the territory of Broncourt (7 miles SE) and the La Quarie to arrive at Port-sur-Saone (on the Soane River) Our arrival about Haut-Chemin revealed a farm situated South (more to the E than S) of Rougeux on a plain that separates Fayl-Billot from Pierrefaites.

Southeast of Chaudenay (8 miles W), we discovered a side road and found traces of this second way South of Rougeux by Maraucheres (village not found) Going from West to East, between Fayl and Charmoy, we named it, 'The Road of the Romans.' It descends the small valley of Pierrefaites, (4 miles E) and at its extremity at the North, it touches ancient Montesson (Montis Statio), appears at Ouge and Biemont (via montis), passes through Vitrdy (via strada) and rejoins at Port-sur-Soane (25 miles SE)

Another Road leaves Bourbonne (29 miles NE) for Guyonvelle and La Ferte (7 miles E), crosses the preceding road at Montesson (8 miles E), and advances to the East of Pierrefaites (4 miles E) by the part of Corps-Marchais, the Homme-Mort, the Chalelet, the Riosseau de Serqueux, the Mouillieres, the Chanois, then traverses the levee of Langres at Rhin between the existing road of Broncourt and the department route of Bourbonne at Champlitte. Its probable route is to Frettes (18 miles S) via Genevrieres where we found vestiges going North and South.

In the map of Roman roads, M. Pistollet has recommended another way to Lavernoy (19 miles SE) by the Bois-Chapiltre, passing at the limit of the territories of Hortes (4 miles N) and of Arbigny (6 miles N), arriving at Maizieres (4 miles N) through the valley of the Amance, crossing the plain at Charmoy, (2 miles E) of that village. We think it cuts the lines to head directly, via the

ROMAN EMPIRE 300 AD

Bois de Cotes, very close to Pierrefaites (4 miles E) Northeast of Pressigny (10 miles NW) we rediscovered it where it subsequently reached Morey (125 miles N) From this road, South of Varness (8 miles N), a side road leading to Julemont (Juli mons) in the territory of Champigny (Campus pugnae), perhaps leading to Coiffy le Bas (11 miles N) along the Pimont, the farm of Chezeaux (7 miles N), and between Soyers (8 miles NE) and Monicharvot at Voisy and Barges at Jussey (20 miles E) .

We find, says M. Pistollet [1], on the territory of Velles a Roman road that passes close to the Abby of Vaux-la-Douce (11 miles E) and crosses the forest of Voisey, climbs the hill of Genrup (18 miles NE) to gain Bourbonne (12 miles N)

We do not recognize any additional road to the South but it (The above mentioned road) diverges to the Cote de Voncourt and the village of Morey (110 miles SW) [2].

A portion of the territory of Farincourt (10 miles SE) is crossed by a Roman Road going from Southeast to Northwest where we found traces on the territories of Valleroy and of Savigny. It is cut close to the village of Valleroy (14 miles SE) by a road that comes from the territory of Fouvent and its region to the North where it passes close to Voncourt (11 miles SE) [1]. It is possible it goes toward La Quarie and Ouge at Vellles (8 miles E) We once again mention a section of a route discovered at Petit-Creux between Poinson and Brussieres. It is perhaps the route of Frettes at Fayl-Billot according to the investigation of M. Jolibois.

Doesn't the name of Grande-Voie given to a road at Vicq (12 miles N) additionally reveal another Roman Road of Langres to Bourbonne via Orbigny-au-Mont, Celles, Lavernoy, Vicq and the forest of Boubonne?

Close to these Roman roads, notably in the territories of Damremont, Lavernoy, Arbigny, Maizieres, Hortes, Rougeux, Charmoy, Soyers, Montesson, Pierrefaites, Fayl-Billot, Poinson, Pressigny, and Savigny, we find a great number of ponds and marshes. These are cavities sunk in to the soil, the top open and form an elliptical circle. Their diameters vary from 36 to 90 feet with a depth of 55 to 95 inches. They always contain water, some not as much depending on the seasons. In some, oak logs have been removed, blackened like ebony, from which carpenters have made planks and furniture. It is thought they were placed in the water before the ancient occupation by the Gauls and Romans. Others, considering the advanced state of Roman roads, presume they were placed there by less ancient peoples and attribute this work during the time the country was invaded by the Barbarians who built shelters against the winter.

Between these two opinions the ponds were inhabited by men and the oak logs served to cover their cabins. But in many of these ponds we did not find any wood; the number of oaks is insignificant; their length was not proportionate to the diameter of the excavation and gives no knowledge of their assembly. After fifteen centuries they have better use in being cut up for boards and timber. Elsewhere we never see the broken debris of pottery or utensils in houses. Even more, the soil is impermeable, and the ground extractions around the edges of the water did not contain debris. How do you suppose these men, these primitives could live in these ditches, veritable cesspits, the greater part of the year?

We think we must attribute the pools to the Romans who dug down to the bottom to conserve the water for their cavalry. In that assumption we can explain the name, 'The Watering Place of Caesar' (Abreuvoirs of Cesar), and their presence on the highlands along the Roman roads among the quartering places of the Roman soldiers; for example as at Montesson (8 miles E) In talking of the camps, M. Pistollet says: "I think we will find retrenchments on the mountains that border the valley of the Amance and the gullies along the valley."

In effect, the historians think there are numerous retrenchments other than on the two hills on each side of the river. Both summits that border the river were fortified; on the right Varennes (9 miles N) that historians call 'Oppidum' and 'Castrum.' On the plateau of Julemont we have found debris of armies as well as tombs and the Varennes noires (?) where the vestiges of a fort have been found in our lifetime.

Debris have also been found near the ancient Montesson (10 miles E), constructed East of its current location; at Ouge (10 miles E) and Vitrey (70 miles N), and at Biemont (13 miles E), a ruined small town remarkable for its beautiful location and its antiquities 3. On the left bank of the river on the magnificent promontory we see Coiffy-sur-Haut (11 miles NE) 4. On the edge of the mountain forest that rises between Champigny and Bize (4 miles NE) exist more remains of Roman camps and the very apparent fossils covering the mounds of soil 5.

La Ferte (7 miles E) is rampant with bricks, and roofing tiles with raised edges.

We must cite another, Fayl-Billot (2 miles South), who possess a Chateaux-Grillot and a Chatelet in which we have seen remains of construction, roof tiles with raised edges and fragments of well sculptured statues; additionally important sites North of Charmes, and Montey, has no less6 than five hectares of surface ruins. There we have also discovered walls of solid construction, some pavements, debris of dressed stone, tiles and mosaics 6.

Additionally, says the M. Vignier, we see at Coiffy le Haut (11 miles N) some tombs upon which was engraved the following Roman inscription:

> D.   M.
> AURELIO SACRO……REM.

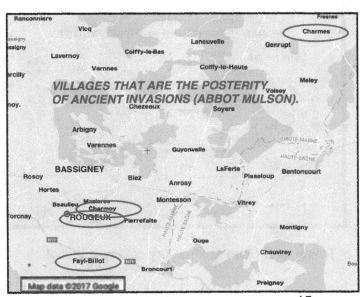

VILLAGES THAT ARE THE POSTERITY OF ANCIENT INVASIONS (ABBOT MULSON).

But our country has not conserved another Roman époque funeral monument that had been deposited at the presbytery at Fayl-Billot. (2 miles S) We reconnoitered in the forest of that village in 1858. Bad news! It is degraded and the figures incomplete. It is made of engraved stone and represents in relief a man and a woman of grandeur in an almost natural appearance. The woman is clothed in an elegant robe with pleats descending to her shoes. Both hands are resting on her breasts; in her right hand is a cup in the form of a chalice. The man is dressed in a tunic descending to a little under his

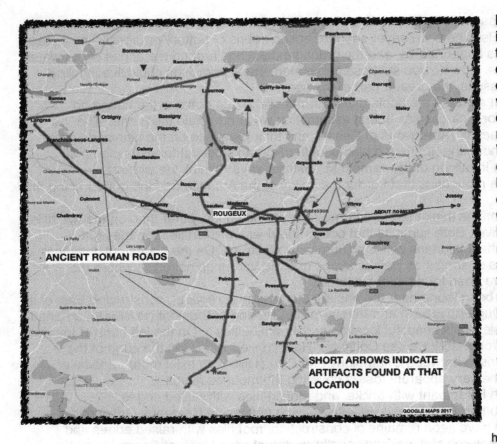

ANCIENT ROMAN ROADS

SHORT ARROWS INDICATE ARTIFACTS FOUND AT THAT LOCATION

GOOGLE MAPS 2017

knees. His left hand is on his brEast and the right carrying an object, but because of the breakage, I was unable to determine the nature of the object. With reference to coins, there have been many discoveries. At Chaumondel, Coiffy le Haut, and Vicq (12 miles N) we have seen many and in the last locality mentioned there has been exhumed a bronze key. At Biemont the age of these coins stops at the regime of Gallien. (Gallienus c. 218 – 268 was a Roman Emperor with his father Valerian from 253 to 260 and alone from 260 to 268. He ruled during the Crisis of the Third Century that nearly caused the collapse of the empire and was unable to prevent the secession of important provinces)

At Ouge, (10 miles E) visages of Roldeboz (unknown personage) have been found on a large quantity of small bronze coins. Coins made between I and III centuries with the effigies of the emperors Trajan (98 AD), Gordien (238 AD), Phillipe, Galle, Volusien, Valerian (253 AD), Gallien; the empresses Salonine (242 AD), (Julia Cornelia Salonina was an Augusta, wife of Roman Emperor Gallienus and mother of Valerian II, Saloninus, and Marinianus) Severa, etc., have been found.

At Montesson (9 miles E), instead of the Tresor (gold coin), we have pieces of gold, silver and leather, some clasps of gold, some mosaics, and an iron spearhead, etc. At Fretes (15 miles S), close by the road of Langres to Besancon, we have recovered many coins of bronze stamped during the rule of Trajan, and close to a military colony, a bull of

ROMAN RUINS FOUND IN THESE VILLAGES.

Map data ©2017 Google

bronze about eight hands in size 6. At Arbigny the Varennes noires (black-its meaning unclear) states there were bronze coins of Nero, Antony and Vespasian.

At Varennes (9 miles N) we also find items from Trajan, Anthony, Severe, Volusien, Galle, Claude, Nerva, Adrien, Faustine, Probus, Constantin, Licinius, etc.(Roman Emperors)

We will continue our resume of the discoveries made upon our territory. There has not been much explored below the surface and there is still an assurance of much historical and archeological discoveries. There has come two brilliant researchers to demonstrate a manner of discovery. They are Mm Doctor Aillet, of Bourguignon-les-Morey and Abbot Rossignot, priest of Argillieres. They have remarked about the number of Roman tiles remaining between Valleroy and Savigny (12 miles S), and as has been said in Asaut-Barbe (unknown historian), they began and executed, in 1881, a thorough search with substantial benefits from the scientific point of view.

The first digging was at a building 24 meters long by 14 meters wide (roughly 78x24 feet) The foundations, using cement between the stones, formed strong forts in the walls at appropriate places. It is on this basis that walls were elevated with close fitting mortar joints, this being possible with the material of this territory. We have not found a wall that has been repaired but the piles of cinders regularly spaced 4 meters apart proves the wooden parts of the colonies were destroyed by fire. Thirty meters of this habitation is a Cella (Latin for small chamber or the inner chamber of a temple in classical architecture, or a shop facing the street in domestic Roman architecture) of 3 meters high, many debris of pottery vessels as well as other more precisely formed objects was found. In an other direction, 50 meters from the first house under a rural road, we found a wall we recognized as still under construction and buried under debris but we did not continue the evacuation.

Between three constructions we saw during various days, parts of walls although we did not designate their location. Do they indicate a large villa or a conglomeration of a number of buildings? Only further digging will provide an answer to these questions. Here is the list of very interesting objects found in these ruins: seven pieces of money; two of Lingons, two of Sequanes and three of Eduens. (Tribes who were pre-Roman in origin but contested, especially the most powerful, the Sequanes, against the Germans and Romans) Seven bronze coins were found; an Adrein and a Trajan, a large bronze, an Augustinan stamped at Lyon, an Adrein, a Vespasian, a young Faustine, wife of Marc Aurele, a medium sized bronze, a dozen of large bronze fasteners of nine centimeters down to ones of two centimeters in the form of birds. The small one was decorated with tiny stones; another was enameled; soon we will conserve the traces of silver covering them. A medallion composed of fine quality and very tiny stones of various colors made a very remarkable brooch. Additionally I found a small pierced purse with a key to open it and a three pointed bronze piece covered with gemstones.

A lot, important enough, of tools of steel and of flint, a hammer, two gouges, two knives, two knives with double blades besides dies, engravers, hooks and scrapers was also discovered. Also found were pieces of furniture made of granite; a considerable quality of fragments of various Roman pottery, the first of a Roman hard clay; a red sealing wax with brilliant luster and glassy appearance, much decorated

with fillets 1.

At Haute-Saone, (36 miles E) some had carved on them relief design that represents good knowledgable of hunting, combat and other subjects. Generally the name of the maker is on the best pieces of this group. The second is a pale red and gray over a black luster and employed for funeral services. The third is made of a gray clay, blackened but without the high luster. The fourth is a yellow clay, pinkish rose with white, all without luster which served for domestic use.

Among the numerous tile-makers two tile examples were found; a plate tegula, measuring 20 by 12 inches and another half cylinder, imbrex, that served to complete the connection of tile roofing plates 7.

----
1. p. 136----History de Jonvelle.
2. Historie de Fayl_Billot.
3. Historie de Vicq, p. 7.

Plagues have tormented the population incessantly throughout history.

The Antonine Plague of 165–180 AD, also known as the Plague of Galen (from the name of the Greek physician living in the Roman Empire who described it), was an ancient pandemic brought back to the Roman Empire by troops returning from campaigns in the Near East. Scholars have suspected it to have been either smallpox or measles but the true cause remains undetermined. (These symptoms are similar to ergotism, its source unknown for another 500 years)

The epidemic may have claimed the life of a Roman emperor, Lucius Verus, who died in 169 and was the co-regent of Marcus Aurelius Antoninus, whose family name, Antoninus, has become associated with the epidemic. The disease broke out again nine years later, according to the Roman historian Dio Cassius (155–235), causing up to 2,000 deaths a day in Rome, one quarter of those who were affected, giving the disease a mortality rate of about 25%.[3] The total deaths have been estimated at five million, and the disease killed as much as one-third of the population in some areas and devastated the Roman army.

Ammianus Marcellinus reports that the plague spread to Gaul and to the (Roman) Legions along the Rhine.

The Plague of Cyprian is the name given to a pandemic, probably of smallpox, that afflicted the Roman Empire from AD 250 onwards during the larger Crisis of the Third Century. It was still raging in 270, when it claimed the life of emperor Claudius II Gothicus. The plague is thought to have caused widespread manpower shortages in agriculture and the Roman army. Contemporary accounts state: *"In 250 to 266 AD, at the height of the outbreak, 5000 people a day were said to be dying in Rome."* St. Cyprian's (Bishop of Carthage) biographer, wrote of the plague: *"Afterwards there broke out a dreadful plague, and excessive destruction of a hateful disease invaded every house in succession of the trembling populace, carrying off day by day with abrupt attack numberless people, every one from his own house."*

Cyprian drew moralizing analogies in his sermon "On the Plague":

"This trial, that now the bowels, relaxed into a constant flux, discharge the bodily strength; that a fire originated in the marrow ferments into wounds of the fauces; that the intestines are shaken with a continual vomiting; that the eyes are on fire with the injected blood; that in some cases the feet or some parts of the limbs are taken off by the contagion of diseased putrefaction; that from the weakness arising by the maiming and loss of the body, either the gait is enfeebled, or the hearing is obstructed, or the sight darkened;—is profitable as a proof of faith. What a grandeur of spirit it is to struggle with all the powers of an unshaken mind against so many onsets of devastation and death! What sublimity, to stand erect amid the desolation of the human race, and not to lie prostrate with those who have no hope in God; but rather to rejoice, and to embrace the benefit of the occasion; that in thus bravely showing forth our faith, and by suffering endured, going forward to Christ by the narrow way that Christ trod, we may receive the reward of His life and faith according to His own judgment!".

CHAPTER III
(300 AD --- 1000 AD)

THE INVASIONS AND THE END OF THE CAROLINGIAN DYNASTY

1. INVASIONS ----- 2. ETYMOLOGIES OF OUR ANCIENT VILLAGES ----- 3. COMMENCEMENT OF CHRISTIANITY ----- 4. GIFTS TO THE ABBEYS OF LUXEUIL AND OF BIZE ----- 5. SAINT GENGOUL OF GENGON ----- 6. TITHES ----- 7. PALACE OF THE CAROLINGIAN -----8. THE SARACENS, NORMANS AND HUNGARIANS ----- 9. ERGOT ----- 10. 800-1315AD-START AND END OF WARMING PERIOD

Constance Chlore
Roman Emperor 293-306

The ruins that we are about to discuss and some other subjects we cannot clearly understand are the effect of the numerous invasions that caused such tragedy near the end of the III century and continued through the IV and V centuries.

The numberless routes cut through our country has contributed to its prosperity during peacetime but favors the arrival of the German population. In 303 AD the Germans arrived like a torrent upon our country and devastated it to a point that it almost became a desert. Constance Chlore (Roman Emperor from 293 to 306) engaged them in combat that resulted in his being wounded and his army routed. Horsemen pursued him and his frightened army all the way to the walls of Langres (15 miles W) As soon as the large number of runaways had entered the village, the gates were hastily closed and the enemy was prevented from entering.

To protect the emperor from imminent danger of falling into enemy hands we threw him a rope that permitted him to scale the rampart. But such humiliation is hard to endure. Reinforcements rapidly arrived; the citizens armed themselves. Two and one half hours after this debacle, Constance fell on the Germans in a surprise attack and inflicted a great carnage seldom seen in Europe where in one day more than 60,000 men fell on the fields of battle1. The captives remained as prisoners. The new inhabitants married the many surplus and fecund

LANGRES

19

females, and repopulated, by the sweat of their brow, the country they came to ravage 2.

Agriculture prospered and the province of Langres began pouring out its abundance, not only on it's neighboring countryside, but also on the capital of the region whose name was Claudian 3. (In 313AD the Edict of Milan is issued. Christians are now tolerated in the Roman Empire)

(On August 9, 378 AD, The Battle of Adrianople (Hadrianopolis) - the beginning of the end of Roman military power)

We see, in 398 AD, Stilicho embarked on the Soane the grains that Bassigny could provide to Rome to alleviate the menace of famine 4. (After many years of victories against a number of enemies, both barbarian and Roman, a series of political and military disasters finally allowed his enemies in the court of Honorius to remove him from power, culminating in his arrest and subsequent execution in 408. Known for his military successes and sense of duty, Stilicho was, in the words of historian Edward Gibbon, "the last of the Roman generals")

December 406 is the often-repeated date of the crossing of the Rhine by a mixed group of barbarians that included Vandals, Alans and Suebi. The Rhine-crossing transgressed one of the Late Roman Empire's most secure limites or boundaries, and so was a climactic moment in the decline of the Empire. It initiated a wave of destruction of Roman cities and the collapse of Roman civic order in Northern Gaul. That, in turn, occasioned the rise of three usurpers in succession in the province of Britannia. Therefore, the crossing of the Rhine is a marker date in the Migration Period, during which various Germanic tribes moved Westward and Southward, out of Southern Scandinavia and Northern Germania.

The full statement of received opinion has been that a mixed band of Vandals, Alans and Suebi crossed the Rhine at Mainz on December 31, 406, and began to ravage Gaul. Several written accounts document the crossing, supplemented by the time line of Prosper of Aquitaine, which gives a firm date of 31 December 406. (Prosper of Aquitaine d. abt 460, was much more famous for what he wrote than for what he did. (Abbé L. Valentin) However, many historians believe his chief fame rests not on his historical work, but on his activities as a theologian and an aggressive propagandist for the Augustinian doctrine of grace)

Other barbarians attempted to penetrate into Gaul. The Romans, under Constantin, Julien, and Valentinien unsuccessfully attempted to stop the barbarians by impressing (unprofessional) ordinary men as soldiers. But beginning at the V century all defenders were dismissed by what remained of the Roman Empire. Our country was then at the mercy of excursions by these hordes. The Burgondes in 407 the Sueves (The Kingdom of the Suebi was a Germanic post-Roman kingdom, one of the first to separate from the Roman Empire. Based in the former Roman provinces of Gallaecia and Northern Lusitania, it was established by the Suebi about 410 through the 6th century), the Alains (The Alans were an Iranian nomadic pastoral people of antiquity. The Alans have been connected by modern historians with the Central Asian Yancai and Aorsi of Chinese and Roman sources and are mentioned by Persian and Roman sources in the 1st century AD. Upon the Hunnic defeat of the Goths on the Pontic Steppe around 375 AD, many of the Alans migrated Westwards along with various

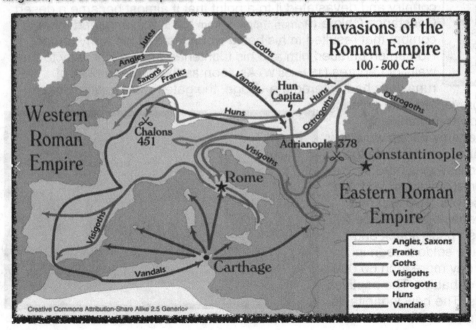

20

Germanic tribes. They crossed the Rhine in 406 AD, and the Vandals in 411. (The Vandals were an East Germanic tribe, or group of tribes, who were first heard of in Southern Poland, but later moved around Europe establishing kingdoms in Spain and later North Africa in the 5th century. The Vandals are believed to have The Roman empire under Hadrian (ruled 117–138), showing the location of the Burgundiones Germanic group, then inhabiting the region between the Viadua (Oder) and Visula (Vistula) rivers (Poland) migrated from Southern Scandinavia to the area between the lower Oder and Vistula rivers during the 2nd century BC and to have settled in Silesia from around 120 BC), all made excursions. The Huns (The Huns were a nomadic people who lived in Eastern Europe, the Caucasus, and Central Asia between the 1st century AD and the 7th century AD), under the leadership of Atilla, were prominent for steel and flame.

A letter of Jerome, written from Bethlehem, gives a long list of the barbarian tribes involved. Some of them, like Quadi and Sarmatians, are drawn from history or literary tradition.(The Quadi were a Suebian Germanic tribe who lived approximately in the area of modern Moravia in the Northern Carpathian Mountains in the time of the Roman empire) (The Sarmatians were a large confederation of Iranian people during classical antiquity, flourishing from about the 5th century BC to the 4th century AD. Originating in Eastern Europe, between the Don River and the Ural Mountains the Sarmatians started their Westward migration around the 6th century BC)

Jerome mentions Mainz first in a list of the cities devastated by the incursion, which is the sole support for the common assumption that the crossing of the unbridged Rhine was effected at Mainz. (A frozen Rhine, making the crossing easier, is not attested by any contemporary, but was a plausible surmise of *Edward Gibbon*) Jerome lists the cities now known as Mainz, Worms, Rheims, Amiens, Arras, Thérouanne, Tournai, Speyer and Strasbourg as having been pillaged.

The Vandal king Godigisel was killed, but the Alans came to the rescue of the Vandals, and once on the Roman side (the Western side of the Rhine), they met with no organized resistance.

Stilicho had depleted the garrisons in 402 to face Alaric in Italy (Alaric I 370 – 410 AD was the first King of the Visigoths from 395–410. Alaric is best known for his sack of Rome in 410, which marked a decisive event in the decline of the Roman Empire)

In 452, and, after being defeated (by the Romans) in the plains of Chalons, (120 miles N) Atilla repassed our country causing vast new devastations. Soon Langres (15 miles W) was separated from the Empire)

The Burgondes conquered and incorporated Langres into their kingdom in (413) The wife of King Clovis, Clotilde, granddaughter of Gundioc and niece of Gondebaud, King of Bourgogne (493), was baptized (496), an indication of increasing civilization.

The Franks also imposed their empire on this part of Gaul (418) (The Franks (are historically first known as a group of Germanic tribes that inhabited the land between the Lower and Middle Rhine in the 3rd century AD, and second, as the people of Gaul who merged with the Gallo-Roman populations during succeeding centuries, passing on their name to modern-day France and becoming part of the heritage of the modern French people)

If one considers the dimensions of the devastation of the bubonic plague of the 6th Century in the midst of the Dark Ages, accompanied by the savage imperial wars waged against the barbarian hordes, the terrible famines, the ubiquity of death and destruction, and finally the unleashing of this cataclysmic epidemic, it should not be difficult to imagine that the people at the time believed that they were being scorched and ravaged by the dreaded Four Horsemen of the Apocalypse. (The Plague of Justinian (541–542) was a pandemic that afflicted the Eastern Roman (Byzantine) Empire, especially its capital Constantinople, the Sassanid Empire, and port cities around the entire Mediterranean Sea. One of the deadliest plagues in history, this devastating pandemic resulted in the deaths of an estimated 25 million (at the time of the initial outbreak that was at lEast 13% of the world's population) to 50 million people (in two centuries of recurrence) Recent investigations relate this severe plague epidemic to extreme weather events of 535–536 considered as an example of volcanic winter)

The learned physicians of Justinian's day, who at the time followed the precepts of Graeco-Roman medicine, were discredited because their nostrums proved useless at the time of the cataclysm. Instead, the people turned for consolation to monastic medicine and the teachings of Christianity. The Christian church did rush in and, as best it could, tried to fill in the medical void. The monks in the monasteries quickly became the spiritual as well as corporeal healers (and victims) by tending both to the needs of the soul and the requirements of the body. They used prayer and only the rudiments of physical or herbal medicine to console and heal the sick.

The humbling of the medical profession because of its impotence to control the plague of the 6th Century, essentially halted the advancement of medical knowledge for centuries.

After the death of Theodoric (613) the Bourgogne (Burgundians) separated into various groups and their territory became part of the monarchy under the authority of Clotaire II (Chlothar II the Young, King of the Franks (b.584)

Such is the brief resume of the long (and very complicated) period of invasions, of wars, of successive calamities and social revolution during these seven centuries.

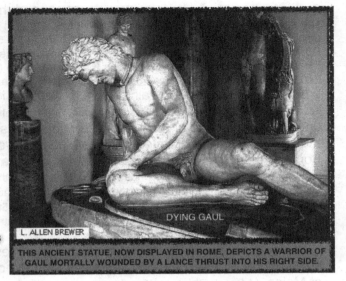

DYING GAUL

L. ALLEN BREWER

THIS ANCIENT STATUE, NOW DISPLAYED IN ROME, DEPICTS A WARRIOR OF GAUL MORTALLY WOUNDED BY A LANCE THRUST INTO HIS RIGHT SIDE.

1. Historie romaine, l. 9.
2. Ita nunc per victorias tuas, constanti Caesar invicta, quidquid infrequens ambiano et bellovaco et tricassino lingonicoque solo restabat, barbaro sudore revirescit (Eumenius, Panegyr. de Consi., c. 21)
3..... Fecunda Tibris ab Arico
Vexit lingoico sudatas vomere maeses. (Eloge de Stilicon)
4. Mathieu, Les Eveques de Langres, p. 1

For those who inquire about the commencement of Christianity in our country, we have little information.

We know that St. Benigue was sent to the Orient during the time of the Gauls by St. Polycarp (69-155), disciple of St. John and bishop of Smyrne. After having baptized St. Symphorien at Autun, St. Benigue came to Langres (15 miles W) where he found Christians. He converted the brothers Speusippe, Eleosippe and Melasippe, constructed an oratory in honor of St. John, and returned to Dijon (40 miles S) where his days terminated by glorious martyrdom under the reign of Marc Aurele (Roman Emperor 121-180 AD) Those three brothers, completely joined in agreement, soon courted martyrdom together with St. Leonille, their grandfather, St. Junillle, and Saints Neon and Turbon 1. *"But did the flames of belief in Our Lord claim the inhabitants of our villages before the end of the III century?" "Perhaps"* (by Abbot Briffaut)

The act that killed paganism was the declaration of as the official religion by Constantin the Great in 313.

The first preachers who evangelized our region did little until the missionaries attached to various communities of clerics constructed Christian churches and gave their spiritual security to the population disseminated over a vast countryside. The ravages of the invasions (Romans and Germans) separated the communities until the time of the monasteries and priories (around 1000 AD)

We think that St. Martin, (316-397) bishop of Tours, and his disciples made a large number of conversions in his diocese of Langres 3. *"What a city, what a church!"* Didn't Suplice Severe say, *"Don't I desire having some priests from the 'parish' of St. Martin?" "That explains why he has so many conversions because of the illustrious miracle-maker!"* (This sentence, by Abbot Briffaut, has been reconstructed to what I think is the meaning. The original contains an unknown word, 'parcisses', and the original sentence structure makes no sense to me)

As a rule, the churches have been rare enough but they are found within the environs of the fortifications, along the Roman roads and in the valleys and fertile places along the rivers.

St. Gregory was consecrated Bishop of Langres (15 miles W) for 35 years, dying in 541 some days after Epiphany and buried in Dijon.

1. La Diocese de Langres, t. I, p.50.
2. LaHaute-Saone, t. I, p. 1.
3. La tradition rapportee a la page 6 of Historie de Fayl-billot, ne repose sur aucon fondemant, Il certain que la paroisse de "Charmoy is moin ancienne que colle de Fayl-Billot

During the VII century, a rural parish was a conglomeration of sparsely inhabited tenant farms administrated by parish priests who lived at the churches. They were the celebrants and the office who distributed the offerings that controlled the destiny of the badly served residents. Ordinarily such a chapel would be the center of the community, surrounded by the cemetery where all the dead of the community sleep for the last time in their caskets of stone; used until the XIV century 1. All the hamlets and villages served the church as best they were able to. Before Mass they ignited a grand fire whose 'splinters' of smoke advertised to all the absentees of the intentions of the priest to say Mass.

Under the regime of the Merovingiens (French rulers during theV to VIII centuries) of which we live, (this part of the history is quoted by Abbot Briffaut verbatim from documents of these centuries) among others, two abbeys were quickly constructed; that of Lexeuil (590) (50 miles E) in the diocese of Besancon (60 miles SE) and that of Bize (630) (4 miles N) in the diocese of Langres (15 miles W) We lured them here through much talking because of the donations that were raised in our region and the relations that were developed with them.

Luxeuil was founded by St. Colomban and named for the second abbot, St. Eustase, who was born close to Langres of wealthy parents and allies to the family of St. Salabergo. He was the son of one of our priests of our epoch, the blissful Miget, whose compositions were divinely inspired 3. At this place schools instituted by that abbot were widely celebrated. There are a number of disciples among whom history mentions, one being the monk St. Agile. He was the son of a grand seigneur, whose domination stretched far into the country called Onorisiacum ou Onoraciacum, or other words, Noroy-les-Jussey (20 miles E)

It is to be believed, says an unbiased savant (Abbot Morey, priest of Baudoncourt) 4, that he was at the abbey of Luxeuil that possessed property located along the river banks of Upper Soane and at the

BIZE

23

Amance until the VII century. An investigation of this is found in a certificate by Charlemagne, carrying the wrong date of 815. The certificate cites Vitery, Ouge, Aurosey, Broncourt, Genevrieres, Jussey, Cemboing, Jonville, Enionvelle, Aigremont, Ravenne-Fontaine, Provencheres, and a number of other innocuous names (Rougeux) as being his property. (These villages were undoubtably very small settlements 2000 years ago—they are still small!)

A religious of Lluxeuil (50 miles E), Valdalen, son of Amalgar, count of Attonar, became the first abbot of Bize that his father had founded about 665. (There was considerable trouble concerning the use of the rules of the order at this establishment he had obtained from Clotaire III (497-561) King of Neustrie and of Bourgogue)

Much later, we don't say which century, (7th or 8th) the bishops of Langres yielded to this abbey the benefice of the priests of Vitrey, of Pierrefaites and their branches Rougeux, Chauvirey and Ouge.

We must not confuse the defender of Bize (Valdalen) with his grandson St. Gengoul of Gengon. This one, say the autographers, was born in Bourgogne. A few others denote the place as Varennes (9 miles N) 2. They point to the

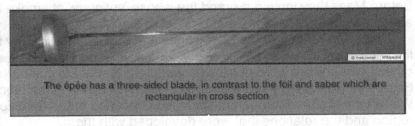
The épée has a three-sided blade, in contrast to the foil and saber which are rectangular in cross section

contradiction with the first ones because Varennes was then part of this province. His family, noble, rich and pious acquired a very strong Christian education. They studied Scriptures, acquired a deep love for religion and carried, with the Grace of God, the practice of virtue as their insignia. They were humble, chaste, sober, and loved charitable endeavors with the poor. At Varennes, they had an ordinary house, and they had built at their cost a basilica in honor of the apostle St Peter (basilica sancti Petri) served by several clerics. To avoid idleness, always disastrous of morals, the family readily exercised by hunting. Soon they embraced an army

career and followed Pepin-le-Bref (715-768) (Frankish king, a Christian, but who practiced brutality) in his wars. Their valor is covered with glory and they soon became a confident and closely connected to the King.

Gengoul became espoused of a girl rich as noble as he was, but she displayed as much viciousness as he was virtuous. She profited by his absence to steal the faith of marriage. The warrior learned of her scandalous conduct and returned to Varennes where he employed suggestions as a means to correct the infidelity of this woman by the use of sweetness and charity. Not proving successful he retired to his property of Avaus (praedium Avalense) four miles from Varennes (9 miles SSW) There he practiced the penance and work of mercy. Learning that he was distributing his wealth to the poor and fearful that he would denounce his wealth to the judge and knowing the severity and finality of the law, she resolved to have him murdered. She employed her valet to assassinate him by night. Gengon, surprised by a cruel strike of a blow from an epee, survived a number of days from the mortal wound.

1. Le Diocese de Langres, t. I, p. 130.
2. L'Abbe Morey, Notes historiques sur le cures de camagna, p.3.
3. Semaine religieuse du Diocèse de Langres, XX année, n 46.4. Godescard, Wies e Saints, 2 vol

But he expired [1] on the day of St. Vitique; a martyr to the justice of conjugal chastity (11 May, 760) His body, first exposed in the church at Avaux, (near Rhiems) was then transported to Varennes with great pomp (then?) to his sepulture in the basilica of St. Peter in Rome. The miracles that have happened at his tomb testified of his sainthood and was soon venerated in France, Germany, and in the Pays-Bas (Netherlands, Belgium, Germany) Soon numerous churches and chapels were dedicated under his name. Then the Normans, after their invasion, transported a part of his relics in their possession to Langres and in 1208, Raymond and Barthelemy de Chisel formed an annuity of fifteen livres for a lamp that was to burn day and night in front of his tomb.

The religious houses and the urban churches were soon finding devotees (donors) On the contrary, the rural churches were quite some time without property. Several councils, in particular that of Tours (560) and of Macon (586) recommended tithing, prescribed at once for Christians and Jews. But we recognize this was not as an obligation but as a voluntary offering of the faithful who felt a little pressure because that is the single method of existence for priests in Campagne. Finding a means of support is too precarious to leave to the pastor who is at the mercy of his parishioners. Struck by this inconvenience and wanting to assure the ministers of the altar of our position that we will provide shelter and food and render them independent. Charlemagne (Catholic) made the tithe the law of the country (779) (lasting almost a thousand years until the Revolution of 1793)

The tithe, despite the significance of the word, has not always been the tenth part of the products. It has varied all the way to thirty percent according to various places. We remember large tithes of grains, of wine and other considerable materials; minor and variable tithes of fruits, novales, (means ground newly cleared of growth) vegetables, etc.

The dynasty of the grand emperor (Charlemagne) seems to have wanted, with our country, a special relationship, if we must believe certain historians. Mabillon (Dom Jean Mabillon, O.S.B., (1632 – 1707) was a French Benedictine monk and scholar of the Congregation of Saint Maur) reproduced two documents from in nostro palatio (our palace) Petrae fictae, (Pierrefaites) one by Pepin, King of Aquitaine (827), the other by Carloman, King of Neustrie (881) He thinks these Acts of Pierrefaites, chief town of the our deanery, described a

chateau and a forest that could agree with royal hunting 1. The abbot Mathieu (lived during the 1200's) is of the opinion of the learned Benedictine (unknown) The royal houses, he says, were so widespread in France they were unable to find even one hunting forest in the Bassigny (our region)

The little town of Pierrefaites (villa Petrae fictae) once had a chateau-fort, and a hunting forest reserve of our kings and a deanery. This antiquity can be proven 2. Additionally, not far from the village is situated the farm of Vau-Martel, (4 miles SE) the farm and the woods of la Reine, used for hunting. The names of the laws have confirmed the aforementioned claim. But we have not seen one document, no trace, from the palace of the Carlovians confirming this. *"This action, it is good for Pierrefaites?"* (No doubt the King had his way!)

We are not surprised by the unavailability of documents that we suppose were destroyed by the ravages of the Sarrasins (Moslems) after their defeat in front of Tours by Charles Martel (732) and by the Normands and the Hongrois (Hungarians) during their multiple invasions throughout 831, 888, 936, 937, etc. Our unfortunate country was prey to looting, of burning, of massacres, famine and the plague. The bishop Geilon died of grief at the sight of the evils that desolated his diocese (891)

1. Chronicon Besuense. ---- Spicilege de d'Achery, t. I, p. 499 --- Pairologie de Migne, t. 162/3. col. 866-870.
2. Baugier, Memories do Champagne, t. II, p. 90 ---Dictionare de Larmartiniere. ---- Dom Calmet, Historie de Lorraine, t. I, p. 138

————————

SUPPLEMENTS FROM ABBOT MULSON AND OTHERS

....

The catastrophic collapse of the 800 year old Roman Empire in 406 AD was primarily brought about by an unconcerned people living in an empire where integrity, honor, patriotism virtue, rampant homosexuality and immorality was common among the population. Citizens were kept content by free food and meaningless entertainment; disinterested patriotism ruled, the army

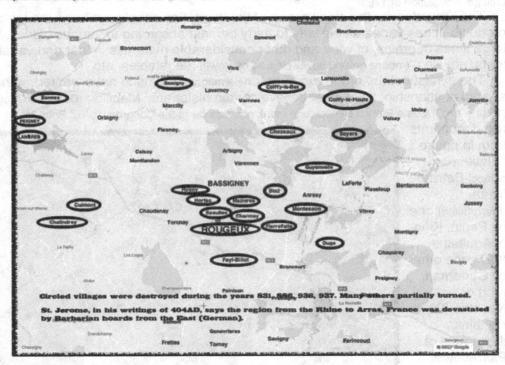

Circled villages were destroyed during the years 831, 888, 936, 937. Many others partially burned.
St. Jerome, in his writings of 404AD, says the region from the Rhine to Arras, France was devastated by Barbarian hoards from the East (German).

composed of foreigners and a booming economy permitted great fortunes to be quickly made. In short, God was rejected by leaders and citizens. The well known Antonine Plague of 165 AD – 180 AD also helped weaken the army and population.

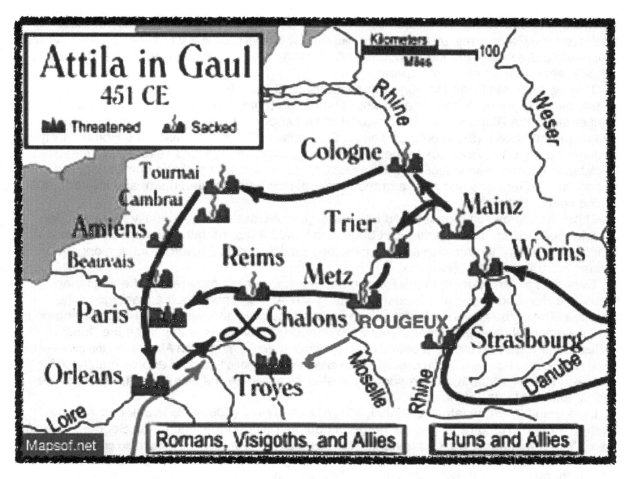

Attila in Gaul
451 CE
🏚 Threatened   🏚 Sacked

Cologne
Rhine
Weser
Tournai
Cambrai
Amiens
Beauvais
Reims
Trier
Mainz
Worms
Metz
Paris
Chalons ROUGEUX
Strasbourg
Moselle
Rhine
Danube
Orleans
Troyes
Loire
Mapsof.net

Romans, Visigoths, and Allies | Huns and Allies

No other nation has ever had such a long history of heroism, patriotic devotion, and dedicated virtue. Long past was the time when a general would execute his son for a victory achieved by disobeying orders. Extensive use of slaves was accompanied by desire for greater accumulation of goods and personal pleasure. Refusal to serve caused the ranks of the army to be filled with Barbarians, potential enemies who did not have Roman interests at heart. The extended borders of the Empire, too great a burden for a series of perverted emperors carelessly ruling an empire of self-absorbed citizens, led to a series of major defeats, opened the floodgates to the hordes of Barbarian tribes to the East and sacking of Rome.

The battle of the Roman emperor Aurelian against Tetricus I, emperor of the Gallic empire, in 274, fought in what is now Châlons-en-Champagne, France

27

(125 miles N) (known as 'Battle of the Catalaunian Plains' and the same place Atilla was defeated in 451), destroyed the Gallic army, (Almost 300,000 men are said to have fallen in that battle." - Hydatius, Chronicon, 150) marked the end of the independent Gallic Empire, and reunified it back to the Roman Empire, after thirteen years of separation.

The many routes forged through the countryside of NorthEastern Gaul facilitated the invasions of Germanic tribes. The torrent of barbarian tribes which poured through the Roman frontier along the Rhine in 303 AD, devastated and killed so many that the country almost became uninhabited. (Enumenius, Panegyr De Const., c 21) They chased the Roman army through the region of Rougeux to the walls of Langres (15 miles W), and severely wounded Constance Chlore, (Roman Emperor from 293 to 306) Within two hours of this humiliation, he turned on the Germans and after a grand carnage, thoroughly routed them, and killed 60,000 on the field of battle.

Other Barbarians who penetrated into our region of Gaul were continually repressed by Constantine, Julian, and Valerian. But beginning in 406 AD a mortally weakened Roman Empire was forced to abandon its centuries-long position on its Eastern frontier along the Rhine, 100 miles East of Rougeux.

Ever alert for an opening in the Roman defenses, the most important of the Barbarian tribes, the Burgundians, came from the North in 407 AD, and soon took advantage of the situation. Their tribes swept into the region around Rougeux and eventually gave their name to one of France's fairest provinces. They were considered by the Romans to be the "most civilized of the Barbarians" and established a kingdom extending from Alsace (on the banks of the Rhine River East of Rougeux) to Provence (South to the Mediterranean Sea) and approximately 300 miles wide. Their occupation was soon contested by other Germanic tribes; the Sueves, the Alians, and in 411, the Vandals.

Less than fifty years later, on 7 April, 451, Attila the Hun, (406–453) leader of a savage Eastern Mongol-Turco race, and his horde of pagans ravaged the land of the Sequani (Rougeux region) "like a wild beast walking upright." (The barbarian nation of the Huns became so great that more than a hundred cities were captured ... And there were so many murders and blood-lettings that the dead could not be numbered. Ay, for they took captive the churches and monasteries and slew the monks and maidens in great numbers. — Callinicus, in his Life of Saint Hypatius) Attila had a fetish for constructing pyramids of human heads as well as being known for 'fire and flame.'

He destroyed Rome, looted the European section of the Empire, and held sway until a confederation of Franks, Romans and other tribes of the region (between a coalition led by the Roman general Flavius Aetius and the Visigothic king Theodoric I. It was one of the last major military operations of the Western Roman Empire. The battle was strategically inconclusive: the Romans stopped the Huns' attempt to establish vassals in Roman Gaul, and installed Merovech as king of the Franks. However, the Huns successfully looted and pillaged much of Gaul and crippled the military capacity of the Romans and Visigoths) defeated him at the battle of Calataunian Fields (120 miles N)

Known to suffer from chronic nosebleeds, it is said he drowned in his own blood after falling unconscious into a drunken stupor while celebrating his wedding the night before the battle.

Nine years after its destruction by Attila, Rome was again sacked by a new enemy, the Goths. This event, coupled with extremely high taxation and profound corruption of its citizenry and leaders, led to the final and total collapse of the Roman Empire.

This catastrophe introduced the 'Dark Ages' in which the progress of civilization stopped and began a long slide back into the barbarism of pre-Roman times. Chaos swept over the European continent. Hopeless of escape and without leadership, bovine peasantry and masses of wild warriors endured centuries-long traditions of disorder, localism, and violence until gradual improvements began around 1000 AD

Around 450, the Franks, a group of barbaric Germanic tribes, invaded and colonized the regions North of Paris. In 534 they occupied neighboring Burgundy, and the region of Rougeux. Gregory of Tours lavished much pity for the victims of pillage and arson that were committed during the endless Frankish, Burgundian, Gothic wars and Barbarians from the

28

East. Without funds, the poor had no means of ransoming husbands or sons captured by these savage hordes. Unless prisoners of war were ransomed, they were used as slaves, slaughtered or mutilated to prevent them from further fighting. In at lEast one instance, it has been reported, 15,000 endured the horror of having their eyes gouged out at the point of a sword.

(The Franks are historically first known as a group of Germanic tribes that inhabited the land Roman-held soil between the Rhine, Scheldt, Meuse, and Somme rivers in what is now Northern France, Belgium and the Southern Netherlands in the 3rd century AD, and second as the people of Gaul who merged with the Gallo-Roman populations during succeeding centuries, passing on their name to modern-day France and becoming part of the heritage of the modern French people. Some Franks raided Roman territory, while other Frankish tribes joined the Roman troops of Gaul. In later times, Franks became the military rulers of the Northern part of Roman Gaul. The kingdom was acknowledged by the Romans after 357 AD. Following the collapse of Rome in the West, the Frankish tribes were united under the Merovingians, who succeeded in conquering most of Gaul in the 6th century, which greatly increased their power. This empire would gradually evolve into the state of France.

The Holy Roman Empire (Not to be confused with Roman Empire was a multi-ethnic complex of territories in central Europe that developed during the Early Middle Ages and continued until its dissolution in 1806) The largest territory of the empire after 962 was the Kingdom of Germany, though it also came to include the Kingdom of Bohemia, the Kingdom of Burgundy, the Kingdom of Italy, and numerous other territories.On 25 December 800, Pope Leo III crowned the Frankish king Charlemagne as Emperor, reviving the title in Western Europe after more than three centuries. The title continued in the Carolingian family until 888 and from 896 to 899, after which it was contested by the rulers of Italy in a series of civil wars until the death of the last Italian claimant, Berengar, in 924. The title was revived in 962 when Otto I was crowned emperor, fashioning himself as the successor of Charlemagne, and beginning a continuous existence of the empire for over eight centuries also imposed their empire on this part of Gaul (418) (The Frankish State, by the 8th century, developed into the Holy Roman Empire and had consolidated its hold over the majority of Western Europe by the end of the 18th century)

After defeating the Germans and Rome, Clovis founded the Frankish kingdom, and became the king over what is now Western France and Germany, was baptized a Christian in 496 after he promised to: *"Give up his gods and be baptized if the Lord Jesus would save him from sure defeat by the Germans."* A sudden and unexpected victory prompted his wife to insist he fulfill this vow. She called upon the Bishop of Reims, who baptized Clovis and 3,000 of his soldiers. His baptism inspired the rapid spread of Christianity throughout France and most of Europe during the following centuries. According to Gregory of Tours, 'paganism' still had many followers at the close of the sixth century despite the sweeping conversion to Catholic beliefs.

In 571, bubonic plague ravaged Clermont, Bourges, and Dijon, (40 miles S) Reports confirm that Rougeux was effected by reoccurring invasions of 'the pest' through the centuries and close proximity of villages unquestionably permitted plague carrying fleas to be rapidly transmitted across the countryside. Extremely rapid collapse and total disruption of the superb communication and commerce systems immediately followed the retreat of the Roman Empire and had many severe consequences for the populace.

Social structure in the Empire became divided into small enclaves; each with their own selfish and prideful warlord with unceasing aggression against their neighbors. Civil wars and the specter of famine became rampant. To this chaos was added the loss of normal but critical legal functions; formally common and standardized across the Empire. Recording and enforcement of deeds; distribution of inheritances; resolution of property boundaries; established processes for filing suit and other multitudinous court disciplines disappeared with the Roman collapse. Local customs and variations of Roman and German 'law' began to supplement the customary legal training of the Romans. Successful prosecution of an offender from another location with different laws became impossible. During the next 600 years the incompatibility of Germanic influences and brutish customs, greatly at odds with the Roman system which had previously bound the entire social fabric of the many peoples of Europe into a unified order, was forever lost. It was not until the 11th century that a few scholars began attempts to standardize and codify the enormous variations within the laws and customs of the various regions. Attempts at standardization was commonly met by armed resistance. Much of this work has not been completed today.

Collapse led to the beginning of the feudal system in which peasants became deeply subjugated to every lawless whim of his local master. Gradually this exploitation led to an accumulation of wealth for those aggressive men without consciences whose distinctions of moral values were totally opposed to those of the peasant class. Their prideful ideas of 'right' and 'good' did not apply to the poor. These 'noble' men separated themselves from ones who failed to meet their standards and fundamentally believed all 'common' people were liars. In the opinion of these 'nobles,' they alone were the sole determiner of what was 'truth' and passed judgments, cruelly and shamefully oppressed the poor, while they lived grossly opulent lifestyles. They occasionally helped the poor, not through pity, but through the feeling of plenitude, the consciousness of a great wealth and the super-abundance of power. These arrogant and condescending men began calling themselves 'nobles' and 'kings' with a clearly defined order of importance and authority. Constant conflicts between these jealous and covetous men caused untold misery and death to the poor who were forcefully impressed into their armies. Thankfully, the Rougeux name does not appear on any list of these 'nobles.'

It is abundantly clear the noble ones were the not the oppressed who courageously managed to survive the cruelest of times and still maintain their faith in Our Savior.

Famine was a rare phenomenon during the time of the Roman Empire. The well constructed and maintained road system, which led to the furthermost corners of the Empire, enabled the Roman government to integrate commerce, enjoy rapid postal service and constant communication with every official. *"Along the main roads,"* says Gibbon, *"houses were everywhere constructed at the distance of only four or five miles; each of them constantly provided with forty horses, and by the help of these relays, it was easy to travel 100 miles a day."*

By 398 AD, transportation had so seriously deteriorated that a famine gripped Rome itself, only partially relieved by Stilicho (Cardinal Mathieu, Les eveques de Langres, p. 17), (Flavius Stilicho was a high-ranking general in the Roman army who became, for a time, the most powerful man in the Western Roman Empire) who embarked upon the Soane (River) with vast loads of grain from the region of Rougeux.

chlothar ii king of the franks
fr.wikipedia.org/

(The extreme weather events of 535–536 were the most severe and protracted short-term episodes of cooling in the Northern Hemisphere in the last 2000 years. The event is thought to have been caused by an extensive atmospheric dust veil, possibly resulting from a large volcanic eruption in the tropics, and/or debris from space impacting the Earth. Its effects were widespread, causing unseasonal weather, crop failures and famines worldwide. The Byzantine historian Procopius recorded of 536, in his report on the wars with the Vandals, *"During this year a most dread portent took place. For the sun gave forth its light without brightness... and it seemed exceedingly like the sun in eclipse, for the beams it shed were not clear")*

In 618 our region came under authority of Clothar, King of France. (This action initiated a long period of invasions, wars, and successive calamities, which badly disturbed the lives of the inhabitants) Clovis I, his father, divided the kingdom between his four sons. In the year 511 at the age of about 14, Clothar I inherited two large territories on the Western coast of Francia, separated by the lands of his brother

30

Charibert I's kingdom of Paris. Chlothar spent most of his life struggling to expand his territories at the expense of his relatives and neighboring realms in all directions.
By the end of his life, Chlothar had managed to reunite the Francia by outliving his brothers and grabbing their territories after they had died. But upon his own death, the Frankish kingdom was once again divided between his own four surviving sons. Chlothar's father, Clovis I, had converted to Nicene Christianity, but Clothar like other Merovingians, did not consider the monogamy taught by Christianity should be expected of royalty; he had five wives.

742-814
CHARLEMAGNE

genealogyofpresidents.blogspot.com

In 779 AD Charlemagne, after his successful 30 year war, captured the Saxons and Franks, instituted the tithing (tax) laws of the country of a 10 to 30% tax of all grains, fruits, vegetables, newly cleared land, etc. This burden, falling on the poor, lasted until the Revolution of 1789—a full 1000 years!

At the beginning of 800AD the 'Medieval Warming Period' started and lasted until 1315. The Vikings settled Greenland. English farmers grew grapes for wine. Temperatures rose in Europe and farming did well. The population of Europe swelled. There is no shortage of documents describing the ravages of the Saracens (Muslims) until their defeat in front of

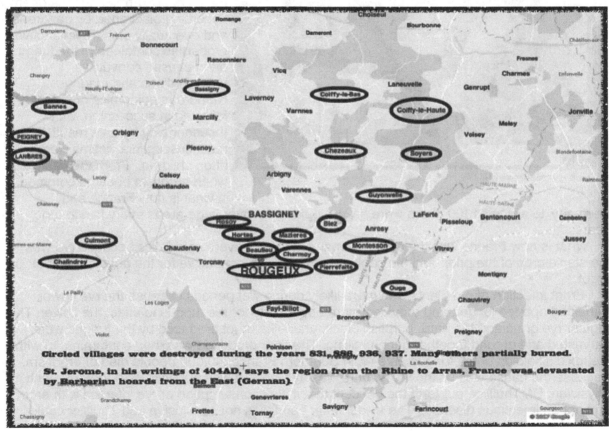

Circled villages were destroyed during the years 831, 926, 936, 937. Many others partially burned.

St. Jerome, in his writings of 404AD, says the region from the Rhine to Arras, France was devastated by Barbarian hoards from the East (German).

Tours by Charles Martel in 732 AD; of the Normans and the Hongrois (Hungarians) during multiple invasions during the years, 831, 888, 891, 936, 937 AD, and beyond. The pillage, burnings, massacres, famine, and pestilence, which followed these invasions are beyond belief.

Charlemagne, between 768 and 814, united most of France and subdued the Barbarians on the East side of the Rhine. While king, he established the various dioceses and parishes which still essentially exist today. However, atCharlemagne's death the region was split into three sections and we were again at the frontier in the midst of considerable fighting between his heirs. Burgundy divided into Eastern and Western sections and eventually, themselves were split into feuding fiefdoms controlled by local warlords. Continuing as the buffer zone between German tribes to the East and those to the West, our region again suffered invasions by the brutish Normans in 883 and again in 923.

Painting by **Matthias Grünewald** (c. 1470 –1528) of a patient suffering from advanced ergotism about 1512-16.

Records of these times mention frequently St. Anthony's Fire, 'burning death' or 'Holy Fire'. It was in the Rhine Valley, in 857 AD, that the first major outbreak of gangrenous ergotism was documented. Called 'Holy Fire' because of the burning sensations in the extremities that were experienced by the victims. 'Holy' because of the belief that this was a punishment from God. Constricted circulation resulted in toes, fingers, arms and legs often becoming blackened by gangrene and eventually die. Psychoactive properties contained in the fungus often caused convulsive hallucinations and madness. Numerous epidemics of ergotism followed in succession, with thousands dying as a result. The most susceptible victims were often children. From the year 900 when ergotism became common in what is now France and Germany, to around 1300, there were severe epidemics over large areas every five to ten years.

What is now France was the center of many of these severe epidemics because rye was the staple crop of the poor, and the cool, wet climate was conducive for the development of ergot.

Ergot infection of rye plants was more likely during wet periods because the rye flower remained opened longer, and provided more opportunity for the fungus to infect the flower. The regular rye grain and the hard, purplish black, grain-like ergot produced by the fungus were harvested and ground together during milling. The flour produced was then contaminated with the toxic alkaloids of the fungus. In 944, in Southern France, 40,000 people died of ergotism. Because the cause was unknown, no cure was available. It was not until 1670 that a French physician, Dr. Thuillier, put forth the concept that it was consumption of rye infected with ergot and not an infectious disease. The evidence at hand was not conclusive and Thuillier could

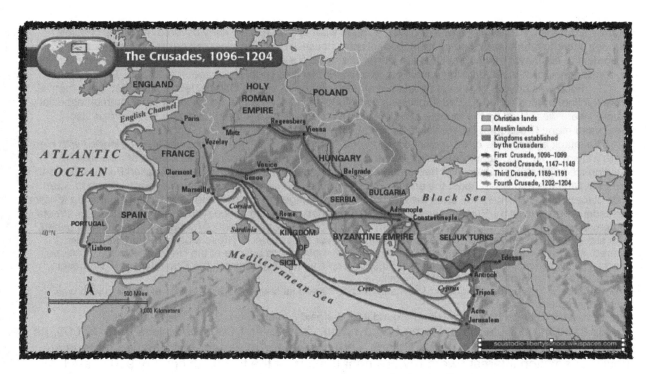

The Crusades, 1096–1204

Christian lands
Muslim lands
Kingdoms established by the Crusaders
First Crusade, 1096–1099
Second Crusade, 1147–1149
Third Crusade, 1189–1191
Fourth Crusade, 1202–1204

not convince the farmers that this was the cause of this dreaded affliction. It would be another two hundred years before ergot was demonstrated to be a fungus causing this terrible plague.

Crop rotation, strenuously resisted and only accepted in the 1800's effectively stopped the reproduction of the spore which gained toxicity during the winter following the initial infection.

Those we call sorceress, those men but mainly women, who gave assistance to Satan and attended festivals or assemblies of sorceress and demons and give assistance to the genie of evil, make for harm those acts that exceed the power of humanity. In 1610 seigneur of justice for Hortes (4 miles N) seized two women accused of evil doing to their beasts and to their children. After a regular procedure one was banished in perpetuity, the other was condemned to the fire. The one who appealed to the Counsel of Paris lost her appeal. The process cost 288 livres.

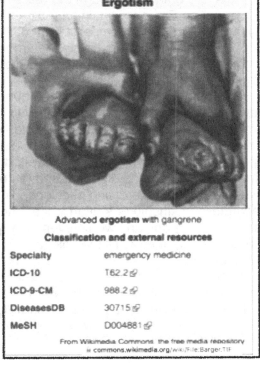

Ergotism

Advanced **ergotism** with gangrene

Classification and external resources

Specialty	emergency medicine
ICD-10	T62.2
ICD-9-CM	988.2
DiseasesDB	30715
MeSH	D004881

From Wikimedia Commons the free media repository
commons.wikimedia.org/wiki/File:Barger.TIF

Convulsive symptoms of ergotism
From Wikimedia Commons, the free media repository

In 926 and 954, the Hungarians invaded and decimated the region. In 1095 Pope Urban II called for the First Crusade. (Many poor peasants embarked on this 3000 mile trek without supplies and failed to survive. They could not use the Mediterranean Sea as the Crusaders did not control the ports on the coast of the Middle East and were forced to go by foot. They travelled from

33

France Southeast to Eastern Europe and then through what is now Turkey. They covered hundreds of miles, through scorching heat and deep snow in the mountain passes. The Crusaders ran out of fresh water and according to a survivor of the First Crusade who wrote about his experiences after his return, some were reduced to drinking their own urine, drinking animal blood or water that had been in sewage.

Food was bought from local people but at very expensive prices. Odo of Deuil claims that these men who were fighting for God were reduced to pillaging and plunder in order to get food. Disease was common especially as men were weakened by the journey and drinking dirty water. Dysentery was common. Heat stroke also weakened many Crusaders. Disease and fatigue affected rich and poor alike.

The attack and capture of Jerusalem started in the summer of 1099. Jerusalem was well defended with high walls around it. The first attacks on the city were not successful as the Crusaders were short of materials for building siege machines. Once logs had arrived, two siege machines were built. A monk called Fulcher was on the First Crusade and wrote about the attack on the Holy City. He can be treated as an eye-witness as to what took place. Fulcher claimed that once the Crusaders had managed to get over the walls of Jerusalem, the Muslim defenders there ran away. Fulcher claimed that the Crusaders cut down anybody they could and that the streets of Jerusalem were ankle deep in blood. The rest of the Crusaders got into the city when the gates were opened. The slaughter continued and the Crusaders *"killed whoever they wished"*. Those Muslims who had their lives spared, had to go round and collect the bodies before dumping them outside of the city because they stank so much. The Muslims claimed afterwards that 70,000 people were killed and that the Crusaders took whatever treasure they could from the Dome of the Rock.

The Crusaders created the Kingdom of Jerusalem in 1099 and its first king was Godfrey of Bouillon who was elected by other crusaders.

The Crusaders held the city and the land around it for the next 87 years.

By 1100 the population of Rome had dwindled from over 1,000,000 to less than 10,000. Its infrastructure, monuments, and buildings were continually mined for construction materials until preservation interests were revived near the turn of the twentieth century 900 years later.

A pestilence broke out in Parijustins in 1129, which in short order swept off 14,000 persons and despite all efforts daily added to its victims. At length, on November 26th, the shrine of St. Genevieve was carried through the streets of the city in solemn procession. That same day but three persons died, the rest recovered and no others were taken ill. This was but the first of may miracles which the city of Paris had obtained through the relics of its patron saint.

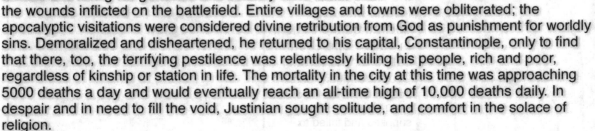

Justinian the Great

www.skate.com/

The Emperor Justinian (482 – 565), was a Byzantine (East Roman) emperor from 527 to 565. During his reign, Justinian sought to revive the empire's greatness and reconquer the lost western half of the historical Roman Empire.

Defeated by the cataclysm of the bubonic plague, he saw with horror the disease demolishing his once invincible armies and killing his generals and soldiery alike faster than the wounds inflicted on the battlefield. Entire villages and towns were obliterated; the apocalyptic visitations were considered divine retribution from God as punishment for worldly sins. Demoralized and disheartened, he returned to his capital, Constantinople, only to find that there, too, the terrifying pestilence was relentlessly killing his people, rich and poor, regardless of kinship or station in life. The mortality in the city at this time was approaching 5000 deaths a day and would eventually reach an all-time high of 10,000 deaths daily. In despair and in need to fill the void, Justinian sought solitude, and comfort in the solace of religion.

In 1629 Anne Carteret, of Guyonvelle, (12 miles NE) convicted of having assisted at rites near the pond of Soyers (7 miles NE) was also burnt at the stake as a common sorcerer, we read in the Croix de Chassus (A type of French dictionary) (Witchcraft was dreaded by the people and pursued by the courts. Recent scientific analysis of 'burning death' caused by rye fungus indicated mental faculties were effected and may have been the cause of bizarre actions leading to an accusation of witchcraft.

CHAPTER IV
(0-1790)
DEANERY

1. INSTITUTION----- 2. ADMINISTRATIVE CENTER----- 3. NOMINATION ----- 4. FUNCTION OF THE DEANERY ----- 5. EPISCOPAL LETTERS ----- 6. DEANERIES

Once the province of Lingonaise, the most ancient of Gaul, extended all the way to the Saouc (River) In 60AD Emperor Galba (3 BC--69 AD) (a homosexual who ruled by extreme cruelty, even killing his youngest son) detached a portion for the benefit of the Sequani (by the formation of the new province at Dijon)

The territory was divided into many cantons (pagi) We call pagi a canton (district) and a contra a country. The first word evidentially comes from the Latin pagus, the way paysan becomes pagans. The pagus Decolatensis (name of the new district) of Partensis (apparently the name of the official who gave the Latin names to the new districts), the name of Port-sur-Saone, resembles that which was heard over all the diocese of Pierrefaites after that time. Hortes was a part of the canton. But the diocese of Besancon (65 miles S) adjoined the parish, while the part of Port-sur-Saone remained in the province of Lingons. They united in canton Bassiniacenssi, where in principal they would exert considerable strength. Lingues and the Lingons separated into the Bassigny of the Lorraine and Champagne Bassigy1. These ecclesiastical divisions then formed the last six archdeacons of the diocese. The other five were, based on their location, the Langrois, the Dijonnais, the Tonnerrois, the Barrois and the Lassois. Each one Included several deaneries. The archdiocese of Bassigny was composed of deaneries of Is and of Pierrefaites.

At what epoch were these administrative districts established? Our historians do not agree on their response to this question. The abbot of Mangin says, *"It is consistently said that during the IV century of the Church, we already see several deaneries in Campagne in one diocese."* During the centuries VII and VII there was established almost all of the rights and Episcopal functions to the deaneries during the visits by judges of all things ecclesiastics and they insured that the Ordinaries (untrained men acting as priests) were no longer in the canton and bishops in name only 2. The bishops, feeling that their authority had been considerably diminished searched for means to restore their authority over the deaneries.

We now arrive at a new century 3.

After Abbot Mathieu instituted the arch-deaneries at the deaneries existing from the VI century, MM. Pistollet and Roussel traced this change to century IX 4 and the savant Abbot Richard himself assigned the same date that concerns the diocese of Basancon 5.

Our opinion is that the deaneries made the final organizations under the regime of Charlemagne (King of the Franks from 768–814 and Emperor of the Holy Roman Empire from 800–814)

The deaneries, as later the civil cantons, gradually returned to the names of their capital cities. We call our own Decanatus Peirae ficias--or Petra fiche, which means stones planted or placed for security in ancient times. Further corruption of the name; Pierreficle, Pierefitte,and

Pierrefaites occurred. (4 miles East of Rougeux)

Fifteen villages in France have the same etymology. Thirteen retained the primitive, Pierrefitte: Pierrefiche (Aveyron) approaches the most liberal usage; Pierrefaites is the only one of

THE HOME OF OUR PRIMARY SOURCE OF MATERIAL FOR THIS BOOK, FRANCOIS JOFFRAIN.

PIERREFAITES

Google Earth

Pierrefaites

PIERREFAITES

Image © 2017 DigitalGlobe
© 2017 Google

such designation. The words Petra ficta are susceptible, we think, of two interpretations. First, a border limiting the provinces and the separate city administrations can be defined. We know this has been done in many localities and Pierrefaites would also (have) placed at the extreme edge of its frontier, markers of its important territorial divisions.

It is also probable to have (had) a Gaulic monument. This served as a center of population and proof of its ancient origin, and for history, a means of explanation of the choice that was made when it was chosen to become the capital city of the deanery. The Church is called the center of the worship of our God over the ruins of paganism and where the evangelizing preachers first planted the cross, established a chapel, a baptismal and cemetery for the people of the country.

Primarily the deans were chosen by the priests themselves as presiders at their assemblies, but confirmation of the election was required by the Episcopal authorities. In the following greater part of the centuries, at Langres it was the same, the name of the person nominated as dean was reserved to each of the Churches. They were always among the most

36

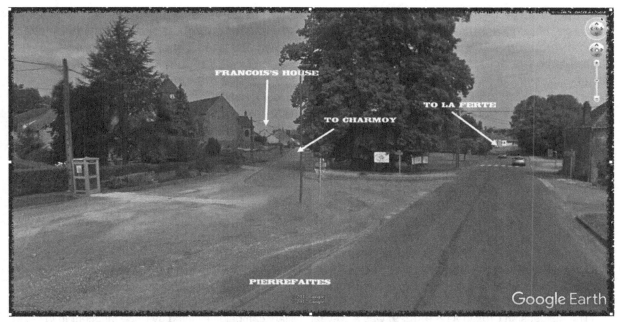

FRANCOIS'S HOUSE

TO CHARMOY

TO LA FERTE

PIERREFAITES

Google Earth

instructed and the most commendable. (In these times assignment of priests and some bishops, and even cardinals was sometimes based on popularity, relationships or politics)

The dignity of the Dean was respected and he was not necessarily attached to the deanery who nominated him. Since we have been united it is never permitted to hinder or prevent a bishop from transferring him to another parish if infirmity disables the assigned inhabitant and prevents him from performing his functions. Elsewhere the commission of rural deans are revocable ad nulum episcopi. (by the power of the bishop) There were also some vice-deans at some of the smaller deaneries who were nominated by the bishop [1].

The word Decannus designated first, in the abbeys, a religious who has the direction of ten monks, and in Campagne the priest in charge of monitoring at lEast ten of his colleagues.

Here are the functions charged to a rural dean:

-----Visit the parishes, provide of Holy Oils, install the priests, supervise their administration and conduct, transmit orders from the bishop, spiritually comfort the sick administer the

Sacraments, provide burial, assist in the Bishops synods (who drew their strength and authority from the Bishop and their effectiveness of their vigilance of the deaneries); promulgate the announcements of the Bishop and precisely report all important issues promptly to the Bishop.

NEAR PIERREFAITES

Google Earth

If the deans found themselves unable to perform, these functions were assumed by the vice-dean [1].

The reproduction of a specimen of an Episcopal letter from Guy de Rochefort from the XIII century authorized the installation of a priest. Written on parchment of small dimension (4 centimeters by 13) it contains six lines in Latin with numerous abbreviations, nevertheless it is clear and precise: *"----Guy, by the grace of God, bishop of Langres, of the dean of Pierrefaites, salvation. Having admitted M. Guillaume, priest to the vacant church at Champigny, upon the recommendation of the prior of Varnnes, who it is known has the right of patronage, we authorize you to accept this recommendation and place Guillaume in corporal possession of this church with all the solemnities and devotion used to place men in such circumstances. Given, this Friday after the Laetare Jerusalem."* (The fourth Sunday of the season of Lent in the Western Christian liturgical calendar from the traditional Gospel reading for the day; the story of the miracle of the loaves and fishes)

The names of the deans are unknown until commencement of the II century. Then Thierry (Theodoricus), uncle to Gillaume, and seigneur of Pierrefaites, appeared and claimed authority over the deanery and signed, in this capacity, a great number of acts. He became a collector of the churches of Frettes and of Tornay and paid ten sols for the abbey of Belmont. He assisted in the foundation of the abbey of Beaulieu (adjacent to Rougeux)

Paganus, priest and dean of Pierrefaites was eyewitness of the donation made by Milon de Rosoy (de Rosseio), the owner of Bussieres, to Beaulieu.

Hugues (Hugo), priest of Saviguy, dean in 1227 AD, signed the waiver that made Sebille, widower of Etienne de Noidant, seigneur of Poinson, killed during the war against the Albigeois, with all the rights and pretensions of the property of Beaulieu resulting from the inheritance of her marriage. (which included the village of Rougeux)

(The Albigensian Crusade(1209–1229) was a 20-year military campaign initiated by Pope Innocent III to eliminate Catharism (a cult) in Languedoc, in the South of France)

1. Pistollet de Saint-Ferjeux, Limites de la Province lingonaise.
2. Illistorie du diocese de Langres, t. II, p. 344
3. Les ereqies de Langres.
4. Les limites de la province lingonaise. ----- La diocèse de Langres, 1. I, p.   28.
5. Historie des Dioceses de Besancom et de Saint-Claude, t. I, p. 122-199.

Blaixe de Rosoy, had given to the abbey of Cherlieu a shipload of wheat, measure of Langres (Langres had its own measuring system, one among many developed during the centuries after the collapse of the universal system used by Roman Empire prior to the IV century) to be collected each year in addition to the one-third tithing and the other revenues of Rosoy. We later see Armand (Armandus) was still dean and cure of Pierrefite in 1265 and 1269.

He drafted an act of borrowing from the sons of Simon, seigneur of Pierrefaites, for the abbey of Beaulieu 1. In 1269 he was an eyewitness, with Aubert, priest of Coiffy, of a declaration made by Henri, priest of Arbigny, whom we call a venerable man. His successor of the deanery was Simon, priest of Hortes (de Orates) 1275 to 1279 (4 miles N) The functions of dean are performed in 1336 by John, priest of Celles, whose ordination we find was done by a letter from the Official of Langres who reports to the parish church of Champigny 2.

For more than two centuries we do not find the names of those who held titles in the churches. From 1516 we find at the same times the names of the priests of Pierrefaitte, John Carieret, (1610), Hector Carieret (1629-1635), of Anrosey, Clement Faullet, priest of Poison (1645-1657), and Claude Bacquet, priest of Vitrey (1749-1768)

1. Historie de diocese de Langres t. II, p. 335 and p. 28. Notes historiques sur les cures de champagnes, p. 21.
2. Guido Dei gratia Lingonensis Episcopus, Decno Petreficiae salutem, Cum nos Dominum Villermum presbyeterum ad curem Ecclesiae de Champiegneie vacantis admiseraverimus, ad praesetationem prioris de Varennis ad quem dictae ecclesiae jus patronatus dignoscitur pertinere, et ispsum incuravarimus de aeadem, Vobis mandamus quatenus praedicium Vitlermum in corporalem possessionem dictae ecclesise inducatis adhibitis solem pnitatibus quae solent et debent in talibus adhiberi. Datum die verenis post Laetare Jerusalem, Anno Domini millesimo ducentesimo sexagesimo quarto.

CHAPTER V
(900-1500)
PRIORIES----- COMMANDERS -----LEPER HOSPITALS

1. PRIORIES IN GENERAL ----- 2. PRIORY OF FAYL ----- 3. PRIORY OF VARNENNES ---- 4. PRIORY OF MAIZIERES ----- 5. PRIORY OF DE LA FERTE ----- 6. PRIORY OF CHARMES-SAINT-VALBERT ----- 7. PRIORY OF ROUGEUX ----- 8. AGRICULTURAL GRANGES -----9. COMMANDERS OF ARBIGNY ----- 10. COMMANDER OF BRONCOURT ----- 11. LEPERS OF PIERREFAITES AND OF FAYL

The establishment (priorates are usually a small community directed by a priest (prior) and dependent upon an abbey). is conventional and regular as long as the religious live under the rules of their Order. In principle all of our priests are conventuals (meaning they have the right to live always in the same abbey or convent) When through default or other reasons, the monks have decided to live a life of seclusion, we have given to their house property, free of encumbrances, which was not given in the name of the Prioress, Sebille, widower of Etienne de Noidant (Killed in the Albigensian war. The Albigensian Crusade or Cathar Crusade (1209–1229) was a 20-year military campaign initiated by Pope Innocent III to eliminate Catharism in Languedoc, in the South of France) So, then this gift removed the power of the proprietor of the canton and of the king when appointments were being considered. (Bypassed the obligation of patronage) The earnings from this gift removed the dependency of the house (from the bishop) but the title holder (Beaulieu) must pay the charges (tithes?), whether by himself or whether by another eclectic.

A parish priest can designate an adjacent parish to join with him in assistance when he has serious concerns 1.

One of the more ancient of our parishes is that of Fayl (-Billot) Around 900 the seigneur, who was at Fouvent, gave some woods and some ground to the abbey of Montieramey in the 2 diocese of Troy to found an abbey in his domaine. Those monks that relocated in the new abbey came under the rule of St. Benoit (480 – 543 or 547 AD. A Christian saint, venerated in the Eastern Orthodox Churches, the Catholic Church, the Oriental Orthodox Churches, the Anglican Communion and Old Catholic Churches. He is a patron saint of Europe. Benedict's main achievement is his ' Rule of Saint Benedict') Later, it consisted of a church dedicated to the Birth of the Virgin then eventually a parish convent. The priest was the superior of the religious and for a long time also performed the functions of the parish priest. He was named by the abbot of Montieramey under the direction of whom he administrated the needs of the parish. We see, in 1264, he demanded permission, in writing, to exchange the Bois de Sainte-Marie for one much closer called Bois-Prieur from which the brush and trees had been trimmed (Mentioned because of the scarcity of fuel) 1.

The conventional life of the monks did not now exist at the parish of Notre Dame at this time (1264) The religious, for what reason we are ignorant, abandoned this life.

After that the abbot conferred a secular priest to this parish. The first name we know that lived there called himself Pierre in 1347. In 1391 the parish elected a priest of Fayl (-Billot—2 miles S) whom we see had ceased to have any monks. However the title of priest was maintained and given to a priest who was not obliged to the residence but who was required to serve at Fayl 'en bon jours' (literally, 'in good days' but probably, fEast days—or possibly, 'because he liked wine?') of the year in order to make the desserie (wine)

The abbey of Montieramey (73 miles S) survived and until 1789 (when the Revolutionaries took command of The Church) the right to name the prior and the priest. Among the eighteen known abbots we find remarkable were Pierre Baudot, archdeacon of Bassigny, official and vicar general of Langres (1643-1662); Pierre-Bernard Baudot, canon of Langres (1662-1717) who donated 16,000 livres from his estate to the hospice of Saint-Anne at Dijon who were responsible for maintaining, in perpetuity, an orphanage for poverty stricken children at Fayl (28 April 1716); finally Louis-Francois Vivet de Monclus, canon and vicar general of Langres during the time of St. Brieuc 1725-1729)

The arable land, meadows and the Moulin-aux-Moines (grain mill at Moines), it has been affirmed, composed of this benefice. The abbot shared with the priests the tithes, but that, with the grain, only amounted to twenty bundles a year 1.

In 1254, Pierre, dean of Moge and John, priest of Fayl, discovered that Girard, mayor of Rougeux, with the assent of his spouse Adeline and her mother Alvis, gave an alms to Beaulieu the amount of the tithe of their property out of love for the abbey. (No less than 10% of their farm) The following year the bishop Gui de Rochefort approved this acquisition.

In 1084 Raynier de Choiseul (1195-1239), who wanted to do some good to remedy the salvation of his soul and those of his ancestors begged that Raynard, bishop of Langres, grant to the monks the church at Moleme d'Varnnes (that had been previously dedicated to the blissful Apostle Peter and of the martyr St. Gengoul) The prelate agreed to the request and gave in perpetuity to St. Maire de Moleme the church at Moleme d'Varnnnes, with all its tithes, offerings, and hundreds of other things that were part of its alter on condition that the religious humbly pray to Our Lord for the church of Langres, and each day during their daily office, pray for him (Raynier) while he lived and after he died. For this concession by the prelate, Raynier added many material advantages to the church at Langres.

Everywhere the men (monks) of that church could find an inhabited terrain exempted from the census they were free to inhabited it. (Apparently they had authority to confiscate property) If such territory had been seeded, the seeds or the price of the seeds was restituted to those who had replanted it. The same monks had the household chores; gathering cattle, harvesting hay, baking bread, and finding honey in the forests (normally peasants were required to request permission to enter the forests and were not permitted to pick up sticks for firewood without permission) The venison that they (these Monks) could find (killing a deer normally was punished by hanging), were permitted to receive for a host or an infirm brother. In all, they could acquire, in whatever manner they could, absolute liberty and freedom.

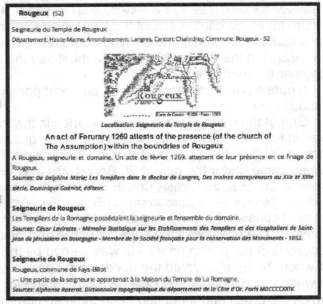

Rougeux (52)

Seigneurie du Temple de Rougeux
Département: Haute-Marne, Arrondissement: Langres, Canton: Chalindrey, Commune: Rougeux - 52

Localisation: Seigneurie du Temple de Rougeux

An act of Ferurary 1269 attests of the presence (of the church of The Assumption) within the boundries of Rougeux

A Rougeux, seigneurie et domaine. Un acte de février 1269, attestent de leur présence en ce finage de Rougeux.
Sources: De Delphine Marie; Les Templiers dans le diocèse de Langres, Des moines entrepreneurs au XIIe et XIIIe siècle. Dominique Guéniot, éditeur.

Seigneurie de Rougeux
Les Templiers de la Romagne possédaient la seigneurie et l'ensemble du domaine.
Sources: César Lavirotte - Mémoire Statistique sur les Etablissements des Templiers et des Hospitaliers de Saint-Jean de jérusalem en Bourgogne - Membre de la Société française pour la conservation des Monuments - 1852.

Seigneurie de Rougeux
Rougeux, commune de Fays-Billot
— Une partie de la seigneurie appartenait à la Maison du Temple de La Romagne.
Sources: Alphonse Roserot. Dictionnaire topographique du département de la Côte d'Or. Paris MDCCCXXXIV.

They were also granted a building for their use, houses, grist mill, and all other edifices. (This unprecedented freedom and those benefits did not last many years!) This extremely indulgent liberty was approved by Raynier, seigneur of Nogent, by Ermengarde, wife of Raynier de Choiseul, and by their children, Roger and Adeline.

The witnesses were Amaury, Voscelme, Robert, Girard, Varnier, Hugues, dean; Payen, Brenger, Bernard; archdeacons.

The Prelate wrote: *"If anyone dares to violate this order he will be struck with the sword of anathema and kept away from the most Holy Body and Blood of Our Lord until the time I am satisfied."* Then he affixed his seal on the act, given in the name of the Sainted and Indivisible Trinity, in the year of the Incarnation of Our Lord 1084 under the reign of Phillipe, King of France, Raynard, Bishop of Langres 1.

The abbot of Moleme, having accepted the order, sent, as soon as possible to Varennes (9 miles N), many religious for establishment a priory who would remain dependent upon his abbey. Then the parish church also became part of the priory.

The bishop immediately gave a part of the tithes of these (unknown to us) villages (whose tithes were owned by Varennes) to the priory and the same rights he had given to the priests of Vicq, Coiffy, of Champigny and Chezeaux.

Various members of the house of Choiseul wanted also to improve their spiritual life contributed to the endowment for the poverty stricken parish (Varennes) Besides his original generosity, Raynier de Choiseul and Raynier de Nogent ceded their seigniorial rights over Vicq and Coiffy (1101) Henri de La Ferte abandoned, with the consent of his spouse Leudegarde and his sons Ponce, Renard, and Heuri, his house at Champigny with the ground, orchard and use of the forest (1102) Godefroi, bishop of Langress, gave the church of Meuse, and Gerard de Dammartin gave his son, Robert, as a monk at Moleme, and gave half of the village and its tithes (1159) (Villages were owned by the purchaser who was either an official or monastery)

Raynard II gave the mill, the village oven and part of the village of Chezeaux (7 miles N), on condition that the religious say a perpetual mass for the repose of his soul (1216) Later, he gave them the alms from three measuring vessels (of the size used in Roman times) of wheat and oats each year from the ground of Saulxures (1226) and confirmed an additional measuring vessel of rye from the tithes of Lavernoy (1234)

Guy de Vignory engaged the priest Hervler as la garde et lauderie (custody and prayer of the office of lauds) of Champigny for forty livres in confidence of his performance. (1239)

However the Sires of Choisuel (24 miles N) did not always act kindly to the parishioners. A parishioner named John Ler caused some damages and protested his condemnation to death by the abbot as unjust, requiring Guy de Rocherfort (Comte de Rochefort) to intervene. John agreed that the prior had total authority of a seigneur over the men of the abbey who live at Varennes and its jurisdiction.

If someone, said John, wants to live at Varennes, they must agree the prior has the right to imprison or free the people who live under his authority. However, when a person is condemned to death, claimed John, the authority of an abbot over a lost member ought to be forfeited and submitted to his seigneur, then to his commander to assure justice.

Guy saw that the justice and seigneur-ship of the abbot extended over the people, woods, plains and water of Varennes and of all his territories. (He apparently became extremely angry that his rule was being challenged by a peasant, weakening of his own position and possibly fearful of an uprising if he weakened the authority of the abbot) The Abbot responded by proclaiming: *"That from the monks who served the seigneur at Varennes had the same liberty as those who served Raynier and his family. Industrious men who could be attracted were welcomed. That from now on if his men who live at Varennes (9 miles N) or his families leave, they shall die without heirs to their corpse and such heritages shall go to the abbot in its entirety."*

The Abbot further proclaimed: *"For the lodging which I required at Varennes, or I had guarded, Guy wants me to annul ten livres langoines (from the tithes given to the peasants); one hundred sols from Saint-Remy and one hundred sols from Paques (Easter donstions?) And you can no longer request for any reason lodgings either at the abbey nor at the village of Varennes. And for all things, Guy wants me and my heirs to quit donating the 2,066 livres 8 sols and all the other fables."* (fables in this context probably means various benefits previously bestowed or goods that have been supplied)

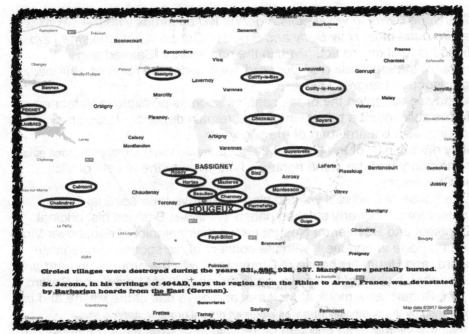

Circled villages were destroyed during the years 831, 836, 936, 937. Many others partially burned.

St. Jerome, in his writings of 404AD, says the region from the Rhine to Arras, France was devastated by Barbarian hoards from the East (German).

In May 1259 this amount was awarded as indemnity to the abbot by the royal court. (Apparently these very harsh acts were inflicted as punishment for Johns' rebellion of the injustice being inflicted on him and was about to be executed without recourse. It was a harsh world for the more than 95% of the population who were living in poverty those many centuries) 1. Le diocese de Langress, t. I, p. 60

There arose a difference between the monks and Bernard, priest of Vicq (de Vico) (12 miles N) That one pretended to have the right to all the tithes large and small and all the offerings made by the faithful to the parish church.

The religious, on the contrary claimed the two-thirds (their normal source of income from the tithes) Pierre Ralon, then priest of Varennes, presented the case in front of the priest of Luxeuil, who was a sub-delegate of the priest of Saint-Gengoul de Langres and who had been appointed by the Pope to resolve matters of this type. The cure did not at all agree the demands of Bernard were legitimate. An act was written in which Bernard could only retain one-third of the tithes and offerings and must bequeath to the parish all his furniture and all he had acquired at Vicq, his houses, ground, vineyards and his directives for celebration on the anniversary of his death in the churches of Moleme and of Varennes. And to make this an anniversary, he said, *"Anyone who owns the vineyard of Vicq must pay annually to the monks at Moleme and of Varennes, for their support, forty sols langrois"* 1 (sols langrois was the local currency) His act is dated November 1263. (Bernard was severely punished!)

In 1316, Guillllaume de Durfort, bishop of Langress, exempted (from tithes) the priest, the religious of the choir and the conventional brothers of his jurisdiction and of visits outside of the parish by the officers (of the monastery) (These monks were Cistercians and cenobites who wanted to live in seclusion)

From the 1517 concordat dated of Pope Leon X (1475-1521 and Pope from 1513 to 1521) and of Francois I, King of France (1494-1547) the priests were nominated, not by the abbot de Moleme, but by the King. The religious were given the benefice of becoming regulars (no longer bound by the strict regulations and poverty demanded by the order of St Benedict) by commendation of their superiors. We do not have a complete list. From the year 1156, the author of 'Le Diocese de Langres' mentions sixty-six.

The history does not say which epoque the monks ceased to be conventual; it seems they still existed until the priest was given that command 1.

Maizieres (Maceriae) (4 miles N) had a priest dependent on Saint-Vivant-sous-Vergy (for his support by tithes) To the year 870, the bishop of Clermont en Auvergne, established between the Saone and Dole a house for the religious that appropriated the relics of Saint Vivant, once abbot of a monastery de Poitiers. We gave them the patronage of several churches between those of Auxonne and de Voisey. It was the church of Saint Vivant who was destroyed soon after by Hasting (English General during the 100 Years War), who was at the head of the Normans. Manasses, duke of Bourgogne had constructed another church close to the chateau of Vergy, and strongly fortified it. He received the initial allocation of property of Sainte-Vivant en Amaous and took the name of Saint-Vivant Sous Vergy 2.

We do not know the date of the foundation of the priory of Maizieres (2 miles NE)

In 1006 the brighest apparent magnitude stellar event in recorded history appeared. (SN 1006 was a supernova that is likely the brightest observed stellar event in recorded history, reaching an estimated –7.5 visual magnitude, and exceeding roughly sixteen times the brightness of Venus. This 'guest star' was described by observers across China, Japan, Iraq, Egypt, and Europe, and possibly recorded in North American petroglyphs. Monks at St Gall provide independent data as to its magnitude and location in the sky, writing, *"In a wonderful manner this was sometimes contracted, sometimes diffused, and moreover sometimes extinguished..."* It was seen likewise for three months in the inmost limits of the South, beyond all the constellations which are seen in the sky. Some sources state that the star was bright enough to cast shadows; it was certainly seen during daylight hours for some time)

In 1178 a bull of Alexander III declared that Saint-Vivant-sous-Vergy possessed the village and the priory of Saint-Clement de Maizieres with its dependancies 3.

The following year, Oliver, priest of Saint-Vivant, ceded to the abbey of Beaulieu (very close to Rougeux), half of its land at Pleticort and of Pontelir with tithes payable at Vergy during the Octave of the Exaltation of the Holy Cross. (The date of the fEast marks the dedication of the Church of the Holy Sepulchre in Jerusalem in 335) During the same time there was a contention between the monks of Maizieres and those of Beaulieu, (2 miles apart) concerning the leagues of land they had seized and held in common.

1.Archives de la cote-'Or, abbeys de Molome, 40 laisse. Historie de Vicq. Le diocese de Langres. La Haute_Marne.
Revne Champenoise.

2. Historie de diocese de Besancon et de Saint_Claude, t. J, p. 171.

3. Villam et prioratum sancti Clementis de Marerils cum appenditilis suis. Historie de Saint_Vivant, p.25 and 26. Archives de la Cote-d'Or.

Pierre, abbot of Marimond, decided, in 1183, that Foulque, seigneur of Choiseul, having a substantial interest in the quarrel and the terms he gave the serfs, proved that at Maizieres (monachi de Maceriis) there are monks. (Am unable to see how this may have resolved the issue) In 1212 we see Robert, priest of Saint-Vivant exchanging a number of pieces of ground with the abbey of Beaulieu. Sicard, former priest of Voisey was made priest of Maizieres in 1179. In 1228 Anselme de Fouvent, canon of Langres was the administrator. Clarambaud was the holder until 1315. This priory (at Maizieres) stopped being a conventual during the XIV century then had to annex itself to Vergy, its dependent. This union is still found operating in 1440. Since that moment, the priest of St-Vivant, who was the grand dean of Vergy, was simultaneously priest of Maizieres, was seigneur of the village, and responsibility for high, average and low justice (the right to administer justice for all levels of crime and their appropriate punishment, including execution) had also the right to bestow a benefice 1.

Those historians were in error when they thought that the villages of La Ferte and de Soyers (Soaeriae) possessed each a distinct priory. There was only one for both.

The authors of Pauilles are also mistaken in saying that this establishment are dependent on Cluny; they should have said Luxeuil.

(The town of Cluny grew up around the Benedictine Abbey of Cluny, founded by Duke William I of Aquitaine in 910. The height of Cluniac influence was from the second half of the 10th century through the early 12th. The abbey was sacked by the Huguenots in 1562, and many of its valuable manuscripts were destroyed or removed) (60 miles SE) (Founded circa 585–590 by the Irish missionary Saint Columbanus. With a grant from an officer of the palace at Childebert's court, an abbey church was built with a sense of triumph within the heathen site and its 'spectral haunts'.The monastery grew so large that the chanting of the office went on day and night. In 731 a raiding party of Moors penetrated into Burgundy and massacred most of the community. The few survivors rebuilt the abbey. The monastery and the small town around its walls were devastated by the Norse in the 9th century and pillaged on several occasions. At the French Revolution the monks were dispersed)

A bull by Innocent II (?-1143) in 1136 enumerated the churches and the priories subject to Luxeuil (50 miles E) La Ferte and Soyers were not included, but a letter of Philippe de Sauabe, dated Haguenau in December 1201 mentioned La Ferte (7 miles E) among the priory lands and seigneurs of this abbey. It is during these two years that will place the origin of this abbey.

The patron of Philippe de Souabe and that of the church of La Ferte is Saint-Pierre are linked. As the church of Soyers (9 miles NE), Luxeuil are under the protection of Saint Valbert, their third abbot. There was probably conventionality in the diocese. Several who were prefects were religious of Luxeuil.

We find in 1266 brother Coliu, priest of La Ferte and of Jussey(18 miles E) The priest of La Ferte with the seigneur of Soyers had the right of presenting candidates for the priesthood at Anrosey, of Chaumondel, at Pisseloup, of Soyers (8 miles NE) and the vicars of La Ferte, at and of (9 miles E)2.

In 1276 a difficulty arose among the monks of Vaux-la-Douce (12 miles E) and those of Luxeuil (50 miles E—its difficult to understand why two locations so far apart would be interested in this pasturage) concerning certain usages claimed by the previous residents of their parish. In virtue of an arbitrary decision Vaux-la-Douce (12 miles NE) continued to enjoy the right of pasturage on the territory of Soyers (9 miles NE) following strict guidelines 1.

At Charmes (18 miles NW) there was a parish under the dependance of Luxeuil. The church was at the same time priory and parish. When it ceased to be conventional the abbot retained the title of primary priest of Charmes. They celebrate or cause to be celebrated by a religious the offices of the saints during the great annual festivities, especially that of their patron saint, Valbert.

During the XV century or later the simple benefice was normally in charge of the prefect of the monastery. The church, annexed to Pressigny, found itself served by the priest of that parish and by a vicar who was a resident of the village.

1. Notice manuscripte sur Maixieres. ----- Manusorits Mathieu, t. X, p. 72. ---- La Haute-Marne, article Maixieres. ----- Revue Champenoisc, p. 338. ---- Le diocese de Langres, t. II, P. 287.
2. Notes de M. L'abbe Foissey, cure de Soyers.

The ancient titles of Beaulieu are important to the existence of a parish at Rougeux. It was originally formed by the religious of Bize. Olger, abbot of the monastery, declared by a written act of 1213: There has arisen a difference between the brothers of Beaulieu and Etudes, priest of Rougeux (de Rugeol) We have decided that our priest of Rougeux or of our men belonging to it, have no right to use the territory of Mont-Refroy, (between Rougeux and Beaulieu) nor of a barn of Beaulieu 3.

After having acquired the tithe of Rougeux (1254) by the appropriation by the bishop, Guy de Rochefort (1255), Beaulieu claimed the rise of the ground adjacent to the land owned by the monastery. This was opposed by the residents of Rougeux.The dispute was settled by the following agreement. (The following from an ancient document of Beaulieu)

In the 13th century, Rougeux, in Latin, ville de Rogeio, belonged to the monastery of Bize. The religious of Beaulieu bought the tax of this village in the year 1255. Guy de Rochefort, bishop of Langres, gave his permission by the following letter:

"We, Guy, by the grace of God, bishop of Langres, make it known to all who will see these letters, whom we greet, agree and confirm this acquisition which the monastery and convent of the church of Beaulieu have paid the tax of Rougeux, from whatever right there be by title of fief or otherwise, providing the tax belongs to the church of Langres, gives from us and our successors all the rights which we have or which we could have acquired on said tax. In faith of this we have attached our seal to the present letters. Given in the year of our Savior 1255 in the month of November."

The abbot of Bize responded:

"To all who see these letters, we, brother Godfrey, humble abbot and all the convent of the monastery of St Peter of Bize greet you in Our Lord. We make it known that a difference has arisen between myself and some of the religious of Beaulieu of the order of Citeaux on the one

party and according of what is said of the abbot and convent of Beaulieu which asked of us a tax and a third of the produce of land already acquired which we have been cultivating on the borders of Rougeux because the said abbot and convent of Beaulieu have had right to the tax and a third of the products of said lands which have been the custom of the inhabitants of the village of Rougeux: we on the contrary are sure that we were not at all held to pay the tax and the third of the products of the land because we have never paid nor have we been used to paying the tax and third of the products which we produce ourselves now and in the future.

Similarly, we have asked of the abbot and convent of Beaulieu to pay the taxes of the church of Rougeux owed on the indebted labor and land which the above mentioned abbot and convent of Beaulieu bought from Girard, the mayor of Rougeux, without our consent and our blessing, and that which was not lawful as we had assumed."

"Similarly in that the abbot and convent of Beaulieu said that our men of Rougeux drove and pastured their animals on their borders of Mont-Refroy, (Land situated between Beaulieu and Rougeux) which grazing belong to the same abbot and convent of Beaulieu, they could not nor should not do as they had assumed.

Lastly, through good and discrete people, and the agreement of the above mentioned parties, peace has been made in this way:

That we can hold, cultivate and own as many as seventy documents (meaning unknown) of this workable land on the border of Rougeux while including in these lands already acquired and owned by ourselves or which we will have cultivated by others at our cost.

Similarly, we, the above abbot and convent of Bize, could exchange the above mentioned seventy documents, one or many, which we believe advantageous to ourselves and to the benefit of the church. But we, the above abbot and convent of Beze, yield and have given up to the above abbot and convent of Beaulieu, the right which we have had, or could have had, to receive forced labor or land sold by Girard, mayor of Rougeux.

For the above mentioned things, the above mentioned abbot and convent of Beaulieu and their successors will be held to pay us and our successors each month in perpetuity, or at our demand after the fEast of the Blessed Andrew, apostle, (November 30) a small portion of cheese, and a measure of Langres as will come and be found in the fields of the village of Rougeux. But, if we the above mentioned abbot and convent of Bize, cultivate the lands on the border in addition to the above, we shall be held to pay in taxes and thirds of products.

Similarly, the men of said village of Rougeux will have the ability and permission to lead and pasture their large and smaller cattle from the horse gate up to the woods as the large road goes and can transport the same providing they do not go beyond the road which leads toward the pasture of Mont-Refroy. However, while leading their animals to pasture, they will be allowed to go past the woods as long as they never damage it, they do not cut it, and do not eat of the nuts or fruit.

We, the above abbot and convent of Bize have wanted and have convened, as the above abbot and convent of Beaulieu have wanted and convened, that if they or us have other letters or titles making mention of that which is contained here that these be of no consequence and of no value. As far as those other things mentioned above we say to the abbot and convent of Bize that we promise for us and our successors to observe these in good faith.

In witness and agreeing to which, we have put our seal on these letters.

Given in the year of Our Savior, 1262, in the month of November.

Shortly after, the village of Rougeux was passed on to The Knights of St. John of Jerusalem.

In 1552, Guy Le Boeuf, knight of that order, commander of the battalions of Romagne, Thors, Avalleure and Broncourt, was the lord of Rougeux. In July of that year, he made a transaction with the abbot of Beaulieu and its inhabitants, the substance of which is given below;

"The inhabitants of Rougeux and the merchants who work in the territory will pay the tax of seven full boxes (size unknown) *As for the country of Faulley and the other lands which have recently cultivated, they will only pay the Tax of ten boxes. They will be held to bringing this tax to the village where the commander of Romagne will have a third and*

the abbot of Beaulieu the other two thirds. Those who will give their boxes before having called the tax collectors will be penalized with a fine of sixty sous paid to the lord. As far as the schedule of taxes go, the religious of Beaulieu will benefit of them as before the transaction. The inhabitants will be able to lead their animals to the pasture on the border of Beaulieu as they have been doing. They likewise will be able to the same in times of drought in the fields of Beaulieu from the area near the mill which is called Boulaye up to the river to the border of Maizieres, except in harvest time during which time they can not lead their pigs and goats in the woods of the monastery; but they can lead their large animals there. For this the inhabitants will each be held to forced labor at the harvesting of wheat at harvest time for the people of Beaulieu, who will feed them during this time or will pay them a dozen farthings for this labor. " Once in possession of the soil, the monks were impatient to clear the land of brush and unwanted growth. But to assist this

important work, they employed men other than the brothers, and they attracted and employed mercenaries who lived in our country. It was they constructed the agricultural houses, numerous barns (grangae) that housed their laborers and the servile employees in charge of planting and tending the soil of the crops, the beasts and instruments of tillage.

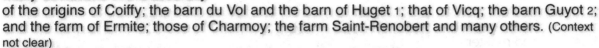

It was evident there are many deviations in the accuracy of the origins of Coiffy; the barn du Vol and the barn of Huget 1; that of Vicq; the barn Guyot 2; and the farm of Ermite; those of Charmoy; the farm Saint-Renobert and many others. (Context not clear)

Through the bottom of the XIII century we read that the priest of Varennes had built at Vicq and at Damremont houses with chimneys (not a common luxury) to serve the inhabitants, some barns to store the wheat, some mills and some baking ovens. The retainers of properties are obliged to provide good and sufficient ox plows for the laborers of the ground. Thanks to the activities of the monks and their organization agriculture is making progress and the hills of the Amance are forming very fruitful vineyards 3.

Under the pontificate of Pascal II and the reign of Baudoin, brother of Godfroy de Bouillon and his successor on the throne of Jerusalem, began an Order religious and military of the

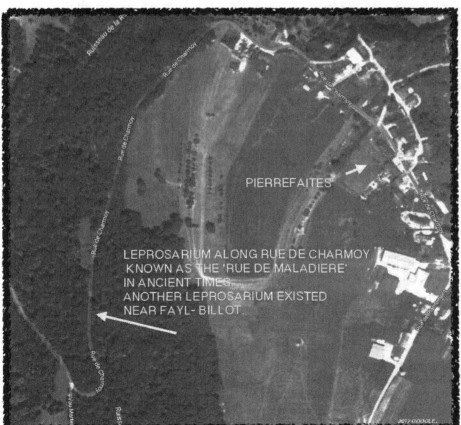

LEPROSARIUM ALONG RUE DE CHARMOY KNOWN AS THE 'RUE DE MALADIERE' IN ANCIENT TIMES. ANOTHER LEPROSARIUM EXISTED NEAR FAYL- BILLOT.

PIERREFAITES

Hospitaliers of Saint-John. We have given the rule of the monastery of Saint-Augustine. Those who are members, obey their obedience of poverty, chastity, of devotion to treating maladies and defending the pilgrim against the infidels. Their uniform is that of knights of that time when a red cross with eight points on a black coat. In 1112 the Pope confirmed by a bull the new Order that reached its definitive form in 1184. We were not tardy in establishing ourselves in France. During the middle of the XII century we had traveled to a new house in our parish.

In Varennes, the priest and the Hospitaliers were disputing about who was the proprietor of the church of Arbigny (5 miles N) To get the patronage and the tithes they agreed to give annually three minots of wheat and three minots (equivalent to 24 gallons) of oats (1153). For this payment the priest must return his rights. Anselme, a brother of the Hospital of Jerusalem and master of Albignes who placed his

REMAINING FOUNDATIONS OF ONE OF THE LEPROSARIUMS ON CHARMOY ROAD NEAR PIERREFAI FOUNDED DURING THE 13TH CENTURY. THE OTHER HOUSE WAS NEAR FAYL BILLOT.

Courtesy of Ron Miller

seal on an act by which the son of Princlinart de Charmoy, gave to Beaulieu the barn of this abbey which is in front of Velars (1250). (I think this is at a farm named Velars near Pierrefaites) Simon had the title of master in 1276.

Brother Jean de Villers, of the sainted house and hospital of Saint-Jean de Jerusalem was in a difficulty with the abbey of Moleme, concerning the right to confer a benefice of the cure of Arbigny. An industrious tribunal decided that the monks alternate the benefice between the hospitaliers and the monks (1282).

Resurgence of leprosy across the population in our region became an additional affliction and continued for the next four centuries before gradually dissipating. (There was a sudden, dramatic increase of leprosy during the 11th century) The origin of this communicable and terrible disease was thought be from the first Crusade (1096-1099) whose surviving members carried the bacullus from the Orient. There was clearly a stigma associated with the language used to describe lepers and leprosy. Lepers were labelled (in Latin) 'leprosus' and 'infirmus', and (in French) 'lépreux', 'ladre' and 'mesel'. There was a strong, albeit complex, relationship between sin and disease in medieval thinking, and leprosy was often associated with sin and divine punishment. Seldomn misdiagnosed, the disease was clearly recognizable, carried a stigma, and provoked strong reactions ranging from pity and compassion to great fear.

Not only Jews could be victims of mass hysteria on charges like that of poisoning wells and was the basis for a large scale hunt of lepers in 1321 France.

In the spring of 1321, in Périgueux, people became convinced that the local lepers had poisoned the wells, causing ill-health among the normal populace. The lepers were rounded up and burned alive. The action against the lepers didn't stay local, though, but had repercussions throughout France, because King Philip V had issued an order to arrest all lepers, those found guilty to be burnt alive. Jews became tangentially included as well; at Chinon alone, 160 Jews were burnt alive. All in all, around 5000 lepers and Jews are recorded in one tradition to

en.wikipedia.org

Advanced Leprosy

have been killed during the Lepers' Plot hysteria.

Symptoms include granulomas of the nerves, respiratory tract, skin, and eyes. This may result in a lack of ability to feel pain and thus loss of parts of extremities due to repeated injuries or infection due to unnoticed wounds. Weakness and poor eyesight may also be present.

One witness is quoted, *"The symptoms were not the same as in the East, where a gush of blood from the nose was the plain sign of inevitable death; but it began both in men and women with certain swellings in the groin or under the armpit. They grew to the size of a small apple or an egg, more or less, and were vulgarly called tumours. In a short space of time these tumours spread from the two parts named all over the body. Soon after this the symptoms changed and black or purple spots appeared on the arms or thighs or any other part of the body, sometimes a few large ones, sometimes many little ones. These spots were a certain sign of death, just as the original tumor had been and still remained."*

Transmission is believed to occur through a cough or contact with fluid from the nose of an infected person and occurs more commonly among those living in poverty and believed to be transmitted by respiratory droplets. Contrary to popular belief, it is not highly contagious.

The deanery (religious region we know as a group of parishes) contained two leper (Maladieres) hospitals, one at Fayl Billot (2 miles S) and one at Pierrefaites (3 miles E) The first one was cited in an act of 1220, by the seigneur Arnout de Reynel who gave the abbey of Beaulieu (Cistercian Abbey 2 mile N) diverse properties with the right of vaine (grazing of horned beasts on unplouged fields) pasture from the barn of Velars all the way to the bottom of the valley on the Maladiere of Pierrefaites. (Obviously an important gesture to have this praise introduced by the Abbot into his narrative at this point)

The second, cited in a document of 1417, permitted the name of a road in Fayl-Billot to be named 'Rue de la Maladiere' ('Road of Illness')

These 'hospitals' served those inflicted in our country with this horribly disfiguring and incurable disease across these centuries. *"At these houses,"* said the Abbot Morey, *"we do not have other administrators than the priest of the parish of the territory in which they are situated"*. He had to manage the property, render reports to the bishop, make the necessary building repairs, provide maintenance for the ill, visit and instruct them, console them, bring the sacraments and give them a Christian burial. He placed himself at grave risk. Control was by isolation. The Third Lateran Council, of 1179, decreed that lepers should be identified and separated. A Mass was held for the leper, (what a sad Mass that must have been)! who became 'dead among the living'. (In some regions, the afflicted was required to stand in a freshly dug grave during the Mass) From that time on, the leper had to carry a clapper or bell to announce his or her presence and to live outside the normal world. In some places the leper had to carry a long stick to use when

reaching for goods or alms and had to wear clothes marked with a yellow cross. In Europe, the disease declined rapidly in the fourteenth century. This has led some observers to suggest that plague so decimated the sufferers that there were not enough to spread the infection. It may have been a factor, however, Maladiere houses were, by design, well isolated from the general population. There is also no evidence that, even taking the worst figures for the effects of the Black Death in the middle of the century, the population fell below the point at which Hansen's Disease was viable.

We see Guillaume de Bellerama was master in 1293 and brother Jena is the master of the sainted house and of the Hospital of Saint-Jena of Jerusalem and commander of the bailiwick, houses and hospital.

This establishment, normally led by a master, depended on the commander of the Romagne, situated on the Vingeanne between Percey-le-Grand (23 miles SW) and Saint-Maurice (9miles W)

The commander was a part of the seigneurity of Arbigny (6 miles N), high, middle and base justice, (authorized to pass judgment on all classes of crime and under the high category of crime could have the person executed) rights of intercession for a non-naturalized person, of fines, confiscations, the laws and sales, the census, the corvees. (A certain amount of days of unpaid work demanded by the prefect of the monastery)

The church, annexed to Pressigny (8 miles NW), found itself served by the priest of that parish and by a vicar who was a resident of the village of Arbigney and the appurtenances thereof (1379).

1. Memories de la Societe hist. Et archdiocese de Langres, vol.2 p. 339.
2. Historie du diocese de Besamgon et de Saint-Claude, 1. II, p. 128. ---- Le diocese de Langres, t. III, p. 378.
3. Archives de la Haute-Marne, abbey de Beaulieu.
4. Historie de Fayl-Billot, p. 303 a 302, etc.

Erard de Beaufremont was commander of Robecourt, Ruetz at Arbigny (6 miles N) in 1448 and seigneur of his vassals and a sixth of the tithes of all the territory and was charged to pay the cure two hemines (unknown measurement) of oats and wheat 2.

The Order has also acquired some properties at Charmoy (2 miles E), because in 1582 they had in the village an attorney, Sir Philibert de Foissy, knight of Saint-John-of Jerusalem, commander of the Romagne. They also possessed, even more, at Broncourt (7 miles SE) a house, because of his title as commander he was therefore qualified. We do not recognize the day or the author of such rights. We can show you the place he occupied and the enclosure is still very visible (1880). We have discovered some tools of the marshal, a battery of kitchen and other objects.

A well executed search could uncover much more to the advantage of history.

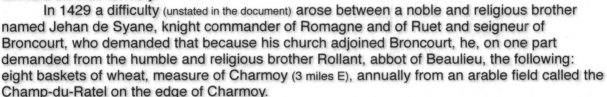

The commander was seigneur of the village; he collected the tithes and instituted a bailiff to render justice in his name. The part of Charmony and that of Arbigny, submitted to the Romagne (a district in France), dependent the bailiwick of Broncourt. This bailiwick also extended on a portion of Pressigny whose subjects or those guilty of crimes or offenses and locked up in the prison at Broncourt.

Other than the seigneur, the order had a certain (uncomfortable?) quality of presense for the farmers on their territory.

In 1429 a difficulty (unstated in the document) arose between a noble and religious brother named Jehan de Syane, knight commander of Romagne and of Ruet and seigneur of Broncourt, who demanded that because his church adjoined Broncourt, he, on one part demanded from the humble and religious brother Rollant, abbot of Beaulieu, the following: eight baskets of wheat, measure of Charmoy (3 miles E), annually from an arable field called the Champ-du-Ratel on the edge of Charmoy.

An act of accommodation was prepared by Prevot, Captain of Fayl, notary, who was an official of the court of Langres and Jean de Bosredon, ecuyer, who (an officer who cuts the meat at the dinner table of a prince, among other similar duties) enjoyed at Broncourt, the rights that extended to the XIII century (Resolution of this dispute is not recorded) We see, in 1553, brother Guy Legoeuf, knight of the Order of Saint John of Jerusalem, was commander of commanders of the Romagne, Thors, Avalleurs, Veribcourt and Arriving 2. The tithe, introduced by Charlemagne 800 years previously, as the legal method of taxing, was difficult to understand, inconsistent and ranged from 10% to more than 30%, was a cause of frequent disputations.

In 1682 a dispute arose about the place of collection (lacking money, tithes were paid in kind by the peasants) and at first they agreed to pay at three barns, on the weight of thirteen sheaf's of grain per load, by counting each load, the last of each being exempted from tax on any harvests made within the percents of each village. But then, in order to subtract a part of the royalty, a certain number of farmers resorted to a stratagem more ingenious than loyal.This was done by each time only 10 or 12 sheafs per load, thus lightening the loads which were taxed and reserving the shortages for the last untaxed load. The owners did not relish these kinds of maneuvers!

They (Probably Broncourt, Rougeux, Bize, Charmoy, Pierrefaites and others in the near vicinity) submitted to the objections of the owners, but in 1722 a dozen farmers refused to continue submission and disavowed the 1578 agreement (Same agreement for over 200 years)! and the community took the cause to themselves, full of confidence of a favorable issue of the process they had begun, then 4 or 5 defected. Two judgments rendered in the bailiwick of Langres gave satisfaction to the owners. Attempts to negotiate with the owners failed. Pushed to the hilt they appealed to the Paris Parliament, who gave its judgment 7 September 1724.

BRONCOURT—LAST HOME OF OUR ANCESTOR.

BRONCOURT—LAST VILLAGE OF OUR IMMIGRANT

The residents, bold in their settlement proposition and offers, were kept in possession of nothing, neither for the last wagon which was restricted to not more than six sheafs after payment of the tithe, the amount of tithes did not increase more than the last ones, and properties in the circumferences of the cross-roads exempt from the tithe. (Cannot determine the rationale for this) Similarly, the flax, the hemp, the millet, and the peas harvested in the parish, if the participants used a third part of their fields for these crops.(This settlement too obscure to accurate evaluate)

The tithe holders were sentenced to pay two-thirds of the legal costs and the residents, the other third.

During this period huge deforesting were being accomplished to the detriment of the inhabitants whose used these for gathering of twigs and dead limbs as fuel for their cooking hearths. Objections were futile.

Toward the end of the 17th century the Minolta family were reunited into a huge estate, the Lords of Rey and Vergy. This united a forest of about 120 hectares, about large enough for the needs of our community but when the new owners having them dug up, it was the coup de grace. The community, frustrated by this threat, raised useless demands.

In the memorandum sent to the Paris Parliament in 1722, the residents pointed out these injurious acts and other more recent usurpations committed by the lord's farmers on the common ground. Dismissed of any power on these items before the tribunals, they did not dare run the risk of a new process and the limitation covering these injustices of which they complained.

Fifteen years later, the community had become more enterprising with the diligence of its councilman, Jean Bessil. It asked the Lt. General of Langres, authorization to commence some suits against the lords it accused of having infringed on 7 quarters of Vernors' pasturage. However, added the petition, the fear of having debates with them shut them up until today.

The complaint states, *"They cut the woods out in Champelds, two in LaRune; they cut out the woods of Verde, and forbade the residents to touch the dead wood or kill the weeds. Finally, the lords took possession of the river which they used to their profit, despite protests and the judgment of the councilmen to conform to the order of the water and forests."*

The complaint, dated July 18, 1772, was precise and clear and the right to pleas not being able to be refused, opened a process grown by debate 28 years. (Until the overthrow of those in power by the Revolution!)

In spite of the pressing hearings of the residents, no solution was given the affair before the Revolution in 1789. After suppression of the Billagrs (Owners or those in power prior to the Revolution), the commune took the dispute before the tribunal at Langres where they were successful in introducing the case on March 25, 1793.

New laws of June 10, 1793, of the Revolutionary forces in Paris stopped the procedure and deferred the matter to arbitration. When the named arbiters arrived at the sites, the objects of litigation, witness were questioned and the claims of the residents examined, they rendered a decree that adjudged the community the major part of its demands. The judgment was interlocutory and not definite.

While these things were being examined, M. De Minette, the defendant, was jailed at Bourbon as a suspect. (During the Revolution people could be arrested for such things as being in favor of the Pope but the author (Abbot Briffaut) knew what the charges were and assumed his readers also knew) Returned to his freedom, M. De Minette was eager to provide an ending to it. His death came at this time. His widow and heirs following the appeal, obtained an annulment of the arbitrary verdict because of an error in procedure, and the procedure reverted before the tribunal of Chaumont, where the de Minolta defense yielded definitely. By a verdict rendered the 27 foamier, an VIII (December 22, 1800) (Revolutionaries renamed the months and began counting 1782 as the year One and had a 10 day week), the community, settled again in possession of its domestic offices, returned (to the village) its rights of usage, and authorized follow up against the forest holders, the damages that had accrued by the non-use of the residents from 17 July 1772, the date of their first demands right up to the end of the procedure (December 22, 1800)

The community was pitiless in its calculation of the damages (a big surprise)! It erected, year by year, a state of all the wagons of dead wood; of brambles; of live wood; of service; returning (due) all to the tenants of the two lordships since 1772. It estimated in money its value; they (no doubt gleefully!) added compound interest to the owed amounts and presented a bill of 63,276 francs and 5 centimes. It was equivalent to the price of the largest part of the forest which remained with the old lords, but with the juridicts having been all exhausted, it was necessary for them to submit. (Just imagine the gloating of the poverty stricken peasants in taking sweet revenge upon those who had long oppressed and cheated them without recourse!)

This action imposed on the district of M. Minolta, by the act of 9 pluvoise an IX (February 1, 1801), gave up all possessions and use of the woods called La Bique (she goat) with an area of 20 hectares, 26 centiares (32 acres), having for its limits, to the East and to the SouthEast, the lands of the Rpue farm; to the North, the road. (unknown location)

As to the expense done in the dredging of our poor stream, we were not able to recover this because of mediocre crops resulting from the thick coating of alluvial sand and mud covering our fields. As for compensation, the farmers profited in all the propitious places in order to establish, in the plain, some natural fields.

CHAPTER VI
ABBEYS
(1000 -- 1400)

---

1. ABBEY OF VAUX-LA-DOUCE ----- 2. SAINT-BERNARD GIVES THE RULE OF CITEAUX ----- 3. THE SUPPORTERS ------ 4 THE DIFFICULTIES WITH THE SIRES OF LA FERTE ------ 5. FOUNDATION OF BEAULIEU ----- 6. DIFFERENCES WITH MORIMOND ----- 7. DONATIONS ------ 8. SERVICES RENDERED BY THE MONKS.

The religious houses of which we have been speaking are not the only ones belonging to the diocese of Pierrefaites. We have possessed two others more important; the abbeys of Vaux-la-Douce and of Beaulieu.

Between La Ferte 2 and Voisey we find a narrow valley. The surrounding hills are crowned with forests, give origin to diverse streams, one is named the Stream of l'Etnat, which after entering into its stream flows through Guyonvelle and of Velles and empties into the Amance. It

is the boundaries of the Champagne, in the Lorraine and the hills of Bourgogne, that we built the abbey of Vaux (Vallis) This solitude, so favorable to contemplation and prayer, was able to attract pious cenobites desiring to live far away from the tumult of the world. Whatever they think, the ancient chronicles, vetrera instrumenta, conserved since then in the monasteries, appraise us that there was a church and an abbey at Vaux. The clerics that inhabit, and we have seen, during the XI century, were governed by members of the same Order.

De P. Benoit, and after him Dom Calmet designated the foundations of this abbey. Adelaide, sister of Lothaire II, emperor of Germany, was the wife of Simon I, duc of Lorraine, who lived a long time in oblivion in the monastery for the salvation of her soul. Converted by Saint Bernard in

GUYONVELLE

1133, she recognized that God wanted her to build a monastery at Vaux. Her godfather, Henri, archdeacon at Langres and bishop of Toul, confirmed the foundation in 1138 1. The year following, the princess becoming widowed, formed a religious house with her sisters Agathe and Berthe in the abbey of Notre-Dame du Tart in our diocese 2.

In 1151, the abbot of Clairvaux (30 miles NE) came to Cherlieu (Possibly near Preigney 12 miles SE) at the moment that Othon de la Roche (d. before 1234. A Burgundian nobleman who joined the Fourth Crusade and became the first Frankish Lord of Athens in 1204. There he lived in his castle atop the Acropolis. There is a hypothesis, proposed for many centuries, that Othon de la Roche acquired the Shroud of Turin during the conquest of Constantinople in 1204) gave to that house a part of the ground at Versions. Our deacons discussed with him their desire to have the rule of Clairvoix. Saint

Google Ear

Bernard applauded their generous desire and in 1152 Vaux incorporated the Order of the Chapitre general that placed them in the line of Morimond under the affiliation of Clairefontaine 3. So you see, without doubt, the abbot of Mangiu affirmed that Saint Bernard himself cast the foundations of this new monastery. Concerning the name of Vaux, he joined the epithet dulcis,(sweet, kind) its full development being Douce-Vanae or Vaux-la-Douce.

During the following year, 1153, Godefronde Rochetaillee, Bishop of Langres, addressed to Lambert, abbot of Clairfontaine, a charter that assured his protection and of his successors and the peaceful jurisdiction of the properties of Vaux-la-Douce. Donations were not slow in multiplying. It should be mentioned numerous benefactors who gave up tithes, the rights of pasturage, wells, fields, etc., on the territory in the vicinity; Guy de Raconnieres, Othon de la Roche, Eudes, Humbert, Renard de La Ferte, Euded and Guy de Jonvelle.

By a bull of (Pope) Honorius III, dated 1216, the abbey was placed under the protection of Saint-Siege and confirmed *"all the property you possess, especially those you receive from Etienne, comte de Bourgogne."* (1065–1102), Count Palatine of Burgundy, shared his father's nickname "the Rash" (French tête hardie). He was Count of Burgundy and Count of Mâcon and Vienne. His younger brother was Pope Callixtus II) The son of Etienne, John, also comte de Bourgogne, comte of Chalons, vicomte of Auxonne, surnamed le Sage, married his son, John, with the daughter of Gauthier II, seigneur of Vignory and brother of Guy II, sire of La Ferte. This alliance, made with the cooperation of the religious of Vaux-la-Duce, included the right to take, each year, ten livres of salt from his salt mines of Salins (The territory of Salins, 75 miles Southeast, was enfeoffed in the 10th century by the Abbey of Saint Maurice-en-Valais to the counts of Mâcon, and remained in possession of their descendants till 1175. In 1477 Salins was taken by the French and temporarily made the seat of the parliament of Franche-Comté by Louis XI. In 1668 and 1674 it was retaken by the French and thenceforward remained in their power), and was charged to celebrate a solemn Mass for the repose of his soul and that of his wife Isabelle.

1. Notes historiques sur les cures de campagne, p. 60.
2. On ecrit maintenance La Ferte en un soul mot; nous avons conserve l'ancinne orthographe.

The good harmony didn't last long between the monks and the seigneurs de La Ferte. Guy II, beginning to regret the liberties of his ancestors, contested certain rights of the abbey despite many years of peaceful proprietorship. Guy pursued his harassment even to violence. The abbot, in dire necessity, appealed to the Church for help. Guy was excommunicated. Then he confessed in detail that the religious had at Velles twenty households of people who were disabled and no longer able to work. At the Moulin-Rogue, workers were suppressed and forced to work under violent threats and forced to grind grain without payment where they had exclusive rights (1224) Peace was restored: ten years later the same difficulties reappeared. Guy was slapped with a new excommunication, under the blow of which he remained for eight years. Then, after the counsels of Simpon de Sexfontaines, V (Winston Churchill's 22-Great Grandfather) with the consent of Alix, his wife, of his brother, the sire of Vignory, he submitted and renounced all his own pretensions and confirmed his ancestors had given land to the abbey. He promised, for the salvation of his soul, to declare himself excommunicated if he does something contrary to his promises. He kept his promises, made in 1282, and his son Gauthier repeated the same promises.

However, he came to a place where he desperately needed money and because the monks desired tranquillity they found a way to obtain a considerable amount of money and Guy ceased to disquiet them. However their successors suffered once again, notably John, Perrin and Philibert during the XIV century and Cleriadus and Victor de Choiseul during the XVII century.

The foundation of the abbey of Beaulieu (2 miles North of Rougeux) was laid in 1166. Gauthier de Bourgogne, governor of the diocese for three years, then declared in his Chapter that he was agreeable to see the Cistercians establish a monastery under his episcopal authority. He was prepared to give to them a number of grounds to realize the object of his desire.

1. Histoire de Toul, p.. 419.   Historie de Lorraine, t. II, p. 8, 9, 26.
2. Canton de Genlis (Cote-d'Or)
3. Canton d'Amance, Haute-Saone.

The Dean Manasses and his cannons responded favorably to his demands and offered their property of Mont-Refroy, (between Rougeux and Beaulieu) situated on the creek that forms the reunion of water of Chaudenay, de Rosoy and of Hortes, which is one of the affluence of the Amance River. (This property is located on the Beaulieu Road #D103 leading out of Rougeux toward Hortes four miles

11TH CENTURY LIVING QUARTERS FOR MONKS AND GUESTS

MONASTERY WALL CIRCA 1200 AD

RECENT BUILDINGS

BEAULIEU FROM THE WEST

NW)

This agreement was communicated to the house of Charlieu 2, daughter house of Citeaux (A Roman Catholic abbey located in Saint-Nicolas-lès-Cîteaux, 72 miles South of Dijon, France. Today it belongs to the Trappists, or Cistercians of the Strict Observance (OCSO) During the Hundred Years' War, the monastery was pillaged in 1360 (the monks sought refuge in Dijon), 1365, 1434 and 1438. In1791, during the French Revolution, the abbey was seized and sold by the government. In 1898, the remains of the abbey were bought back and repopulated by monks of other abbeys)

The abbot Lue accepted with grand benevolence to provide the monks for their new abbey. At a fixed day he received an assignment to read the following:

"Manasses, by the Grace of God, dean of the church of Langress, and of the whole cathedral, to the venerable brother Luc, of Cherlieu, for perpetual memory."

"The best act we can do for the good of the church is to let it serve for the good of the poor and everywhere that there is ceaseless work for the good of God. It why we judged it good to build on our territory a tabernacle of God of Jacob, which can, in our region can let the faithful servants, by their prayers and their merits, achieve graces for us, for temporal affairs and the continued uninterrupted contentment of our prayers and piety."

"It is for this and by the request of our bishop and the consent of all the Chapter, we donate to our Venerable brother Luc and his successors the Mont-Refroy with all its dependancies for his construction of a monastery of the Order of Citeaux." (St. Bernard was founder of the Cistercian order)

MONKS QUARTERS

RECENT

ENCLOSURE WALL

Google Ea

And to render our union more durable, we have made this convention: "*Those religious that die that are one of us, they are obliged to pray for them, and the same for them. In solemn Chapter at Langress, in the year of the Incarnation, 1166.*" The witness are: Garner, Goulques, Ponce, Gerard, Hugues, archdeacons; Arnauld, Pierre, Lamberl, priests; Durand, Arnould, Hubert, deacons; Ulric, Milon, Girard, under deacons; Thierry, deacon of Pierrefaites Guy, laborer and his sons, Durfort and Lambert. The bishop confirmed this liberality, freed the tithes until the monks can cultivate their land with their own hands and find protection within the nascent monastery.

However noise was widespread that a new monastery was going to be built so far from Langress. The religious of Morimond were claiming that their rights were being infringed upon. They addressed to the abbot of Cherlieu their concerns in pressing terms; "We have learned, they wrote, that you have approved the founding of a new abbey on the border that the

A RUINS OF ANCIENT CHAPEL AT BEAULIEU

Chapter General of the Order has fixed for our community. We lift up our voices in formal opposition."

Luc responded that, in veracity, *"My intention was to found a new abbey on a terrain that you gave to us for this result, but when we accepted this donation, I had no thought to harm or displease and had only been guided by the desire for aggrandizement and prosperity of the Order.* 1 *Rest assured, I do not, he added, want to approve of an enterprise without your full and entire consent. Therefore, I humbly supplement you to approve our new enterprise and fix the boundaries beyond which we would not be able to accept as a gift nor use. Finally, we agree to permit arbiters to trace a line of demarcation between the properties of the two monasteries."*

"Given this day for Morimond ward of Lambert, ancient abbey of Citeux; Martin, under-priest; Albert dean of Aigremont and other lay persons; on their part, the abbot of Cherlieu, as do the monks, Barthelemy and Gerard, Guy de Bonnercourt and Bouchard, the lay brother."

"It must also be decided which roads will follow the limits of Langress to Morcily; from Marcilly to Varennes and passing Montmort; to the Battlements; then Morimond; then to Varennes at Soyers and finally from Soyers to the barn at Vaux."

This difficulty flattened, Luc sent from Cherlieu, under the control of the abbot Guy, a colony of monks who took possession at Mont-Refroy. The establishment changed the name to one more poetic, Beaulieu. (Bellus locus)

Very soon persons contributed to its construction. The Abbey of Bize who had a priory at Rougeux, abandoned his possessions from Mount Larris all the way to Mondelente, their new forest on Mount Loual, and further, to the ground of the Chum, including the right to pasture on all their properties, but kept the valley of Rougeux. In return Beaulieu contracted to pay the abbot of Theuley, one hundred quarter livres langrois each year between Ash Wednesday and the first Sunday of Lent. The witnesses were; John, priest of Citeaux; Jean, knight; Constant, dean of de Beze; Thiery, dean of Pierrefiate; Gerard, abbot of Theuley.

The first donations were confirmed in a bull of Alexander III who took the abbey under the protection of Saint-Sege, according the religious the right of refugem (exemption) from tithes for the property or the goods produced by their hands, and menaced the rash who would violate their persons, animals or attack their house.

Manasses, dean of Chapitre, and bishop of Langress, gave Beaulieu all he held at Fraces. Thierry de Salvamento, 1 with the agreement of his wife Agathe and his son Guillaume committed his tithes from Mont-Refroy, of Hortes, of Rougeux, and all his properties situated on the flanks of the mountain to the West of the abbey for twenty livres langroises and seven livres estevenantes (A currency used in the Champagne region until about 1500)

Gerard d'Achey gave the right to pass over his property and permission to take from his forests wood for heating (1180).

Simon de Grancey made alms of his tithes of the Chenee and the Larris (1183).

Milon de Chatearvillain (1186), Pierre de Bonnecourt, Guy de Coublanc, Guillaume de Pierrefaites (1190), Milon de Rosoy, Eudes and Hilduin de Montlandon (1202), Arnault de Reynel (1220), Gauther de Vignory, Etienne de Noidant and others, abandoned to the Abbey various freeholds, rights of usage, pasturage on the Amance and on territories of Montlandon, Chaudenay, Rosoy, Marcilly,

Clemence de Fouvent, widow of Guillaume de Vergy, ceded her house situated on the road under the walls of Chamlitte, and the facility to acquire vineyards within the parish with the franchise of all rights and responsibility for the festivities of the day after Notre-Dame of September (February 1252) 1

The year following, his son, Henri, approved the gift of the tithe of Orvigny-au-Mont, by Guillaume de Genevrieres. Phillippe de Chauvirey gave three muids (288 pints of liquid measure) of grain, wheat and oats, etc. (1262).

MONKS CHAPTER HOUSE

REMAINS OF ENCLOSURE WALL

Google Ea

1.Histoire de Toul, p.. 419.   Historie de Lorraine,
 2. Canton de Genlis (Cote-d'Or)
 3. Canton d'Amance, Haute-Saone.,t. II, p. 8, 9, 26.

Add this reflection about our religious establishment: the cenobites that live at Beaulieu, at Vaux-la-Douce and on our priories find solace in all their conditions. They place themselves in a community under a monastic rule and find a fraternity, equality and liberty missing in this century. They make a vow of poverty, of chastity and obedience some time after their arrival to the religious perfection required and await the eternal beatitudes. With respect to society, they render services by their prayers, their mortifications, their work, their examples of works of mercy that cannot be fully appreciated.

The monks pray, day and night, not only for their benefactors but for all those living outside of their monastery until they acquire their celestial reward.

Because of their hard and austere life and their penance, they gain forgiveness for the sins of the people. The Masses of atonement are related to the forgiveness of the crimes we commit. Yet among the guilty some do not expiate at all while others do in an insufficient manner. This requires that the holy souls, in the hope of obtaining glory and happiness in heaven, accept by a heroic devotion through the principle of the solitary and hard work, to maintain equilibrium between transgressions of

SITE OF MONASTIC RUINS OF BEAULIEU
FOUNDED IN 13TH CENTURY
ABANDONED IN 19TH CENTURY

Google E

Chapel ruins

Enclosure wall

Beaulieu Abbey Ruins
1166-1844

© 2017 Google

divine law and reparations so that the terrible blows of divine justice may be deflected.

The work of our religious have transformed the valley of the Amance. Clearing of the fields, removal of rubbish, digging canals, cleaning the ponds, construction of grain mills, renewing of the farm land, raising beasts, tilling the fields, planting vineyards, and gardens, and teaching the people proper agricultural techniques that has given them intelligence and taste. This is the grand gift that has been marvelously accomplished. For example, with patience and virtue the different classes of society have been influenced on the proper way to improve their farms much to their happiness.

Because there are no hotels in our champagnes where is the pilgrim or the traveler going to find shelter and food? At the monastery. There they will find welcoming friends, all the attention, sympathy and delicacies of Christian charity. We never refuse anyone for a night; neither the pedestrian or the knight are refused. At Beaulieu the Logis des hotes are composed of six furnished rooms. The proximity of the water of the Bourbonne and the road of Allemagne occasion frequent passages of officers, persons of distinction and others; service for such men, their domestics and their horses are very costly. Each day we give alms to the poor who present themselves. On Holy Thursday we had a crowd of villagers surrounding us. In 1750 we counted 1500 at the Abbey of Beaulieu.

Therefore it is at our religious house that we have the local historical materials. We conserve with care, within our cabinets of oak, the papal bulls, the charters of seigniors, the tithes of properties and all the papers most important and interesting. The archives are for the historian and for his information and publication; a source close and inexhaustible from which information can be precisely drawn.

1. Cette dame donne aussi a l'eglise de Langres, pour son anniversaire sionante sold sur ses lour de
   Fayl.
2. L'abbe DuBois. History de Morimond.

MT. REFROY

ANCIENT HORSE TROUGH AT BEAULIEU

© 2017 Google
© 2012 Google

SUPPLEMENTS FROM ABBOT MULSON AND OTHERS.

The Abbey of Notre-Dame of Beaulieu of the order of Citeaux 1 and of the affilication with Charlieu, caused the founding in 1166 in the parish of Pierrefaites between Rougeux and Hortes but on the ancient territory of Rougeux, four leagues from Langres. This was done by the Dean Manasses and the chapter of Saint Mammes with the enjoyment of Bishop Gauthier de Bourgogne. Discussions between the abbot of Beaulieu, the chapter of Saint-Mammes, and the religious of Beaulieu resulted in the decision to have a service for each Cannon upon his death.

The abbey of Beaulieu, formed solely for the customs and privledges of the Cistercians, a domesticated parish for the religious farmers and servants of the monastery. This parish had for their service a religious man provided by his superior who could be recalled at his will. The parish church of the diocese of Pierrefaites was by any standard, a smaller representation of Notre Dame. With respect to Beaulieu, who bit by bit the farmers of the monastery set up a special community to the time of the Revolution (1788) but managed to survive until 1844 when they had to depart due to lack of sufficient resources to continue the regular community.The territory of Beaulieu was divided between the community of Hortes, of Rougeux and Rosoy.

In 1568 the Monestary was pillaged by the Reitres (bands of roaming, pillaging former soldiers) Even greater devastation in 1711 by a band of pillaging Germans that considerably diminished their resources by the damage and thefts. The church by this period was ancient but a modern convent had been constructed. The church walls still existed in part but the church was in complete disrepair.

In 1730 the net revenues generated were 4,933 livres. The historian Baugier, who wrote during these times, carried them 2,000 livres. (Not sure what this means) According to l'Europe ecclesiastique of 1757 the abbot of Beaulieu possessed 4500 livres of revenues. At the beginning of the Revolution (1788), since the Concordat of Francois 1st, at the nomination of the King, he decided on a rent of 5,000 livres per year (Their total income!) The abbey was also taxed an additional 200 florins by Rome. (This punitive tax was typical of the revolt against religion and greed of everyone. This income cold only have come from heavy tithes required from the villages owned by the monastery, Rougeux certainly being one of those)

In our time (1850) the farm of the ancient monastery of Beaulieu is not independent of Hortes.

After the Revolution there only remained four or five religious. (Before being abandoned in 1844)

1. From La Diocese de Langrres: history et stastistique, Volume 2

CHAPTER VII

THE SEIGNEURS AND THE COUNTS OF CHAMPAGNE (1100-1460)

1. THE SEIGNEURS. ----- 2. ASSOCIATION OF THE MONKS OF MOLEME AND THE COUNT OF CHAMPAGNE ----- 3. DESPITE THE OPPOSITION OF JEAN DE CHOISEUL, WE CONSTRUCTED A CHATEAU AT COIFFY ------ 4. VILLAGES THAT WATCH AND GUARD ------ 5. PROVOST OF COIFFY ------ 6. VANCE-LA-DOUCE AND LUXEUIL PLACE THEMSELVES UNDER THE PROTECTION OF THE COUNT ----- 7. THE SEIGNEURS DECLARE THEIR VASSALS ------ 8. THEY REND HOMAGE TO THE BISHOP ----- 9. THE PRIOR OF VARENNES FURNISHES SUBSIDIARIES FOR THE CRUSADE ----- 10. REUNION OF CHAMPAGNE WITH THE CROWN ----- 11. EXEMPTION OF NUMEROUS COMMUNES.

Among the seigneurs who reside on the Amance, the most considerable are at La Ferte. They constructed, on the site of the ancient Castrum a chateau of high walls that dominate the valley. The first was known as La Ferte. By the marriage of Elizabeth, whose seal calls her a countess, with Gauthier de Vignory La Ferte as her husband, passed into that house. Gauthier was one of the knights-banner (entitled to carry a banner in a war) of King Phillippe-Auguste and his crusade of 1190. (Philip II, known as Philip Augustus, (1165 – 1223), was King of France from 1180 to 1223, a member of the House of Capet. Philip's predecessors had been known as kings of the Franks, but from 1190 onward, Philip became the first French monarch to style himself king of France. Philip transformed France from a small feudal state into the most prosperous and powerful country in Europe. He checked the power of the nobles and helped the towns to free themselves from seigniorial authority, granting privileges and liberties to the emergent bourgeoisie. He built a great wall around Paris,

OLD WALLED CITY

LANGRES

re-organized the French government and brought financial stability to his country)

But the two seigneurial families who were the most powerful families in our country were the one of Choiseul (24 miles N) and that of Fouvent, which succeeded the Vergy.

The house of Choiseul descended from ancient counts of Bassigny and recognizes as one of their ancestors Saint Gengoul and Saint

LANGRES

Salaberge. Raynier de Choiseul, who lived at the end of the XI century was married to Hermengarde de Vergy, who was part of the first Crusade. His sons Roger and Conon followed his example and also rose, with Macelin and Dukes of Hortes, for the pious expedition to the outer seas. (Jerusalem) The Haute-Amance, all the way and including La Frete (9 miles E) was under the suzerainty (control) of the seigneur of Choiseul, who rendered homage to the bishop of Langres. His war cry was: *"Bassigny a la resconsse"*. (Bassigny *(the region)* to the rescue!)

The family of Fouvent, also an original count and one of the more ancient in the country, where, under their authority, were villages, among whom were: Frettes, Tornay, Pierrefaites,

LANGRES

Moutesson, Charmes-Saint-Valbert, Pressigny, Rosoy. The family possessed Fayl and they built a Chateau to which was attached various fiefs and the guard of Arbigny and of Montlandon.

During this epoch, the quarrels between the barons, and hostilities between neighbor and neighbor, occurred, often leading to pillaging, devastation and incendiaries causing the monasteries to be the principal victims. (In 1977 the mayor told me that during a lost battle with Hortes, during the 13th century, Rougeux was burned to the ground. I have not been able to confirm that but the village was certainly devastated on more than one occasion) The religious who lived at Varennes, at Vicq, at Coiffy and other environs strongly complained to their superior, the abbot of Moleme. The Abbot saw fit to confer with Thibauit IV, count of Champagne and king of Navarre. The King's wife, Marguerite de Bourbon, pointedly responded that the monks should place themselves and their property under the protection of Thibaut, but, in secret, she charged her agents to counsel the count to work for possession of the properties of the monasteries, using the excuse that the count had some interest as to what happened there and could be more attentive and

LANGRES

have concern and comfort for the abbey. Then the monks addressed a demand to Robert, bishop of Langres, who recognized their claim (20 January 1239) and wrote for them: Considering that the ecclesiastical leadership was powerless to impose respect on the property of the parish of Varennes, he consented that the villages of Coiffy and of Vicq, be placed under the guard of Thibaut IV, Count of Champagne. This decision having been (made) known, Thibauit IV, into whose custody these villages had been entrusted, proved unsatisfactory to him. He, afraid of diminishing his authority and influence and of being ultimately responsible for such a rural place, remained in his life near the bishop (at Langres 15 miles W), the count and the king and nothing changed for the monasteries; they were spared neither menaces nor promises. They forgave even twelve crimes that were committed against each hearth (household) of the

CONSECRATED IN 1196

Coiffys (1247). The debates will last ten years but nothing will be obtained.

Employing his Episcopal authorization, the abbot, Christopher, ceded, and his name is on the covenant, to count Thibaut, half of the rights he had at Coiffy and at Vicq, his men, his women (slaves?), census, territory, forests, etc., etc.

This act of association, dated the month of July 1250, gave to the count of Champagne the guard of the parish of Varennes and its dependancies, naturally entailing the construction of a chateau to provide protection to the religious, resulting in assured protection for them. Also, very soon the question arose of a fortress crowning the mountain of Coiffy that would dominate the surrounding environs. (The burghers of the tenth and eleventh centuries were ruthlessly harassed, blackmailed, subjected to oppressive taxes and humiliated. This drove the bourgeois back upon their own resources, and it accounts for the intensely corporate and excessively organized character of medieval cities. The walled city represented protection from direct assault at the price of corporate interference on the pettiest levels, but once a townsman left the city walls, or if his village had no walls, travelers were at the mercy of often violent and lawless nobles in the countryside. Because much of medieval Europe lacked central authority to provide protection, each city had to provide its own protection for citizens both inside the city walls, and outside. Thus cities and rural villages with and without walls formed communes, a legal basis for turning them into self-governing corporations. Every town had its own commune and no two communes were alike, but at their heart, communes were sworn allegiances of mutual defense. When a commune was formed, all participating members gathered and swore an oath in a public ceremony, promising to defend each other in times of trouble, and to maintain the peace within the city proper. The commune movement started in the 10th century and gained strength in the 11th century and then spread in the early 12th century to France, Germany and Spain and elsewhere)

The discontentment of Jean de Choiseul (Lord of Langres) knew no bounds. He declared formal opposition to the execution of the project. He searched for allies to make war against Thibauit IV, the Count of Champagne. But Thibauit IV's death (10 July 1253) stopped the hostilities. His widow, Marguerite, mother and tutor of the young Thibaut V and Jean, connived to submit their contestation to Guy, bishop of Langres and to Jean, count of Bourgogne, seignior of Salins. A common accord between the villages of Vicq and Coiffy was needed for them to remain under Marguerite, her son and heirs, and who, in their fortressed beds, could make an accord that would hold the bishop in their control.

At the same time, Jean de Choiseul claimed transfer and transport for him, his brothers and sisters, for Marguerite, widow of Thibauit IV Queen of Navarre and Countess of Champagne, and to her son ThibautVI, the right of guard and the other rights that they could appropriate from the villages of Vy and of Coiffy and to return the fief of Pouilly that the sire de Ray had given to Thibauit IV. On their side, the Countess and her son have recognized that homage to the Bishop of Langres was necessary.

1. Andre Duchene, History de Vergy

The question finally being settled, (No description of the terms are available) the regent authorized the foundations, at the end of the year 1255, of the fortress of Coiffy that was ready for a state of defense after four years.

The two seigneurs, the count and abbot together and gave a charter of the mainmort (Because of the condition of those who cannot render the service or duties which is required of the fiefs, they are therefore not subject to mutilation) and to form districts for protection. (1260). The villages that divide the guard and the lookout of the chateau are: Coffu-le-Haut, Coiffy-le-Bas, Laneuvelle, V, Rougeux, Arbigny, Bize, Anrosey, Montesson, La Ferte, Guyonvelle, Soyers, Neuvelle-les-Voisey, Barges, Blondefontaine, Enfonvelle and Melay.

The hamlet of Genrupt was in agreement to meet their obligation, but in 1582 the governor of Coiffy, Christophe de Choiseul-Lanques, who required the watch of the villagers (from which they apparently rebelled) went, with Philibert de Foissy, commander of the Romagne, and of the same level of responsibility, seigneurs of Genrupt, Neuville, Arbigny and Rougeux and obtained from the Parliament of Paris and the duke de Guise, arrest warrants to make examples of those villages who refused to do guard duty at the chateau and fortress of Coiffy.

66

The act of the association provides that, with the consent of the monks and count, provisions to render justice have been established. Recently in possession of Coiffy, ThibautVI hastened to establish a provost who depended primarily on the bailiwick of Chaumont. It was comprised of a provost, a prosecutor, a police lieutenant, a

GENRUPT

commissioner inquirer and examiner, an advocate and a clerk. Its jurisdiction, not well defined, extended to Coiffy-le-Haut, Coiffy-le-Bas, Laneuvelle, Damremont, Vicq, Chezeaux, Soyers, Montchrvol, Genrupt, Vaux-La-Duce, and Guyonvelle.

There have already been a number of years that the count assumed responsibility for the guard of Vaux-le-Douce according to the following surviving documents:

Google E

"To all who sees these letters, F. Etienne and all the community of Vaux-la-Douce, the order of Citeaux, salute our Lord. We are here to tell you your church is not being guarded by anyone and we fear its total destruction by mercenariness, and do not know each day if we are going to be prevented from doing our religious duties according to our Order. By consent of our venerable priest, the abbot of Clairefontaine, we have addressed the illustrious Thibaut VI, King of Navarre, (1201-1253—he had a complicated life full of wars, a Crusade, three marriages and endless family problems)

VAUX LA DOUCE

Google Earth

count of Champagne and of Brie, prayerfully requesting that he take your abbey and all its dependancies under his guard and protection."

ThibautVI, granting the request in view of the mercy of God and the remission of his sins, said, *"He desires to increase your monastery and wants to engage in your protection, him and his successors if we, and our descendants promise not to permit the passage of the guard to other hands. Done in the year of Our Lord 1241."*

ThibautVI acquitted himself of his promise with dedication and also for our testimony of gratitude, the monastery engaged under the government of the Aubert, in the month of January 1267, to say each day, a mass for the Virgin Mary, for the count of Champagne, and after his death, and for the dead. The abbot of Clairefontaine approved this action.

The abbey of Luxeuil imitated this example. The protection of the abbeys by the counts of Bar and Champagne in virtue of an agreement of protection between Thibaut V (1160-1229) and the convent was concluded in 1258.

Ten years later the same Thibaut VI made with the monks of Moleme and of Varennes, a new association for the village of Monicharvot. Then Vicq, Damremont, the two Coiffy and Monicharvot formed the Company de Coiffy (Compagnie de Coiffy) for their villages.

In 1255, Rougeux, (Rogiolum, Rubeolus) was made a part of the region of Champagne and in the bailage of Langres. In 1255 the abbot of Bize, who owned the tithes of Rougeux, decided to sell the tithes to the abby of Beaulieu. It was only after his death that they were sold to the Knights of Malta who shared the tithes with Beaulieu. This agreement lasted until the Revolution of 1789.

Jean de Vergy, sire of Fouvent, (The Lord of Vergy, Guerin, brother of martyred St. Leodegar, who was stoned in 681. They were one of the most prominent families in France until the 17th century) seneschal of Bourgogne, did demand an assembly of serfs from Henri de Champagne for Pierrefite and Montesson. (Probably to help harvest the crops) In return he will pay the sum of five cents (hundred) livres, and gives him quittance the Thursday after the fEast of the beheading of John the Baptist, 1273. The same year the count of Bourgogne, Othon IV, found himself constrained by the bad condition of his finances, and made an offer to Henri for his chateau of Jussey (18 miles E) in return for a thousand livres tourneys. 1

Thibaut VI, count of Campagne and of Brie, King of Navarre, was promised a tribute (public honoring and blessing) from the Bishop of Langres for what he had donated to his diocese.

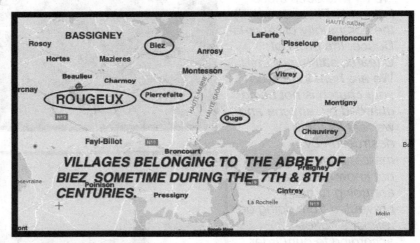

VILLAGES BELONGING TO THE ABBEY OF BIEZ SOMETIME DURING THE 7TH & 8TH CENTURIES.

The tribute made Thibaut VI say to Guy de Rochefort (bishop of Langres, of the dean of Pierrefaites) that the Grand Songmaster, Guy de Geneve (famous singer, musical director, and a chief of ceremonies) must do the same formalities prescribed by Feudal Law as was done in 1167. (He wanted an equal public approval) The ceremony took place in the open land of the bishop in the beautiful valley situated between Luzy and the Val-des-Ecoliers. Thibaut VI, bare headed, without weapons, flexed his knee in front of the bishop, made the sign of the Cross, his hand joined with that of the seigneur who reciprocated with a kiss. He had (with him) his vassals from Bar-sur-Seine, Bar-sur-Aube, La Ferte-sur-Aube, Chaumont, Nogent, Montigny, Coiffy, Vicq, and the guard of Moleme. Among the witnesses of were, archdeacons, canons, the bailiffs of

Langres and of Chatillon, Eustache de Coublanc and many seigneurs, and notables of the sire of Choiseul. This scene made a grand impression (exactly the political power he wanted) on the barons and knights who were preparing a new expedition to the Holy Land. (8th Crusade) . Thibaut VI wasted no time in demanding that the abbot of Moleme contribute to the future Crusade.

He warned all the priests who were dependents of his monastery to come to his aid.

The religious of Varennes made a considerable offering. Independent of us who already made contributions, Thibaut VI made still more demands on the ecclesiastics, including ransom for their vocations (excused from the Crusade because of their religious vocation). Eventually, in April 1270, Thibaut VI departed on the campaign. On (the eighth and last crusade to the Holy Land) the following 5 December he succumbed at Trapani, (Sicily) struck by the same disease that killed King St. Louis in 1270 (dysentery on the eighth crusade in Tunisia).

Thibaut VI had no children, and the kingdom of Navarre and the counts of Champagne and of Brie, reverted to his brother, called the Gross, seigneur de Rosnay, and who rendered homage to the bishop of Langres, the 18 of October 1271. Three years after, he died at Pampelune, his capital, and left a year old daughter named Jeanne. She inherited and married Phillippe-le-Bel, son of the King of France.

The abbot of Moleme reclaimed, during this new epoch, a confirmation of part of the act of 1250 (This act of association, dated the month of July 1250, gave to the count of Champagne the guard of the parish of Varennes and its dependancies,—see page 76-77 for complete details) that gave formidable possibilities of breaking or canceling it. (to regain the half he had originally given for protection) Phillip and Jeanne (Thiabut), in a document given in Paris in the month of December 1284, made the ratification permanent and simple with promises of confirmation of all the act. (took 34 years and a final move that thwarted the plans of the abbot of Moleme to escape the demands of his part of the Act of 1250!) The following year the death of Phillippe-le-Hardi called to the throne Phillipe-le-Bel. By this reunion of Champagne and the crown was realized. (Who had fought against each other in former times)

It seems that in the early years of the XIV century certain localities, overburdened by the rights of the seigneurs, strongly pleaded for the rights of the poor and miserable. After a time, exasperated families, who found it was less difficult in other places, abandoned their native villages and the number of the peasants significantly reduced.

1. Le texte de ce traite est imprime dans l'Historie de Vicq, at reproduit dans les Chateau et citadelle de Coiffy, ou nous avons puise plurieurs de documents de ce chaptrr.

2. Les Chasteu et citadelle de Coiffy, p. 83.

3. Vicq a-t-il ete forte, sous aux temps gallo-romains, soit sous les comptes de Champegne? L'histoie ne nous l'apprend

pas. Mais, l'auteur de Chasteau, et citadelle de Coiffy etait applee, a l'epoque romaine, Regalis ou regius mons, et qu'on en a la preuve dans le registre des hommages faits a Thibaut V de 1256-1270, sous le n 612 ou on lit: Feoda regalis montis vel Cufei quod idem est (Hist. Des comtes de Champagne, par d'Arbois de Jubainville), plus a la table, placee a la fin du registre (n 707), Regalis mons. ---- Il s'agit de la montagne de Vicq, maintenant converie de bois, nommee ce vulgairment Regemont, et, par corruption, Rougemont.

This happened at Fayl (2 miles S), (and probably at Rougeux too) at Vicq, at Damremont and Coiffy-les-Bas. (Villages 12 miles N of Rougeux) Fayl and Morey had given their rights to Jean I de Vergy and his daughter Helissent who returned to the Duke of Bourgogne the chateau of Fayl, and the chapel and its dependents, in August 1300.

After losing her husband, Henri de Vaudemont, Helissent married Gaucher de Chatillon, count of Porcein, the premier military officer of France. It was their son, Guy de Chatillon, who the inhabitants of Fayl addressed and supplicated for the end of the burden of the excessive size of the tithes he had arbitrarily imposed two years earlier. Guy inquired of the value of the territory from his friends and found his property fronted on the frontier of the counts of Champagne and Bourgogne, (and populated by local peasants) who could enter his property if it became deserted. Therefore by a charter of July 20, 1324 that freed the community of all tithes and other servitudes and replaced those extremely onerous burdens with the following: three cents for each fire (meaning the cooking fire in each of the peasants huts), four cents for each plow, three cents for each horned beast, and six cents for each work horse, if they promised to never leave to serve under another seigneur. For those peasants who had no plow, and if they periodically work the ground on a day to day basis, twelve deniers, for two or three days, two sous, and more than three, four sous payable the day of the Toussaint. (All Saints Day, usually at the end of October)

1. Hist. de Jussey, p. 13
2. Revue champenoise, p. 501

The Lenten fast, the barn work, the fork and the rake and the plow, military service whether on foot or horseback, were exempted from tithe. Eudes de Bourgogne (1231-1266- Duke of

Bourgogne) after having examined this charter, approved and confirmed it by a letter signed the Villers-le-Duc, July 1327. 1

By that regard Coiffy-le-Bas, Vicq and Damremont took the initiative to join Fayl in this form of taxation and wrote to their seigneur for approval. Philippe V (Philip V (1293 – 1322), King of France and King of Navarre (as Philip II) He reigned from 1316 to his death and was the penultimate monarch of the main line of the House of Capet) requested knight Pierre de Tiercelines,

VICQ

VICQ

bailiff of Chaumont to make an inquiry about the knowledge that would profit or damage that would follow if the mainmort was abolished (Mainmorte is a French term which means the lord's right to a share of his men's personal estate after death. During the medieval days, when a peasant tenant died without a direct heir ready to assume his tenancy and debts, the peasant's property reverted to his landlord. The heirs who lived away from home had to pay huge tax to assume possession of the deceased peasant's possessions)

Upon the report being presented and after consideration accorded their request. The agreement was sent to Paris in November 1337, *"We, considering the poverty in our region that is causing the depopulation of our villages and remedies that can be used, therefore have quitted in perpetuity the condition of mainmorte of those inhabitants and their successors in the villages of Coiffy, Vicq and Daremont 2."*

But in renouncement of the mainmorte, the King reserves the right of property sold, consisting of forty livres for every one sold. *"This shall be shared between the King and the priory. Before the buyer can enjoy his purchase he must have permission of the mayor of the village. The King ordained that in addition to what each house paid beyond the ancient rights, they should pay one chicken each year."*

1. Hist. De Fayl-Billot
2. La demande du prieur a de etre faite avant 1331, car Pierre de Tierelines fut bailli, pour la troisieme et derniere fois, de 1320 a 1331. (Hist de. Chaumon

CHAPTER VIII

DURING THE WAR WITH THE ENGLISH
(1340-1460)

From the year 1337 there was a rupture in the relationship between England and France. Our country (Champagne) did not suffer directly from this struggle but suffered the serious consequences of levees of men, passage of diverse troops and the required contributions of the process. To cover the costs of the war, Philippe de Valois (Philip VI, (1293–1350) considerably augmented import duties on salt, already established under Philippe-de-Long, (Philippe V) and made permanent a salt tax (1345) known as the 'grande gabelles'. (Reigning at the outbreak of the Hundred Years' War (1337–1453), he had no means of imposing on his country the measures necessary for the maintenance of his monarchical power, though he continued the efforts of the 13th-century Capetians toward the centralization of the administration in Paris. To raise taxes for war, he was obliged to make concessions to the nobility, the clergy, and the bourgeoisie; hence his reign witnessed the important development of the political power of the estates. The bourgeoisie, profiting from the king's power, proved grateful and loyal; among the clergy and nobility, however, a movement for reform of finances took root)

A repressive state monopoly, it was made doubly so by obliging every individual above the age of eight to purchase weekly a minimum amount of salt at a fixed price. Citizens are forced to buy up to 7 kilograms of salt per year. Further, they are prohibited to use this salt for making salted products (meat), which was illegal and could lead to charges of faux saunage, or salt fraud. Failing to adhere to this could lead to imprisonment and, if repeated, death. Each province had a Greniers à sel—a salt granary—where all salt produced from that region needed to be taken in order to be bought (at a fixed price) and sold (at an inflated price). It created a heavy burden to those who lived in Champagne because as the largest population of the six (divisions of the country) it had not only the highest salt prices but also not exempt from the mandatory salt duty for all people over eight years (of age) One-third of France's population resided within our region yet we had to pay two-thirds of all salt revenue but only consumed one-fourth of all salt. Because extreme disparities in tax rates and salt consumption existed between the six regions, opportunities for smuggling were ripe within France. The obvious means of smuggling salt was to buy it in a region where it was cheap and to sell it illegally in regions where it was expensive, at a higher price, but still less than the legal price. Customs guards tasked with arresting the smugglers were called gabelous, a term obviously derived from the gabelle (salt tax) they sought to uphold. They were despised by common folk as they were, without cause, able to search people and their homes in order to find illegal salt. The gabelous carried weapons and were known to grope women for pleasure under the guise of looking for salt. However, women were often used to smuggle salt under their dresses and sometimes used false derrières known as faux culls.

Smugglers were known as faux-sauniers, from faux ('false') and the root 'sau'-referring to salt.

Acrss the following centuries penallties for violations of this oppressive tax became stricter and more extreme.

Under the 1640 codification of gabelle law by Jean-Baptiste Colbert (Jean-Baptiste Colbert, (1619, —1683, Paris), controller general of finance (from 1665) and secretary of state for the navy (from 1668) under King Louis XIV of France. He carried out the program of economic reconstruction that helped make France the dominant power in Europe. He remained a faithful Catholic) Participating in salt smuggling warranted a range of harsh punishments.

Merely housing a faux-saunier could lead to imprisonment, fines, and, if repeated, death. Faux-sauniers could be sentenced to up to ten years on a galley if they were caught without weapons, and to death if caught while armed. Other forms of faux-saunage included sheepherders letting their flock drink from salty ponds, traders overly salting cod during transportation, and fishing at night (so that fisherman with great knowledge of waterways couldn't smuggle salt)

Each year, through the end of the 18th century, approximately 3000 citizens (men, women, and children) were imprisoned, sent to the galleys, or put to death for crimes against the gabelle. All the while, religious persons, nobility, and high-ranking officials were often exempt from the gabelle or paid much lower taxes (and could easily afford).

By the end of the eighteenth century, female smuggling was so common in some areas, especially in the West, that more women were arrested than men. It has been estimated that between 1759 and 1788, out of the 4,788 arrests in Laval, 2,845 women and children were arrested, amounting to more than half.

In 1789, following the ascension of the National Assembly, the gabelle was voted down and abolished throughout the entirety of France. Later, in 1790, the National Assembly decided that all persons imprisoned by for breaking laws pertaining to the gabelle were to be freed from prison and that all charges and convictions were to be permanently dropped.

This freedom would be short lived, however, as the gabelle would be reinstated by Napoleon Bonaparte in 1804, this time without major exemptions for regions such as Brittany. (The gabelle would stay part of France's legislation until abolished in 1946)

During the 1300's those villages dependent on the count and duchess of Bourgogne were not subject to this law because they assembled and refused to ever accept this tax.These two Burgogne's were governors for Eudes IV, son of King Philippe-le-Long (Philip V of France) (This relationship protected them from being forcibly required to pay the tax)

Fearing the visits of the requisitioners of the armies, the monks of Cherlieu placed themselves under the protection of Phillip, King of France, (a significant move in that France and Burgundy were not united and frequently fought each other. France wanted to capture Burgundy to which the duc of Burgundy, EudesIV, was opposed)

At the same time, by recommendation of their council, the inhabitants of Semmandon, (not a part of Burgundy) justifiably belong, they claim, to Henri de Borgognem, (not a good idea!) cousin of Eudes, (Duke of Burgundy and son of King Phillip of France) equally with the other peasants of Philippe de Valois and declared themselves litigants. Their request and claim was made to the provost of Coiffy. (12 miles from Rougeux)

They, in effect, signified to the camp at Rochelle their eligibility to also being included in the guard the judicial authority of Cherlieu and Semmadon. But the bailiff had much hate for the French who were gaining control over his county (Champagne and our region was not part of France prior to this time) and would not suffer what he called a felony. To deter others from having the desire to imitate this example, he sent, in the morning, a detachment of soldiers to pillage and wreck Semmadon. The soldiers returned to the camp with prisoners and booty, and celebrated for several days.

One of the bad results of the wars was the beginning of what was called the 'peste noire' (Black Death) It spread everywhere in 1349. That year became known as the year of the grande mort (large death).

1. Jussey (Historie, etc)

In the villages, on the roads, we could see those with maladies with a livid tint, whom we saw were dead. We saw those whose skin was covered to its extremities with black, red or blueish ulcers, cadavers recumbent and without burial. It was dreadfully horrible. Coiffy, in particular, was cruelly tested in 1347. Eudes IV (son of King Phillip of France), Duke and Count of Bourgogne, became a victim of the terrible scourge.

The states of the prince were inherited by his little son, Philippe de Rouves, who was just four or five years old. His grandfather Jean-le-Bon (John the Good was a monarch of the House of Valois who ruled as King of France from 1350 until his death) naturally became his tutor and assumed authority for the two Bourgognes. But he was unfortunate in the battle of Poitiers (1356) and was made prisoner by the English and anarchy desolated the provinces. The Valley of Amance was delivered (with its villages, including Rougeux), for a period of ten years, to the mercy of the foul adventurers and brigands known as the Routiers.

When John II came to power, France was facing several disasters: the Black Death, which caused the death of nearly half of its population; popular revolts known as Jacqueries; free companies of routiers who plundered the country; and English aggression that resulted in disastrous military losses, including the Battle of Poitiers of 1356, in which John was captured. While John was a prisoner in London, his son Charles became regent and faced several rebellions, which he overcame. To liberate his father, he concluded the Treaty of Brétigny (1360), by which France lost many territories and the enormous ransom of twice the income of France was unable to be raised and he died in British captivity.

Among the bands of English, were men from Lorraine, France, and many others. Undisciplined soldiers forcibly entered the abbeys, roamed the fields and woods, pillaged the huts of the peasants and killed, raped, and burned as they pleased. They murdered Eudes of Pierrefaites, the abbot of Cherlieu, ravaged and delivered to the flames Fayl (two miles S from Rougeux), Bourgogne, and a great number of villages and burgs during these ten years. They captured and ruined the chateau's, poorly guarded by ill trained and badly equipped guards. We suppose the chateau at Fayl was destroyed during this epoch. Duguesclin ('The Black Dog of Brocéliande', was a Breton knight and French military commander and enemy of our region during the Hundred Years' War) delivered France of their presence by his entry into the war between Spain and England (1366) (The English were also fighting the Spanish, who were allies of the French, during this 130 year war 1337-1453). Nevertheless, we see, in 1371 the Germans and in 1374 the English again invade our country and cause great harm to our citizens, however, the militia of Langres finally chased them away.

Thomas de la Rochelle imitated the Routiers. He committed his fiefdom without the authorization of his king and to punish him, Philippe-le-Hardi (Duke of Burgundy, 1342–1404 and a younger son of King John II (the Good)) confiscated the ground of his manor.

la Rochelle got vengeance by devastating the fiefs (homes of poor peasants) that belonged to the duke and of Champagne. Then he took refuge in the chateau of

Chateau Dessus

Chauvirey. But on the 17 of August 1374, under the banner of Jussey there arrived at that place three hundred policemen, twenty arbaletriers (men who had crossbows) and twenty companions on horseback. But, assisted with mercenaries, he managed in some manner to escape. The following year the provost captured him and he was obliged to serve 13 years in prison. Chauvirey-le-Vieil belonged to Renaud du Chatelet (d. 1429) As at Chauviery-Le-Chatel, he also had Jean II as his seigneur, who was married to Jeanne de Salins. It was he who built the chateau Dessus, and sometime later the chateau Dessous, so that his two children, Jean III and Gaucher, could each inherit a chateau. To Jean III, the firstborn, he gave his chateau, Dessous and the Eastern part of his chateau Dessus.

In 1398, as an example to those who remained with him when he lived elsewhere, he returned to fief the abbey of Cherlieu for three hundred florins of gold, the same as that of Chauviery. Gaucher received the Eastern part of the chateau Dessus.

(In Medieval feudalism a fief was a favor awarded to a vassal and was his source of income, granted to him by his lord in exchange for his services and to whom he paid homage and swore fealty. The fief usually consisted of land and the labor of peasants who were bound to cultivate it. Dignities, offices, and money rents were also given in fief)

During the wartime slaughter of 1385 and again in 1406 he declared held in fief the sovereign, the chateau with its pits, squares and gardens that are in the environment, the ground with two plows and twenty-five first cuts of hay, eighty-eight households, reduced to thirteen due to the result of war, all tillable to friends who have been wounded, and divided in half with his brother the woods, and selling the tithes to whomever paralyzes (captures) and gives justice on those strangers by the time of the days of fairs and markets. (It is unclear who are the people being targeted but could be attempting to get revenge on Thomas de la Rochelle and his followers)

Previously, in a very strong house at Vitrey, fifty-four families were sheltered, now reduced to twenty-two because of the casualties of the repeated invasions.

The wars have reduced the tithes to a quarter of the ovens (communal ovens for baking of bread) and a quarter of the tithes of wheat, oats, and wine, and of the fiefs of Thiebaud, Favez, de Gevigney, and of Jean de Cemboing, and giving justice to their subjects, they could not produce more.

At Ouge there were only twenty-eight feu (fires/hearths/houses) remaining.

That seigneur had an ancient free-hold (tax free), but when the counts of Bourgogue, revoked their rights of suzerainty Gaucher felt obligated to furnish the admission-feudal (I was unable to find an explanation for this term but it appears that he is doing an equal revocation to his vassals)

During those times lived Jean-le-Gros, born at Coiffy-le-Bas near the end of the XIV century and regarded as a man of merit. He was canon of Langres, of Sens and of Reims, counselor and secretary of (Mad) King Charles VI (1368-1422) In 1392 he founded the chapel Saint-Catherine in the church at Coiffy. He made many important donations were also made to the church of Langres. Jean-le-Gros was the first member of a family who attained a high rank from our valley.

Under the administration of Louis de Bar, nominated bishop of Langres in 1396 and cardinal in 1397, there were beautiful religious festivals. Numerous notables of the town declared to the prelate that the main part of the corpse of Saint Gengoul, their compatriot, had been, because of the wars, hidden in a humble tomb in the priory. Though (the faithful of) Varennes, they said, frequented with fidelity and honor the good hearted martyr, his relics remained ignored except for a few reliable men who secretly transported it at a moment favorable for this. We do not think of moving him, (because it) wounded our conscience. After prayers and pious research the bishop moved his body to Varennes where it was placed in a casket made of silver and accorded an indulgence of forty days if a good confession and contrition for sin is made. It was thought that the casket would be brought into the church on the fEast of the saint however it was found to be legitimately impossible because a letter from frere Barthelemy, Abbot of Moleme (what could have been in that letter?) That religious presided over a grand ceremony for the saint on 11 May 1404.

We see that the seigneur of Fayl belonged to Gaucher de Chatillon. He sold it, on 12 May 1360 to Etienne, count of Montbeliard. Agnes de Montbeliard brought it in marriage 14 May 1398 to Thiebaud VIII, seigneur of Neuchatel, count of Bourgogne. The count encouraged population increases and gave the results of his census to the duke Jean-sans-Peur (John the Fearless was born in Dijon on 27 May 1371 to Philip II "the Bold," Duke of Burgundy. For a period of time, he served as regent of France on behalf of his first cousin King Charles VI of France, who suffered from severe mental illness in 1407 and in 1408)1.

He held the fief for the duke which consisted of the chateau, the village of Fayl, and all its legal authority. He enumerated all the various rights of the inhabitants. Each household must pay three sous d'eschief on Toussaint (All Saints Day at the end of October), one hen each Careme (46 days in which the Church ordained fasting from meat) All, except the clerics, must perform three corvees, (days of work), one of haymaking and two of harvest. The laborers must pay, for each four legged animal, six sous; for each plow, four sous, and for each plow three days (corvee) of work. Each pair of oxen must bring a wagon load of hay 2 before Maizieres (Feast of Corpus Christi) Two horses must bring three wagon loads of hay each year, one at All Saints Day, one at Christmas and one at Bordes (unable to locate the meaning of this word), one cartload of wood and three other wagons of material for repair of the chateau each year. To the chateau (at Fayl) belongs the guard of Montlandon (unknown meaning), and for that the inhabitants must pay twenty-five sous, in the coin of Arbigny-sous-Varennes (6 miles N) by the fEast day of Saint Remy (unknown saint) and accompanied by twenty-five hemines (a regional unit of measure, according to some authorities, was unknown in Paris) of oats. But because the villages were poverty stricken and deserted by the ravages of war and high mortality, these requirements were reduced by half (however ability to obtain coinage remained a great difficulty) The seigneur has the right to sell all the merchandise bought or exchanged at the weekly market and the annual fair.

1. Archives de la Cote-d'Or, abbey de Moleme, 40, laisse.
2. Archives de la Cote-d'Or. ----- Charte d'affranchussenebt de Fayl. ----- Historie de Fayl-Billot, etc.

He extended his suzerainty over many vassals and because of him there are a dozen fiefs situated in Fayl, Bussieres, Genevrieres, Tornay, Bourguignon and Staint-Maurice. In summation, the chateau of Fayl was one of the most considerable in the country.

Jean-sans-Peur, (John the Fearless, murdered in 1419) Duke of Burgundy, to whom Thiebaud rendered homage, wanted to overpower his cousin Louis, Duke of Orleans, brother of the mad King Charles VI of France and cuckold of the Kings wife, Queen Isabeau, with whom there was much enmity. In the end Jean-sans-Peur had Louis assassinated (1407) (The mad king, the infidelity of the Queen, and the assassinations led to civil wars while at the same time the country was engaged in the 100 Years War with England who each year inflicted annual invasions and pillage on the inhabitants)

The king of England profited from these internal wars and completely defeated the French in the famous battle of Azincourt in 1415. In 1419 Jean-sans-Peur was treacherously killed, in

turn, on the bridge of Moatereau, by the people of the Dauphin. In revenge for the death of his father, the new sixteen-year old Duke, Philippe-le-Bon, joined the English and in concert with Queen Isabeau (The wife of mad King of France Charles VI) signed the Treaty of Troys for the demented king, in which the French Royal succession was given to the English. Our territory was immediately invaded by English and Bourguignons. The fortress of Coiffy, say the historians, could not resist the attacks of Thomas de Montaigu, count of Sailsbury (England) and fell under his power in 1428 and into which entered a garrison of strangers while forcibly living off the peasants, pillaged and sacked all the farms of the region.

We are not sure how long the English occupied Coiffy. It is certain it extended beyond 1431 based on the following events. (Because of confusing inferences and assumptions of events, errors in identification of the principals, scrambled sequences, and four untranslatable words (fourny, garny, tenoye, estoit), I have rewritten the events of this chapter based on historical events)

THE RIVER.

VIEW OF THE VALLEY OF THE AMANCE RIVER

The Battle of Bulgneville (July 1431) (Fought between Renee(1409-1480), King of Naples (Italy) who claimed inheritance of the deceased Duke of Lorraine and the count of Vaudemont, Antoine de Vaudemont (1400-1458) who also claimed the duchy and allied with the English) With Burgundian help Vaudemont defeated Renee and took him prisoner along with a number of his officers, high officials and soldiers, who, in an attempt to rescue the Rene, also became prisoners and like their unfortunate master, have languished eighteen months in the dungeon of Antoine de Vergy (1375-1439), at Champlitte (9miles S)

Erard du Chatelet, knight and seigneur of Deuilly, and marchal of Lorraine, and Pierre de Chauviery, Vansillot of Saint-Veroune and their other gentlemen and companions of arms were also fellow prisoners (of those allied with the English)

After 18 months the Duke Rene was able to obtain his liberty on parole by yielding up his two sons as hostages. This angered the King (of France) and the Duke was re-imprisoned and was held two more years while he raised a heavy ransom that impoverished him and his duchy.

Duke Rene finally bought his liberty at thousand florins, and for surety of payment Pierre-de-Chauviery (also a prisoner) was obliged to pledge to deliver Chauviery-le-Vieil, Betoncourt and Vitrey.

VALLEY OF THE AMANCE

Google Earth

Duke Rene's title was confirmed by the (French) King in 1434, however his impoverishment was not alleviated (and his very complicated and generally unsuccessful life and those of his children continued to his death) We found these brothers (sons of Rene and hostages for him in the dungeon of Vergy) on the 2 of July of this year (1434) who this traitor (Antoine de Vergy)-(A Burgundian allied with the English who was wounded as he assisted in the assassination of Jean-sans-Peur in 1419), before discussing their ransom, demanded the surrender of the castle of Coiffy, such as it was, and the twelve men penned up there.

(The Vergys were an ancient and powerful family in the region. Known from the 7th century, the first known lord of Vergy is Guérin de Vergy, brother of Saint Leodegar. Guérin was stoned around 681 at the foot of the rocky spur at Vergy, shortly after his brother's martyrdom. The first house of Vergy arose in the 9th century with (760 –

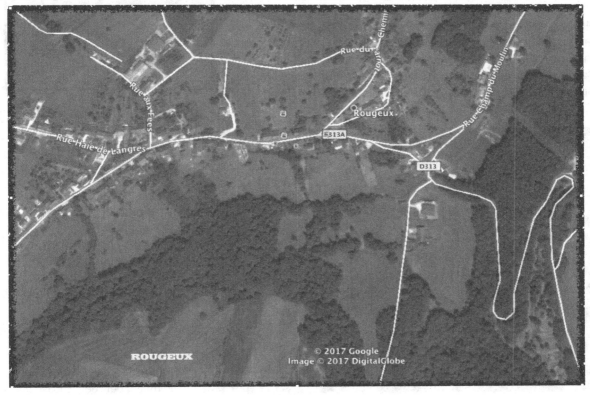

ROUGEUX

© 2017 Google
Image © 2017 DigitalGlobe

Mr Marechal in front of his barn   1979

819), who was count of Chalon and count of Mâcon, then count of Auvergne.
(In the 12th century Vergy was considered one of the most impregnable fortresses in the kingdom by Louis VII of France. Pope Alexander III took refuge there in 1159. It was during this era that the church of Saint-Saturnin was built, still to be seen today)
(The Vergy family is the first historically attested owner of the Turin Shroud. It was Jeanne de Vergy who, in accordance with her husband Geoffroy de Charny's vows, put on the first showings of the relic at Lirey. The relic was twice absent in her castle at Montfort)

This Antoine de Vergy, seigneur of Champlitte and his nephew Jean de Vergy, sire of Fouvent, was in great favor with Vaudemont, duke of Bourgogne, after the above events.

Gaume de Chateauvillain, baron of Chalancey became very jealous (The reason is not clear) Leaving the party of Vergy (allied with the English) he submitted to the King of France (opposing the Vergy's and those who had joined the English and Burgundians) who made him a lieutenant general and gave him full authority to negotiate the surrender of the places in Champagne occupied by the English and the Burgundians (allies against France) Suddenly he found himself strong enough to attack the villages and chateau's of the Vergy's and ravage their territory. Abruptly, Jean de Vergy returned with his prince and submitted to the obedience of the King of France (Swapped sides again!) and directed his forces against his former allies (Vaudemont) who did not want to surrender the

THE ASSUMPTION OF OUR LADY   ROUGEUX, FRANCE   1979

chateau's and his authority in their region. De Vergy then forcibly chased them (Vaudemont) from Coiffy, of Montigny and of Nogent, These fortresses were immediately occupied by the garrisons of the Vergy. This was part of another war during the anarchy that desolated the environs around Langres (and Rougeux)
The treaty of Arras (1435) detached Philipe-le-Bon (Duke of Burgundy) from the English. During his reign he alternated between English and

Note stove pipe
Catholic Church at Rougeux France   1979

80

The Marechal home
Mrs Marechal
Rougeux 1979
OWNED BY AUTHOR

French alliances in an attempt to improve his dynasty's position. The Treaty of Arras, signed in 1435, became an important diplomatic achievement for the French in the closing years of the Hundred Years' War. Overall, it reconciled a longstanding feud between King Charles VII of France and Duke Philip of Burgundy. Philip recognized Charles VII as King of France and, in return, Philip was exempted from homage to the crown and Charles agreed to punish the murderers (Charles VII had been at lEast complicit in that crime) of Philip's father, Jean-sans-Peur. By breaking the alliance between Burgundy and England, Charles VII consolidated his position as monarch of France against a rival claim by Henry VI of England. The political distinction between Armagnacs and Burgundians ceased to be significant from this time onward. France already had Scotland as an ally and England was left isolated. From 1435 onward, English occupation in France underwent steady decline)

SS troopers billeted here during WWII
MME Marechal's house
Rougeux
F 1309 PH 92
OWNED BY AUTHOR

The poor people, delivered from the oppression of strangers, hoped to live in peace but it did not happen. Bandits and pillagers and scoundrels and again the terrible Routiers of the previous century covered the

Madam Marechals house   hotel   church

1987

countryside with bereavement and ruin. We named them the Ecorcheurs because they even take the shirt off our backs. They have at their head Villandras, and Antoine de Chabannes (1408?–1488) (Chabannes was a French soldier in the Hundred Years War. He served with Joan of Arc, distinguishing himself at the siege of Orléans in 1428–29, fought as a captain of écorcheurs, or armed bands, and took part in the Praguerie revolt (1440) Pardoned by King Charles VII, he was appointed to various offices and presided over the committee that procured the conviction of the financier, Jacques Cœur. After the accession (1461) of King Louis XI he was imprisoned. He escaped and joined (1465) the League of the Public Weal against Louis XI, but was pardoned once more and became one of the king's most trusted officers—proving, once again, there is little justice in this world)! and the bastard of Bourbon (Villandras), both grand seigneurs, whose brigandage became so notorious that Parliament stopped it by banishing them. Their steps were marked by rape, murder, incendiary and of all kinds of cruelties. At their approach the inhabitants of our countryside abandoned their homes and sought refuge in the forests and chateaus. The fields remained uncultivated and famine and the black death followed closely behind them. The air was so corrupted by an odor so awful that life itself was endangered. The mortality was very immense, notable during the years 1437 and 1438.

In 1439 Jean de Vergy surprised one of these bands in Bassigny (24 miles N), routed them and seized their booty. Charles VII arrested Villandras at Bar-sur-Aube (36 miles SE), and had him enclosed in a sack and thrown into the river. Troops began to appear more frequently and confronted these ravagers, who during a period of ten years reappeared during each spring. But the soldiers were charging so much for their services that we called them the Retondeurs (cutting off the best part of the meat)

Shirley walking the main street in Bourbonne 1979

As a result of all the civil unrest and wars, all of our villages find themselves ruined and reduced to the last extremity. Fayl-Billot (2 miles S), the locality most populated, was pillaged and burned numerous times, lost more than half of its inhabitants. The Ecorcheurs inflicted numerous reprisals and caused irreparable damages and ills.

From 1430 the village was unable to pay any of the twelve francs due each year to the Duke of Bourgogne and he was forced to cancel it and searched the 'attic' of

Dijon for the necessary salt that the cattle required. Upon the request of the inhabitants, Philippe-le-Bon, by an edict of Hesdin in 1448, quitted the running eighteen year fines for default of payments. Moreover he decided that during the forthcoming ten years, the day after the fEast of the Naivety of Saint John the Baptist (June 24, three months after the celebration of the Annunciation) the village would only be required to pay six francs in place of the twelve. At the end of the term, the deviation would return to the ordinary.

(Hesdin was a fief of the counts of Artois, vassals of the Counts of Flanders until 1180. When Philip, count of Flanders gave Artois as dowry to his niece Isabella of Hainault when she married Philip Augustus of France in 1180, Hesdin and the other seigneuries passed to France. Though subsequently the territory passed to the Dukes of Burgundy, Hesdin remained one of a handful of French strongholds, until in 1553 Emperor Charles V ordered the utter destruction of the old fortified town on a rise of ground and built the present town the following year, some 6 kilometres (3.7 mi) from the original site, on the banks of the Canche. The unfortified village of Vieil-Hesdin was later built on the original site. In 1639 the French laid siege to Hesdin and under Louis XIII, it was recaptured for France. Thus, though Hesdin has an ancient name and 16th century structures, there is nothing left of the medieval town)

As the long and hard calamities subsided, some of us began to talk, and some men of Maizieres were thinking about getting rid of some of the easements they dislike. For example they want permission to marry in front of the justice of the peace and elimination of the requirement that on the evening of their wedding they had to lie in their wedding bed and make their residence at Maizieres under threat of confiscation of their property. They tried to execute their project but they were arrested and imprisoned.

One of them, Odot Gerard, who had a wife and infants, escaped. He wandered in the woods from one escapade to another until Jean Jeofroy, abbot of Luxeuil and grand dean of Saint Vivant-sous-Vergy arrived to reestablish order.

Learning of this new order, Odot surrendered. An act of September 2, 1452, passed in front of Vignarded, guard of the seal of the provost of Coiffy and Perron, notary, consultant noted that Odot threw himself to his knees and asked for pardon for his disobedience and the injuries uttered against him and his person, and that he recognized him as his true lord and submitted himself to his judgment. Odot, as a fine, then swore on day of Saint Evangiles that he would be a loyal subject of the grand dean and never move to another seigneur.

Then the Reverend Father condemned the payment to the provost the gross fine of Coiffy to amend the prison violation, and defended the situation of the prisoner as being totally destitute in that he had lost all the heritage he possessed at Maizieres and had no means to support his family. The justice of the sentence pronounced by the seigneur overcame the misery. The tears of the mother of the infants touched the heart of the religious; they remitted the property seized as payment for the penalty. (Massive depopulation from war and black death was an ulterior motive in this judgment because the labor of the surfs generated income for the seigneurs)

Six years after this affair MM. De Saint-Vivant (grand dean of Saint Vivant-sous-Vergy) refused the request of the royal prosecutor of the bailiwick of Chaumont. They claimed, in a provisional sentence rendered to this bailiwick, the 13 of November 1458, the immediate possession and use of the facilities of that ground and to give a discharge of the seizure made against them. (The reason for this action is not stated however probably Odot had not paid his tithes) (This seems heartless of the Abbot however those were brutal times with little good will anywhere)

SUPPLEMENTS FROM ABBOT MULSON AND OTHERS

Famines were familiar occurrences in Medieval Europe. Localized famines occurred in France during 50-52BC, 470, 613, 831, 888, 896, 937, 1095, 1126, 1142-46, 1161-62, 1172, 1186-96, 1304, 1305, 1310, 1315–17 (the Great Famine), 1330–35, 1349–51, 1358–60, 1371, 1374–75 and 1390. (Abbot Briffaut mentioned famine 55 times in this translation)

83

ROUGEUX. 1979.

Poverty, understood in the usual sense of destitution, was a permanent condition of the Dark and Middle ages. Considered inescapable, it was accepted as an inevitable part of the social structure. By 470, in Reims, in countless other cities, at their monasteries and churches, the poor were being registered and multitudes gathered for food distribution. During the next 1200 years, churches and monasteries were the primary source of what little relief was available. We do not lack for sources of information regarding the scope, persistence, and variety of poverty in the period surrounding these centuries.

In 1095 a severe drought only yielded the equivalent of two months worth of food for the year. In 1126 AD the 'Chronicle,' of Sigbert of Gembloux, reported a great famine where multitudes

Rougeux 1977

died of hunger. Less than 20 years later the 'Annels of Lobes' reported in 1142 of a long rainy spell that hampered the harvest and led to severe shortages and an exorbitant rise in prices. In 1144-45 severe windstorms, rain and an extremely cold summer, lead to continued famine through 1146. The 'Acts' of Pope Alexander III heralds how in 1161-62 all France trembled in fear as another famine swept across the country. The 'Annels' of Holy Cross, in Coimbra, speak of a universal hunger during an even more serious recurrence in 1172 that spared neither man nor beast.

From 1186 through 1196 excessive rainfall everywhere across Europe spoiled the harvests and through erosion, the supplies of potable water became polluted. Many died at the gates of monasteries as their supplies became exhausted. A few years of warmer weather led to respite from about 1200 to 1250. For most people, even during this period, there was often not enough to eat, and life was a relatively short and brutal struggle to survive to old age.

Rougeux 1977

According to official records about the British Royal family, an example of the best off in society, for whom records were kept, the average life expectancy in 1276 was 35.28 years.

Between 1301 and 1325, during the Great Famine life expectancy was 29.84 years while between 1348 and 1375 during the Plague, it was only 17.33 years. The figures do not necessarily mean the average lifespan of an adult, as child mortality was extremely high in pre-industrial societies and if one survived beyond the teen years the odds of living several decades more were substantially increased.

Yield ratios of wheat, the number of seeds one could eat per seed planted, had been dropping since 1280, and food prices had been climbing. After favorable harvests, the ratio could be as high as 7:1, but after unfavorable harvests it was as low as 2:1 -– that is, for every seed planted, two seeds were harvested, one for next year's seed, and one for food. There was little margin for failure. By comparison, modern farming has ratios of 30:1 or more.

The Great Famine of 1315-1317 started with torrential rains and cool weather, perhaps the result from a volcano, in spring of 1315. Universal crop failures lasted until the summer harvest of 1317. Throughout the spring and the summer, it continued to rain, and the temperature remained cool. Under such conditions, grain could not ripen leading to widespread crop failures. Grain was brought indoors in urns and pots to keep dry. The straw and hay for the animals could not be cured so there was no fodder for the livestock. The price of food began to rise; prices doubled between spring and midsummer. Salt, necessary for livestock, was difficult to obtain since it could not be effectively evaporated in wet weather. Wheat prices grew by 320%. Stores of grain for long-term emergencies were limited to lords, nobles, wealthy merchants and the Church. Because of the generally increased population pressures, even lower-than-average harvests meant large numbers would go hungry; there was little margin for failure. People began to harvest wild edible roots, plants, grasses, nuts and bark in the forests. All segments of society from nobles to peasants were affected but especially the peasants,

Valley where Rougeux was located before 13th century   1977

who represented 95% of the population and who had no reserve food supplies. To provide some measure of relief, the future was mortgaged by slaughtering the draft (horses and oxen needed to plow) animals, eating the seed grain, abandoning children to fend for themselves and, among old people, voluntarily refusing food for the younger generation to survive.

Hunger did not abate until 1322. The famine marked a clear end to the period of growth and prosperity from the eleventh to the thirteenth centuries. Extreme levels of crime, disease, mass death and even cannibalism and infanticide was widespread. The crisis had consequences for the Church, state, European society, and for future calamities to follow in the fourteenth century.

They did not know it, however this period marked the beginning of 'The Little Ice Age" which would begin abatement for more than 500 years.

Historians debate the toll, but it is estimated that 25% of the population of many cities and towns died. While the Black Death (1338–1375) would kill more people, it often swept through an area in a matter of months, but the Great Famine lingered for years, drawing out the suffering of the populace.

A number of documented incidents show the extent of the famine. Edward II, King of England, stopped at St Albans on 10 August 1315 and had difficulty finding bread for himself and his entourage; it was a rare occasion in which the King of England was unable to eat. Recent analysis of skeletal remains discovered in Lorraine, a few miles East of Rougeux, not only show evidence of violent death but also of atrophy, rickets, and serious vitamin deficiencies. Although no data has been found to indicate the birth rate, these ancient cemeteries, not surprisingly, contain a large proportion of child remains, confirming a high mortality rate.

In a society whose final recourse for all problems had been religion, and Roman Catholicism was the only tolerated faith, no amount of prayer seemed effective against the causes of the famine. That undermined the institutional authority of the Church and helped lay the foundations for later movements that were deemed heretical by the Church, as they opposed the papacy and blamed the failure of prayer upon corruption within the Church.

During the 1300's there were thirty-four years of war; 16 famines caused by late spring frosts, lack of rain at needed times, excessively cool summers; continuous summer and fall rains, and early frosts. By 1317, people were so weakened by diseases such as pneumonia, bronchitis and tuberculosis, and so much of the seed stock had been eaten, that it was not until 1325 that the food supply returned to relatively normal conditions and that the population began to increase again.

Most of the half-naked poor had only had a knife as an eating utensil and in many cases this was the total inheritance for their children. Few had spoons and none had forks. Before Columbus reached the West Indies, the Old World had no corn, squash, tomatoes, potatoes, or peppers. Anything that wasn't eaten fresh was dried, smoked, salted, fermented, or pickled. Spices such as pepper, cinnamon, or any other seasoning was not locally available and far too expensive for any but the nobility. Cooking and baking were done in a communal village oven (necessary due to scarcity of fuel) Their diet, handed down from ancient times, was deficient in supplying essential nutrients, particularly Vitamins A, D, E, K, but especially Vitamin C.

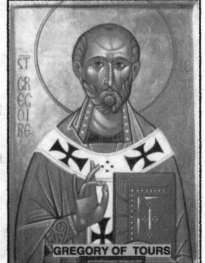
GREGORY OF TOURS

According to Gregory of Tours (538-594), the diet of the poor consisted of grape pips; hazel flowers; fern roots; periodically available oatmeal, eaten without milk, salt or sugar; heavy gray or rye bread; and occasionally, home made beer; all accompanied by common field grass. Meat and salt were rarities and spices; sugar or sweets were never served at those poor tables and did not change until introduction of new foodstuffs from South America by Columbus.

Poaching in the forests of the seigneur or abbey was punishable by blinding and/or long imprisonment in the hulks (rotting ships anchored along the seacoast where prisoners were kept secure by having an iron collar riveted around the neck and arm and a cannon ball fastened to the right ankle)

Failure in repayment of debts to Jews or Lombards could often result in mutilation.

A license was required to gather firewood (dead tree limbs and combustable twigs found in the woods), another impediment in the bitter struggle to remain alive.

Failing all too frequently to fill a craving stomach, peasants ate their scanty meals in their one room, dirt floored windowless huts, with bare hands from a bowl placed on a rough table.

The following description of·a meal at Duke Philip's (Duke of Burgundy) palace in Dijon, only forty miles South of Rougeux, illustrates the polarized lifestyles of nobles and peasants. Otto Cartellier's, 'The Court of Burgundy,' records that:

"They were not unacquainted with the finer aspects of exquisite cuisine, which would have been an epicure's paradise. Duke Philip submitted himself unconditionally to the laws of etiquette and demanded a like submission from the highest to the loWest of his servants. The napkin with which the prince dried his hands was kissed when the sommelier delivered it; in the same way the valet-servant touched his lips to the handles of the two large knives which were laid at the Dukes place; the fruitier in like manner kissed the torch which was intended for the ruler. Bareheaded, the valets and pages carried the dishes from the kitchen to the dining hall and knelt frequently before the prince. The manner in which the various articles were to be held was carefully prescribed; the salt cellar between the foot and girdle, the drinking vessel at the foot. Food and drink were brought in solemn procession. All eyes were upon the prince; a nod sufficed and when the cupbearer presented the gold, jewel-encrusted cup to the table, he held it high above his head so that it would be untouched by his breath. When the prince had finished drinking the cupbearer received it with great reverence. A buffet was close by, the six shelves of which were loaded with gold and silver services and crystal and glass of all colors and shapes studded with pearls and jewels. On the table lay cloths of solid damask reaching to the floor and on the benches were cushions with embroidered coats of arms. At the extreme end of the table golden fountain spurting water had been erected. Twenty-eight musicians played while forty-two courses of meat and other foods were served. At the end golden bowls of spices, encrusted with jewels, were passed to the guests, etc."

Charles the Bold, Duke of Burgundy.   1477
commons.wikimedia.org

"Some choice dishes demanded by nobility included the superiority of chicken drowned in wine, rather than killed the usual way; of game caught in mild weather, rather than cold; of fruit plucked while the moon was on the wane; and the delight of being served roasted peacock, with its full plumage displayed." "But not until the time of the Reformation in the 1500's did people begin to feel ashamed at the sight of others living in conditions unworthy of human beings and organized efforts gradually implemented to help the poor."

By the 1700's potatoes, because of their high nutritional value and resistance to poor weather, began to be an important crop and major factor in alleviation of famine in Europe.

Acceptance during the 1800's by hard headed peasants, reluctant and highly resistant to change, gradually began, with implementation of crop rotations and replacement of the ancient system of letting their land lay fallow for up to seven years, became widespread. This was a critical advancement and vastly increased food stuff production.

In 1833, five rich young Parisian men, on a dare, went into the slums of Paris, and were heart struck by what they encountered. They banded together, founded the Saint Vincent de Paul Society, and dedicated their lives in attempts to alleviate the dismal poverty of their city.

The *Palais des ducs de Bourgogne*
General information
Type
Ducal Residence, Royal residence
Architectural style
Gothic architecture, French Baroque architecture
Location
Dijon
Construction started
1364 (for the Medieval palace)
Completed
1737 (completed by the grand escalier)
Client
Philip the Bold, Duke of Burgundy

Palace of the Dukes and Estates of Burgundy

Palais des ducs et États de Bourgogne

Necessary intervention from government agencies was not implemented, however, for an additional 100 years.

Throughout many, many centuries, multitudes of the indigent, starving, sick, and disabled; widows, orphans and unemployed—the poorest of the poor—were driven from the land by ravages of war; epidemics, plague, leprosy, scarcity, debt, hunger and crop failures. Many roamed the roads, feared, despised, and untrusted by all (These poor must have been the filthiest, malodorous, ragged, necessarily thieving, unhappy, hopeless, desperate, fearful, possibly dangerous and seriously emaciated imaginable. Surviving outdoors in the elements without shelter would have been an awful life)

Countless numbers lived in the woods, eating grass and other growth they could find, too weak to take to the roads. The paupers, slightly more fortunate, managed to stay on small plots of land and lived in rude thatched huts with little or no furniture. Many had no tools and worked the soil with their bare hands. Ravages of war, freakish weather and other misfortunes pressured them to borrow seed crop money from Jews or Lombards at usurious rates. The Council of Paris in 829 AD left a striking description of the situation stating, *"It was not uncommon to demand for a single modius, three or four modi at harvest time. Foreclosure of the property and/or tools was the result of failure to repay as agreed. Failure to repay often forced the husband to flee to avoid mutilation, imprisonment or slave ships; abandoning his wife and children to their fate."*

Astonishingly, worse was yet to come!

Costs of perpetual war beginning in 1290 and ending the mid 1500's required every cent available. Heavy taxes were imposed that smothered any nascent beginnings of commerce.

In October 1347, during a famine beginning in 1335, a group of twelve Genoese ships landed at Ancona, an Italian port along the Adriatic Sea, the entire crews either dead or deathly ill. Because of recent reports by a Franciscan monk that, *"A plague of unparalleled fury was decimating the Far East,"* it is thought that the crews had made contact with this illness at the Indian port of Caffa. Within a few days, the entire Italian city was infected and the enraged populace forced the ships to set sail. They unsuccessfully tried to land at other ports in Italy and France, but only succeeded in spreading, over a wide area, rats infested with plague bearing fleas.

Plagues were not unknown prior to the middle ages. The great plague of 160 AD, known as the 'Antonine Plague,' (also known as the Plague of Galen, who described it), was an ancient pandemic, of either smallpox or measles, brought back to the Roman Empire by troops returning from campaigns in the Near East. The epidemic claimed the lives of two Roman emperors — Lucius Verus, who died in 169, and his co-regent who ruled until 180, Marcus Aurelius Antoninus, whose family name, Antoninus, was given to the epidemic. The disease broke out again nine years later, according to the Roman historian Dio Cassius, and caused up to 2,000 deaths a day at Rome, one quarter of those infected. Total deaths have been estimated at five million. Disease killed as much as one-third of the population in some areas, and decimated the Roman army. The epidemic had drastic social and political effects throughout the Roman Empire, particularly in literature and art.

The year 1349 is known as the year of the 'grand mort de la peste noir' (great year of the Black Death) in the Rougeux region. Along the roads, in the villages, and in the fields, could be seen people, with the typical livid complexion, already classified as dead. The Plague took two forms, pulmonary with spitting up blood bringing death in three days, or bubonic, covering the body with running pustules and carbuncles, and death within five days. Multitudes died without being buried.

In 1315 the Little Ice Age began, causing food shortages and additional woes on the afflicted population, not moderating until 1850—and in fact the last vestiges ended during the lat 1930's. This 1920's era photo illustrates the amount of ice clogging the river during the spring thaw. This river, the West Branch of the Susquehanna near Frenchville, still froze over when I was a child during the '30's. It has not frozen over since that time. Dad told me of one summer when he was young, about 1898, when he plowed the fields during a June snowstorm.

A Viennese chronicler wrote in 1354, *"Neither relatives, nor friends, nor priests, nor friars accompany the dead to the grave nor was the office of the dead recited. No bells were rung and nobody wept as everyone expected to soon join their loved ones and believed this was the end of the world. In many places in the city trenches were dug, very broad and deep, and into these bodies were thrown and covered with a little earth and thus layer after layer until the trench was full."*

"And I, Jean Detorue, with my own hands, buried five of my own children in a single trench, many others doing the like. Many were dug up by dogs who dispersed their limbs throughout the city and consorting with the sick or merely touching their clothes meant certain death. Mine own eyes have seen dogs who, in a brief time, died after touching or eating part of the dead."

Estimates of deaths in France ranged from 26% to 55% of the total population during the first three years. The rate varied by location, but the number of deaths, exacerbated by a populace weakened by the ongoing famine, was appalling. Covering windows with heavy blankets and

Note denuded mountains formerly densly forested with the greatest white pine forest in the world.

Coudley post office and store P/O established 11/29/04 and closed 11/30/36

1920 frozen Sesquehanna at Deer

Note denuded hills in background
DeerOffice has been shoved over the tracks
1920
owned by author

abstaining from any type of bathing (which was not done very frequently anyway) was recommended as treatment to prevent opening of the pores and subsequent entrance of "vapors" into the body. The Faculty of Medicine in Paris also recommended "Eating good white bread, white meat and young lamb while avoiding leeks, turnips and onions which engender flatulence. Other 'light and subtle foods' were also to be avoided for this same reason." Further recommendations included advice *"that one should work less, sleep on good, fine-smelling sheets, use costly aromatic disinfectants and sprinkle rose water around the room."* (Chances are good the poor starving peasant never saw 'good white bread' during his entire lifetime and for years was even prohibited from even eating his own chickens. It would take more than 'sweet smelling sheets' to hide the odor of his pallet of rotten straw. This is a good example of the complete oblivion of the upper class to the suffering of the poor)

The uneducated and superstitious peasantry assumed the plague was a punishment from God. They were excited by the deaths of communities of monks and clergy, which caused, among other things, the Church to suffer a loss of credibility for many years. Figures indicate over 45% of the clergy died within a two-year period.

For a substantial number of years after the diminution of the plague, commerce was seriously disrupted by the vast number of farms, businesses and other occupations abandoned by the death of farmers and burgers. The plague gradually abated over a period of five years after being blamed on 'vapors' or 'mists'. It was not until 1365, sixteen years later, that the epidemic finally ended and 150 years before the population regained its previous level. (The continent was afflicted with numerous and periodic bouts of the plague over many centuries)

From 1337 to 1453, France endured especially tumultuous times. During this time, 'The Hundred Years War' between England and France (and ally Spain), and a vicious civil war between the Burgundian nobles (the Eastern part of the present country of France, including Rougeux) and the French nobility (the Western part of the present country) managed to keep France so weakened they were unable to mount an effective resistance against the English. The British, acting under the pretext that English kings were the rightful rulers of France through inheritance, annually mounted feebly opposed raids in all parts of the country, inflicting pillage and rapine throughout most of the 116 year war. Payment of large ransoms to free noble captives and looting enriched England at the expense of the French. The victorious Anglo-Saxon savages captured a large part of France and Burgundy. Irishmen known as 'knifers' slit the throats of the wounded and pillaged the dead after a battle. British raiders were in the habit of tying human heads to their saddles and in some cases those of babies were strung like fish on a line. Constant looting, plundering, and scorched earth policies by all three contestants prevented the population from rising above extreme poverty and starvation.

It was during the Hundred Years War that Joan of Arc (1412-1431), born (at Domrémy 55 miles N) in the nearby region of Lorraine, helped the French king defeat the British. The Burgundians, allied by a treaty with their traditional enemies, the British, against the French king, captured her and to their later shame and regret, turned her over to the British. The British were not long in extracting their revenge, and burned her at the stake. British troops were finally expelled

90

Domremy-la-Pucelle
BIRTH PLACE OF JOAN OF ARC – 20 MILES NORTH OF ROUGEUX

from the soil of France in 1429 AD, but the invasions continued into Normandy until 1453.

When the French, at the battle of Poitiers, captured the king of the two Burgundies, Jean-le-Bon, in 1356, the Rougeux region was left at the mercy of brigands who called themselves 'Routiers.' Included in the band were Englishmen, men from Lorraine, men from France and undisciplined soldiers. For ten long years they ruthlessly and impudently strode through villages, burning, pillaging, raping, and destroying the meager crops. One chronicler stated: *"The peasants are like men walking around in a pond with water up to their noses and the smallest depression causes them to drown."*

In 1397 AD tax rolls show 83% of the 'hearths' (households) were classified as miserable and were not subject to taxation in the region of Dijon, forty miles South of Rougeux. During this epoch, quarrels between neighboring villages led to mutual pillage, devastation and fire. Monasteries were frequently the principal victims. In past centuries, Rougeux had suffered various degrees of devastation, but by the end of this conflict, Rougeux had been burned to the ground.   (Acts de Comtes de Champagne)

In 1435, the treaty of Arras freed King Philippe and our region from the English, but when he attempted to return to our region from his captivity, several years of powerful resistance by an army of Jean de Vergy, a powerful local noble, left the region in deeper ruins and crushed the hopes of the poor for freedom to return to a more normal life. Raids followed this period by Villandras and Chabannes, bastards of the Bourbons, the rulers of France. These two were both grand seigneurs in the court of the King of France, but had been banned from the court because of their previous history of rape, killing, and burning. Calling themselves 'Eorcheurs,' (flayers, burners) and even more savage than the 'Routiers' of the previous century, they roamed our region inflicting bereavement and ruin during the years 1437 and 1438. The fields went uncultivated and the air was foul from vast numbers of dead and unburied bodies. The poor inhabitants, upon seeing an approaching band, dropped whatever they were doing and fled into the woods. Jean de Vergy, in 1439, put an end to the brigands by capturing their leaders, placing them in a sack, and throwing them into the Amance River.

After these wars the villages in the region of Rougeux were in total ruins to the extreme. Fayl-Billot, (2 miles South) the village with the most people, was totally destroyed. From 1430 to 1448 the residents were unable to pay even a dozen francs to the duc of Bourgogne, Phillip-le-Bon. He finally dispensed with the tax and forgave the eighteen ecoules ten years, and for the next ten years reduced the tax to six francs.

In 1464, Guy Bernard, seigneur of Hortes (4 miles N), after building a strong house, assumed the right of hunting, war, escheats, property title changes, confiscations, division of property, vantes(?), heritage of bastards, corvees (forced labor) of plowing, of the woods and forests of the valley, thereby more severely controlling the lives of our fathers.

In 1470, the French king, Louis XI, declared war on the Burgundian duke, Charles the Bold, and invaded our region. In April 1471 the duke's army gathered at Jussey (close to Rougeux) and marched to attack the king at Jonville (24 miles NE) The resistance of the French king to this attack, destroyed Jonville, killed the inhabitants, and resulted in complete victory for the French. Supplies for these armies were stolen from surrounding villages, including Rougeux.

In 1465, Count Henry Proudon, treasurer of Foruvent, instituted by letter of the commission donated provisions through Jean Joard, Chief of the counsel and president of the parlement of Bourgogne. This siegneur, allied to the dame Marguerite de La Roche-Guyon, was the recipient of the dowery given to her by the duc of Bourgogne. Gifted by the the product of the vines, she had given the following: one hundred (?) to Roigeul (Rougeux) in an appropriate manner. (Rougeux and surrounding villages had been pillaged and burnt).

Throughout history mankind has been afflicted wirth typhoid fever. Caused by ingestion of human fecal matter on food, in fecal contaminated drinking water, or by a person carrying the live typhoid bacteria in their gallbladder and many times conveyed on the feet of house flies. It claimed millions of lives throughout the centuries (and still prevalent in the water supplies of underdeveloped countries).

Our region was not exempted from this endless scourage as well as other fevers and diseases that periodically swept across the population. sometimes decimating whole families within days. (The cemetary at Frenchville has a number of such tragedies related on existing tombstones).

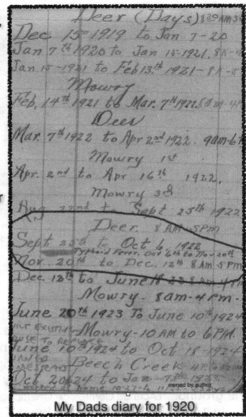
My Dads diary for 1920

A graphic description of typical well contamiantion leading to typhoid.

CHAPTER IX

FROM THE ADVENT OF LOUIS XI UNTIL THE WARS OF RELIGION.
(1461-1562)

Louis XI (1423-1483) who mounted the throne in 1461, promised his daughter Anne, still an infant, to Nicholas, duke of Lorraine, with a dowery of five hundred thousand livres. A part of this amount was to be acquitted by the transfer of Coiffy, Montigny, Nogent, Chaumont, (and very probably Rougeux since these towns were in a region surrounding Rougeux 50 miles in diameter) and others to new seigneurs as part of the reunion of Lorraine and our Bassigny property.

The marriage was not realized (when Nicholas repudiated her) and the dismemberment fortunately did not become reality (since this action would have undoubtably led to conflicts with those of neighboring seigneurs)

The seigneurs continued to make donations to the parishes and to the religious houses to obtain prayers for the repose of their souls. Also, we see that in 1461, Jacques de Doncourt, seigneur of Bize, (4 miles NE) ceded to Thomas, abbot of Beaulieu (2 miles N) many presents.

Construction of the chapels and the churches, monuments of their time and of their piety; Simon de Montreuil, seigneur of Mont and of Anrosey, in part a man of arms of the large ordinance of the king, caused construction of the church in the village of Anrosy. Additionally, he founded, in concert with his wife, demoiselle Platel d'Ogres 1, a chapel especially for their family that an inscription attests that we see again inside that church that ends with these words: Pray to God for them.

Some years afterward, the bishop Guy Bernard, seigneur of Hortes also had rebuilt the church that the village consecrated with a grand solemnity (1455)

We see, by the drastic reduction of the population, the bishop, in 1464, assigned a dignitary at Hortes for the direction of the parish who was a member of the abbeys of Beaulieu, Rosoy, Corgirnon, Torcenay or Chatenay-Vaudin. The bishop had full authority. The location of the defensive house was on property he owned and to make an opportunity (for financial gain) He built, as well, the market place where sales were customarily held at Montsaugeon. He had the rights of the hunt, of war, les eschiefs (meaning unknown) epaves (meaning unknown) confiscations, profits, consignments, inheritance of bastards, mandatory free work days (corvees) of plows, of the forests, etc. He could require mattresses made of chicken feathers at a price of six deniers

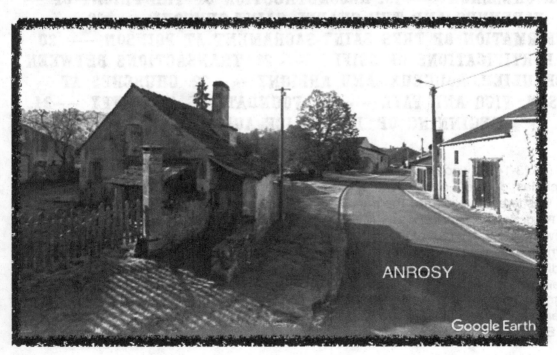

for him without bailli (meaning unknown) or his receveur (meaning unknown) Additionally he had wells, ground, and hundreds of other rights of a seigneur.

The 10 of March 1468, Henri Benoit, provost of Hortes intervened in a difference that had

been raised between the abbey of Beaulieu and the priest of Pierrefaites, Claude Briseon. Briseon claimed the right to the tithe or annuity of twelve sheaves, this amounting to four days work, from a piece of arable land called Champ de la Franchise, close to the barn of Velars near Charmoy and belonging to the convent (probably of Beaulieu) The abbot Thomas of Saint-Marcek, and the prosecutor Dom Pierre Blanchot, supported, to the contrary, the person who had given free census, tithes and other valuables. The parties openly presented at Langres the sworn official tabulations. We named the arbiters, we took information, and we consulted letters from donors. It was decided that the field in question would remain for the benefit of Beaulieu, free and clear of the cure' of Pierrefaites1.

Philippe-le-Bon died in 1467 and left his estate to his son, Charles-le-Temeraire (the-Bold) At Peronne during negotiations with Louis XI, Charles learned of a revolt (instigated by Louis) of the

Liegeois (People of Leige who lived 300 miles N) and that the Burgundian governor had been killed. (Charles was furious. The Duke's advisors had to calm him down for fear that he might hit the King. Louis was forced into a humiliating treaty, giving up many of the lands he had acquired and to witnessing the siege of Liege in which hundreds were massacred. But once out of Charles's reach, Louis declared the treaty invalid and set about building up his forces. His aim was to destroy Burgundy once and for all and end a feud which had lasted over three generations since the murder of Louis, Duke of Orléans in 1407. War broke out in 1472, but Charles's siege of Beauvais and other towns were unsuccessful and he finally sued for peace)

Upon Charles' return it is reported he saw a miraculous vision of Saint Hubert, the patron saint of hunters. St. Hubert (d. 727) was the bishop of Maestricht and of Liege, and buried in the church of the Benedictines of Saint-Pierre and canonized there about ten years later.

1. Historie de Fayl-Billot, ------ La Haute Marne, art. Maizieres --- Archived de Dijon et documents divers.

In 1470 King Louis XI (of France) declared war against the Duke of Bourgogne, Charles-the-Bold (1433-1477) The French were led against the Count by Villare-Saint-Marcellin. Those supporting the Count hastened to join forces to resist the forces of the King who had entered Champagne, incinerated Coublanc (15 miles SW), and terrorized the countryside, including the Abbey of Beaulieu, (and certainly Rougeux) until March 1471. But, in April the Lorraines, the Varrois, the Liegois and others joined at Coiffy (11 miles N) with their captain, Antoine de Livron, and marched with the garrison to a certain place against the Count. The village of Jonvelle (20 miles E) was taken in the assault and placed under fire and blood, Voisey, Villers, Fignevelle, Godoncourt, Ormoy, Corre and Ranszevelle were pillaged, incinerated and their inhabitants slaughtered, taken prisoner or dispersed about the countryside.

It was a disastrous campaign for the Duke (not to mention the hapless villagers of the Amance Valley)! and he was finally killed at the Battle of Nancy on 5 January 1477, ending the Burgundian Wars.

(Abbot Briffaut severely truncated the history of the events surrounding this ambitious and blood thirsty Duke and concentrated his History to events directly effecting the Amance Valley)

Count Charles-le-Temeraire (Charles the Bold 1433 – 1477) was killed 2 January 1477, not leaving any heritage for Marie de Bourgogne. (He was Duke of Burgundy from 1467 to 1477. His early death at the Battle of Nancy at the hands of Swiss mercenaries fighting for René II, Duke of Lorraine, was of great consequence in European history. The Burgundian domains, long wedged between the growing powers of France and the Habsburg Empire, were divided, but the precise disposition of the vast and disparate territorial possessions involved was disputed among the European powers for centuries)

King Louis had destroyed his sworn enemy. Other lords who still favored the feudal system gave in to his authority. Others like Jacques d'Armagnac, Duke of Nome's, were executed.

(French King) Louis XI (1423-1483) took complete possession of the duchy and searched for the heirs and seigneurs subject to the Count. He sent troops under surrender orders to the seigneur of Craon and of Charles d'Amboise, sire of Chaumont-sur-Lorie. They attacked Vesoul (36 miles SE) in 1479. The inhabitants opposed with heroic resistance, but a breach was made and were able to enter the city, and after massacring a great number of persons burnt everything to the ground.

The war done because of lack of defenders, Louis XI took title of the Count of Bourgogne and engaged (1483) the Dauphin (his son and heir Charles VIII (1470-1498) and only surviving child of Louis XI by his second wife)) to young Marguerite, (arranged when he was 13 and she 5 years old as part of the peace treaty of Arras) daughter pruned (taken) from the Archduke Maximillen and Marie de Bourgogne (of Austria)

But Charles VIII thought he (now 21) could find a richer wife and married the reluctant (14 year old) Anne of Brittany, who, unhappy with the forced marriage arrived at the wedding with her attendants carrying two beds! There still remained, however, the matter of Charles's first intended, young Marguerite. Although the cancellation of her betrothal meant that she by rights should have been returned to her family, Charles did not initially do so, intending to marry her usefully elsewhere in France. It was an abominable situation for Margurite, who informed her father in her letters that she was so determined to escape her situation that she would even flee Paris in her nightgown if it gave her freedom. Eventually, in 1493, 10 years later, she was returned to her family, together with her dowry.

Maximillen, (of Austria) angry at this treatment of his daughter, who would have inherited the property of the count of Bourgogne (by the proposed marriage), enlisted the help of his eldest son, Philippe-le-Beau and endeavored to attack the garrisons of the French (1491) Maximillen, after three years of fruitless war, finally abandoned his pretensions to Bourgogne and signed the treaty of Senlis 22 March 1494 with the King (Charles VIII (1470-1498), forever ending the separation of France and Bourgogne (36 miles NE of Rougeux) The marchal Guillaume de Vergy, seigneur of Champlitte, was nominated governor of that province. In 1498 it was at Villersexel with Maximillen as emperor, that gunfire and the clash of arms resounded. Without wasting any time, Guillaume set out, his route passing through Bassigny, and seized Bourbonne (17 miles N), Coiffy (10 miles N, Aigremont, and Montsaugeon. But the French returned to these places to take revenge by burning.

The chateau of Coiffy situated on the frontier of Bassigny, had its premises always exposed and took the first blows of the enemy.

(King) Louis XI, in letters from Blois (a city and the capital of Loir-et-Cher department in central France), 31 March 1499, charged Jean de Dominarien, Seigneur of Pailly (127 miles E), to fortify them (Bassigny, Bourbonne, Coiffy) comparable to those of Montigny and Nogent. Under the orders and the intended direction, important work was commenced and continued during many years.

In 1510 Francois I pressed for completion because of the fight with Charles-Quint, brother of Philippe-le-Beau, future count of Bourgogne, (1530), king of Spain (1556) and emperor of Germany (1559) Antoine de Livron had from Marguerite de Noailles, two sons: Jacques, abbot of Morimoud, d.1491, and Bernard, Squire of the Stable of the King and Captain of Coiffy. He married, 18 August 1477, Francoise de Vauffremont, who brought him the dowery of the seigneurs of Bourbonne, Parnot, Chezeaux, Torcenay, etc. (nearby villages of Rougeux) Their contract of marriage passed in front of Thevenin de Rangecourt, Squire, and guard the of the seal of provost of Perron and Neuilly and notary of Coiffy (11 miles N)

1.Une ferme sur le territorie d'Anrosey porte le nom de Platel.
2. Archives de la Haute-marne.

Under the regime of Louis XII (1462-1515) the peste (black death) and famine dispersed in Bassigny (the name of the immediate region around Rougeux) as a result of prolonged drought, lasted a number of years. When the ground is not refreshed with rain then fruits are not produced; mice and divers insects ravished what did grow. We said prayers, the young processed, with many prayers, through the villages. In 1514 the dearth of rain ceased, and oats was sold as normal, six sols the bushel. During this epoch the Bishop of Langres, Michel Boudet, permitted the usage of butter, milk and cream during Lent due to the shortage of oil 1. (Imagine that kind of fasting today!)

Letters patent of the King, given at Paris 2 September 1503, to Pierre de Bosredon, commander of Romagne, d'Arvigny, etc., granted safeguards in favor of the householders, possessions, usages, and franchises. His successor, Francois de Franel, ceded, in return for twenty-five sous annually to brother Pierre Javernault, religious of Malta, priest of Arbigny, a proper place for construction of a mill and other pieces of ground (1516) M. Guy de Dree is also seigneur and many disputes about many of their decisions was common. One of 15 December 1516 permitted M. De Franel to put up a gibbet with only two drops (capable of only executing two victims at once) at a place called Champ des Fourches. (Unable to locate this remote road)

Another, in 1518, determined the portion of the parish over which each seigneur had jurisdiction. We also find, on 15 April 1518 a transaction between M. de Dree and his subjects. Each inhabitant, he stated, will have the right to feed his large and small beasts in all the woods from Saint-Michel all the way to Saint-Andre in payment of two sous six deniers the day in the coin of Saint-Remi. For the pigs that are taken out of season, there will be a fine for him if it escapes; this is fixed by the custom of Chaumont if it is garde faite (unknown meaning) All can search for (standing) dead wood and for dead wood on the forest floor and even the clearings and those in cultivation, for a rent of grain of twenty gerbe or of 17 pints of wine, one or the other. No one is allowed to fish in the river, ordered the seigneur, under pain of fine. The seigneur retains the Registry for the profit of the village. This allows, that henceforth, it will be possible (for him) to construct on ground outside the village any house or barn without the consent of the inhabitants. It is specified that all this does not nullify or prejudice or is derogatory to the rights of the commander.

A Maizieres the principal seigneur was always the prior of Saint-Vivant, and he had a type of fief in which the possessor took the title of Grand-Marie. This manorial contained the right to name the judge, the sergeants and dismiss them at will and assessed some ground and royalties with certain amounts of grain and silver coins, the amount being mercenary. Jena Baudesson, Squire, has for quite a long time permitted it to remain as a heritage of Jean Lelievre, Nobel and Squire of the king who sold it in 1519 to Simon Gousset, merchant at Langres. The following year he sold it to Mongin Petitjean. M. De Saint-Vivant then bought it for the sum of three cents livres and rejoined it to his domain (1522) 1.

In 1524, war was declared between Francois I, (1494-1547) (King of France) and Charles-Quint(1500-1558) (Archduke of Austria), in collaboration with Charles de Bourbon(1490-1527), (Constable of France), (Due to a dispute with King Francois I, who mistrusted the Constable, he turned traitor and joined the Archduke of Austria against France, his country. He was killed attacking Rome) who revolted against his country and tried to bring the hostilities into Champagne, and in concert with the Archduke of Austria and the Count of Frustemburg, arrived in front of Coiffy with twelve thousand Austrians and Spanish troops. The governor of the chateau saw that he could not defend the chateau against such enormous numbers, surrendered at the first demand. From there, the fanatical Germans descended upon Monteclair, who made no resistance, then headed for Montigny. Upon receiving such news, the King gave an order to Claude de Lorraine, Count of Guise, which is in Bourgogne, to provide for the defense of the country. Even though his forces were well inferior in numbers, he began a rapid offensive. Within the space of six weeks he forced the enemy to abandon the two places he had captured and cut to pieces his rear guard in the passage to the Muese.

The same year, the two brothers, Felix and Guillaume de Wirtemberg (Germans) burned Coiffy and numerous other villages and ravaged Bassigny. Among the victims of that German invasion we cite in particular the priory of Varennes, which was totally devastated. It already had been pillaged by the seigneur of Choiseul, by the knight Livron de Bourbon, and by his master. Once again it was the Count de Guise who saved our unhappy country where the heavy frosts have caused a famine.

On 6 January 1523, the prior was informed that the abbot of Moleme was authorized to make an investigation of this event. The affair was reported to Rome. In 1529, Guy, priest, and doctor, with civil as well as cannon rights, archdeacon and official of Langres, formulated a letter to (Pope) Clement VII against those who have committed these excesses and of the pillages.

A pontifical censure (by Pope Clement VII) (the primary and proximate end of censures is to overcome contumacy or willful stubbornness in order to bring back the guilty person to a better sense of his priority by depriving him of the benefits of the Church, among others; the secondary and remote end is to furnish an example of punishment in order that other evil-doers may be deterred) was issued against Nicholas I de Livron, seigneur of many houses, baron of Bourbonne, knight of the order of the King, captain of fifty men at arms of the order of His Majesty, and governor of Coiffy and Montigny. During a full census of 15 January 1538, Nicolas de Livron also declared Chezeaux (7 miles N) in full fief (to the King) and made homage to the King because his chateau was the important one at Coiffy (11 miles N)

Near 1540 we reconstructed the monastic buildings and on the foundation of Saint-Genogoul, a little chapel dedicated to that martyr. (Saint Gangulphus of Burgundy-died May 11, 760 AD. Full story in Chapter III p26. Venerated as a martyr by the Catholic Church.)

In that same year, 1540, we instituted in the church Saint-Martin de Poison-les-Fayl (5 miles South) a brotherhood of Tres-Saint-Sacrement. Renault Auger, cleric of the diocese of Langres, obtained, on 16 October, for the members of that association, the privileges and indulgences accorded by Pope Paul III, the same as the Dominican Fathers had received at Rome in the church of Minerve.

At his elevation to the throne (French King) Henri II (1519-1559) (died from injuries in a jousting tournament when splinters from the shattered lance of his opponent punctured his eyes) sent Admiral d'Annebault, who visited Coiffy and ordered a large stronghold be added to the chateau (1547) In 1554 we added more fortifications until it became the bastion of the North. Francois de Champluisant was captain of that place and commissary of fortifications at a cost of forty livres each month.

By the terms of the concordat of 1517 between the Saint-Siege and of France the superiors of the abbeys and the priors were nominated by the king and confirmed by the Pope. We recall the commendatory (men appointed by others and not approved by the Pope) abbots and priests.

In 1552 Francois de Hodicq was a very commendatory abbot of Beaulieu. He made, 6 July 1552, a transaction with the inhabitants of Rougeux and Guy Leboeuf, knight of the Order de Saint-Jean-de-Jerusalem, commander of the Romagne, of Broncourt and Arbigny. He settled a dispute that had arisen with respect to the tithes. Here is the covenant that was made between Nicolas Lergros, notary public sworn to the King at the manor of Coiffy:

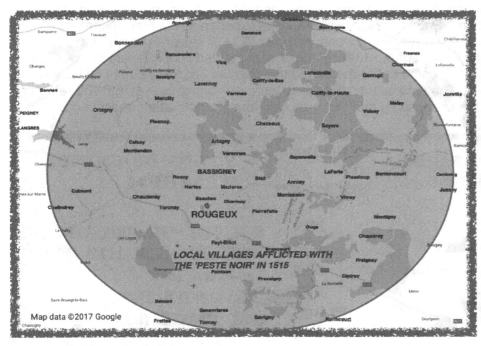

LOCAL VILLAGES AFFLICTED WITH THE 'PESTE NOIR' IN 1515

Map data ©2017 Google

"The inhabitants of Rougeux and the itinerant who plow on the territory pay the tithe or seven sheaves, one or the other. For the country of Faulley and the their new territories recently cultivated, they will only pay but ten sheaves (grebes) a year. (About 2 1/2 days of work) They will be required to bring to the village that tithe and give the commander one-third and the abbot the other two parts. Those who deliver and unload their sheaves before they notified and were inspected by the inspector of tithes will be fined sixteen sols that will be paid to the seigneur. (Apparently the peasants had learned that if they could unload their wagons before inspection they could claim a sheaf or two more than actually delivered) As to the small tithes, the religious of Beaulieu will continue to enjoy the same as that of the past."

"The inhabitants are permitted to lead their large and small beasts to empty pastures around the edges of Beaulieu the same as they have always done. They can also conduct, in times of empty pastures, in the prairie of Beaulieu, from the place where the mill called Boulaye stands on the side of the river all the way to the territory of Maizieres, and except for the time of grain harvest, can lead their beasts to the forests of the abbey. For these concessions, the inhabitants each must make a corvee of the drudgery of harvesting with the sickle for the poor venerable of the abbey of Beaulieu for their nourishment during this time. Those who do not want to do the corvee must pay twelve deniers tourneys 1."

1. Registre de paroisse de Maizieres.

During the middle of the XVI century we constructed in the parish of Pierrefaites: a church at Poinson (1544); with a single aisle and transept: one at Vicq with three aisles and massive pillars and a choir similar to the one at Fayl-Billot, which with a multitude of ribs represents well the style of this epoch. This last construction was executed by Jean Noirot, mason of Neuvelle-les-Voisey (1555)

Jean Thierry, priest, and choir leader of Langres, by his testimony, near the year 1560, by a good estimate, paid twenty-two ecus and six to Maizieres, to have celebrated, on Friday of each week, a low mass in the church of Coiffy-le-Chateau and to be buried in the tomb with his ancestors. Nicolas Thierry des Verrieres, cannon of Langres, his nephew, executed the disposition of the will in 1587. They both were probably born at Coiffy.

1. Archived de la Haute_Marne--Historie de Fayl-Billot--Beaulieu et La Haute-Marne

----

SUPPLEMENTS FROM ABBOT MULSON AND OTHERS

The 15th century was marked with periodic returns of the plagues, famines, and various wars with France, Holland, Prussia, and Austria. Europe experienced its first influenza epidemic in 1510. Typhus, a disease not mentioned before 1477 swept France but it was the rapid expansion toward the end of the 15th century that presented a severe test of medicine of the time. Whether syphilis existed in Europe before the discovery of America in 1492 is still a matter of doubt but in 1463 a prostitute testified in a court at Dijon (40 miles S) that she refused an undesirable customer because he had the 'gros mal', but it is not further described in the

YEARS OF PLAGUES AND EPIDEMICS	YEARS OF FAMINE	YEARS OF UNUSUAL WEATHER
1500 & 1501	1513,	1504,–1505,–1512,–1513,–1516,–1517
1522, 1523, 1529, 1530	1521	–1518,–1523,–15,15,–1526.–1527.–15
1557 (6 MONTHS OF GRIPPE)	1565,	34,–1535,– 1838
1562, 1563, 1564	1567,	1540 UNTIL 1575
1578, 1580, 1587, 1596, 1597,	1582,	1580, UNTIL 1600
1600	1589,	– DEEP COLD-LATE FROST/SNOW- FLOODING–RIVER FROZEN SOLID– EARLY FREEZE-EXCESSIVE RAIN

OWNED BY AUTHOR

record. On March 25, 1494, the town crier of Paris was instructed to order all persons suffering from 'la gros verole' to immediately forsake the city but we do not know what this great pox was; it may have been syphilis.

Soon after the French invasion 1495, the Italians accused the French of bringing into Italy an outbreak of 'French Disease,' which rapidly spread among the population. When the victorious soldiers returned to France in 1495 they scattered it among the people and after 1500 it was described as 'morblis gallicus' and came to be know throughout the continent as syphilis. Treatment consisted of an application of an ointment of mercury and continued as the only remedy until the first half of the 20th century.

Under the rule of Louis XII, 1462-1515, the 'peste' (Black Death) and a severe drought lasting several years, caused famine to return across our region. The soil was not refreshed with rain and could not produce fruits either from the ground or trees. The lack of rainfall produced hoards of various insects which ravaged the leaves. Prayers, processions, and masses were said, begging for relief. Finally in 1514, the famine ended, lush fields of wheat once again grew as in the past and once again wheat sold for six sols the basket, however, in 1515 the 'Little Ice Age' struck Europe. After the Medieval Warming Period, when climate was ideal for raising grains in Europe, temperatures started to fall, and with them the fortunes of many in Europe. Crops failed and many starved and froze to death. Temperatures remained low until the mid 1800's.

During this epoch, the eveque (bishop) of Langres, Michel Boudet, permitted the peasants to use butter and whole milk because of the rarity of oils (probably lard) (An inadvertent revelation of the amount of minute control the Church and Seigneurs had over the vast proportion of the population)

In 1524, a revolt by Charles de Bourbon against the king, again brought the war into our region. (Charles de Bourbon (2 June 1489 – 25 March 1537) was a French prince du sang)(of blood) and military commander at the court of Francis I of France. He is notable as the paternal grandfather of King Henry IV of France)

The Count de Furstemberg, with 12,000 German soldiers came against Coiffy, (11 miles NE) After just six weeks he was repulsed, but in revenge burned Coiffy and many villages (including Rougeux) in the region. Theft of seed stocks accompanied by an especially cold and long winter created a famine (la disette) lasting several years. A letter from Pope Clement in 1529 condemned these actions and threatened the Count with excommunication unless reparations were made. (There is no record that the count obeyed)

On July 6, 1532, Francois de Hodicq, abbot of Beaulieu, made an agreement with the inhabitants of Rougeux and Guy le Boeuf, commander of Romagne, Broncourt and Arbigny, (translated to the best of my ability) as follows:

"The inhabitants of Rougeux and the foreigners who toil on the ground pay tithes of seven sheaves (of grain) to one (14%) On the contrary the Faulley, and the other new territories, recently cultivated, it is said, pay ten sheaves the year. They haul their other sheaves to the village and to Beaulieu. Those who declare their tithes before seeing the register of the tithes (To probably cheat on the amount) will be punished by a fine of fifty sous to be paid to the seigneur."

"The inhabitants are permitted to graze their large and small beasts on the property of Beaulieu as they have been doing. They can, in the times of pasture, use the prairie of Beaulieu from the right of the mill, named Boulaye, to the river all the way to the edge of the Maizieres except for the time of the grain. Also they cannot let their pigs and horses into the woods of the abbey, but they may let their large beasts into the woods. For this the inhabitants will each do a corvee (labor) with the sickle at harvest time for the venerables of Beaulieu in order to feed them, and we will pay you for this corvee twelve deniers tournois."

A massacre at Wassy (72 miles N) in 1562 was the inauguration of a civil war between Calvinists and Catholics. (The 1549 Consensus Tigurinus brought together those who followed Zwingli and Bullinger's memorialist theology of the Lord's supper, which taught that the supper simply serves as a reminder of Christ's death, and Calvin's view that the supper serves as a means of grace with Christ actually present, though spiritually rather than bodily. The doctrine of justification by faith alone was a direct inheritance from Luther.[Due to Calvin's missionary work in France, his program of reform eventually reached the French-speaking provinces of the Netherlands) This event did not immediately effect the Valley of the Amance or Rougeux, but it served as a conduit for other events (deep into following centuries) that would.

In 1562 the Calvinists preached a sermon at Pressigny, (five miles SE), to recruit partisans to their cult. The battle of Saint Denis on the 25th of October 1567, led to the introduction of 14,000 armed German Huguenot (Calvinists) foot soldiers (Led by the future King of France, Henry IV who led the first charge of the Huguenot cavalry during the long campaign through the ravaged provinces, extending from Poitou in the heart of Burgundy to the region of Rougeux) Their retreat resulted in much pillaging and destruction in our area and the Abbey of Beaulieu was pillaged. The (religious) civil war recommenced in 1569 with battles between Langres (Catholic) and Chamont (both about 15 miles W) being won and lost through the years 1583, 1586, 1589, and 1591.

In 1577, the French king, (Calvinist) Henry III, again seized our region and forbade peasants to eat any meat, even from their own chickens. Continued oppression of the peasants caused a number of uprisings; the unsuccessful rebels soon marched to the gibbets on the 'hanging road' near Broncourt. The disturbance of 1586 led to loss of seed stocks and a great famine once again combined with 'la peste.' This blight on the valley of our ancestors lasted many years.

On the 17 of January 1593 (Calvinist) King Henry IV's declaration of war on (Catholic) Phillipe II King of Spain again prompted war to sweep over our region. Many villages were destroyed but the most drastic devastation was inflicted upon Maizieres, (2 miles NE), in which the inhabitants were killed and the village leveled by those allied with Spain. (After long hesitation, Henry undertook a final conversion back to Roman Catholicism in July 1593)

This turmoil among a people stirred up by the claims of various cults created an atmosphere of intense fear and bewilderment. People, mostly women, began to have assemblies where they tried to communicate with Satan and slaughtered animals during their worship of him. In 1610 two women in Hortes, (4 miles N) were accused and one, Anne Carteret, was condemned to be burned at the stake.

No comments about this infection at Rougeux were found, however there were undoubtably less aggressive residents who shared these same fears across Europe.

CHAPTER X
THE START OF THE WARS OF RELIGION AND THE PEACE OF VERVINS
(1562-1598)

1. THE BARONS OF FERTE ----- 2. THE PROTESTANTISM AT PRESSIGNY ----- 3. PASSAGE OF REITRES ------ 4. INVASION OF WOLFGANG ------- 5. MAKING OF THE CHATEAU OF CHOISEUL ----- 6. REPEATED PASSAGE OF REITRES ----- 7. LA PESTE ----- 8. LETTER OF THE MAYOR OF LANGRES TO THE CAPTAIN OF COIFFY ----- 9. THE SEIGNEUR OF GUYONVELLE BAILIF OF CHAUMONT ----- 10. LETTER OF HENRI DE NAVARRE TO ROUSSAT ----- 11. COIFFY TAKEN BY THE LUTHERANS ----- 12. PILLAGE OF CHAUVIREY----- 13. CONDUCT OF PHILIPPE DE GUYONVELLE ----- 14. MAIZIERES RUINED ----- 15. HUBART JACOB

The Seigneurie of La Ferte (8 miles E) who had owned successively houses in Joinville, Neuchatel and Ray, passed his property, at the beginning of the XVI century, to the family of de Choiseul by the marriage of Anne de Ray with Antoine de Choiseul. Antoine, son of Philibert, who was seigneur of Langres (16 miles W), and Louise de Juilly. He was a baron of La Ferte, seigneur of Pressigny and Pierrefaites, and seigneur in part of Autreville, Daillecourt, Vercourt, etc. He died 21 December 1549. His sons divided their heritage, Jean, the oldest, received Langres. Edme became Baron of La Ferte and Francis became seigneur of Pressigny, Pierrefaites, Chamarandes, Rougeux, etc.

Edme, captain of one hundred light horse arquebusiers, was wounded in an encounter in front of Thionville, breathed his last at Meiz, 13 January 1558, and was buried in the cathedral at this village close to the choir. He bequeathed La Ferte to his brother Jean, knight, gentlemen ordinary to the Chamber of the king. He was also lieutenant of fifty lances of ordinances to His Majesty.

When Jean was commandant of the arquebusiers during the defense of Meiz against Charles-Quint, he distinguished himself by his courage and killed, with his epée, a German captain who had dismounted to fight.

On 1 February 1562 he assisted at the mass of Saint-Spirit in the Cathedral of Langres. As a result he was one of a dozen deputies that the nobility called to supervise the election of Jacques d'Helvis, nominated by the King as bishop of Langres. His death arrived in 1564.

Francois de Choiseul and his spouse did cowardly abandon the Catholic religion to embrace the Protestant (Lutheran) religion. They, at the same time, were very active in spreading propaganda in favor of their cultic reforms they introduced into their chateau. During the year 1567 there were secret meetings held at Chamarandes. On 28 April 1568, the Calvinists preached at Pressigny and tried to recruit some partisans from the restless and curious, however the vast majority remained faithful to their faith of old.

CHATEAU AT LA FEITE-SUR-AMANCE

The massacre of Wassy (70 miles N) was the signal of the beginning a civil war between the Catholics and Protestants. (On 1 March 1562, a faction of armed soldiers under Francis, Duke of Guise attacked and killed worshippers at a Huguenot service, called the Massacre of Wassy, which marked the start of the First War of Religion in France)

Fortunately, our country suffered very little direct involvement (in that engagement) But after the battle of Saint-Denis (25 October 1567) (near Paris) proved a defeat for the Calvinists, Jean Casimir, son of the elector Palatin, went to Germany to gather forces to relieve them. His army was composed of thirteen to fourteen thousand men, according to the history, under the name Reitires.

It was said he had horsemen and also Lansquenets (refers to 15th- and 16th-century mercenary German foot soldiers; the lansquenet drum is a type of field drum used by these soldiers) and infantry. After rejoining the French heretics in Lorraine, the German cavalry surrounded the garrisons of Joinville (60 miles N) and Chaumont (35 miles W), captured Chateauvillain, and sacked Auberive (25 miles W)

A peace treaty was signed at Longjumeau, 2 March 1568, and the band of Germans retreated to the Rhine, passing for many days through the valley of the Amance, and burning Plesnoy, Andilly, Celles, Hortes, Rougeux, pillaged the abbey of Beaulieu, etc. (This may be the incident that resulted in Rougeux being rebuilt on the upper reaches of the hill above the valley floor of its previous location because of excessive wetness of the soil at its location. The church was not relocated to its present place for more than a century later)

The war recommenced in 1569. In the month of March the Lutherans of Germany, in combination with the Huguenots of France, under the command of Wolfang, Duke of Bavaria and the Deux-Ponts, (A German-French infantry regiment) with Guillaume, Prince of Orange-Nassau and the Count Ludovic, his brother, entered the region of the Count of Bourgogne through Montbeliard and Lure. Their invasion was rapid and furious. They pillaged and burned all the villages that bordered the Lanterne and the Soane, destroyed Bourguignon-les-Morey and devastated a part of our parish. The place of Chauviery was unsuccessfully attacked by the fanatic troops; the peasants of the neighborhood found an inviolable and precious refuge for their persons and goods and escaped with their lives. (no explanation of what this refuge could have been. Churches were not sacred to the attackers)

After the fEast of Saint-Barthelemy (24 August 1572) the Protestants furiously arose once again. By the end of April 1573 bands of armed men, joined the Germans and returned into the Ardennes and Champagne with the approval of Emperor du Perthois. Having failed to succeed they arrived at Choiseul, and instead of preaching they seized the chateau and its fortifications. This coup of arms sounded an alarm throughout the territory. But Charles de Guise, cardinal of Lorraine watched their movements and sent an army which prompted Langres to furnish soldiers, artillery and rations. Soon that place was invested and taken (May 1573) We think the rebels obeyed the orders of their king and destroyed the chateau, except for the chapel.

Jean Lebon, of Autreville tells the facts in his booklet, 'The Tumult of Bassigny,' (Referring to our region) that says that at Saint-Gengoul, whose relics were guarded and honored at Choiseul (24 miles N) by faithful Catholics, were stolen by the rebels and polluted by the manure of those men. (Deep hatred of the Catholic Church by the Lutherans)

Near the end of 1575, Casimir, who was searching in Germany for reinforcements for his Protestant army, penetrated a second time in France through Lorraine. He retired after having foraged through Bassigny, (our region) passing in view of Langres. To besiege Dijon, 10 May 1576, (French King) Henri III made peace with the Huguenots and German auxiliaries who were with him, and bought their departure by payment of three million six hundred thousand francs (and gave the Huguenots many liberties to practice their religion. This treaty was called the Edict of Beaulieu les Loches and repudiated by the States General in December 1576. It was replaced by a much less generous treaty in 1577)

During the month of July these foreigners retired to the environs of Langres until payment was fully completed. They lived at their discretion in our unhappy land like conquerors, pillaging, burning villages in their entirety, and we could do nothing. Casmir had Marcilly burned because all he could find was a rooster.

During this terrible time we not only just suffer from the wars but from another outbreak of the 'peste' (The Black Death plagued Europe for many centuries. During this century alone there were 20 outbreaks in France-an average of once every five years. Between and overlapping these were 7 famines, each lasting several years (famine describes starvation, malnutrition) resulting from wars and severe fluctuations in temperature both in summer and winter that either froze or burned the crops) The sterility of 1586 brought a dreadful contagion and widespread famine. This scourge lasted several years. (In 1589-1590, 45,000 deaths occurred from famine in Paris alone)

Sentiments of deep faith and patriotism gave birth to the League of Faith. (Much political maneuvering, murders, and religious wars surround this organization however for all its political and internecine wrangling, the League was still very much a Holy Union. Its religious role was significant, as the League was the conduit between the Tridentine spirituality of the Catholic Reformation and the seventeenth century devots. Often overlooked is the emphasis the League placed on the internal and spiritual renewal of the earthly city. Duke Henri de Guisc was the soul of this organization. A powerful opponent of the Queen Mother, Catherine de' Medici, he was assassinated by the bodyguards of her son, King Henry III in his presence. By this murder Henry turned the League against the Royalty and thereafter the League fought a civil war against the Royalty as well as the Protestants) Six days later the mayor and aldermen of Langres wrote (obviously fearful of possible consequences) to the magistrates of Chaumont to notify them of the situation that caused the death of the Duke but it did not effect their obedience to King Henry III. They wrote the same to the captain and commandant of the chateau of Coiffy to guard their village against any surprises.

Langres and Coiffy remained royalists; Chaumont embraced the League in opposition to King Henri III (thus assuring the civil war would continue even more bitterly between these close neighbors)

In February 1589 we nominated as bailiff of this village (Langres) Philippe d'Anglure, knight, seigneur of Guyonvelle, Voncourt and Rosoy.

Despite the protestations presented by King Henry III and the counsels of friends and the remonstrates of Roussat, Philippe accepted the office of leader offered him by the League (and an opponent to King Henry (Royalists and Protestantism) He became an ardent Leaguer who marched at the head of armed men against the Royalists. On a quick battle, close to Valentigny, he took as prisoner the Baron de Lanques. He besieged Chateauvillain, defended Nogent, signed passports in the name of the League, chased from Chaumont suspected Royalists and confiscated their property. (Later, in 1591, as captain of cavalry for the Duke de Mayenne, surprised the old Marquis de Brion in his mansion of Mirebeau. Under pretext that the son of the Marquis was in the service of Henry III, and had killed eight of his men, Philippe demanded from him twenty-five thousand ecus, one hundred fifty horses, precious furniture, provisions for his army and placed the Marquis himself in prison)

Hearing this news, (1789) Henri de Navarre, came to unite with Henry III (still a Protestant) against Philippe and the League. Having been appraised that Langres had encouraged and secured the garrison of Coiffy, wrote to the mayor of Langres (who, with Coiffy, had remained united witht the King and Protestantism), Jean Roussat, the following letter, dated Beaugency, 16 June 1589: *"I find good order in what you have done to make provisions for the lives of men of war who are in the chateau of Coiffy."* (On 1 August 1589, King Henry III had lodged, with his army, at Saint-Cloud, Hauts-de-Seine, and prepared to attack the Catholics of Paris, when a young fanatical Dominican friar, Jacques Clément, carrying false papers, was granted access to deliver important documents to the him. The monk gave the King a bundle of papers and stated that he had a secret message to deliver. The King signaled for his attendants to step back for privacy, and Clément whispered in his ear while plunging a knife into his abdomen. Clément was killed on the spot by the guards.

At first the King's wound did not appear fatal, but he enjoined all the officers around him, in the event that he did not survive, to be loyal to Henry of Navarre as their new King. The following morning—the day that he was to have launched his assault to retake Paris—Henry died. Chaos swept the attacking army, most of it quickly melting away and the proposed attack on Paris was postponed. Inside the city, joy at the news of Henry's death was near delirium; some hailed the assassination as an act of God)

On the 5th a messenger approached Langres with the news and cried: *"Viva Henri IV!"* (Announcing the assumption of the throne of France by Henri de Navarre)

Charles III, Duke of Lorraine, who had entered the (Catholic) League, entered into relations with the Chaumontais and in concert with the Sire of Guyonvelle (8 mles NE), he tried to surprise Langres (15 miles W)(Protestant Royalists), 20 August 1591. The attempt failed. Then the Sire of Guyonvelle went to Montigny, and was repulsed but only after having set fire to the village. For his part, the Duke of Lorraine marched upon Coiffy to seize it, but they observed him and established their defense and he decided not to attack and took the road of La Mothe. His son, the Marquis de Pont-a-Mousson, returned close in front of Coiffy with some considerable forces. One of the principal officers of his army, Colonel de Salin established a siege of the village and after a number of months he mastered them. During an attack through the breach in the wall he was killed. The governor of the chateau, Erard de Livron, Baron de Bourbonne, found himself in a very delicate position because he was a Chamberlin for the Duke of Lorraine, who 1 was attacking him. He capitulated 1 April 1593 and was permitted to keep his chateau. The Baron de Livron was the last to submit and he retired to the chateau and permitted liberal passage to all the bands of pillagers.

On 17 January 1593, Henri IV declared war on Philippe II, King of Spain, who supported the Catholic League against him. He had discovered that they were planning the invasion of France-Compte (Our region) (In July 1593 he reconverted to Catholicism at the request of his new bride) The king permitted them to take from Chalons and Langres the necessary cannons and other necessities. They then threw themselves with thousands of men against the Count of Bourgogne. The two Chuavirey (9 miles SW) villages suffered horrible pillages. Fauquier surrendered his attachment to his chateau at the instigation of Philippe d'Anglure, sire of Guyonvelle. (This is a contracted history of these convoluted times and requires a careful reader to follow the events!)

This famous (Catholic) Leaguer, (Fauquier) was then a partisan of King Henri IV. But soon he quitted the service of that prince for that of Philipp II, King of Spain. (From 1590 to 1598, Philip was also at war against France, joining with the Papacy and the Catholic League during the French Wars of Religion. Philip's interventions in the fighting – sending Alessandro Farnese to end Henry's siege of Paris in 1590 – and the siege of Rouen in 1592—thus saving the French Catholic Leagues's cause against a Protestant French monarchy. In 1593, Henry agreed to convert to Catholicism; weary of war, most French Catholics switched to his side against the hardline core of the Catholic League, who were portrayed by Henry's propagandists as puppets of a foreign monarch, Philip. In June 1595 the redoubtable French King Henry defeated the Spanish-supported Catholic League in Fontaine-Française in Burgundy and reconquered Amiens from the overstretched Spanish forces in September 1597)

Fauquier, the Catholic Leager, who had obtained for himself the title of Governer of Jonvelle, pleaded the cause for his half-brother, Philipp (d'Anglure), both of the same mother, and through intrigues, Philipp was named commandant of Jussey (19 miles E)

Mieux resigned because of charges of conspiracy, and the archduke withdrew his commission the following year. Then Philipp (d'Anglure) took refuge first at Beaulieu, but soon he bought, close to Vesoul, the chateau of Vairve which was inferior until he could have it repaired. (Since he was on the losing side of the war, he had reason to fear fatal recriminations) He established himself near the Count because he wanted to escape the just anger of the young Marquis de Brion who was burning for vengeance for the robbery and imprisonment Philipp had done to his father, Marquis Brion, five years earlier.

A restless man, already advanced in age, quarrelsome and audacious, without a penny nor stitch to support his place as grand seigneur, and always ready to sell to the highest bidder, Philipp (d'Anglure) was badly seen by all the people. At the end of 1596, he negotiated a new reconciliation with Henri IV, through the intermediation of the advocate, Le Gros, promised to reveal the names of five hundred gentlemen who were still devotees of the King of Spain (and

In 1589 the Captain of Coiffy assumed responsibility and worked for two years as seigneur. The greater part of the remaining inhabitants who had not paid their tailles, subsidies or taxes were imprisoned in the chateau of Coiffy after an order came from Chaumont. To rebuild, he borrowed seventy-three ecus. He found it impossible to repay to the profit of Jacques Monginot de Coiffy, to whom they had guaranteed, but with some other minor amounts, sixty-five pieces of ground, with the trees and bushes situated close to the woods of the King (he cleared the debt) The purchaser paid the tithe and taxes. The verbal process and the final process was done 16 September and approved by the priest of Saint-Vivant 1 October 1592.

Claude de Vergy died in 1560. His son Antoine II, killed in the war of 1593, and his successor came and reclaimed the goods and rights of lordship of Vergy and Pierrefaites (and Rougeux) This claimant, William, married to Catherine de Vergey, had some long disputes with the inhabitants of Pierrefaites and Rougeux, his subjects under his marriage contract. He brought an action against them demanding a payment of a tax of 18, of 22, and 25 pounds which he claimed had been levied on them and as subjects were due as rent and tax on millet, hemp and 'other secretly grown things'. He apparently succeeded in his demands.

Before the battle of Fontaine-Francaise (5 June 1595), the Constable of Castille and the Duke of Mayenne defeated a detachment composed of Albanians, Italians and Spanish who had become masters of the chateau of Fouvent, and ravaged our country. They attacked Maizieres and burned a great part of the village. On 18 September 1596, we made at the bailiwick of Langres an investigation of this devastation committed by these men of war. The country between France and Spain, according to the treaty of Vervins, should be restored (2 May 1598) During this time there lived Hubert Jacob, born at Anrosey (6 miles NE), who became a master surgeon celebrated for his knowledge of medicine. He composed a work entitled, matter. We found the interesting details related to the therapeutic properties of these thermal waters and the enumeration of the various illnesses healed at these springs.

'Discussion of the admirable virtues of the hot water of Burbonne-les-Bains, en Basing', which was printed in Lyon in 1570, is the most ancient and the first written book on this subject. ------------------

SUPPLEMENTS FROM ABBOT MULSON AND OTHERS

————————

The French Wars of Religion, or Huguenot Wars of the 16th century, are names for a period of civil infighting, military operations and religious war primarily fought between Roman

Catholics and Huguenots (Reformed Protestants) in the Kingdom of France. It involved several pre-modern day principalities around the borders of today's France, like the Kingdom of Navarre and parts of Burgundy, and occasionally spilled beyond the French region.

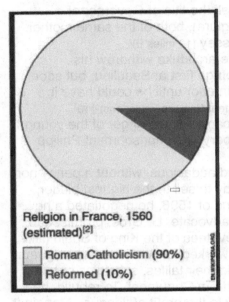

Religion in France, 1560 (estimated)[2]

- Roman Catholicism (90%)
- Reformed (10%)

Approximately 3,000,000 people perished as a result of violence, famine and disease in what is accounted as the second deadliest European religious war (behind the Thirty Years' War, which took 8,000,000 lives in present-day Germany) Unlike all other religious wars at the time, the French wars retained their religious character without being confounded by dynastic considerations.

The conflict involved disputes between the aristocratic houses of France, mainly the Reformed House of Condé (a branch of the House of Bourbon) and the Roman Catholic House of Guise (a branch of the House of Lorraine), and both sides received assistance from foreign sources. Protestant England and Scotland supported the Protestant side led by the Condés and the Navarrese faction (led by Jeanne d'Albret and her son, Henry of Navarre), while Hapsburg Spain and the Duchy of Savoy supported the Roman Catholic side concentrated around the Guises.

Politiques, consisting of the French kings and their advisers, tried to balance the situation and avoid an open bloodshed between the two religious groups, generally introducing gradual concessions to Huguenots. Catherine de' Medici initially held that stance until she sided with Roman Catholics after the St. Bartholomew's Day massacre, (a frenzy of slaughter rarely seen in the most savage battles of war in which Catholic mobs killed as many as 30,000 Protestants throughout the entire kingdom)

On 1 March 1562, Francis (François), the second Duke of Guise, traveling to his estates, stopped in Wassy (70 miles N) and decided to attend Mass. He found a large congregation of Huguenots holding religious ceremonies in a barn that was their church. Some of the duke's party attempted to push their way inside and were repulsed. Events escalated, stones began to fly, and the Duke was struck. Outraged, he ordered his men to fortify the town and set fire to the church, killing 63 unarmed Huguenots and wounding over a hundred. This event is generally used as the beginning date of the war, officially ending in 1598, however the massacre provoked open hostilities between some followers of each religion, sparking the first war of a long series of French Wars of Religion, which continued largely uninterrupted for more than a century.

With the Counter Reformation initiated by the Council of Trent (1545-1563), positions hardened and a strict Catholic orthodoxy based on Scholastic philosophy was imposed. Some humanists, even moderate Catholics such as Erasmus, risked being declared heretics for their perceived

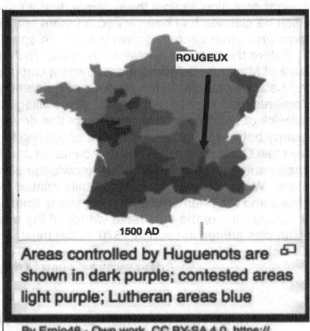

ROUGEUX

1500 AD

Areas controlled by Huguenots are shown in dark purple; contested areas light purple; Lutheran areas blue

criticism of the church.[19]

The historian of the Renaissance, Sir John Hale, cautions against too direct a linkage between Renaissance humanism and modern uses of the term humanism: *"Renaissance humanism must be kept free from any hint of either 'humanitarianism' or 'humanism' in its modern sense of rational, non-religious approach to life ... the word 'humanism' will mislead ... if it is seen in opposition to Christianity. Its students in the main wished to supplement, not contradict, through their patient excavation of the sources of ancient God-inspired wisdom."*

At the conclusion of the conflict in 1598, Huguenots were granted substantial rights and freedoms by the Edict of Nantes, though it did not end hostility towards them. The wars weakened the authority of the monarchy, already fragile under the rule of Francis II and then Charles IX, though it later reaffirmed its role under Henry IV.

Pope Pious II

Some of the first humanists were great collectors of antique manuscripts, including Petrarch, Giovanni Boccaccio, Coluccio Salutati, and Poggio Bracciolini. Of the four, Petrarch was dubbed the 'Father of Humanism' because of his devotion to Greek and Roman scrolls. Many worked for the Catholic Church and were in holy orders, like Petrarch, while others were lawyers and chancellors of Italian cities. Some of the highest officials of the Catholic Church were humanists with the resources to amass important libraries. Such was Cardinal Basilios Bessarion, a convert to the Catholic Church from Greek Orthodoxy, who was considered for the papacy, and was one of the most learned scholars of his time.

There were several 15th-century and early 16th-century humanist Popes one of whom, Aeneas Silvius Piccolomini (Pope Pius II), was a prolific author and wrote a treatise on The Education of Boys. These subjects came to be known as the humanities, and the movement which they inspired is known as humanism.

CHAPTER XI
OF THE PEACE OF VERVINS AND THE WAR WITH FRENCH-COMTE
(1598-1636)

1. LA DAME DE PRESSIGNY ----- 2. FOUNDATIONS RELIGIOUS ----- 3. SORCERIES ------- 4. TROUBLES IN BASSIGNY ------- 5. THE BARON DE FERTE IS CHARGED WITH MAINTENANCE OF ORDER ----- 6. THE REBELS ----- 7. THE GOVERNOR OF LANGRES MARCH AGAINST ----- 8. NEW SEIGNEURS ----- 9. ARREST OF LORD MONTAIGU ----- 10. DESCRIPTION OF THE FORTRESS OF COIFFY----- 11. ITS DEMOLITION———12. 1614 FIRST RECORDED ROUGEUX ANCESTOR

Peace was signed between the representatives of Henry IV of France and Philip II of Spain, on 2 May 1598, at the small town of Vervins in Picardy, Northern France, close to the territory of the Habsburg Netherlands, ending the vicious War of Religion that had raged across Europe since 1562. The terms were worked out under the auspices of the papal legate of Clement VIII, Alessandro de' Medici. By its terms, Philip recognized the formerly Protestant Henry IV as King of France and withdrew his forces from French territory, depriving the remnants of the Catholic League of their support.

(Philip died on 13 September, but his heir Philip III respected the terms of the treaty. Carlo Emanuele, duke of Savoy, who had held back from the treaty, was defeated by Henry IV in 1599. He signed a separate Treaty of Lyon with Henry in 1601.

The parties to the treaty were hosted by Guillemette de Coucy, co-seigneur of Vervins, in her Châteauneuf de Vervins. Close to the Spanish Netherlands, the Thiérache region had suffered much damage in the recent fighting. Its numerous 16th-century fortified churches still bear witness today)

The efforts of the Huguenots to establish Protestantism in the parish of Pierrefaites, did not lead to the desired results.

We contemplated war by the partisans of the reform who are at Pressigny. The lady of this place, after having employed every means in her ability to implant this heresy, did not seem quite so happy when she saw that most of the population kept the faith (and remain Catholic until recent times when there is little religion of any kind))

After death struck that woman, in 1601 her co-religious came to bury her corpse in the church despite the resistance of the cure and the Catholics.

110

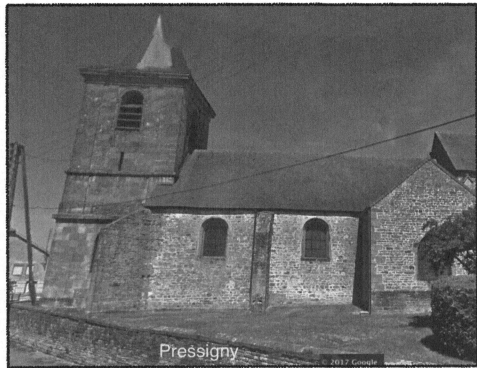

Pressigny

Then the bishop placed an interdict on the church, and would not consent to removal of the remains until after an exhumation of the cadaver which was done at the end of the year. During this epoch there were many religious reconstructions. We saw a reconstruction of a church at Rosoy (1600) Antoine Chevillot and Jeanne Pelletier, his wife, established at Pierrefaites, for their testament, on 10

PRESSIGNY

© 2017 Google

December 1610, the Hours of the Cross for the Fridays of Lent. An ordinance of M. Facenet, vicar general, on 5 November 1613, reorganized the Confederation of the Conception built at La Ferte, January 1408 and confirmed by a bull of Pope Alexander VI.

Claude Legros, Counselor to the Kings Provost of Villare-le-Pautel, and Agnes Vosgien, his wife, founded in 1618, the chapel of Notre-Dame-de-Pitie at Coiffy-le-Chateau (11 miles N) The same year, Martin Chalochel, priest of Genevrieres, donated the chapel of Saint-Sacrament de Poinson-les-Fayl, (6 miles South) place of his birth. The church of this last village who was

formerly a branch of Pressigny, was made a curial parish by M. Zamet near the year 1621. Henri IV was assassinated 14 May 1610. (After 13 attempts, was ultimately assassinated in Paris on 14 May 1610 by a Catholic fanatic, François Ravaillac, who stabbed the King to death in Rue de la Ferronnerie, while his coach's progress was stopped by traffic congestion for the Queen's coronation ceremony. Henry was buried at the Saint Denis Basilica. His widow, Marie de' Medici, served as regent for their 9-year-old son, Louis XIII, until 1617) His son, Louis XIII, became King when he was sixteen. During the minority of the King, the great feudal lords revolted and this agitation communicated itself among the provinces. Bassigny (our region) was troubled by the disorder caused by Philippe d'Anglure, seigneur of Guyonvelle. This seigneur, pressed by his creditors, was obliged to place for sale his ground at Bonnecourt, purchased by Jules de Boulogne, governer of Nogent. He thought the moment was favorable for raiding and threw his lot with the party of the princes and, with his cousin Aurillot, seigneur of Essey-les-Eaux, decided to raise a company of light horse soldiers. With a small number of arms, at Bonnecourt, (14 miles N) Aurillot made himself master of the chateau without much penalty and burned the defenses of Bassecour (unknown today) A farmer, his wife and infants tried to flee but were thrown back into the flames. We ran to Nogent (25 miles N) to implore assistance. Boulogne, called by the Queen, was in Paris. Pontis, lieutenant of the place was exceedingly afraid of those attackers, therefore he had the young men of the area mount horses and with fifty musketeers, it was enough to chase the enemy who abandoned all their booty (1614)[1].

That little victory failed to give tranquility to the population. These rebels made intrigues, looked for alliances, and prepared for fighting. In September 1615 Guyonvelle and Clinchamp (36 miles N) led their companies all the way into Luxembourg, The Prince of Conde, (Henri II of Bourbon 1588-1646) informed of those who were invading, charged Henri de Choiseul, baron of La Ferte and seigneur of Pressigny (assassinated 1632), to maintain order within our country.

On the date of 31 October, he (Conde) wrote him (Choiseul) a letter from the camp at Couvressant, that said: *"We desire that the chateau of La Ferte-sur-Amance remains subject to His Majesty, because it is well placed to provide grand service for the conservation of Bassigny, keep the people safe and guarantee against oppression. So that the enemies of the State do not press the King by force, surprise or otherwise we have considered that, for the service of the King, we should find someone capable, and of sufficient experience in arms to prepare for war. We cannot make a better choice that you since you have all the qualities and the inclination to do good for the State is well known. We just have, therefore, to commission you to be commander in this place and adjacent counties and with the previously mentioned men of arms seize and take possession strong places and chateaus occupied by the enemies of His Majesty contrary to the good of the State; take prisoners and draw ransom after the judges have made a good appraisal; place in prison, etc...; begin work on repairs to the fortifications at La Ferte by the inhabitants of the parishes and surroundings; take from the tax contributions of the neighboring villages; take sums from any that are convenient, in other words do all you judge necessary for the service of His Majesty and his State to provide defense against his enemies and all the things you choose to do we will provide amply."*

This letter was read back by Paul Michelin, royal notary at the chateau de Pressigny. On the bottom we read: *"We, Henri de Choiseul, captain of one hundred light horsemen and master of the camp of two hundred carabins for the service of the King have given provisions to Richard de Chabut, sire of Percy, to make a gift of twenty-five carabin (?) for the service of the King..Given this day in our garrison of Pressigny [1]."*

Choiseul and Chabutwere prepared for the war. But learning that Prince Conde (Henri II of Bourbon 1588-1646, a French prince) was arrested and imprisoned (from 1616 until 1619) by order of Count de Concini (1575-1617), postponed their plans.

By 1617, Louis XIII, incited by his favorite Charles de Luynes, was tired of Concini's tutelage.

Instead of defending the interests of Prince Conde, Choiseul and Chabutwere followed the advice of malcontents and rebels. They made common Clinchamp (36 miles N), Courcelotte (54 miles SE), and with Sauix-Tavannes (8 miles W)

This last named (Chabutwere) seized the parish of Grosse-Saure and that of Varennes, where they established their quarter-general. Clinchamp and Courcelotte occupied Bize (4 miles NE) and environs (certainly would include Rougeux) Out of this came the decision that led to inflicting tribulation and ravishment upon the villages and territory. Varennes was strongly maltreated. Vicq was incinerated (1616) (12 miles N)

Indignant at such a revolt and plunder, the Mayor and Aldermen of Langress quickly alerted the King who promptly took the arms of the peasants of the Montagne (possibly meaning the arms of those living in Langres which is situated on a small mountain) and supported by some horsemen of the Baron, attacked and captured, close to Bize (4 miles NE), the Lords of Clinchamp, and Courcelotte and conducted them to Chatillon. At the same time, others joined the garrisons of Nogent and Montigny, and marched upon Pressigny with artillery. But informed that this expedition was being organized against them, Choiseul, Guyonvelle, and Chabut evacuated that place without interference. The rash Aurillot resolved to defend Pressigny. It must be recognized that he retired into a peculiar house and barricaded himself in a room. We broke through the barricade and door without effort. He finally surrendered to the lieutenant of Pontis, named M. De Francieres, who to him Aurillot remitted his epee. Taken to Langress, he was met with boos from the crowd and one member drew on him a musket. However the nobles protested and to escape the crowd the commander had Aurillot conducted to Chaumont (40 miles NW) where the justice condemned him to beheading. Aurillot appealed this sentence and was transported to Paris. The judgment was confirmed, then we cut off his head. Carved on the place of Greve is written, 'Pour brulements' and incendiaries' (For burning and incendiaries)

Henri de Choiseul died by assassination in 1632. He left the baronage of La Ferte to his nephew Cleniadus. As at the seigneurie of Pressigny, he sold to Jules de Bollogne, consular to the King, governer of Nogent, Seigneur of Bonnecourt, of Poiseun and of Andilly. Because this was such a new royal family, we must mention two others who established themselves in the kingdom. Around 1600, Catherine de Fauquier, married Andre Bernard de Montessus and brought with her the illustrious house Shivery and La Quarie (Neither place can be found today) This last village, began to form itself after clearing four hundred acres of woods.

Among the seigneurs of this epoque, the Livron played a significant role in our country. Charles, son of Erard, Marquis of Bourbonne, count of Hortes, etc., captain of seventy men of arms, and as governer of Coiffy, was pledged a hundred livres per month for our protection.

In 1627, he attracted the public attention by the arrest of Milord de Montaigu.

1. La Haute-Marne, passim, etc. wife, Leonora Galigaï (1571?–1617),

That personage (Montaigu) had been sent by the Duke of Buckingham (of England who now ruled France) to conclude, against the good of France, a league into which had entered England, Spain, Lorraine, Savoie and Bavaria. (1585-1642), But Richelieu learned of this and, speaking for the King, ordered M. De Bourbonne to observe the movements of Montaigu and, if possible, arrest him. (Armand Jean du Plessis, Cardinal-Duke of Richelieu and of Fronsac 1585 – 1642, commonly referred to as Cardinal Richelieu was a French clergyman, nobleman, and statesman. Consecrated as a bishop in 1607 and was appointed Foreign Secretary in 1616. Richelieu soon rose in both the Catholic Church and the French government, becoming a cardinal in 1622, and King Louis XIII's chief minister in 1624. He remained in office until his death in 1642. He sought to consolidate royal power and crush domestic factions. By restraining the power of the nobility, he transformed France into a strong, centralized state)

His Grand Eminence
**Armand-Jean du Plessis
Cardinal de Richelieu**

Cardinal, Bishop of Luçon

https://commons.wikimedia.org/wiki/File:Holyromanempire.png

The Marques (De Bourbonne) desirous to do the bidding of Cardinal Richelieu, (and Buckingham), ordered two Basques to go to the location where he knew the Duke of Montaigu was staying. The Basques, disguised as locksmith companions, managed an encounter with Montaigu (who they apparently arrested) and his valet de chamber, Okenham, (and apparently others) whom they did not arrest. When they were near Barrois, close to the frontier of France, one of the accomplices of Montaigu came to tell his captors the place to meet the emissary of Richelieu (who was coming to take Montaigu to Paris)

Immediately, De Livron (Marques de Bourbonne) mounted a horse, and accompanied by a dozen of his friends, came to the place on the highway that enabled him to encounter the emissary. He was arrested, in the name of the King, at the village of Roux. All resistance was impossible. The prisoner, in whose valise we found the treaty, objected to his movement, however, permitted us to take him to Bourbonne where we fed him his supper. That same evening, at eleven o'clock, Livron assembled one hundred mousquetieres and led them to the citadel at Coiffy, (11 miles N) and reduced it with one blow of the hand. He told the prisoners, *"You have eaten your last supper and have taken the trouble to sleep your last night in the house of my master, the King, in his house at Coiffy".*

The 21 November, (1627) Charles De Livron, Marques de Bourbonne, who had arrested the English Lord on orders of His Majesty, wrote to the mayor of Chaumont, warning him that the Duke of Lorraine was threatening to besiege the chateau at Coiffy where the English were being detained. He requested munitions but we had to refuse because we had insufficient arms to defend our village. (The Abbot Briffaut and author of this history resided at Pierrefaites)

The regiments who were in Bourgogne and in Champagne rapidly approached Coiffy to reinforce him. Some time later, Montaigu, apparently free in appearance, but without his epee or spurs was placed on a small horse, and in the middle of eight or nine hundred cavaliers, obviously in plain daylight, but at the same time preventing the troops of Lorraine from attacking. At the same time the prisoner was removed from the chateau, we fired two shots from a cannon to distract the enemy and advise the besiegers to depart. We arranged our troops in battle formation to permit the enemy to engage in an affair, but they remained in their quarters. By then the escort, commanded by Livron and Anglure, his grandfather, were well on the route to Paris (10 December) where his Lordship was conducted to the Bastille in Paris and the door locked. This important arrest vaulted the Marquis de Livron to lieutenant of Champagne[1].

The fortress of Coiffy was composed then of the old chateau and the citadelle. The old chateau was forty fathoms long and fifteen wide. From both sides the thick foundations

COIFFY LE HAUTE.

advanced all the way into the precipitous escarpment of the mountain. It was also equipped with three large round towers. The front of the chateau faced a plateau, upon which was constructed the burg. Entry to the chateau was over a draw bridge. The rear was defended by the citadelle, separated by a ditch six feet wide. The chateau possessed a chapel, whom Choiseul (a Protestant) had made into a butcher shop but was restored by Livron. The citadelle, with work more modern than the chateau, formed a parallelogram protected by four large boulevards between stone walls that were twenty-two feet thick at the base and eighteen feet to the summit.

The Leaguers had fired against the wall facing Lorraine more than two thousand cannon shots. Livron had it repaired and placed into good condition.

1. Archives de 'Hotel de Ville de Langres

But Richelieu judged that it is difficult and dangerous to seriously oppose the enemy by disseminating his forces among a number of chateaux. (In order to further consolidate power in France, Richelieu sought to suppress the influence of the feudal nobility. In 1626, he abolished the position of Constable of France and ordered all fortified castles to be razed, excepting only those needed to defend against invaders. Thus, he stripped the princes, dukes, and lesser aristocrats of important defenses that could have been used against the King's armies during rebellions. As a result, Richelieu was hated by most of the nobility) In addition the annexation of Lorraine (1634), he removed Coiffy from the frontier and as a place of importance. This clever Minister, Richelieu, obtained from the King in April 1635, an order for the demolition of the Chateau of Coiffy and charged M. De Choisy, steward of Champagne, to be the executor of his order.

The dismantlement, begun this same year, was promptly made achieved. The burg was left defenseless but the villages saw that their fortress was so often in ruin that they saw it fall without regret. The place occupied a surface of six thousand six hundred sixty-eight yards. The king ceded it to the inhabitants subject to an annual fee on condition they permit the way between the citadelle and the chateau to be free space.

SUPPLEMENTS FROM ABBOTT MULSON AND OTHERS

Ninety of the 17th Century's 100 years were consumed by endless and overlapping wars in Europe. No country was spared the ravages of these mindless conflicts ending only by the total exhaustion of them all. Prior centuries were endless affairs of turmoil with never-ending fears of well documented starvation and other miseries and it was thought that things could not get worse. The 17th century proved that assumption false.
In 1600 after the eruption of a volcano in Peru in 1600 created a volcanic winter, reduced amounts of sunlight reached the Earth's surface, which scientists believe contributed to bitterly cold winters, loss of crops and animals, and massive famine around the world. As a result, people killed many animals with their bare hands to preserve their furs for warmth. Two million died in Russia.The famine was documented across the world; in France, the 1601 wine harvest was late, and wine production collapsed.

Assumption of the throne by the nine year old son of the assassinated King Henry IV sparked a revolution by the nobility that communicated itself to our region.(In a third assassination attempt, King Henry IV, a Protestant, was killed in Paris on 14 May 1610 by a Catholic fanatic, François Ravaillac, who stabbed him in the Rue de la Ferronnerie. Henry's coach was stopped by traffic congestion related to the Queen's coronation ceremony).

The usual destruction was suffered until the revolutionaries abandoned the fight in 1614. But this was a hollow victory and did nothing to pacify the situation.

116

The rebels continued with their intrigues and in September 1615, these actions started the '30 Years War' Beginning as a religious civil war between Catholics and Protestants, it quickly grew into a war between the French Bourbons and the Hapsburgs of Austria. Armies stationed seven miles Southeast of Rougeux at Pressigny focused the activity on our region. The continual retreat and advancement of both armies during this vicious thirty-year turmoil, finally ending in 1639, decimated both countries and led them into famine and economic ruin. This was the same period when the mania for tulip bulbs 100 miles to the North was in its full rage among the rich who paid the equivalent of the finest house in Amsterdam for one tulip bulb.

In 1636, on September 14, an invading army of 42,000 from Franche-Compte began a civil war with Burgundy, that centered in our region. In one of its first actions, this army, consisting of men from Franche-Compte, Croates, Germans, Spain and England, laid siege for six weeks to Fayl-Billot, two miles South of Rougeux. The survivors, in spite of surrendering to a code of honor, were immediately fell upon, stripped of what they had, run through with the epee (thin flexible sword) and the remaining buildings leveled, leaving utter desolation. Mounted enemies, only six days later, while headed toward Hortes (4 miles N) and Rosay (4 miles NW), and massacred fifty residents of Rougeux, the remnants survived by fleeing into the woods. The part of the village rebuilt on the side of the hill was burned to the ground. As the enemy surrounded Hortes, musket fire from the residents wounded some. In great anger, the horsemen began to massacre the residents with knife and sword, many of whom found refuge inside the church. Flames, spreading from nearby houses eventually engulfed the church, killing even little children and all those who had sought protection in the house of God. Some of the residents continued firing at the enemy, killing a large number, but in the end everything of value was stolen and flames had devoured two churches, five pavilions, 105 houses, three or four chasts(?) and a large number of prisoners were taken. Soon after, French forces, attacking at night before the enemy had an opportunity to form defenses, routed them, and captured munitions, gold, the baton of the commandant, his gold chain, many horses and chariots and burned their tents. Furious at this defeat, using hatchets, the enemy butchered fifty of their prisoners.

During June of 1636, 'la peste' recommencing in Langres, spread Eastward through Rougeux and adjacent villages. This plague, the war, and a terrifically hot summer led to widespread famine, not ending until the fall of 1642.

On the 22nd of February 1638, the Croates, and Germans returned once again to ravage Hortes and Rougeux. The priest of Hortes found shelter under an overhanging rock in the stream, but he was forced to remain there for such an extended time that he suffered exposure and died the 20th of March 1638.

There are numerous accounts of repeated attacks during the following year on Coiffy, Jonville, Jussey, Fayl-Billot, La Rochelle, Saucourt, and other villages surrounding Rougeux in the Valley of the Amance, which, for the sake of brevity, are not included in this recounting.

CHAPTER XII

ABOUT THE BEGINNING OF THE WAR WITH FRANCE-COMTE UNTIL THE TREATY BETWEEN THE TWO BOURGOGNES
(1636-1643)

From the time that King Louis XIII (King of France) became emperor of Lorraine (East of Rougeux along the Rhine), the dispossessed Duke, Charles IV, served Austria and Spain within Franche-Compte (Our region) To obtain his vengeance against the King of France, he placed, near the end of April 1636, at Darney, Richecourt and other localities, certain garrisons designated to ravage the frontier. The companies of Lorraines (Germans), commanded by Baron de Clinchamp, and one of his officers invaded the Bassigny (Region surrounding Rougeux) The companies of Lorraines, commanded by Baron de Clinchamp and one of his officers, he place, near the end of April 1636 at Darney (36 miles NE), Richecourt (90 miles N), and other localities certain garrisons destined to ravage.

The first week of May many villages were ravaged and burned. At Fresnoy (25 miles N) and at Montigny (15 miles E) these brigands, after pillaging and the incendiary, passed their epee through all those that did not have enough to pay a ransom.

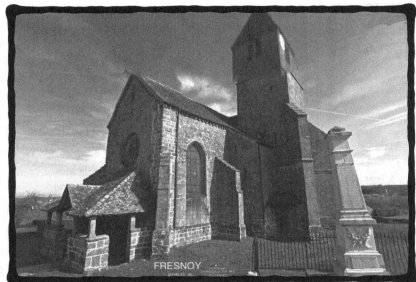
FRESNOY

Clinchamp, at the head of one hundred cavalry, tried to seize the priest of Varennes (8 miles N)
Our troops captured Clinchamp who decided to render himself and promised that he would not kill anyone or burn anything on condition for his freedom.
M. De la Notte, Commandant, recognized the perfidy of his enemy, and rejected in total this proposal, but he finally yielded to the tears and supplications of the inhabitants who feared the murderer and the incendiaries.

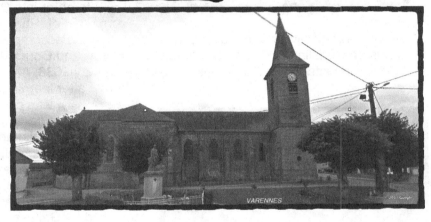
VARENNES

After having received the parole of honor from Clinchamp, we opened the doors of the house and he came out. But what cruelty! In an instant we jumped on him and disarmed him and by order of the commandant, we hung him on the first tree we could find, without giving him, says Macheret, time to confess his sins and say an act of contrition. Soon he died with tears in his eyes, begging mercy from God and accepted death gladly (!) for the love of the passion of Our Master Jesus Christ.
The soldiers of Clinchamp immediately began to set fire to the village and continued their devastation.

Varennes

Clinchcamp had imposed a general taxation over the entire territory and raised more than thirteen million pistoles. The community of Hortes was taxed twelve hundred, but obtained a reduction to fifty. Nicolas Voinchet, cannon of Langres, himself loaned this amount. The (Pistole was gold money valued at ten francs)
Seeing that Franche-Comte (reversing their alligence) had accepted the Duke Charles IV (who wanted return of his property after losing it when Franche-Compte joined with France) without notification King Louis XIII broke the peace treaty that had existed for twenty-nine years, since

BARON DE CLINCHAMP.

12 September 1610, and he signed, at Chantilly (Chantilly is just North of Paris) 7 May 1636, a declaration of war.

(Military expenses of the 30 Years War and civil wars, had placed considerable strain on the revenues of French King Louis XIII. In response, Cardinal Richelieu raised the gabelle (salt tax) and the taille (land tax) The clergy, nobility, and high bourgeoisie were either exempt or could easily avoid payment, so the burden fell on the poorest segment of the nation. To collect taxes more efficiently, and to keep corruption to a minimum, Richelieu bypassed local tax officials, replacing them with officials in the direct service of the Crown. Richelieu's financial scheme, however, caused unrest among the peasants; there were several uprisings in 1636 to 1639. Richelieu, (and the King) crushed the revolts violently, and harshly dealt with the rebels)

An army of six thousand infantry and two thousand cavaliers, received an order (from King Louis) to enter into Champagne under the command of Prince de Conde (1621-1686), (French general) governer of the duchy of Bourgogne, and accompanied by de la Melleraye, the Marquis de Coaslin; de Gassion, Marquis de Villeroy, and Count Ranizau.

Conde invested Dole (85 mi South of Rougeux) 28 May 1636. After a siege of six weeks he withdrew after learning that the Duke of Lorraine (French enemy) was on his way to rescue the place with numerous cavalry. Soon the Germans, Huguenots, Croats, and Spanish were joining the Duke of Lorraine against King Louis.

They totaled sixty-five thousand accompanied by a multitude of valets, providers and women, trailing in an immense baggage train. This formidable army, led by Gallass, field-general of the Empire (Austrian), caused trembling in Champagne and Bourgogne.

LOUIS PRINCE DE CONDE

Matthias Gallas, Graf von Campo und Herzog von Lucera 1584 – 1647) was an Austrian soldier, who first saw service in Flanders, then in Savoy with the Spaniards, and subsequently joined the forces of the Catholic League as captain during the Thirty Years' War.

At the great battle of Nördlingen (August 23, 1634) in which the army of Sweden was almost annihilated, Gallas commanded the victorious Imperial forces. His next command was in Lorraine, but even the Moselle Valley had suffered so much from the ravages of war that his army perished of want.[3]

Gallas's ineffectiveness severely damaged the Habsburg cause in the latter stages of the Thirty Years' War. Over the years his army had earned for itself the reputation of being the most cruel and rapacious force even during the especially bloody 30 Years War. Like many other generals of that period, he had acquired much wealth and great territorial possessions . Victorious in the first of the battles of Nördlingen (1634), carelessness and drunkenness thereafter marred his conduct of the war. He later became known as the 'destroyer of armies,' especially after his disastrous campaigns of 1637, 1638, and 1644, each of which resulted in the annihilation of his troops.

For the defense, King Louis XIII (by name Louis the Just, 1601-1643, King of France from 1610 to 1643, cooperated closely with his chief minister, the Cardinal de Richelieu, to make France a leading European power. Although Louis had displayed courage on the battlefield, his mental instability and chronic ill health undermined his capacity for sustained concentration on affairs of state. Hence Richelieu quickly became the dominant influence in the government) had sent twenty-five thousand French and Swedish troops divided into three corps. Under the order of Cardinal of La Valette, 20,000; of the Duke of Saxe-Weimar, 15,000; and of M. De Vaubecourt, 6,000.

On 8 September these generals were at Langres (15 mi W of Rougeux) impatiently waiting for General Conde.

Finally, Conde arrived in the evening and the next day, a council of war decided that La Valette and Weimar would occupy Coublanc, Brussieres, Fayl-Billot, (2 mi S of Rougeux) Poinson (5 mi SE of Rougeux) and Pressigny. But they ran out of time because these diverse points had been occupied by (German) general Gallass. French Cardinal La Vallette sent the Viscount de Turenne against this (German) general with 1500 horsemen, 1500 men on foot and three cannons. Turenne grabbed Jussey (20 mi E of Rougeux) and Cemboing (19 mi E of Rougeux) and sacked them (2 September)

Gallass, who had his headquarters at Purgerot (25 mi E of Rougeux) hastily sent his sergeant of battle, Lamboy, with one thousand horsemen and approached Jussey, confident that Turenne had abandoned the place.

On his side, (French General) Weimar had advanced against Champlitte (17 mi S of Rougeux) (14 September) which had closed its doors. Weimar began a siege but upon the immediate arrival of Gallass, retreated back toward Langres (14 miles W) Then Weimar occupied Bourbonne, (18 mi NE of Rougeux) Coiffy (12 mi NE of Rougeux), La Ferte (34 mi N of Rougeux), and surrounding villages. French General La Valette camped his troops in the Montsaugeonnais (22 mi SW of Rougeux)

(Obviously, Rougeux was at the geographic center of these armies and battles and could not have escaped the same treatment as the villages noted in the text) These developments inspired terror throughout the territory, as their villages were laid in ruin and man and beast were slaughtered by both sides. A great number of the inhabitants hid themselves in the forests. The others, more courageous, raised barricades to defend their villages. Lavigney, (16 mi SE of Rougeux) part of the vanguard of the imperial army, jumped on our territory (14 September) and found no resistance except at Coublanc (180 miles South), Bussieres (48 miles South) and Fayl-Billot (2 miles South) because these communities organized stiffened distance and entrenchments against them. But the Germans and Croats attacked with much violence until they were forced to surrender. The attackers killed many persons, indulged in pillage and inflicted horrible injuries on the living and burned many of the houses. A detachment of the army came to Fayl-Billot (2 miles S) and installed themselves for six weeks, consuming all the grain, beasts and left nothing but desolation and ruin.

Lamboy (German), posted at Jussey (24 miles E) made incursions across France with an audacity and with incredible anarchy. During the early days they surprised the chateau of Pressigny (8 miles SE) where they found a large supply of munitions and victuals that they sold to Comtois (local seigneur) Then Forkariz, camped at Poinson (7miles S) was joined by two thousand Croats and together they burned (the region of) Bassigny (abutting Rougeux NW) all the way to the doors of

Gallas, detail from an engraving

Courtesy of the Heeresgeschichtliches Museum, Vienna

Langres (14 miles W) We could, on top of the ramparts of that ville, follow their March by the light of their incendiaries and they advanced all the way to Montsaugeon (22 mi NE) and encountered battle near La Valette.

Of the 17 September, Gallass had his headquarters at Champlitte (30 miles South), His army occupied all of the country all the way from Jussey, Gray, the frontier of Langrois, of Amance at the Vinageann (?) To find food and shelter, the soldiers scoured the territory in small bands and in large companies using greed and force on everything they saw at their convenience.

On Tuesday 23 September 1636, certain Croates presented themselves at Hortes (4 miles N) not far from the church of Saint-Dieter. They were chased by the inhabitants but three hours after, twelve cavaliers appeared upon the road of Barre. We repulsed them promptly and they had the courtesy to provide us with a number of bottles of wine as a gift from the village. The next day they returned by the way of the hill from Rosoy (4 miles NW) with about four hundred and stole, we read in 'Batre deux Vesvres', fifteen hundred horned beasts and three thousand sheep.

The village (Hortes) was barricaded and guarded, and required forced entry. The peasants bravely resisted for some time, but eventually fearing they would be classified as war prisoners or that their houses would be burned they promised to give ransom, not to reclaim any of their beasts, and lay down their arms and to be absent to permit the soldiers to have complete liberty of Hortes (4 miles N) so that the soldiers could take whatever they wanted. Two persons immediately raised the ransom which had to be carried to Rosoy. But this generous treatment had not been approved by the whole community and there was serious blame against those not approving who wanted to continue to defend

because of the extremely high ransom cost. The defenders observed, at nine o'clock in the morning, an enemy corps of four thousand men with wagons that had been directed, on order, to pass through Rosoy for forging and to have refreshment following the conditions of the treaty. To overcome the resistance of the villagers this corps of enemies forced the barricades close to the house of the Knight de Theon, at Hortes, and advanced in a file along the rue de Pont, arriving just next to the hall where they ransacked all the living quarters of the peasants.

The peasants discharged into them a dozen volleys of the guns, wounding and killing a great many. However the soldiers set fires along two roads, the first the du Pont and the one under the church whose smoke soon choked the ones inside the church. The fire gained the bell tower and roof of the nave. None wanted to surrender and resisted valorously the house of God which had become a fortress. The enemies precipitated themselves near the gallery and in front of the portal and proceeded to demolish the mural, fired a vast amount of muskets that reduced the defending men and immediately the enemy entered with sabers and knives and

massacred all they could find, broke and burnt seats, books, cross, images, sacred vases, ornaments, vestments, coffers and precious papers until nothing remained recognizable and, says Macheret, *"dug themselves a pit of eternal fire."*

Suffering through the fire and smoke were a number of men on the vault continuously firing upon those enemies of God and killed about two hundred. Officers were exasperated that they

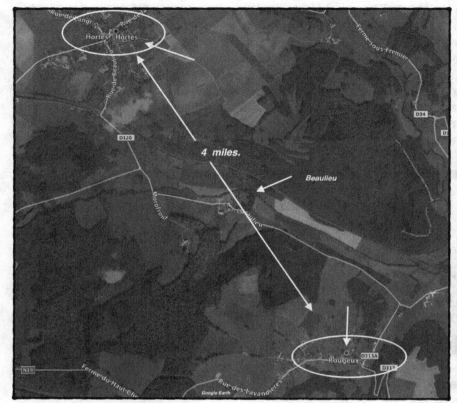

had permitted the fire to traverse the village, consuming small infants. The number of inhabitants put to death in the fields, on the roads, in the houses and inside the church was above four hundred, among whom are forty infants who were hiding in the church that were mutilated, roasted or crushed under the ruins.

Four days after, the venerable cure, Nicolas Joliot, himself picked up the scattered remains of these innocent victims and had them buried in a large pit dug in the middle of the cemetery.

The flames had devoured two churches, five pavilions, one hundred five houses and more than one hundred that were composed of three or four rooms. What other losses of gold, silver, beasts, furniture, grains, forages, wood, etc! We expected a harvest of more than two thousand muids of wine which we now will not have to sell. Hortes, that once was one of the best and most prosperous villages is now one of the most poor and heartbroken.

(Cardinal) La Valette resolved to surprise the Croates in their quarter between Leffond (17 mi SW of Rougeux) and Coublanc. He made a party one afternoon and at nightfall, the Count Rantzau with fifteen hundred horsemen, and the Count de Guiche with eight hundred. The Count Guiche diverged with the Duke de Weimar (between the villages of) Leffond and Champlitte in an attempt to cut the retreat of the Croates and to oppose any assistance that might come to their aid from the camp of Gallass. Rantzau, favored by the darkness and very obscured, arrived close to the enemy without being seen and commenced the attack before La Valette or Weimar arrived at their post. They made a charge so rapid that the Croates were unable to have time to prepare their defense. Isolny and his officers delivered their salute with the agility of their horses. Weimar pursued them all the way to the door of Champlitte (20 miles S), where they killed the ensign and raised their standard. A part of the (Croate) soldiers fled with precipitous disorder, while the others were cut to pieces or made prisoner.

The French entered their camp and burned their tents. They found a great number of horses, chariots and coaches, munitions, general equipages, their dishes of silver, the commandants baton, his gold chain, etc, Furious at this defeat, the Croates massacred with axes sixty-five prisoners and sent soldiers in every direction to ravage the country and commit atrocities whose story makes one shudder.

Gallass had his foot upon France, nevertheless he did not want to march before having been able to reunite all his people. Therefore when the division of Marquis de Bade arrived, and he had no pretext for further deferring attacks. He held council at chateau de Susucourt where Charles de Lorraine, Forkatz, Lamboy, Baron de Scey, Seigneur de Ville-sur-Illon and other chiefs of corps (17 October 1636) were reunited. He attempted to learn if it would be better to attack Champagne to the North or from the South through Bourgogne.

The Prince of Lorraine, Duke Charles IV (German), wanted to place a siege around Langres and take that village by a direct attack even if it sacrificed a thousand men. He aspired to reconquer his lost duchy in that manner.

On their side, the officers of Franche-Compte (The region of France encompassing the Eastern Départements of Jura, Doubs, Haute-Saône, and the Territory of Belfort. Bounded by the regions of Rhône-Alpes to the South, Burgundy (Bourgogne) to the West, Champagne-Ardenne to the NorthWest, and Lorraine and Alsace to the North. Switzerland lies to the East. The capital is Besançon) strongly supported this view of the situation that grew decidedly in the allies who were situated a long way in the heart of enemy territory.

But Gallass who did not want to make any advance other than one of low risk, declared they would commence by the way of Bourgogne, the Southern route in which they will encounter no other than the Prince de Conde.

To gain acceptance of their plan, Duke Charles IV and his partisans conferred with all the council on the mountain of Morey where he showed them the village of Langres (questionable because it is roughly 15 miles on a direct line between Morey and Langres) and of Bassigny, places as though, he claimed, were in his hands. The field general opened his lunette (field telescope) and better contemplated what he had to do make Fayl-Billot (2 miles S) level with the ground, to make arial shots and studied the formidable position of the place that the two powerful armies of Valette and Weimar stood ready to attack.

The instrument fell from his hands. *"Leave Langres, he said, and March against Dijon "* (60 miles directly South of Rougeux rather than moving West to Langres) All the generals approved, and like puppets this view was master and prevailed. In the evening before the next day, the general in chief dispatched orders that everyone must prepare, at rising of the morning, to have the various corps in movement, with arms and baggage.

After having taken the chateau of the Romagne, surrounded Fontaine-Francaise, forced Mirebeau, and devastated by iron and fire the edges of the Duchy, Gallass went to blockade Saint-Jean-de Losue. He planed to storm this small, poorly fortified, village that does not even have a garrison. But the inhabitants defended with a heroic courage, and when the French army came to their succor they put Gallass to rout (3 November 1636) Obliged to retire in great disorder, harassed by our troops, marching with endless difficulties in the middle of a country flooded by the deborderments of the Soane River, they lost half of their people and equipage. After having persevered all the way to the frontier of Franche-Compte our general wants us to take a position behind L'Amance around Coiffy (10 miles N) and Bourbonne (18 miles N)

Because Gallass wanted to try again another enterprise to cover the humiliating dishonor of his retreat, he moved his army along the Soane near Jussey (20 miles E) He sent an advanced guard, a regiment of German-Lorraine troops under General Marcy to that village with a mission to reconnoiter the army of Bassigny.

General Marcy was asleep in the defenses of his lodgments and on the 16 November, Torubadel, Major-General of Weimar's army surprised Marcy's army by falling on so swiftly they did not have time to fire a shot from their muskets. They fell upon the Lorraines, Germans and Croates and cut them to pieces, took prisoners while the rest fled in wild disorder. The inhabitants retreated to the monastery of the Capucins, which they considered an island of mercy, but the army (Germans and Croates) soon broke down the doors and demanded 14,300 francs and took four bourgeois as hostage for the sum which was to be paid within one week. In the meantime, Lamboy (English general) (enemy of French and ally of the Burgendoians) arrived with four thousand horsemen, forcing Tourgbadel (German) to retreat into the monastery and defended themselves for a long enough time that permitted Weimar himself to come to their aid and help them disengage and escape. Lamboy hotly pursued them during their retreat to Coiffy and came so close to the Duke of Saxony (German general Weimar) that he was obliged to turn around and defend himself with his epee. Just at that moment, however a brigade of one

CLINCHCAMP

Google Earth

thousand horseman attacked and Weimar escaped capture by pulling on his bridle and racing away to the headquarters of Gallass.

The ransom not having been paid, Swedish soldiers, using four cannon and much armaments, with pillaging and flames (24 November 1636) leveled the place. (Coiffy) They then turned and threw themselves on Jonvelle (24 miles NE), who now without any soldiers, were well caught, but despite the clever defense tactics of Fauqueir-d'Aboncourt-Chauvirey, their governer (27 November 1636), happily for them the Swedes found themselves masters of all the

CLINCHCAMP

munitions amassed inside the fortress. Weimar established a good garrison and established his winter quarters at Torcenay, where he rested until 15 December.

On 25 December Gallass returned suddenly in front of Jonvelle with Colonel Picolomini. They chased the Swedes and pushed them, with his epee at their kidneys all the way to Bourbonne (about 5 miles NE of Rougeux) Satisfied with this thin and tardy victory, he immediately returned to his winter quarters in

Jonville where he reposed quite a number of days. Eventually he took to the road back to Germany, leaving a contingent of six thousand soldiers for the defense of the Franche Comte(65 miles SE of Rougeux) (21 January 1637)

The traces of the passage of Gallass in our country was funeral and deep. A long time Bassigny continued to tremble in remembrances of those six weeks that they had been subject to the ravaging of the Germans and after they left the devastation that lasted during the following years. We say that during the awful terror, the inhabitants of Coiffy added to their litany of Saints the following supplication; *"From Gala et a Forka libers nos Domine; de Gallass and de Forkaiz, deliver us, Seigneur."*

Many of the villagers of the Amance Valley have given their bad ground the name of Gallass. That word has become a synonym in our language for glutton.

The field general was gone but the war did not stop, The governors of the Compte have decided that the national garrisons would be placed in the villes and the chateaux of the interior and that these strangers would guard the frontier. Jussey, (20 miles E) Chauvirey, La Rochelle, Saucourt, Artaufontaine, Champlitte, etc., were within the border of the Germans. Lodged at Jonvelle (24 miles E) was Bornival (German General) with a regiment of Croates. The Lorraines are posted along the Soane. As far as the French are concerned, they have abandoned our country and have thrown us into the country of the enemy. During the month of March, the Duke of Longueville (with troops from Germany and Lorraine) invaded the bailiff of Aval from the South-West and Grancey, governer of Montbeliard, advanced on Doubs. (About 80 miles SE) The Duke of Saxony and of Hallier followed the route of Besancon, for the purpose of giving a hand to Grancey under the walls of that village. After having taken Romange (18 June) (50 miles N) he presented himself in front of Chamlitte who had the courage to undergo artillery fire, but finally capitulated with 90,000 livres (21 June 1637) ransom. Bassigny (our region) found themselves open to devastation of the Comtois, Lorraines, and the Germans, who pillage and incinerate our villages, massacre the peasants or make them labor with the beasts. On 22 February 1637, the Croates returned to once again ravage Hortes, (4 miles N) killed two persons and committed other terrible acts. The priest, Nicolas Joliot was forced to hide himself in a cave of a creek.

The cold water so incommoded him that he died 20 March 1637. On 26 June forty-five those Croates brought six prisoners from Hortes, three from Rosoy, and a large amount of cattle. On 9 July, Bornival (German), head of a detachment surprised Fayl-Billot a half hour before daylight and sounded the tocsin. The population, distraught, sought refuge in the church. The enemies identified the hiding place, shot twenty

persons, took one hundred twenty, including the priest, M. Carbollot, and all the beasts they found in the village. In the meantime a party of soldiers conducted the prisoners to Jonvelle, while others went directly to Corgirnon and Torcnay where they committed the same acts. Descending down to Chaudenay (75 miles SE), they threatened to burn the village unless they were paid one hundred pistols. The seigneurs of the village were unable to immediately

JUSSEY

furnish such an amount so the soldiers started fires that ruined it from top to bottom. Only two houses escaped destruction. They then passed to Rosoy (3 miles N) where they made the priest a prisoner with his nephew, Simon Millot, who is brought with them to Jonville (24 miles NE) The priest of Rosoy (5 miles W) is jailed for six weeks and was not released until payment of sixty pistoles for his ransom and for his nourishment. Three weeks after, in the night of 29 and 30 July 1637, the sieurs Chevillon and Fauquier of Aboncourt accompanied by six hundred men of the garrison of Dole, Gray, Chauvirey and Jonvelle and arrived in front of Langres and burned the suburb of Aages-aux-Moines, killed an old gardener. They then retired to Chauvirey (100miles SE) with a grand booty and many prisoners in addition to two demoiselles from Langres who had gone to the fauberg (suburbs) to escape the 'peste noir' (black death)

The history of this sad epoch was recorded in a style clear, correct enough, and with a naiveté that has charmed us, by the author whose name is Clement Macheret. He was born at Hortes in 1605 of Claude Macheret, laborer and of Etiennette Bourrier. How he showed good dispositions toward piety, for studies one of his uncles, a monk and under-prior at Clairvaux (Cistercian) was charged with his education. He was placed at the college at Chaumont, and at Dijon and from there placed on pension (room and board) in 1623 under the canon Bernard Meguin. The young man then was received at Clairvaux in the habit of a novice. But he did not embrace definitively the religious life.

His uncle died and he returned to Hortes and Langres. Ordained around 1630, he was made chaplain of Saint-Pierre and rector of the hospital of the Chapter, called today the hospital Saint-Laurent.

We know few details of his life relating to the functions of his ministry, the main constraint due to the bad and unhappy events we suffered during his life time. In 1633, as an indication of the qualities of our last priest, he returned to our village and began picking up the pieces and try to begin returning to a better life. The Sunday 6 May 1635, upon the request of Prince Conde, upon his arrival at Langres, on his way to Nancy, the abbot Macheret celebrated a mass in presence of this high personage in the Episcopal chapel to honor the restoration of the precious ornaments of the reverend seigneur bishop.

By virtue of a patent, delivered by M. Zamet, retired at Bar-sur-Seine, M. Baudot, vicar general conferred upon our abbot, 23 March 1637 the office of cure of Hortes, vacant since the pastor, M. Joliot, had finally died March 20 from hiding in the freezing stream a month previously. As soon as circumstances permitted, after his assignment to Hortes was announced, he carried to his native church the consolations and comfort that they sorely needed. To have Jena Parisel, his vicar, released from prison, who had been taken all the way to Salins (100 miles S) by the Coates, he furnished forty livres. In 1647 there was no longer a priest at Hortes. We find that he was in charge of other offices he filled for the bishop at Langres as a result of the siege and wars. His death arrived in 1669. He had composed six works of history, remains of manuscripts and in the last one, reaching even as far as us, was a book edited for Doctor Bougard. 1.

To attract Divine benefits to France, Louis XIII was happy to place his royal personage under the protection of Tres Saint-Verge. His declaration is dated 10 February 1638. On 2 May of the same year, by letter given at Compiegne and addressed to the bishop of Langres, he expressed the desire, that every year, on the day of the glorious Assumption of the Virgin Mary, Mother of God, we make, with all the solemnity possible, a general procession that includes all the magistrates as well as the people. Consolation is needed for our forefathers who have been struck with all the horrors under the sun.

The 15 May of the same year(1638), the soldiers of Duke of Lorraine and the Croates of the garrison of Jonvelle, under Captain Bornival appeared and have extorted eight hundred pistoles at Bourbonne, and returning extorted more ransom at Coiffy-le-Haut (11 miles N) One inhabitant, from a hidden place, fired a gun shot at the officers. The troop, furiously indulging in pillage, and rape, set fire to our houses, massacred without pity three hundred fifty-eight persons of both sexes and all ages, among others the venerable cure, Jean Goirot, and took a great number of prisoners. The report is that a stream of blood ran all the way to the bottom of the mountain. We see in the church and inscription that recalls this awful event. The following day the nearby communities, especially Coiffy-la-Ville, (13 mi NE) Laneuvelle, (12 mi NE) Chezeaux, (7 mi NE) Lavernoy, (8 mi SE) Varennes (8 mi N) and Arbigny (6 mi NE) were, in their turn, ravaged and burned.

The incursions continued. On 24 March 1639 fourteen Croates of the garrison of Raucourt captured two laborers of Hortes with their plows. On 16 April, one hundred twenty cavaliers came to Bougey, (30 mi NW) penetrated into the village at two o'clock in the morning, made a siege of the church, killed Julien Virey who was meditating, and stole twenty-six horses hidden in the base of the chapel adjacent to the church. The theft of these horses, valued at three thousand ecus, prevented the inhabitants from plowing and cultivating their fields. At dawn on 3 June, the soldiers of Jonvelle entered Marcilly, (8 mi NW) seized the priest, Jean Gauthier; the prosecutor, Facenet, and fifteen other persons and a number of beasts. During their retirement they burned a large part of Chamigny-sous-Varnnes.

CHEZEAUX

The 14 of July the detachments of Jonvelle, Jussey and Vesoul pilfered the Franchisis-sous-Langres (7 mi NE), the two Orbigny and Plesnoy. They divided their booty close to Lavernoy (12 mi N) and rejoined their garrisons without concern. During the early months of 1640, the country was relatively tranquil but on the 8 of June a traitor of Coiffy, named Chateauneuf, who the Langrois had hanged in effigy, came with the Croates and devastated Plesnoy (9 mi NW)

129

They seized many beasts, burned a dozen houses and killed three men. On 25 August soldiers from Gray (30 miles S) were seen close to Noidant-le-Chatenois and were put to flight. They were followed as far as the hills of Pailly, Chanlindry, Torcenay, Rosoy (4mi NW) and Hortes (4 miles N) They thought to retreat to the woods of Beaulieu (2 miles N) but the inhabitants of Hortes were waiting. A young apothecary accompanying the outlaws, to save his life, promised two hundred pistoles; but he had to pass, like the others, at the end of a sword. None survived to carry the news to the Count. Having learned that the seigneur Yves, governor of the chateau of Pressigny (8 miles SE), had been called by the King at Dijon, the enemies came to take beasts from the village (of Pressigny) The garrison of Jonvelle burned Bonnecourt (13 miles NW) , brought

CHEZEAUX

all the horses of Andilly, pillaged Bourbonne and attempted to take the strong house of La Ferte (7 miles E) At Suaucourt (17 miles SE) six men and twenty-six beasts were removed. Other soldiers stole everything they could at Coiffy-le-Bas (10 miles N) and Rougeux; but they were chased by the peasants. On 1 February 1641, they took from Rougeux two men and two women. Some days after they seized some beasts at Torcenay and three men there and one at Fayl-Billot and one at Bize. They effected a night raid on horseback as far as Chezeaux (7 miles N) They seized the 18 April

CHEZEAUX

two men and six horses from Hortes (4 miles N) On their side, they fell, twice, into ambushes, near Jonvelle (24 miles NE), of the Marquis de Bourbonne, governer of Champagne and rescued sixty-five prisoners. The seigneur of Yves also charged them on the hill of Pressigny and killed or took many prisoners men who had hidden inside the church of Savigny.

The poor laborers were exhausted and desolated. Those who had recovered by the sweat of their brow, now were sunk in despair; they found everything ravaged. The horses, cattle and other animals, in addition to all their labor had been ravaged or ruined. The furrow's remain unplowed and consequently unproductive. During this general distress in place of the beasts that had been stolen, it was necessary for the peasants to harness themselves and pull the

LOUIS XIII

plows with their own strength, their energy greatly lessened by the scarcity of food that had been stolen or consumed by the soldiers. Prominent at Fayl-Billot, Torcenay, and Choiseul was a father and three of his sons who would plow a bichet of ground each day for thirty sous. (A biche, called 'raz' in earlier centuries, is a container that will contain a given amount of grain and was widely use during these centuries. The size of the container varied from place to place and was very inconsistent. The area of a bichet of ground is impossible to calculate today. Some writers say it the area that could produce three sheaves of grain; others say it was the amount that could be sown, however this would seem to require a considerable amount of prepared soil because broadcasting seed is not a time consuming job. Obviously manpower could not exceed that of an ox which traditionally could plow one acre per day and from which comes our current dimension of an acre)

Increasing the misery was the extensive damage to the vineyards of the Amance by the soldiers but also from the intemperate weather. On 22 April 1639 a deep freeze burned all the vines, then on 22, 23,

24 June freezes destroyed all hope of a harvest. Wine became scarce and very expensive. The year following, on October 8 and 9 all the raisins and even the wood on certain (grape) species, such as the gamets and whites were frozen. The cold was so intense that on the 28 of October the ground was covered with a foot of snow, any snow being rare.

The priest of Hortes, to whom we discussed these details, recalled the intolerable things the barbarous garrison of Jonvelle had inflicted upon their prisoners. They threw them, pell-mell into tight cells without air or light and they often had to eat grass raw and they had nothing to bandage their wounds. They give them the strappado, a punitive military punishment consisting of

The strappado.

lifting the prisoner by his hands, which are tied behind his back, up on a high pole of wood and then dropping him just to near the ground, savagely destroying their shoulder joints. The (Germans) soldiers engage the women in acts that are greatly revolting; many die under their hands; others were murdered by having explosives ignited inside their entrails.The governer, Fauquier de Aboncourt, seigneur de Chauvirey, Ouge, La Quarte et Vitrey, was not an accomplice of these tortures and atrocities committed by the Germans, but he was nevertheless one of the boldest and most determined to do business in the territories of France.

On 23 July 1641, taking with him his men of Chauvirey, he (Fauquier) fell on Torcenay at eight in the morning and returned with forty-three beasts. Six days after, he reunites in his chateau, with two hundred fifty pietons and one hundred knights, provided by the garrisons of Gray, Jonville, Ray, Suaucourt and Chaivoreu and conducted them to the doors of Langres (14 mi W of Rougeux) Having found both Aages-aux-Moines(?) behind the houses of the Franchises (French) and herds of sheep and other beasts belonging to the butchers of the village and others, which they herded to their Count. During the height of the tour of Fergeux four volleys were fired from cannon. Then the Langrois (German), indignant at such presumption, began a pursuit and chased them to the village of Rougeux, a dependent of the parish of Hortes. The Comtois were on top the hill and the Langois below and they fired a discharge so vivid that they forced the Langois to cease their project, wounding and killing many men, including mortally wounding the chief of the troupe, Governer Fauquier de Aboncourt. On the eve of his departure his spouse knelt before him to pray that he be forgiven for the terrible job of partisan. He responded that he could not avoid going out this time but promising, to console her, that this would be his last time. And henceforth, he did not ever attack the French. He told the truth without knowing it.

Dependent on our troops, who had already taken, the year previously, Champlitte and Montureux-sur-Soane prepared themselves to once again invade Franche-Compte. The General du Hallier, governer of Lorraine, Charles de Livron, governor of Champagne, the Count de Grancey, the Baron de Marey, knight of Tonnerre, etc, reunited at Bourbonne to form an army of seven to eight thousand men with a large number of cannon. On 15 September we appeared in front of Jonvelle whose garrison had burned more than six thousand houses in France and depopulated Bassigny (the Amance Valley region) Bornival was gone and since the death of Fauquier d'Aboncourt, Gaucher du Magny was now commander (against the French) of

YEARS OF PLAGUES AND EPIDEMICS	YEARS OF FAMINE	YEARS OF UNUSUAL WEATHER
1601, 1602, 1604, 1605, 1607, 1608,1609, 1610, 1611, 1612, 1613, 1614, 1615, 1616, 1624, 1625, 1626, 1627, 1627, 1629, 1630, 1631, 1632, 1677, 1638, 1644, 1645, 1646, 1647, 1648, 1649, 1650,1651, 1652, 1653, 1654, 1664 1665, 1670, 1680,	1621,-1648 1649,-1650 1651,-1652 1694,	1603,-1698—EXTERMELY COLD,-16.8C IN PARIS, LITTLE ICE AGE DEEP SNOW—DEEP COLD-LATE FROST—SNOW IN JUNE-FLOODING-RIVER FROZEN SOLID—EARLY FREEZE-EXCESSIVE RAIN—EXTREMELY HOT SUMMERS MIXED WITH VERY COLD SUMMERS AND VERY WET SUMMERS-

OWNED BY AUTHOR

132

the army. We invested the place, took it by assault, and the soldiers were passed through with the sword or hanged from the battlements (butchered)!

The governer was brought in front of de Marcy, first at Langres then at Grancey. We demolished the great tower and burned the soldiers quarters of the village. The army then moved in front of the two Chauvirey Monday 23 September (100 mi SW) Chauvirey-le-Vieil and the Chateau-Dessus, owned by Antoine du Chatelet, made their submission. Forty cannon shots fired against the walls of the Chateau-Dessus were enough to open a mouth sufficient to allow penetration. Meanmoins, the captain, persisted in its defense. Eventually, around noon, he rendered discretion and found himself hung from the door opening of the chateau for having continued such a futile resistance. The enemy soldiers were spared and came out without baggage or arms each carrying a white flag in their hands. We did no harm to the vicar of the parish and retired into the fort where we gave him a safe conduct pass to go wherever he wanted to go with the objects of the church because the chateau had to be destroyed by orders of the King. After the enemy had been taken away, the French and inhabitants of the village tried to tear down its heavy walls but the prevot of Langres objected and set fire to the battlements. The incendiary spared neither the chapel or the hall of arms. A large house of the village, in which we could have defended ourselves, was also consumed by flames.

The Seigneur de Trestondans liked better to abandon his chateau rather than deal as a traitor with the French. At the approach of the French, the garrison made their escape, abandoning everything, including the noon meal at which they were being served bread, meat and wine still on the table. But the soldiers did not trust those enemies and were afraid the food had been poisoned. They decided to test some of the food on their dogs, and in very little time they perished; all had been poisoned.

The fortress was burned and fell into ruin (25 September) The next day we seized the chateau of Artaufontaine, who lost only his big tower and the roof of his house. We saved the rest to have a place to lodge the troops of Marquis de Francieres, governer of Langres.

Vesoul (36 miles S of Rougeux) capitulated and Scey-sur-Saone were taken and a garrison was recruited under the orders of Baron de Saint-Clair. Ray surrendered, and the Seigneur of Yves, Captain of Pressigny, at the head sixty men was placed in charge of guarding. We report other advantages: soon the places of our country, except Gray, were in the power of our army. The Count de Grancey took measures necessary to secure our conquests. After a halt at Champlitte, he came to lodge at Fayl-Billot (2 mi S of Rougeux) and villages surrounding to better occupy the posts that His Majesty had assigned to him

The following year 1642, with General Hallier, La Mothe (8 mi S) was attacked. The defending garrison was captained by the famous Clicquot, who ravaged Bassigny by his frequent excursions. He was resting at that place on from 25 July to 12 August.

Then, after an order of the court, he departed for Lyon to maintain peace during the execution of Cinq-Mars 12 September 1642 (Henri Coiffier de Ruzé, Marquis de Cinq-Mars was a favorite of King Louis XIII of France. Cardinal Richelieu had introduced the young Cinq-Mars to Louis, hoping the king would take Cinq-Mars as a lover, apparently with success. The Cardinal believed he could easily control Cinq-Mars. Instead, Cinq-Mars pressed the king for important favors and tried to convince the king to have Richelieu executed. He led the last and most nearly successful of the many conspiracies against the king's powerful first minister)

Jacques de Thou, was also scheduled for execution September 12. (he was a councillor to the parliament of Paris in 1626 and a consular d'État shortly afterwards. He was unwise enough to link himself to Cardinal Richelieu's enemies. His guilty deed between Anne of Austria and Marie de Rohan was pardoned, but he fell in the conspiracy between Spain and Cinq-Mars, King Louis XIII's favorite. For not revealing what he knew of the conspiracy, his silence was taken as proof of guilt and he was beheaded on the same day as Cinq-Mars on Richelieu's orders.)

The Duke of Lorraine informed the governor of Comte, Claude de Beauffremont, Baron of Scey-sur-Soane and exhorted him to chase the French from the village of Amnont. He eagerly assembled an army in order to reconquer the chateau that Count Grancy had grabbed. He advanced near Scey. The captain of Saint-Clair, absent, had given the commandment to

Romprey, his lieutenant, who, after the preliminary bombardment laid down his arms. Saint-Remy, that same day, was carried and the next day Artaufontaine (18 mi SE of Rougeux)

Beauffremont immediately invested the village of Ray, (30 mi W) and launched fifty volleys of cannon which made a large breech through the wall. Subsequently the Seigneur of Yves, through his large trumpet shouted, *"What good are these walls that you now hold that you took from us as easily as we retook them from you?"* The brave captain responded with despair, *"I don't have anything more in France, and I stay in the chateau as a place to live. I have decided to be buried gloriously in these ruins rather than be dragged into a shameful miserable old age."*

But Count Grancy returned from Lyon and found himself at Voisines before he passed into Franche-Compte. As soon as he called governer de Bourgogne and the cavalry of Tavannes and of Bassiguy and the horses of Hallier, they captured Langres and took munitions and set out for Fayl-Billot (2 mi South) where they arrived at night on 18 September.

The cannons (apparently those of Fayl Billot) grumbled, and he shouted, *"Gentlemen, courage, it is us."*

At two hours in the morning, he sounded the horn and after a March of six grand leagues (24 mi SE of Rougeux) arrived at the chateau Ray and fell unannounced upon the enemy. Then they captured Champlitte (18 mi E of Rougeux) Upon this victory they retired to the hill of Varnnes (9 mi NW) and during this March, with much impetuosity, charged and captured twenty-two principal seigneurs, captured their cannon, munitions and baggage. The captain of Yves, after resisting a siege of three days, occupied himself in attempts to repair the breech with the hope that assistance will arrive in time. He was resisting just for the honor of a victory. During the combat, on 9 September 1642 the Count de Grancy was wounded in the leg and the captain of Saint-Clair killed with five knights and eight infantry. On the 22 September at six o'clock in the morning Grancey entered Langres in triumph and the cannons taken from the enemy fired in salute to Saint-Ferjeux in celebration of the victory. At the request of the bishop, we remained until 11 October 1642 and assisted in repairing the Episcopal palace. That day we promenaded the prisoners to release them upon their oath not to pick up arms again. We then permitted them to return to their homes.

As for the Count (Count de Grancy), he directed himself toward Paris and we accompanied him as far as Saint-Loup where an escort of honor, composed of the noblemen and the militia of Langres. Arriving at the capital he felt more keenly the pain of his wound. Louis XIII and Cardinal Richelieu made his visit one of felicity of his victory. In recompense of his services, they rewarded him with the baton of Marechal.

1. Ces ouvrages sont: Cataloge historique des doyens de l'eglise cathedrale; 2. Sacra Lingonum ditis a Deo plantata, terram implens ac operiens montes umbra sus, quae estendit palmites sous usque ad mare, etc. (Il s'agit ici des hommes illustres de l'eglise de Langres, devenus abbes, eveques, au cardinaux); 3. Vie de Saint-Urgbain, eveque de Langres: 4. Recueil de pieces curieuses tirees du chartrier de l'eveche de Langres: 5. Vers a la lauange de eveques de Langres. 6. Journal de ce qui e'est passe de memorable a Langres et aux environs depuis 1628 jusqu'en 1658 (Voir Revue Champenoise, p. 355

This defeat wiped away the Comtois, however those that remained continued to be impatient to continue their excursions and their brigandage.

On 26 September 1642 a number of soldiers of the garrisons of Rupt et de Scey-sur-Soane killed in cold blood a man of Pressigny (20 miles South) who was using a plow to labor on the territory of the village. They stole, likewise, all the beasts of Pierrefaites (4 miles E) that consisted of three horses, a cow and three goats. The 20 October 1642, twenty-five knights hid in ambush close to the farm of Haut-Chemin in order to surprise the inhabitants of Rougeux. The inhabitants knew, and called some cabinets (soldiers?) in the neighborhood, who killed one and put the others to flight. Nine days afterwards twenty men of Scey-sur-Soane came during the night to pillage the abbey of Beaulieu (2 miles N) But they were discovered before they could execute their project and hid in the woods until after dark. When darkness fell they entered Maizieres (2 miles NE) and stole four hemmes(?) and all seven horses. We pursued them to the edge of the Amance where one drowned in his attempt to cross, and we made four prisoners.

In January 1643 they ravaged Varennes (10 miles N) and took a number of prisoners and twelve beasts; at Hortes (4 miles NW), after destroying three houses, they took a boy, a servant and three horses; at Rosoy (5 miles NW) they demolished two houses and stole six horses, a cow and six hundred livres.

The 8 February 1643, a Sunday, some soldiers of Gray (30 miles S) penetrated the primary door of the church in Chaumont (36 miles NW), and took all the contents the believers had but the peasants so tellingly defended themselves that the enemies were obliged to retire without any booty. Others tried to force, in vain, the door in the chapel at Celsoy but seized one unfortunate woman, then went to sleep in the woods of Hortes, ruined the lodge of the tree cutters, laid hands on the servant guarding the woods and on the beasts of Francois Roux, merchant of wood.

The 25 February, they presented themselves in front of the barricade of Balesmes (120 miles N) We repulsed them but they dared to plunder up to the doors of Langres (15 miles W) The 23 March, twenty-five knights of Rupt appeared at Celsoy and at Montlandon, took six men and fourteen horses, at Torceny a plow and at Corgirnon, another plow belonging to Seur Robert, surgeon of the Marechal of Estree. The 15 May the garrison of Scey scaled the walls and burned the church at Anrosey and took those who had taken refuge there and also took twelve

135

people and killed three others. Ten days after they stole the beasts of the lady of Laneuvelle and a part of those at Bourbonne. The soldiers of Saint-Remy and Demangevelle fought with the inhabitants of Rougeux, Maizieres, Hortes and Rosoy (30 May 1643) and at the end six of the enemies found rest in the terrain. A great deal more would have been massacred if the Captain Romprey, in garrison at Varennes had not arrived. He stopped his men and removed the men, under guard, any who lied to him and bound their hands like prisoners of war. In June and October new raids were inflicted on (surrounding villages of Rougeux) Torcenay, Corgirnon, Les Loges, Fayl-Billot, Charmoy, etc.

Since the enemy have been ravaging our country, we must, to wit, says Macheret, with our garrisons we have inside our chateaux of France, and make parallel war on the poor peasants and the beasts of the Count. During the night of 19/20 January 1643, thirty partisans leave Pressigny under the orders of Seigneur Boulanger, crossed the woods of Preigney and of and arrived unexpectedly in front of the chateau of Bougey. (30 mi NW) In an instant they had penetrated the wall with levers and picks, and entered the fort, shouting, *"France! Victory! Render your arms or you are dead!"*

Suddenly awakened, the troop bravely defended itself without confusion. The trumpeter and the tambour sound the alarm, we run to the church, the tocsin called the population and our men are repulsed, and lost some killed and some wounded or prisoners.

On 6 August (1642) of the same year the Captain Ducerf, quit guarding the chateau of Voncourt (12 miles S), and undertook again a course in Comte (The Franche-Comté, the former 'Free County' of Burgundy, which bordered Switzerland and the Alsace, and an enemy of France) He was at the head of several men and was promised assistance in France, but unhappily he encountered a detachment of the enemy who forced them to drop their arms and rendered them prisoner of war in the ville of Gray (30 miles S) The seigneur of Montcot, Captain de Rolampont, at the head of fifty men, was more successful at the environs of Ray.

The Baron de Marmier-Lonwy, whom we wanted to arrest, made battle but we made him prisoner and exchanged him for Ducerf.

A month after Captain Romprey left Varennes with his knights and his soldiers, advanced all the way to the environs of Sacey-sur-Saone. But the Comtois ambushed them in a place favorable to them and killed one man, captured six and put the rest to flight.

On the 14 September 1636, the troops of Gallaus entered the villages of Rougeux and Montesson took what they wanted and left the villages in flames.

This scourge raged our settlement at Langres, and also in our villages. The war, the famine, the great amount of hot weather of the autumn of 1636 caused and encouraged severe epidemics of maladies extremely contagious. There was a great number of victims; the country was depopulated. The 'peste noir' did not finish until 1637.

SUPPLEMENTS FROM ABBOT MULSON AND OTHERS

At two o'clock in the morning of March 24, 1639, fourteen Croates attacked Hortes (4 miles NW), and Julian Virey, praying inside the church, was run through by their swords and his blood spilled on the steps of the sanctuary. The murderers stole all the valuables from the church, including the chalice and twenty-eight horses the villagers had hidden in the basement. The loss of these animals made it impossible for them to till their fields but in spite of losing their most valuable possession, they courageously attached themselves to their plows and attempted to plant their life supporting crops. A father and his three sons hired themselves out for this work at thirty sous the day. But the misery was not to end. On 22 April 1639 the poor were singled out for further suffering due to an extreme frost which killed all the vine buds and again on 22 June, 23rd, and 24th, (Killing frosts in June!) killing all hope for a harvest. The price of wine grew very high due to its scarcity and then in the following year on 8 and 9 October all the grapes, blue and white, were ruined by a profound frost and a cold so intense that on the 28th the ground became covered with one foot of snow. (Snow being a rarity in this region)

On July 23rd, 1639, an army gathered from Gray, Jonville, and Ray, attacked Langres. After firing four volleys of cannon and stealing a number of sheep and cattle, the army was surprised by a sudden counter attack of the inhabitant's, was defeated, and driven East through the village of Rougeux. Brigandage continued on a regular basis throughout 1642. On October 20th, twenty-five horsemen, who had prepared an ambush near the edge of Rougeux, were sighted, and calling those men who had guns, the villagers in turn surprised the horseman, killing one and causing the others to flee. The day after, twenty men came in the night to pillage Abbey of Beaulieu but were discovered in the midst of their plot and fled to hide in the woods. The next day they entered Maizieres (about one mile from Rougeux) and captured four men and seven horses who were never seen again. On 25 February 1643, six soldiers of Saint-Remy et de Demangevelle were killed in a battle with the residents of Rougeux, Maizieres, Hortes and Rosoy.

Depravations by bands of malcontents who roamed the countryside, continued even after the treaty between Franche-Compte and the two ducs of Burgundy was signed in 1643. During the night of 20 January (1643) the Militia of Pressigny (9 miles South), under the orders of Boulangier, secretly traversed the woods of Progeny and of Charlier (60 miles South) Led by a traitor of Augicourt, named Claude Moniot, just under the walls of the chateau of Bougey, (30 mi NW) and aided by diverse weapons, pierced the walls and ran into the fortress shouting, *"France! France! Victory! Death to those who do not surrender".* The garrison alarmed, took up their arms, blew their trumpets, sounded their drums and spread the alarm. One soldier entered the church and sounded his tocsin which alerted the inhabitants who took up their arms and attacked the assailants, killing 22 and capturing 18. On May 7, troops of Demangevelle struck Basingny and completely defeated by the Militia of Rougeux, Maizeries, Hortes and Rosey. The contest continued on both sides causing incalculable injury and suffering.

CHAPTER XIII
OF THE TREATY OF 1643 AND THE PEACE OF 1659

1. TREATY BETWEEN THE TWO BOURGOGNES ----- 2. INCURSIONS OF THE GARRISON OF LA MOTHE ----- 3. REMISSION OF TAXES ------- 4. PRAYERS FOR GOOD WEATHER------ 5. THE GARRISON OF AIGREMONT----- 6. PASSAGE AND STATIONING OF TROOPS ------- 7. AMBUSH OF PRESSIGNY. ----- 8. BRIGANDAGE IN LORRAINE ----- 9. FAMINE ----- 10. KING STANSLAUS. ----- 11. NOBILITY AT SAINT-PEREGRIN------- 12. THE GARRISON OF BELFORT RAVAGE OUR COUNTRY. ---- 13. TRANSLATION OF RELIQUES OF SAINT DIDIER ----- 14.THE PROCESSION OF FAYL-BILLOT TO LANGRES. ----- 15. CONCLUSION OF THE PEACE

The open war with Spain (The 30 Years War (1635-1648) started with a promising victory for the French at Les Avins in 1635) The following year Spanish forces based in the Southern Netherlands hit back with devastating lightning campaigns in Northern France that left French forces reeling and the economy of the region in tatters.The Parliament of Dijon and that of Dole concluded, 1 October 1643, a truce that lasted until 19 November.

In the month of May 1643, the famine encompassed the environment of Langres (The result of the wars and the extreme cold and deep snow into June followed by incessant rain of 'The Little Ice Age' from 1603 to 1693) The starving and poverty stricken have noting to eat but dogs and horses. The same at Mussy where all they had was the gross carcass of a horse. No one had ever before seen a similar rarity of grain over such a large region. The people of Langres (15 miles W) wanted to buy bread but two days passed before the bakers house before they could buy any but the price was as much as ten bichet which they cold not afford.

The lapse in temperature stopped the hostilities in Franche-Compte, in the duchy of Bourgogne, the Bassigny Champenoise, the villas of Langres and the Chaumont region. This suspension of arms that, according to the terms of the treaty, which the kings of France and Spain were not required to ratify, was made public at Dijon 7 October 1643 and prolonged to 1 January 1644.

Then, instead of returning to Franche-Compte, the provocateurs and friends of war began an advance against La Mothe, a fortress deep inside Lorraine. The 6 November they killed the Seigneur Regnier, lieutenant of justice of Orbigny-au-Mont, captured his brother, his son, their horses and carriages. On 13 December it was invested. We suggested to Captain Ducerf that he request the Lorraines partisans to approach and protect La Mothe but it was finished. After a resistance of seven months La Mothe capitulated on 1 July 1645. The 7th, the garrison came out and they were permitted entrance into the hands of the French. The peasants of the election of Langres were taxed for the maintenance of the army. The counsel of the King had regarded the complaints we had sent him and determined to resolve the siege of that place and placed in charge, Magalotti, marshal of the camp.

After the destruction of La Moth, Bassigny (our local region), considering the times, enjoyed a period of tranquility. To facilitate the sale of the harvest in 1644 it was necessary to form a protective militia to be paid by the public.

The 18 of the same month, while the inhabitants of Coiffy-le-Bas (10 miles N) were visiting the seigneur of La Neuvelle, the enemy arrived at his chateau. Those terrible marauders, about two hundred fifty in number, fell on the village with sixty wagons, stole all the clothes, linens, vestments, one hundred twenty muids (approximately 300 gallons) of wine and hauled it all to La Mothe. During the night of 5 and 6 February 1644, they took, at Chezeaux, (7miles N) four men and seven horses. The 24th they encountered Claude Gorges, of Hortes, (4 miles NW) Reverend of Langres, and took him with two plows in their chariot. They brutalize, at the same time, Montigny, Orbigny-au-Val, Bannes, Culmont, Chalindrey, Celsoy, Montlandon, Noidant-Chatenois, etc., and force the villages to pay exorbitant contributions and capture prisoners for ransom.Our region was so ravaged and ruined a great number of times with a great number of other villages that they found themselves unable to pay their taxes. They had a forgiveness from 1639 until 1 January 1645. But at the end of July 1647 twenty of them notably Varennes, the two Coiffys, and Hortes had not yet paid their tax. The reduction was continued by the bailiffs because they were still reduced to begging.

At the frontier, there was still violence committed by certain brigands who retreated with their booty into the woods known as Trou de la Quarte between Champagne and Franche-Comte. The envoy of the king and prevot of the Marechaussee de Langres ordered the assembly of the neighboring communities to cut the trees. The French and the Comtois wanted to cut the trees (to improve their security) in their respective territories themselves.

In June 1649 the rainfall was so abundant and continued so that we were afraid we would not be able to harvest the fruits of the ground. To obtain cessation of the scourge (reoccurrence of the Black Plague) Monseigneur Zamet ordered prayers, processions and commission of other good works, particularly invocation of the saints of the Diocese. They opened the casket of Saint Gregoire, bishop and Saint Gengoul, martyr, and carried their relics on the grand altar of the cathedral, upon which climbed the people who venerated them with a very edifying devotion. Under the demands of the inhabitants of Varennes, the Chapter donated to their church two pieces of these reliques of their glorious patron and gave a small container to carry these in processions, and the other, on their side, gave permission to lodge, on the hunt on the day of the saint, on their property. We prayed for intercession of the saint that the rain stop. Soon after the people of Langress had made a procession to his chapel, the rain stopped and the temperature raised so that it was very pleasant and perfect for the harvest.

Our territory was made more trouble because of the affairs of Aigremont (22 miles N) During the month of August 1650, the Count of Rosnay sold his place to Charles de Lorraine who hastily installed a garrison. In reaction, a thousand Langroise, conducted by Captain Ducerf, with cannon and munitions surrounded him and began a siege. But the nobles of Bassigny spread a rumor that they were sending a large contingent to raise the siege, causing Ducerf to lift the siege and hurry back to Langres. Ducerf thereafter, with sixty men left Langres and went to Mirecourt to hinder the activities of the soldiers of Aigremont.

The Viscount of Corval also arrived with one thousand men and an equal amount of horsemen. After having passed a day at Fayl-Billot they lodged at Varnnes (9 miles N), the 23 August, and caused a tremendous of damage to everything and demanding supplies of bread and wine. On the 29 August he received an order to identify what it would require to seize Aigremont (22 miles N) and raze it to the ground. The next day at noon he was already at their hill. At the same time two hundred men, with two cannons, went to Langres. Ducerf was still occupied, even after two days, in cutting the trees and ruining the roads through the woods close to Lamarche, to oppose the arrival of reinforcements; but the seigneur de Marey, Baron of Clefmont, had determined the movement of the troops and carried to Langres a letter of the Duke of Orleans, found a pretext to lift the siege a second time. (Duc d'Orléans was a title reserved for French royalty, first created in 1344 by Philip VI in favor of his son Philip of Valois. Known as princes of the blood (princes du sang), the title of Duke of Orléans was given, when available, to the oldest brother of the king. Thus, they formed a collateral line of the French royal family, with an eventual right to succeed to the throne should more senior princes of the blood die out) The militants were still at Saulzures when we told them to turn back on that road. That singular act emboldened the garrison at Aigremont (22 miles N), who, 5 September went all the way to Chatenay-Vaudin (8 miles W) and stole one hundred twenty beasts and imposed a severe contribution from the surrounding villages. At the same time they demanded from Langres two hundred pistoles every month, but the tambour who was charged with this mission was captured and thrown into prison because of his timidity.

Sixty men of the militia under the command of the seigneur of Yves and du Bois posted themselves at Ranconnieres (12 miles N), at Meuse, then Fresnoy (27 miles N) Despite such precaution the Lorraines continued their depravations. The cavalry of Ligneville, stationed at Breuvannes and at Damblain, carried the ravage and incendiary to Gannes, Neuilly-l'Eveque, Bonnecourt (18 miles NW), Meuse, Serqueux, and capture prisoners, Claude de Bollogne, Seigneur of Bonnecourt and the cure of Neuilly. The last was soon redeemed with a passport defending priests from being captured.

The Saturday 29, October, there arrived three hundred men who captured Coiffy-le-Haut (10 miles N), killed the youngster Habigand, burned completely Laneuvelle (12 miles N), except for the church and the chateau, devastated Pouilly, Choiseul, and ignited the fire at the extremities of Parnot (21 miles N), the day of All-Saints (November 1st) Ten others went all the way to Chalancey (31 miles SW), captured three men at Esnoms (24 miles W) and pillaged the barn at Petasse.

We caught them at Belmont (9 miles S), four who are stunned, four at Langres, and two others fleeing are arrested at Fayl-Billot (2 miles S) The 11 December, a Sunday, the soldiers of Aigremont (22 miles N) presented themselves in front of the chateau of Ranconnieres (14 miles N) We fired on them and they set fire to the village and six large houses are consumed; two infants are burned to death. They also burned a great part of Vicq (12 miles N) and Choiseul (24 miles N) Then on 11 January 1651 the captain of Yves had his forty militia surprise the enemy at Aigremont (22 miles N) They threw themselves on a place and grabbed it, despite resistance from the garrison. Soon they began demolition of the chateau. All the villages participated in this work which they have demanded for a long time, and on 31 January, there remained nothing of the antique fortress. The Count de Rosnay and his wife Marguerite de la Baume are convicted of treason and condemned to death with effigies at Langres.

The war was still not done in our country and we had to endure more passages of diverse French troops. In March 1651 the colonel of Champagne was quartered at Marcilly (12 miles N) and his soldiers caused much harm to the peasants.

On Ascension Day 1651, (The observance of this fEast is of great antiquity-probably the 4th century celebrated ton Thursday, the fortieth day of Easter) Marcilly, (12 miles NW) was pillaged, and much preserved food, twenty-five jugs of wine, 300 (hemines) of wheat, a quantity of clothing, kitchen utensils, wagons, harnesses, and 100 animals stolen. They contaminated (with feces) the choir of the church to the extent that the priest felt fire was the only means of decontamination, being incorrect in his assumption that the vault would withstand the conflagration.

The day of Ascension they delivered Hortes (4 miles N) to pillage. They stole one hundred twenty beasts, large and small. Forty-five muids (about 100 gallons) of wine, three hundred hemines of grain, a quantity of linens, clothes, kitchen, chariots, plows, harnesses, etc.

On 8 May 1651 General Rose, ally of Paris and Strasbourg (French and German), with one hundred forty-two cavaliers, three coaches and five chariots of baggage, came to sleep at Fayl-Billot. On 4 June, arriving in Langress vicinity, were thirty companies of the garrison of Stenay, called the regiment of Turenne. They established their headquarters at Thivet (24 miles NW), Nogent (24 miles NW), Montigny, Coiffy-le-Bas (11 miles NE), Coiffy-le-Haut, Poinson-les-Fays

140

(5 miles S), Burrieres-les-Belmont. Chalindrey (5 miles W), Heuilley-Cotton (40 miles S) and Heuilley-le-Grand. These friendly troops, were, to refresh themselves, stationed six weeks and received twelve thousand livres each month taken from the residents of Langres (15 miles W) The presence of this army depleted the local resources without intimidating the enemy.

Twenty-five cavaliers of the garrison of Chatear-sur-Moselle, came the morning of 13 July, (1651) and pillaged Pressigny (9 miles SW) They seized many men and thirty-nine beasts. Ten brave men, mostly young, began a pursuit and caught up with them wading in the Soane. They attacked the cavaliers, killed one, wounded others and returned, safe and sound, with all that had been stolen except one chicken. The Lorraines (Germans), furious, followed their trail, and with reinforcements pulled from Conflans, in all seventeen cavaliers and many foot men they thought to surprise the chateau of Pressigny (7 miles SE) and burn the village, but the peasants, who knew of the project, called to their help volunteers from Savigny, Belmont, Genevrieres, Bellefonds, Tornay, Savigny and other communities surrounding them. The soldiers improvised. Sixty of them prepared an ambush. They massacred ten, wounded five and put the rest to flight. Each of the vainqueres (victors), for his part of the booty had six livres, six sous.

One of the wounded had received several mortal wounds without surrendering his soul. We demanded of him if he had a caricature, that is to say, a marque, a charm, a sorcerer that helped him be contrary to death. *"No, he replied with hauteur, but you won't find me dead until I have been confessed of my sins"*. One of the spectators, full of compassion, called Claude Mathey, cure of Pressigny, who conferred his blessing and after he confessed, gave his absolution, he thereupon immediately died. The assistances intoned the dishabillerant and in the chapel of Notre-Dame-du-Mont Carmel obtained, by the protection of the Very Sainted Virgin, his happy death.

A truce was concluded with the Lorraine. The French army who were besieging Chateau-sur-Moselle was sent to Bassigny (24 miles NW) It stayed there from the 7 to 23 September then it left because it could not survive in that ruined country. The year following 1652, La Fauche, lieutenant of Charles de Lorraine arrived in the environs of Luxeuil and Saint-Loup, came to Alsace and marched against Langres with an army of 6,500 men.

Trailing behind this army was a suite of numerous vivandiers, thieves, women, infants, induced by hunger and for robbery. This troop detached four hundred cavaliers who fell on Morey, Charmes and Bourguignon (93 miles SE) in which the inhabitants experienced the latest brutalities, and their bread, wine, grains, clothes, dishes, money, beasts, in effect, all they possessed were stolen. The brigands used the caves to hide the barrels of goods they could not take with them. It was the 19 April. On the 23 the army camped around Jonvelle (25 miles E) The next day it entered into Bassigny through Bourbonne (17 miles NE) and continued its passage, with all sorts of excesses, including murder, pillage and incendiaries of the nearby villages. At Ranconnieres (14 miles NW) they killed the priest, a venerable old man of sixty years. Langres (14 miles W) feared a reoccurrence and resorted to the divine mercy. The Sacred Sacrament was exposed during two days in each of eleven churches (11 Catholic churches in this small city!) The mayor requested the celebration of nine masses in front of the relics of Saint Didier. At the same time the bourgeois, domestics, teachers, and men of business took to arms. We soon had 2,000 foot soldiers. This good appearance imposed sufficient deterrent to La Fauche, that he turned and descended the Marne ravaging the Valley-des-Ecoilers all the way to Saint-Dixier (86 miles NE)

But another desolation of the fleau (plague) plus the terrible famine swept over our country. The years 1650 and 1651 were extremely wet having given very little grains. On 16 May 1652 the snow fell in abundance, the vines of Vicq, Laneuvelle, Coiffy, Varennes, Anrosey, La Ferte, Hortes, Rougeux, and Rosoy were frozen. Never, in the memory of man, have we seen wine so scarce or so expensive. Wheat sold for six livres the bichet, measure of Langres; rye sold for five livres; barley, four livres, ten sous; wheat, three livres; a michette of bread sells for six

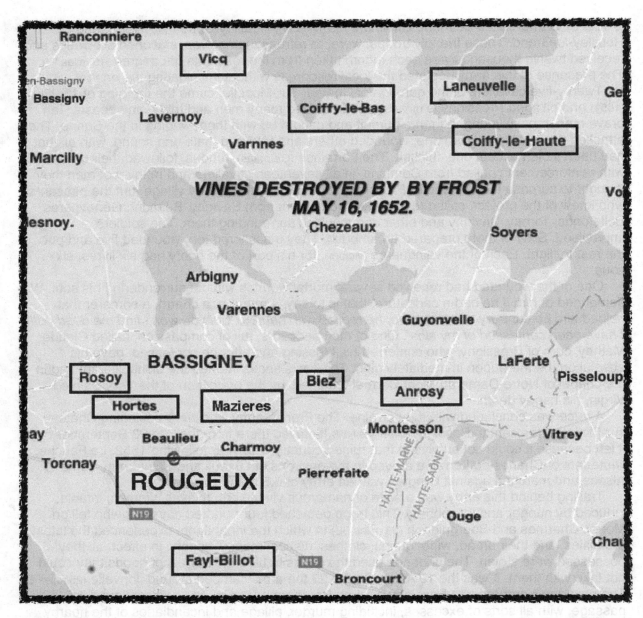

VINES DESTROYED BY BY FROST
MAY 16, 1652.

Ranconniere
Vicq
Laneuvelle
Ge
en-Bassigny
Bassigny
Coiffy-le-Bas
Lavernoy
Coiffy-le-Haute
Varnnes
Marcilly
Vo
esnoy.
Chezeaux
Soyers
Arbigny
Varennes
Guyonvelle
BASSIGNEY
LaFerte
Pisseloup
Rosoy
Biez
Anrosy
Hortes
Mazieres
Montesson
Vitrey
Beaulieu
Charmoy
Torcnay
ROUGEUX
Pierrefaite
HAUTE-MARNE
HAUTE-SAÔNE
Ouge
N19
Chau
Fayl-Billot
N19
Broncourt

sous six deniers. We see crowds of hungry people, hands clasped in supplication, begging the baker to sell them a morsel for their money. They will stand for two days for a tiny quantity of bread. The others, without money and unable to get even a small amount are forced to return home starving and in despair and search for grass in the field as their nourishment. We found a woman dead, her mouth full of grass and holding grass she had gathered, her little infant still alive in her arms. On the roads, we encounter malnourished people looking like skeletons and too weak to continue walking and fall broken. There are a great number with maladies and dead.

In 1653 the regiments of Streuffe and of Bouillon stayed within the region of Langres from 13 February to 7 June. They taxed, for their subsistence four hundred thousand livres. Habitually, they repaid nothing that they took. About this time, the day of Ascension, 22 May, one hundred thirty cavaliers of Bouilon, forced entry into the village and church of Poinson-les-Fayl (6 miles South) where many persons were refugees because it was a part of the Duchy of Bourgogne, and empowered a looting that yielded twenty two thousand livres, a considerable sum for the region during those days of time. (They certainly did not get it from the poverty stricken peasants!)

Two months after, we arrived at the most grand party of the noblesse of Bassigny. There were there, among others, Count de Tavannes, Seigneur of Pailly and of Prangey; de Couvlanc, Seigneur of Piepape; de Lanques, Baron of Fouvent and of La Ferte; de Grecia, Seigneur of Dammartin: de Livron, Marquis de Bourbonne; de Laneuvelle, Seigneur of that place; and Boissier, commander d'Aumonieres. They retired to the hermitage of Saint-Peregrine, with the prior who inhabits the place.

(Saint Peregrine Laziosi (1260 – 1345) is an Italian saint of the Servite Order (Friar Order Servants of Mary) He is the patron saint for persons suffering from cancer according to the Catholic Church. He was born in Forlì, Northern Italy, of a wealthy family. His parents and almost the whole city was anti-clerical. Once, the pope sent a special representative to Forli to preach a sermon and try to win the people's hearts over to God. This representative was a saint and preacher called Philip Benizi. At first, things went well and the people listened. Then, Peregrine showed up with his gang of troublemakers and they drove Saint Philip from the pulpit. Peregrine went further than all of them and slapped Saint Philip in the face. Saint Philip offered the other cheek and forgave him. Peregrine was so full of remorse that he went back to Saint Philip and apologized. After this, Peregrine spent more time in prayer. The Virgin Mary once appeared to him and directed him to go to Siena. There he joined the Servants of Mary or the Servites. The superior who received him was Saint Philip Benizi. There he did penance for his sins)

(One of the special penances he decided on was to stand whenever it was not necessary to sit. It is said that St. Peregrine did not sit for thirty years, which caused him to develop varicose veins and then cancer on his leg and foot. The sores became painful and an assembly of doctors prepared to amputate his foot, but the night before the surgery was scheduled to take place Peregrine dragged himself to the foot of a crucifix and spent many hours in prayer. When he fell asleep he received a vision of Christ touching his foot. In the morning his foot was completely healed. He is therefore considered the patron saint of those suffering from cancer)

The Count of Harcourt, (enemy) came to accompany the Frondeurs (rebels/malcontents) and the Fronde of the nobles held under his hand (owed alligence) at Philisbourg, Brisach, Belfort, and other intermediate places. The timing of the outbreak of the Fronde of the parlements, directly after the Peace of Westphalia (1648) that ended the Thirty Years War, was significant.

(The Fronde was a series of civil wars in France between 1648 and 1653, occurring in the midst of the Franco-Spanish War, which had begun in 1635. The Fronde was divided into two campaigns, the Fronde of the parlements)

(A parlement was a provincial appellate court in the France of the Ancien Régime, i.e., before the French Revolution. After 1443, 13 parlements existed until they were abolished in 1790, the most important of which was the Parlement of Paris. They consisted of a dozen or more appellate judges, or about 1,100 judges nationwide. They were the court of final appeal of the judicial system, and typically wielded much power over a wide range of

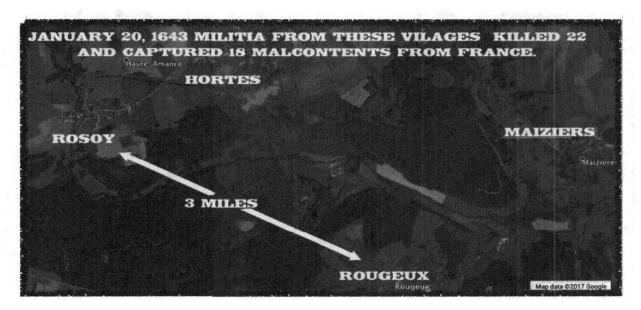

JANUARY 20, 1643 MILITIA FROM THESE VILAGES KILLED 22 AND CAPTURED 18 MALCONTENTS FROM FRANCE.

HORTES

ROSOY

MAIZIERS

3 MILES

ROUGEUX

subject matter, particularly taxation. Laws and edicts issued by the Crown were not official in their respective jurisdictions until the parlements gave their assent by publishing them. The members were aristocrats called nobles of the crown who had bought or inherited their offices, and were independent of the King)

(The parlements spearheaded the aristocracy's resistance to the absolutism and centralization of the Crown, but they worked primarily for the benefit of their own class, the French nobility. The parlements were the chief obstacles to any reform before the Revolution, as well as the most formidable enemies of the French Crown.

The Parlement of Paris, though no more in fact than a small, selfish, proud and venal oligarchy, regarded itself, and was regarded by public opinion, as the guardian of the constitutional liberties of France)

The nuclei of the armed bands that terrorized parts of France under aristocratic leaders during this period had been hardened in a generation of war in Germany, where troops still tended to operate autonomously.

On 23 September, they took at Torcenay (25 miles N) thirteen horses and each stole twenty ecus. A month later they pillaged Rougeux and stole twelve of their best horses then devastated the village and chateau of Bize (4 miles NE) The Marquis de Seunterre went to form a siege at the fortress of Belfort (75 miles SE) A corps of the army commanded by the Marquis de Ussel attempted to help in the operation and in traversing Bassigny, caused great damage, He burned seven houses (22 December) at Recourt (15 miles N) and Avrecourt (16 miles N) and ravaged Chezeaux (7 miles NE) and Hortes (4 miles NW) during the night of Noel.

Belfort (78 miles SE) was being returned to the King of France 7 February 1654 and in return to Alsace, their troops were permitted to pass, during the new year, through our unhappy country. As a result soldiers wanted to enter into the Chateau de Ranconnieres (17 miles N) We prevented them. They killed five people and threatened to kill many others (12 June) In 1656 and 1658 there were more passages of soldiers and bands that reduced our country to misery.

During these years of calamities, Monseigneur the bishop Zamet made generous alms to the poor, widows and orphans. The parish of Hortes (4 miles N) was one of the most afflicted of the diocese. The bishop intended to visit and comfort them when death struck him (2 February 1655) He had opened the hut of Saint Didier, to give a party for the religious at the churches of Avignon, at Frettes and for Hortes, since their illustrious martyr is their patron.

A place was reserved at the festival for Clement Macheret who chose the 23 May, the fEast day of the saint, to carry to his ancient parish the precious relic (of St. Didier) The procession left Langres (15 miles W) the 22 May, then went to Tres Saint-Trinite and arrived in the evening at Rosoy (4 miles NW) At a quarter of a league from the village they encountered the priest of Hortes and he accompanied them to Rosoy where the procession had advanced to honor the reliques and accompany it to the church. The next day residents of Hortes, Rougeux

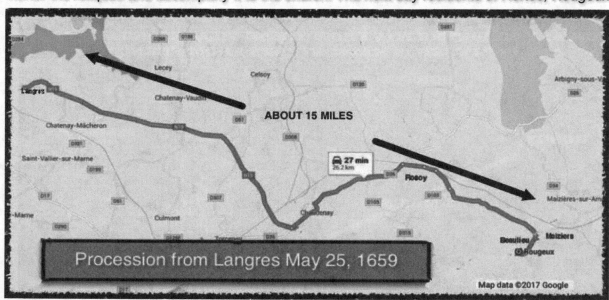

Procession from Langres May 25, 1659

144

and Maizieres and the abbey of Beaulieu formed a truly beautiful procession with a canopy from the church at Rosoy. After praying numerous times the cortege, augmented with the faithful of Him, arrived at Hortes. We placed the reliques on the principal altar of the church. We said the Mass of Sainte-Trinite. The assistants celebrated the fete with a devotion extraordinaire and with a joy really Christian. We well needed the protection from the sky!

It is impossible to describe the suffering of the people during this epoque of sad memory. In this state of our country, struck countless times by the famine and the peste, frequently set on fire and shedding blood, and continuous prey of the affronts of soldiers. How many rapes, ravages, cruelties! It is not only during recent times but for twenty-five years we have been without expectancy. It seems consolation is in the distance. God wants us to be able to improve ourselves; He allows these evils to improve us; he will reward us in a better world. We serve him with resignation in affliction. We want peace but they asked always to their Father in Heaven. To obtain divine mercy they make many prayers during processions all the way to Langres. In 1659 during the Octave of Pentecost (approximately May 25), the parish of Fayl-Billot distinguished their procession above all others by their religious demonstrations. The priest, Claude Huot, organized a solemn procession composed of men, women and infants to a number of three or four hundred representing, with their distinctive attributes, the personages most remarkable of ancient and new Testament from the patriarchs all the way to the martyrs, virtuous theologians and cardinals and the eight beatitudes. The hallebardiers marched in rank. We marched two by two in good order: the women, lowered their eyes, showing exemplary piety. We entered into the church Saint-Mammes. After chanting a Salve Regina in front of the image of Notre-Dame-la-Blanche under the tribune under the gallery, we made a tour of he choir and stopped at the chapel of the cloister, the priest celebrated a saintly Mass. At the end of Mass we went to eat what each had brought to eat and all returned home at two in the afternoon in the same manner as they had entered the ville. The Langrois flocked their path, happy to see such a beautiful devotion for the country expectant that God has not forgotten his people.

The supplications of our ancestors was not later than the answers. Following the victories at Turenne, Spain decided to immediately conclude a treaty of the Pyrenees (7 November 1659) She retained Franche-Compte. The Duke of Lorraine withdrew from the possession of his state. France expanded on the other side (SouthWest toward Spain and Italy) Louis XIV espoused Marie-Therese, infanta of Spain with five hundred thousand ecus of dowry. Conde submitted to the King who honored him with several titles. This peace was made public at Langres 18 February 1660. There was great rejoicing, The priest of Anrosey (6 miles NE), Arthur Hurtault, who was a poet composes at this occasion of verses, anagrams, currencies, couplets, reproduced in prints telling of the cavalcade made by the constabulary.

Supplements from Abbot Mulson and Others

On Ascension Day, 1651 Marcilly was pillaged, and much preserved food, twenty-five jugs of wine, 300 (hemines) of wheat, a quantity of clothing, kitchen utensils, wagons, harnesses, and 100 animals stolen. They contaminated (with feces) the choir of the church to the extent that the priest felt fire was the only means of decontamination, being incorrect in his assumption that the vault would withstand the conflagration.

On the 13 June 1651 a band of horsemen appeared and pillaged Pressigny, taking a number of men captive and twenty-nine beasts. Ten brave young men hid themselves in ambush where the bandits were preparing to cross a stream of the Soane River. They attacked the horsemen, killed one, and wounded others, returning with all that had been looted except one chicken.

The Lorrains (Germans from Alsace-Lorraine) returned, furious, with seventeen horsemen and a number of soldiers, planning to surprise the village, but in the

MARCILLY

meantime reinforcements from the nearby villages came and they were ready for them. The attackers lost ten killed, five wounded, and the others were put to flight.

One of the wounded had several mortal wounds and was asked if he had charms or a pact with the devil that would keep him from dying, but he haughtily responded that he wanted

Marcilly Church

to see a priest. Feeling compassion for him, the priest was called, he confessed his sins, and expired.

Not finding any succor from their misery, the inhabitants were again inflicted, when, as a result of the constant pillaging of their seed grains, famine once again descended upon the whole region. Extending their unbelievable misery, the years 1650 and 1651 were terribly wet and what few crops were planted, failed to flourish and did not yield their fruits. In May 1652 a snowfall, (Snowfall seldom occurs in this region, even in winter) accompanied with a deep frost, fell in abundance over Hortes, La Rosoy, Coiffy, and Rougeux. The price of wheat rose to ten livres the bichet, measure of Langres; oats, three livres; barley, forty sous; rye, five livres. A loaf of bread sold for six sous five livres. One saw mobs of families, hands joined in supplication, begging the baker to sell them a piece of bread for the little money they had. Some waited as long as two days for a small quantity; the others without any money returned home in despair and attempted to find nourishment in the fields. A woman was found dead, her mouth full of grass with a near dead infant in her arms. On the roads one found men as thin as skeletons, and unable to walk any further, died where they fell.

The year 1653 was not an improvement. The Count of Harcourt, holding under his hand a number of villages and excited by the Duc of Lorraine, brought the garrison of Belfort to reconnoiter our impoverished valley. On 23 September, they pillaged Torcenay and seized a number of animals and a month later pillaged Rougeux, taking all the remaining animals, afterwards pillaging the Abbey of Beaulieu. In December they returned and ravaged Hortes on Christmas Eve.

During these years of calamities, the Bishop of Langres helped his most afflicted parishes, Hortes, and Rougeux. On May 23, 1653, he organized a religious event to implore assistance from Our Lord through the intercession of Saint Frettes, patron of the church at Hortes. Carrying a precious fragment of the saint, on May 24 the Bishop began a procession at Langres (11 miles W), arriving in the evening at Rosoy, less than a mile from Hortes. The next day parishioners from the surrounding churches, joined the procession. It continued to grow as it progressed, passing through Hortes, Rougeux Maiziers, finally arriving at Beaulieu, where a High Mass and many prayers for relief were said.(There may have been an ancient road that passed through the region of Rougeux and Maiziers at that time since the current road locates Rougeux on the road after Beaulieu) It is impossible to more fully describe the suffering of the people of this region during this epoque of sorrowful times of reoccurring plague, famine, and unending torment. Hit by seemingly endless calamities during the past years they were not without hope. Their firm faith led them to believe these events were from His hands in order to improve them and they would be fully rewarded in the next world. There were at lEast thirty churches and chapels within a few miles radius of Rougeux. They did not falter in beseeching God for forgiveness. In 1659 during the Octave of Pentecost, 400 solemnly processed, marching two by two, to Fayl-Billot, the women, with eyes lowered kept the infants quiet while selections from the Old and New Testament were read. After entering the church named after Saint Mammes, on their knees they sang Salve Regina in front of the statue of Notre Dame la Blanche, and after a procession around the church, the cure said the Holy Mass. After singing more songs, they ate a common meal with what they had brought, and returned to their homes at two thirty in the afternoon. On 7 November 1659, a treaty was signed with Spain (Ending the war (1635-1659) between France and Spain), in which Spain retained Franche-Compte and our region.

In the middle of the 17th century, as a result of the wars, various families who had roles more or less important of the local magistrates and in the army, seized possession of the seigneurs of our territory. (The nuclei of the armed bands that terrorized parts of France under aristocratic leaders during this period).

Pierrefaites ceased to be a part of the family of Vergy, and a large number of villages changed obedience to a new seigneur, but the commander of the Romagne, Rene de Ham, maintained his rights over Rougeux as well as Broncourt, Maiziers, and Charmoy. With Charmoy, Rougeux was also under the Abbey of Beaulieu.

With the death of Phillipe IV (of Spain) in 1665, his son, now the king of France, pretended he had a heritage to Franche-Compte and to contest his right he came at the head of 20,000 men and took possession. Within three weeks, on February 12, 1668, a treaty was signed. However, on February 23, 1674, Spain and Austria began attacking Gray, just thirty miles South of Rougeux, with cannon. By April, the French forced them to retreat to Besancon where they were forced to capitulate. This loss failed to bring an end to the war and the constant foraging for food and feed dragged on until a treaty was signed at Nimegue, in 1678. This was a major event that redefined the destinies of France and Franche-Compte to this day, for at the end of that war the region of Rougeux became a permanent part of France. (The 30-Year War between Spain and France, rebellion of arrogant local princes in France,and Austria, and a convoluted mixture of unrest and attacks by various groups coupled by invasion by England are far too complicated for this brief account. Needless to say it was the poor who suffered the results of this pride, hate, and ambition of kings and nobles who instigated these centuries of turmoil and death)

CHAPTER XIV
BETWEEN THE TREATY OF THE PYRENEES UNTIL THE REVOLUTION
(1659-1789)

1. FAMILIES OF THE SEIGNIORS ----- 2. CONQUEST OF THE FRANCHE-COMPTE BY THE FRENCH ----- 3. FAYL-BILLOT BURNED ------ 4. PROJECT OF UNION OF THE PRIEURE OF VARENNES OF THE COLLEGE DE VITRY-LE FRANCIS ------ 5. FRERE JEAN-JACQUES AND THE HERMITAGE DE SAINT-PEREGRIN ----- 6. ROGER DE CHOISEUL, ERMITE AT SAINT-NICHOLAS ----- 7. RECONSTRUCTION OF THE BATTLEMENTS OF VAUX-DE-DOUCE----- 8. FROST AND FAMINE ------ 9. BEAULIEU DEVASTATED BY THE GARRISON OF TRAERBACH ------ 10. POLICE ORDER AGAINST SMOKING ----- 11. PASSAGE OF THE KING THROUGH PROLOGUE ----- 12. HOSPICE AND SCHOOLS AT FAYL-BILLOT ----- 13. CHAUVIREY BUILT A BARONY 15. CONSTRUCTION OF AN CHURCH AT L'QUARTE ----- 16. CHAPELS OF THE DIOCESE ----- 17. FREE EDUCATION ----- 18. REVENUES AND CHARGES OF BEAULIEU ----- 19. VISIT OF THE PRIEST OF VARENNES.

During the middle of the XVII century the seigneuries of our territory were owned by various families whose members played roles more or less important in the magistrate or the army.

Pierrefaites had ceased to belong to the houses of Vergy, of Ray, and of Choiseul, only to move into the hands of Ternan, plus those of Bourrelier and Chevillot, advocate of Parliament of Dijon, of Jacqunot-Duval, etc.; finally Jacques de Minee de Beaujeu bought it in 1672.

We found the Chauvirey (as owners) of Chauviey, Vitrey, Ouge, La Quart,; the Lullier and the Montessus, (as owners) at Pressigny; the Heudelot de Lettancourt (1661) (as owners) at Frettes; the Petit (as owners) of Savigny; the Girault (as owners) at Bourguignon; the de Rye (as owners) at , Velles and Pisseloup. And the Poinctes (as owners) at Cexeau and at Hortes; the de Livron (as owners) at Rosoy; du Molinet (as owners) at Varennes, with Vicq, Coiffy, Champigny dependent, as previously, on the King and the priest of Varennes in 1665. Arvigny was sold to M. De Saint Balm, Count of Biesles, in 1666, to Humbert de Rosieres. At the same

PISSELOUP

time, the commander of the Romagne preserved his rights over Atrbigny, Broncourt, Maizieres, Charmoy and Rougeux. These last two (Charmoy and Rougeux) recognize also the abbey of Beaulieu.

At Maizaires, the principal priest is the principal seigneur of Saint-Vivand-sous-Vergy. It is not around Maizaires that the seigneur claims the ground and small fiefs, but those situated at Andilly, Avencourt and at Poiseul whose proprietor is Jean Lemoiue, of Chaumont, knight of the Royal Order, who, in 1665, sold it to Antoine de Ham, Seigneur of La Neuvelle, Cusey. That one then made the acquisition in the name of his brother, Rene de Ham, Knight of Malta and commander of the Romagne.

Poinson and Bize are possessed by Andre de Froment, Squire sergeant of battle, who obtained from the King a safeguard exempting the village of Poinson from lodgments and racing by the men of war (1659) and from the prior general of Charteux, a participation in the good work of the religious of that Order (1666)

The barony of Fayl-Billot who appropriated the illustrious house of the Baume-Montrevel, and that of La Ferte of the ancient and noble family of Choiseul, is master of the camp. He removed the army that, under the orders of King Louis XIV was in possession of Franche-Compte.

At the death of Philippe IV (1665), the King of France, his son,(Louis I of Navarre, called 'le Hutin', 'el Obstinado', 'the Quarreller', 'the Headstrong', or 'the Stubborn') claimed to have a heritage of France-compte (Our region) The way he contested his right was by bringing 20,000 men and took possession. All the villes surrendered within three weeks. We offered to His Majesty King of France the key of Gray. The mayor said: *"Sire, your conquest is more glorious because you were disputed."* (February 1668) But the vast treaty of peace concluded at Aix-la-Chapelle, the 2 May following, between Spain, England, Portugal, France, Ireland, and The Holy Roman Empire, involved the possessions of these countries, including North America, Iceland, East Indies and many other lands around the world.

This treaty returned the province to its ancient master (the Hapsburgs)

Five years later, in 1673, Spain, Austria and other powers declared war on France. In the month of December the incessant advances of the Spanish upon the frontier obliged the inhabitants of Montcharvot to seek refuge at Coiffy-le-Haut, (11 miles N) who, however did not prove to be a protector. French King Louis XIV resolved to (regain and) be the emperor of Franche-Compte.

The Duke of Navailles attacked near Gray (18 miles South) (23 February 1674) He surrounded the lines, opened trenches, and established his batteries. The Visitandines, (Roman Catholic order of nuns founded by St. Francis de Sales and St. Jane Frances de Chantal at Annecy, Fr., in 1610) found three young ladies in the mansion of Choiseul, implored the support of the Marquis of Langues, That one demanded for them a safeguard in case of pillage in case the captains of artillery turn their pieces toward the mansion. No assurances could be given that this would not happen. He was standing by with all his cannon in every attack, with a lit fuse in hand and he will indicate to the soldiers to fire on the mansion if obliged.

On the date of 2 April, the French landed all their forces at Gray (18 miles SS) to spread the news to all the province that the King was firm in his desires. Louis entered the 30 April and spent the day. The next day, he directed his army toward Besancon (60 miles SE), which quickly capitulated (15 May) Dole (49 miles South) and Salins (100 miles W) surrendered a few weeks later and at their submission terminated the campaign. The treaty of Numegue (Nijmegen) definitively determined the destiny of Franche-Compte as a permanent part of France.

(These were peace treaties of 1678–79 that ended the Dutch War, in which France had opposed Spain and the Dutch Republic (now the Netherlands) Spain gave up Franche-Comté, Artois, and 16 fortified towns in Flanders to France)

After the bad times of the war, other disasters which no one expected, overcame Fayl-Billot. (2 miles South) In 1668 an awful incendiary overwhelmed Fayl-Billot. No one could determine the cause but it completely burned the ville to the ground, not even leaving a piece of ruin. The inflammable debris, caught by the wind carried them as far as Charmoy, (2 miles NE) and set that village on fire at a distance of 2 miles, where it consumed two houses, Nineteen years after, the very same disaster was renewed.

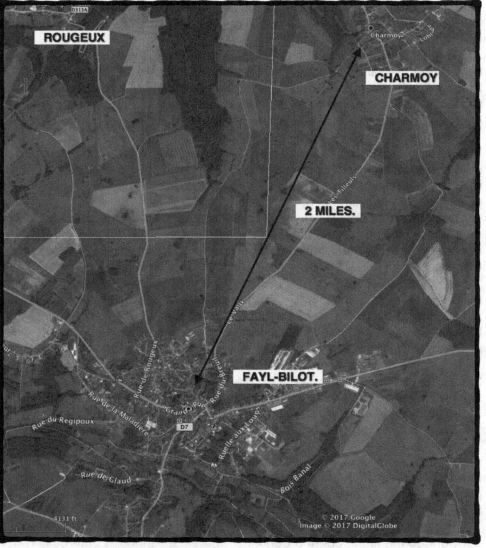

Verbal discussions by the officers of the village uncovered the cause and they declared, on 18 February 1687 at one hour past midnight the fire started in a house situated at the extremity of the road of Mont-d'Olivotte. Since most of the all the habitations were covered with thatch and they did not have pumps to extinguish, unnecessary efforts were made. The wind pushed the flames with such violence that in an instant all the quarters are embraced in flames. We cannot even save any furniture. The land titles, minutes of notaries, records of justice, and registers of the parish are all burned. Amazing! In less than a quarter of an hour three hundred houses had been the prey to those flames 1.

During this epoch, the bishop of Chalons-sur-Marne, Felix de Vialart de Herse, enjoyed the command of the priory of Varennes (9 miles N), where the tithes were 3,300 livres. In 1665, when this prelate established the college of Vitry-le-Francois (90 miles N), the fathers of the Cistercian Order promised for their support the revenues of the priory that would benefit the college. To this end they made a number of steps. But for reasons that we do not know, and perhaps because of earnings, it was situated in the diocese of Langres. At his death, arrived in 1672, the project was necessarily abandoned.

In 1670 Gontier, vicar general of Langres, gave possession of Poinson-les-Fayl (6 miles E) to a pious anchorite, known by the name of Jean-Jacques. The walls had fallen into ruins but the religious repaired and elevated new walls. Soon young men migrated to their direction. They imposed a rule and established a novitiate for an eremitic life. The time was divided between spiritual exercises and work with hands and journey not infrequently to the church for

150

prayer but even more on Fridays of Advent, Lent and fEast days of Our Seigneur (Our Lord), and of Notre-Dame and the days of the other principal saints. All had vestments of a robe that extended to the toenails, a scapular of the same length, a leather belt from which was suspended a rosary, a square hood with a point and a mantle whose length covers the knees. All was natural wool dyed brown. They had bare feet with sandals but wore no hat except on a voyage. But many vagabonds came dressed in much the same manner because they recognized the of the great esteem the villagers had for the monks. They went about the villages using their name, especially at La Ferte begging under the name of the monks of Saint-Peregrin. These circumstances determined Jean-Jacques to change the color of their habit. At the example of the religious of Saint-Sabine, he took the white and it was thought so important that reform was necessary that Mgr de Simiane de Gordes imposed on all the eremites in his diocese, by an ordinance made at Varennes.

September 1687, Frere Jean-Jacques, was designated catechizer of the infants from neighboring parishes. He was elected visitor-general in a synod held by the eremites of the diocese in 1673. The obedient will accept this change 1. He is going to visit all the hermitages, and stay for two or three days each for instruction of the brothers, listen to their complaints and correct the abuse. He revived among them the attendance at work, love of prayer, and silence during the retreat. In a word, he made such admirable advances in coordinating the practices of the monasteries that the bishop published it in 1688.

A noise was repeated that Jean-Jaques was the natural son of Henri IV and of Jacqueline de Breuil, comtese de Moret, and as a result he sought and obtained (22 April 1676) permission to quit Saint-Peregrin. He retired to the diocese of Angers and constructed the hermitage of Gardelles and passed fifteen years in the austerities of the penitence and died in the odor of sainthood the 24 December 1691.

Our Squire possessed another hermitage under the term of Saint-Nicolas. He was situated in the woods called Montigny in the territory of Coiffy le Bas (11 miles N) Following tradition, he was living, in the XVII century as a member of the house of a Choiseul, named Roger, son of the Marechal de Choiseul-Praslin. He was a military, having killed the Comte de Soissons at the battle of Sedan (also known as Marfee) (1641) Seriously wounded himself, he left a number of dead and was saved by miraculously escaping. He resolved to embrace the eremitic life. He settled at Saint-Nicolas and after a long penitence, was reunited with his family and died in the odor of sanctity (1680) His name is inscribed on 9 October in the calendar of Langrois 2. By a decision of 26 September 1772 the bishop of Langres had fabricated at Coiffy a hermitage consisting of a house, chapel, cave, library, and other buildings with a garden, kitchen garden, orchard, and vine yard.

Following the war, Vaux-la-Douce (6 miles E) was depopulated and ravaged. Claude Regnault, who was made abbot from 1607 to 1650 sent the religious in various monasteries and the house (at Vaux-le-Douce) to retire at Langres.

1. Il s'agit probablement de Saint-Prix, Sanctus Praejectus, eveque-martyer de Clermont, en Aivergme, dont la celebre la fete le 25 janviers. Philippe Grisot, ne a Poinson, cure de Fresnoy, fonda en 1736 des prieres en cette chapelle.2. Le diocese de Langres et notes particulieres.. Historie de Fayl-Billot.

The buildings fell into ruin. His successor, Pierre Viard, honorary title of protecter-general of the Order in Heart of Rome, made by testament an important donation to the abbey. He died in 1669.

Frances Mathie who replaced him, could not collect the inheritance immediately. Cleriadus de Choiseul, Marques de Lanques, unjustly retained the money and was even accused of forgery. The quarrel heated up and the religious were able to expose all sorts of transgressions. Cleriadus died without having terminated the affair, and his son and inheritor, Victor Amedeo continued the fight 1. There were 45 hermitages in this diocese. The abbey (suffered) a physical assault (by Amedeo) that resulted in a legal process against him. This caused warning signs to be issued that the arms of the King were to be on the all the grounds of the community. Eventually the return of good harmony was made possible with the house of Choiseul (1689) by the work of the ancient clearer (who?) of Clairvaux. This abbot was distinguished by his knowledge of science and his life. He was visiter and vicar general of his Order who began reconstruction of the walls of Vaux-la-Douce, rejuvenated the tithes and donations of the abbey even though it was stripped. He restored the discipline. On 10 February 1706, he made a transaction with Victor Amedeo, concerning Moulin-Rouge and the chateau of La Ferte (8 miles E) His successor was Roger de Laglee, nominated in 1708, who worked twenty-nine years repairing the abbey. He constructed a chapel and church (at La Ferte in1720)

The history (Abbot Briffaut here is again quoting an unknown source) must mention the exceptional rigor of the winter of 1709. *"By 6 January it had, during the past three weeks, frozen so fiercely strong that we have never experienced before. It was impossible to remain in our unheated houses* (with twigs, gathered only with permission, as the only fuel this not surprising) *and many persons died on the roads from the cold. The wheat, vines, fruit trees, all died. To add to the misery, famine exercised its ravages. Those who transported food met men who took it from them. On 3 April a wagon from Bussieres* (8 miles SW) *was filled with peas; in an instant after arrival the sacks were carried and emptied of all it contained."*

" Before the famine the price of a bichet of peas was four livres, six sous. On October1 (1709) *the same measure of oats was fifty sous; barley, four livres ten sous; wheat, which on 1 October sold for three livres, five sous elevated to five livres ten sous. We have established that at Hortes* (4 miles N) *and La Ferte* (8 miles E) *stores sold pints of wheat at five and one half sous. It was truly a great misery and because of the food shortage, many people died, as evidenced by the parish registers."*

Two years after the last war (War of the Spanish Succession (1701–1714)) started by Louis XIV, a party of enemy, composed of forty men, came out of the garrison of Traerbach-sur-Moselle, traversed Lorraine without encountering an obstacle of their excursion, fell, during the night of 16 August, 1711 (This date does not agree with the earlier statement of this paragraph) on the abbey of Beaulieu (2 miles N) The pillagers, burned ten mounds of hay, killed two sons of a farrier, Pierre and Denis Jobelin, the guard-forester, the retired gardener of the abbey, and a woman who was fleeing up the road of Rougeux. The injury could have been far worse if the tocsin had not called the inhabitants of the village and neighbors, who armed themselves. Joseph Jobelin, put to death the leader of the band. M. De Savigny commandant of the frontier, aide of many peasants, followed the soldiers. *"We recount, sadly, at Fayl-Billot, five hundred fifty fires (houses) burnt."*

Fourteen were made prisoners in the woods of Melay and were brought to Langres but the others escaped. (In 1700, Charles II, the last Habsburg king of Spain, died, bequeathing his kingdoms to Louis's grandson, Philip of Anjou (Philip V) Louis, who desired nothing more than peace, hesitated but finally accepted the inheritance. He has been strongly criticized for his decision, but he had no alternative. With England against him, he had to try to prevent Spain from falling into the hands of the equally hostile Holy Roman Emperor (Germany/Austria region) Leopold I, who disputed Philip's claim. Finally, a palace revolution in London, bringing the pacific Tories to power, and a French victory over the imperial forces at the Battle of Denain combined to end the war. The disasters of the war were so great that, in 1709, France came close to losing all the advantages gained over the preceding century. The Treaties of Utrecht, and of Rastatt and Baden, signed in 1713–14, cost France its hegemony but left its territory intact. It retained its recent conquests in Flanders and on the Rhine)

It seemed that this time it was the impudence of smokers who started the fire at Fayl-Billot. This is why M. Dulyon, Judge of Maizieres defended the right of the inhabitants to smoke in their barns, stables, roads and all other locations except in their rooms, stoves and kitchens under penalty of ten livres. (Doesn't seem to make sense unless the thatched rooves of their houses were more incendiary than their barns) The fathers and mothers, the masters and maitresses were declared responsible if their infants and their seryiteurs (?) break this law and will contravene their defense. Made public by order of M. Martin, cure of the parish and vice-cannon of Pierrefaites (1719)

The 2 October 1725 a brilliant cortege arrived at Fayl-Billot. Stanislas, King of Pologne (Poland) had gone to Paris to celebrate the marriage of Louis XV with his wife, the pious Marie Leckzinska. The steward of the duchy of Bourgogne had made, to receive His Majesty, the prince and the princess, his mother, magnificent preparations.

Stanislas was accompanied by the steward of Franche-Compte, and Champagne. The ville of Langres sent a deputation of Aldermen; MM. Deserrey, MM de Grenant and M. De Monclus, priest of Fayl-Billot, cannon and vice-general, who represented to the King the homage of the religious. After having soup with the King, the steward of Champagne and the Aldermen presented their gifts and retired to their posts. The prince with all his suite passed the night at Fayl-Billot. The next day around five in the evening, Stanislas entered the ville of Langres at the sound of bells and cannon. He put his foot on the ground in front of the episcopal palace, where M. De Monclus recounted all the honors that he had won. Stanilas cordially embraced him twice.

There were very many poor and only one school for infants of both sexes at that village. Renoud, cure of the parish suggested the project to form an establishment for the ill and for instruction of uneducated children. Aided by the communal administration and by liberalities of M. Seurrot and other notables, there was founded in 1730 a house of charity controlled by three religious of the congregation of Saint-Charles of Nancy. Two strove to heal the sick poor in their homes. They distributed the remedies and the food and the others instructed gratuitously the small ones. *"We do not get weary of appreciating the good being done at this institution, the sick and the well both prosper."* Mgr. De Montmorin approved by ordinance this organization 14 May 1738 and Louis XV authorized by letters patent in November of the same year.

The barony of Fayl-Billot was sold in 1689, by the house of Baume-Montrevel to M. D'Argouges, knight, councilor of the State, Baron of Plessis. At his death, arriving in 1696, his son, Alexandre d'Argouges, knight, inherited it. He humbled himself and made homage between the hands of the chancellor of the King who accepted 1 his submission and honored it with the title of Count (18 May 1699) He ceded it, 26 March 1714, to M. Theodore de Custine, knight, Count de Wiltz, Baron de Chemilly.

He quickly made two primary changes in the ownership of the fief, the first 6 July and the second 16 November. He claimed that one-third of the community forests were his. The inhabitants denied it. He started a legal process that lasted twelve years and involved the most celebrated avocets in Dijon and was finally settled amicably that recognized the rights of the community (1728)

 Madame Therese de Custine sold the barony 13 June 1754 for the sum of fifty-

CHAUVIEY

thousand livres to M. Michel d'Attricourt, captain of a regiment of Rouergue who married Bernnarde de Froment, daughter of the Seigneur of Bize and of Chaudenay. At Chauviey, the chateau-Dessus belonged to M. D'Ambly Marquis des Ayvelles and the chateau Dessous belonged to M. Salomon-Bernard de Montessus. Salomon obtained in the month of February 1740, election to Baron of the ground of Chauvirey and his son Antoine-Francois was created Earl in 1770; these two families had the rights of Vitrey, Ouge and La Quarte.

Ouge was a vicarage dependent on the priest of Pierrefaites and La Quarte, a hamlet made part of Ouge (10 miles E) But the hamlet was expanded; it had sixty fires (houses) It was difficult to go to the sacraments at Ouge and to carry the sacraments for the sick to Ouge from LaQuart (2 miles apart) On the other hand the travelers who pass on the great road found it difficult to find a church at Fayl-Billot or Combeaufontaine where they could hear mass.

These motives determined the inhabitants (of Ouge) to build another church. Didiere Cardinal, widow of Jean Pierron, gave sufficient terrain for the chapelle, the sacristy, the cemetery,a house for the vicar and a garden (1 June 1729) Jean Boicelle, stone mason at Ouge, constructed, for the sum of six hundred forty livres, an edifice, forty feet long, twenty feet wide and fifteen feet high. Mgr. Gilbert de Montmorin, bishop of Langres ordained a survey de commodo et incommodo (quickly but secretly) done by M. Dresserey.

LA QUARTE

PROSPEROUS FARM AT LA QUARTE

Google Earth

We assigned, to get his opinion, MM Rogert, cure and dean at Pierrefaites and Chalochet, vicar of Ouge and de Montess and Ambly seigneurs of La Quarte. Their report was presented and they approved and authorized the cult in that new church, under the protection of the local patron, Saint Gilbert. It will be served by M. Doribee, vicar of Broncourt. The inhabitants engage themselves to find lodgment for him and he was paid annually, the sum of two hundred livres and at the Passion (Good Friday) five sous. (1738) In 1740 La Quarte formed a distinct community.

Our church had the normal chapels although several of them were special gifts of bishops, seigneurs or inheritance of the founding families. We should indicate (for praise?): The Saint-Trinity at La Ferte;1 Notre-Dame at Coiffy-le-Haute, La Ferte, Chaumondel, Maizieres, Poinson, Frettes; Saint-Anne at Chauvirey, Vitrey; Saint-Croix, at Coiffy-le-Haut; Saint-Gengoul, at Varennes; Saint Hubert, at Chauvirey; Saint-Jean-Baptiste, at Pierrefaites; Saint-Nicholas, at Chauvirey, Coiffy-le-Haut, at Frettes; the Trois-Rois-Mages, at Vicq 2.

Two others, distinct churches were likewise beneficiaries: Saint-Catherine, situated on the cemetery of Coiffy-le-Haut; Saint-Anne at Norte-Dame-de-Liesse at the Northern extremity of Fayl-Billot.

Varennes had a chapel deducted to Saint-Genogoul at the end of the road of its name. It was restored in 1869 by the care of M. Belime, cure-dean.

The hamlet of Montsols, territorie of Frettes, possessed a chapel of Notre-Dame where we went on pilgrimage to obtain relief from illness of fevers. It is on a farm of Velars, and a chapel that the inhabitants of Charmoy provide assistance at mass. Actually, it is a bakery oven. We see the hermitage of Coiffy-le-Bas, the chapel of Saint-Nicolas and at Poinson that of Saint-Peregrin now transformed into a barn and stable. Saint-Barbe North of Varennes, is found within the new cemetery of that parish.

Christian charity attends to all that is needed for instruction and education of the poor at Fayl-Billot since 1730; all the little infants have been taught without fee 3. In 1745, Marie-Charlotte Moniot, of La Ferte gave the fabric of her parish, a product that produced annually thirty-five livres from fifteen people, to the school for assignment to the indigents, and fifteen to the sick poor on condition that a Mass be said for her the 4 Novembre and that her name be perpetually in the necrology. In 1771, Pierre Hologne, merchant at Coiffy-le-Haut founded an organization with a provision that paid of a rent of forty-five livres for provision of indignant scholars 1.

1. Archive de La Ferte.

2. Historie de Vicq.

3. Bannes, Bize, Bussieres, Champcourt, Champigny-les-Langres, Champlitte, Charmes, Charmoy, Chatenay-Vaudin-a-Chaudenay, Chauviry, Cohons, Corginon, Corlee, Fayl-Billot, Fontaine-Francaise, Fouvent, Henilley, Hortes, Langres, Lecey, Lescheres, Maizeries, Montlandon, Neidant-Chatenoy, Orbigny-au-Mont, Peigney, Poinson, Rolampont, Rosoy, ROUGEUX.

4. Le derniere abbe de Beaulieu, Pierre de Villefray, deving, apres la Revolution, cure de Port-sur-Saone, ou le mort en 1823 a l'age 73 ans.

A wheelwright of Vicq, Francis Humblot, gave the church a principal of five hundred livres of rent payable to the master of the school for care of six poor infants (1776) By testament on 1 June 1786, Marie Rouge sister of the cure of Vicq, gave the sum of five thousand livres placed into the hands of the school master with the approval of the bishop for instruction of all children of the parish.

The abbey of Beaulieu, (constructed 2 miles North of Rougeux some 500 years previously) reconstructed in part before 1633, possessed some benefits and rights on a number of localities 3. Since a judgement 17 August 1625 the abbey had two tiers of income, one for the abbey and one for the religious. In 1737 the total income was 11,744 livres. Upon the declaration of the prior, Dom Denis Cornot, in 1751, the part of the religious, the mens convent, was 4,689 livres and they dispensed 4,618 livres.

The community at this time was composed of five religious. Five others, professed at Beaulieu, were scattered in other houses of the Order. The commanding abbot, not a resident there, nominated Pierre-Louis Savary dean and vicar general of Evreux 4.

On 22 November 1775, Dom Gerard-Marius Landelle, grand prior of Notre-Dame of Moleme, and visiter of all the parishes was received at Saint-Gengoul de Varennes.

Accompanying was MM. Mariet, notary of baillage of Langres of our parish. He made a visit to the church (Beaulieu), the edifices and dependencies of the parish. He recognized that the structure, coverage of the tower, the capping, the buildings, the failed truss above the choir, the barn roof, and that part of the wall had fallen and demanded repairs. These should be done by the prior messire Marie-Gabriel-Louis Texier de Hautefeuille, commander de Order of Malta, living in his chateau of Hautefeville and Gatines.

The income of the abbey (Beaulieu) was divided as follows:

The greatest part of the tithes of wine and grains to Varnnes, Champigny, Arbigy (a sixteenth), Chezeaux, Coiffy-le-Haut, Coiffy-le-Bas, Laneuvelle, Vicq, de Amremont,and Lavernoy; fifty five journaux of laborable ground; forty six mowing swaths; the tithes that seigneurs and others choose at Varennes and at Champigny, the right to charge to Vicq, Damremont, Coiffy-le-Bas; half of the forty five acres of wood brush, undivided with His Majesty, on Vicq, Coiffy and Montcharvot; two hundred fifty acres situated at Varennes.

The charges consisted of 1,400 livres, the bare minimum to survive; 2,720 livres of tenths; 250 livres of pledges to guards; 80 livres in honor of the clerk of justice.

SUPPLEMENTS FROM ABBOT MULSON AND OTHERS

In 'Historie de la Ville' by M. Mulson, 1889, is recorded further misery. *"An unassuming chronicler of the time, Rene Luquet, from Rougeux, has conveyed to us, day by day, with deep feelings, the agonizing incidents of the cruel winter of 1709 AD"*

"The autumn sowing was made late because of rains and the fields were poorly planted; it was a bad omen already. The winter, in addition, arrived early, was long and excessively rigorous. During the month of January especially, it was impossible to stay outdoors and they found dead men frozen on the roads. The alternating freezing and thawing caused a complete

156

disaster. All the country's products, fruit trees, wheat, vines, perished underfoot. Spring did not bring life to either flowers or harvest. One doesn't know an idea of the misery that erupted among the people. Today, (speaking in 1889) the ease of transports, the resources of provisions, the variety of harvest would prevent a parallel calamity. Potatoes, the poor people's bread, were not yet introduced and at the same time had used up the meager provisions of wheat, rye, barley and oats, the farmer found himself to be without a means of existence. One saw bands of miserable folks, pale faced, emaciated, taken to ambush and pillage the provisions and envoys, which circulated. Some efforts were made to lessen the bad times. They opened markets at Hortes, and at La Ferte where wheat was sold by the quart. The price was unaffordable to the poor people, it was worth ten lbs a sheaf, and money was scarce. This frightful scarcity did not end until after the 1710 harvest, happily abundant. In September, wheat came down to thirty cents per bundle, the price of common years. The excessive privations lead to a great death rate, noted in the register of the parish. One counted forty-nine deaths, when the average is six or seven, in the previous years."

A year later King Louis XIV, a committed enemy (due to resistance against the French take over of Franche-Compte and the region of Rougeux), and a party of horsemen, forty in number, made a wide excursion across the countryside. With little opposition, they arrived at Rougeux on the night of 16 September 1711. During the pillaging of the Abbey of Beaulieu, they burned six barns and killed Pierre and Dennis Jobelin, two sons of a nearby farmer, the forester, the gardener of the abbey, and a woman they met walking on the road at Rougeux. The tocsin was sounded and the village rose in arms. Joseph Jobelin killed the leader of the band and M. de. Savigny, commander of the frontier, aided by a number of peasants, pursued the outlaws and made prisoners of fourteen in the woods near Langres. (Their fate is unrecorded)

During this time Fayl-Billot burned to the ground by a fire of unknown origin, the fire so hot that hot embers, floating in the air, ignited and also burned level, a nearby village (Charmoy) In reaction to this calamity, the seigneur forbade the inhabitants to smoke their pipes in any barn, stables, on any road and all surrounding lands except in their own rooms and kitchens under a penalty of ten livers fine. (Tobacco, introduced into Europe sometime in the 14th century, had even made its way to this remote village)

During the following sixty-seven years (approaching the Revolution) the absence of war descended upon the valley of L'Amance but the population was repeatedly struck with plagues, epidemics and famines caused by endless attacks of horrible weather with temperatures ranging from -40 to 104 degrees F interlaced with late and early freezes and vastly excessive amounts of rain were unable to improve their living conditions while the seigneurs and abbeys increased their oppression and wealth. The tithes required of the peasants were savagely increased according to the following examples: twenty days labor in the fields, one month of free road labor (usually during the summer when crops needed attention), forty cuttings (of something), the rights to mutation (meaning unknown), and half of all cut wood. Suffocating taxes on salt and other products as well road tolls were unceasingly required. The residents were permitted to graze cattle only within specified boundaries, and were told the location and exact quantity of vitally needed firewood that could be gathered.

Every pound of milled grain had its tax. The hated custom houses were a worse burden than a foreign garrison. Transportation of grain without an official permit, whose cost was dependent on variable factors, was prohibited, even across a streamlet to a neighboring farm. This control made it easy for the speculators to force the peasant to sell his grain at reduced prices.

The 'gabelle,' or salt tax, had been a standing temptation to the miserably poor to engage in smuggling, a capital crime summarily punished on the gibbet.

The abbeys had the privilege of grazing (vaine pature) their cattle anywhere they pleased, and took the peasantry to court if they failed to pay the tithe in money, goods, or labor.

Consequences for minor infractions were harsh and frequently barbarous. In one form the hapless offender was spread-eagled with his arms and legs pinioned to the ground. A block placed under the ankle and knee of one leg assured that when the heavy wagon wheel was dropped, the shattered bone would result in permanent injuries, if not death from infection. In either case survival of the family was placed in great jeopardy.

Deportation to penal colonies or to the 'hulks' or mutilation were common punishments for this and other infractions. These oppressive measures, implemented and strictly enforced by the higher clergy in league with the nobility, assured dire poverty and total domination for the peasants.

It was not until this era, that crop rotation was being considered as a way to obtain more production from the available farmland. Prior to this time, land had to lay fallow for at lEast three years and sometimes up to nine years in order to produce a successful crop, assuming a cooperative growing season.

The document on this page indicates that sometime in 1712 a branch of Rougeux's, relocated to Pierrefaites.

In 1730 a free Catholic school was started at Fayl-Billot and in 1745 a large government donation was used to pay for help to the indigents and sick poor.

Living in Rougeux in 1750, were sixty men and 130 women and children, slightly more than the current population. (Note the large unbalance between the sexes)

The new cemetery at Rougeux was started in 1760.

In 1783 the Icelandic volcano, Laki, erupted. The direct effects of the erupting lava and poisonous gases immediately killed more than 9000. The ash, carried away by the wind poisoned the land and the sea, killing half of the Icelandic cattle population and a quarter of the sheep and horse population. Nothing would grow on the fields and fish could be found in the sea. In the resulting famine (1783-1784) an estimated twenty-thousand people; one-third of the population of Iceland died. But the Laki eruption had possibly even more widespread effects. In the years after the eruption the climate in Europe deteriorated, characterized by cool and rainy summers. The resulting crop failures were one of the triggers to one of the most famous insurrections of starving people in history — the French Revolution of 1789-1799.

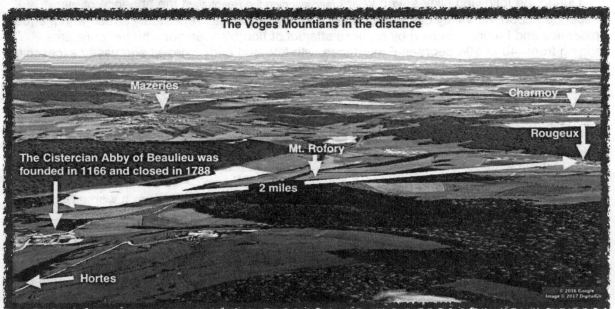

Until 1778, Rougeux had always been included in the diocese of Langres and the deanship of Pierrefaites in the province of Champagne. Soon, however, Rougeux became the seat (residence) of the priest.

The marriage record of Great-great-greatgrandfather John Baptiste Rougeux (JB1) and Anne Caulot records them as testifying as being unable to sign their names. We know from the marriage documents that JB1 (1756) JB2 (1794) and JB3(1831) were able to sign their names, but they certainly were not educated.

Financial records of 1790 show only 25,000 francs was budgeted for education of the entire 25,000,000 subjects of King Louis XVI. Yet, a witness at the baptism of JB3, a John Baptiste Mulson, 69 years old, and probably an uncle, is listed as a primary school teacher. In any event reading was a low priority issue.

There were no newspapers in the region and it is highly unlikely access to a library or books was possible. Additionally, there was no lighting after nightfall nor leisure time to sit around reading a book during daylight hours.

CHAPTER XV

THE REVOLUTION
(1789)
1. ABOLITION OF FEUDAL RIGHTS ----- 2. DESTRUCTION OF THE ANCIENT REGIME ----- 3. THE MISERY ------ 4 CONFISCATION OF THE ASSETS OF THE ECCLESIASTICS ----- 5. PERSECUTION AGAINST THE CLERICS ----- 6. SPOLIATION OF THE CHURCHES ----- 7. THE SCHOOL.

While there are multitude of reasons for the occurrence of the French Revolution, the unfair taxes and their financial burden; widespread discontent of the Catholic Church; the successful 1777 revolution in the U. S.; disastrous losses from the 7 Years War; widespread crop failure caused by savagely cold weather and widespread starvation caused by sale of

Storming the Bastille. July 1789

commons.wikimedia.org

wheat to England by a King on the brink of ruin with debts so heavy it is impossible to pay them, imposed pressures upon the lower-classes that eventually exploded into a bloodbath for Europe.

Near the end of the XVIII century, pressure for governmentaType to enter textl reform, everywhere inspired for In May 1789, forced King Louis XVI to convene the first Etats General since 1614 (which he erroneously thought he could control) to propose solutions to his government's financial problems.

The subsequent turmoil, had widespread, unintended consequences on world history. Arousal of an independent fervor among numerous of the small states in central Europe let to unification and origin of Germany a hundred years later —and subsequent events even today. The information herein is an extremely sketchy outline of the general events.

The Revolution is an extremely complicated affair passing through a number of phases and consuming its leaders each in their turn—as well as millions of others in France and Europe. Even today books are still being written by analysts of those terrible decades.

The Estates-General (or States-General) of 1789 (French: Les États-Généraux de 1789) was a general assembly representing the three French estates of the realm: the Church, (First Estate), the nobility (Second Estate), and the common people (Third Estate)

On 5 May 1789, amidst general festivities, the Estates-General convened in an elaborate but temporary Ile des États (meeting place) set up in one of the courtyards of the official Hôtel des Menus Plaisirs in the town of Versailles near the royal château. Many in the Third Estate (the peasants) viewed the invitation to attend as equal representatives to the nobles and Church as a revolution already peacefully accomplished. However, with etiquette of 1614 strictly enforced, the clergy and nobility ranged in tiered seating in their full regalia, and the physical locations of the deputies from the Third Estate at the far end, as dictated by the protocol. When Louis XVI and Charles Louis François de Paule de Barentin, the Keeper of the Seals of France, addressed the deputies on 6 May, the Third Estate discovered that royal decree granting equal representation also upheld the traditional voting 'by orders', (i.e. that the collective vote of each Estate would be weighed equally), causing their voting representation (the vast percentage of the population) to be vastly diluted as a result. The apparent intent of the King and of Barentin (a counter-revolutionary) was for everyone to get directly to the matter of taxes without the influence of the commoners (Third Estate) The larger representation of the Third Estate would remain merely a symbol, while giving them no extra power. Director-General of Finance Jacques Necker had more sympathy for the Third Estate, but on this occasion he spoke only about the fiscal situation, leaving it to Barentin to speak on how the Estates-General was to operate. Trying to avoid the issue of representation and focus solely on taxes, the king and his ministers had gravely misjudged the situation. The Third Estate wanted the Estates to meet as one body and vote per deputy ('voting by heads' rather than 'by orders') The other two estates, while having their own grievances against royal absolutism, believed—correctly, as history was to prove—that they stood to lose more power to the Third Estate than they stood to gain from the King. Necker sympathized with the Third Estate in this matter, but the astute financier lacked equal astuteness as a politician. He decided to let the impasse play out to the point of stalemate before he would enter the fray. As a result, by the time the King yielded to the demand of the Third Estate, it seemed to all as a concession wrung from the monarchy, rather than a magnanimous gift that would have convinced the populace of the king's good will.

The Estates-General reached an impasse. The first item on the agenda involved the verification of powers. Honoré Mirabeau, noble himself but elected to represent the Third Estate, tried but failed to keep all three orders in a single room for this discussion. Instead of discussing taxes of the King, the three Estates began to discuss separately the organization of the legislature. Shuttle diplomacy continued without success until 27 May, (22 days later and tempers had risen) when the nobles voted to stand firm for separate verification.

The following day, Abbé Sieyès (a member of the clergy, but, like Mirabeau, elected to represent the Third Estate) moved that the representatives of the Third Estate, who now called themselves the Communes ('Commons'), proceed with verification and invite the other two Estates to take part, but not to wait for them. On 13 June 1789, the Third Estate had arrived at a resolution to examine and settle in common the powers of the three orders, and invited to this effort those of the clergy and nobles. On 17 June, with the failure of efforts to reconcile the three Estates, the Communes (Third Estate) completed their own process of verification and almost immediately voted a measure far more radical: they declared themselves redefined as the National Assembly, an assembly not of the Estates but of the People. They invited the other orders to join them, but made it clear that they intended to conduct the nation's affairs with or without them. As their numbers exceeded the combined numbers of the other Estates, they could dominate any combined assembly.

The King tried to resist. Under the influence of the courtiers of his privy council, he resolved to go in state (dressed in his full royal regalia) to the National Assembly, annul its decrees, command the separation of the orders, and dictate the reforms to be effected by the restored Estates-General. On 20 June, he ordered the Salle des États, the hall where the National Assembly (3rd Estate) met, closed. The National Assembly moved their deliberations to the King's tennis court 'Jeu de paume'), where they proceeded to swear the Tennis Court Oath (Serment du jeu de paume), under which they agreed not to separate until they had settled the constitution of France. Two days later, deprived of use of the tennis court as well, the National Assembly met in the church of Saint Louis, where the majority of the representatives of the clergy joined them: efforts to restore the old order had served only to accelerate events. The king foolishly gave the people more fuel to keep going and make change happen.

In the séance royal of 23 June, the King granted a Charte octroyée, a constitution granted from the royal favor, which affirmed, subject to the traditional limitations, the right of separate deliberation for the three orders, which constitutionally formed three chambers. This move failed; soon, that part of the deputies of the nobles who still stood apart joined the National Assembly at the request of the king. The Estates-General had ceased to exist, having become the National Assembly (and after 9 July 1789, the National Constituent Assembly) signaling the outbreak of the French Revolution.

The agitation in the capital had not as yet spread into our territory before July. In the month of July, the inhabitants of Rougeux invaded Beaulieu, menaced the religious if they did not sign an act that end the vaine pature. (the right of the abbey to pasture their beasts on the land being cultivated by the inhabitants of Rougeux that damaged their crops and consumed pasturage they themselves needed)

This was an ominous sign of things to come. (Actual physical movements against the

NAPLEON BONAPART. 1768—1821

en.wikipedia.org/wiki/File:Jacques-Louis_David_-_The_Emperor_Napoleon_in_His_Study_at_the_Tuileries_-_Google_Art_Project.jpg

Church were unheard of and indicates the weight of oppression being laden on the backs of the poor) (The wave of revolutionary fervor and widespread hysteria quickly swept the countryside. Revolting against years of exploitation, peasants looted and burned the homes of tax collectors, landlords and the seigniorial elite. Known as the Great Fear ('la Grande Peur'), the agrarian insurrection hastened the growing exodus of nobles from the country and inspired the National Constituent Assembly to abolish feudalism on August 4, 1789, signing what the historian Georges Lefebvre later called the 'death certificate of the old order.')

The Premier decreed that the Assembly destroy the privileges of the villages and provinces. This act abolished in one night six centuries of the ancient political order and feudal rights of the seigneurs (4 August). Courts were abolished, towns and cities had their ancient rights abolished, and hundreds of other restrictions and changes passed.

Soon there was a famine of grains, work, credit cash and commerce. The economy did poorly in 1790-96 as industrial and agricultural output dropped, foreign trade plunged, and prices soared. The government decided not to repudiate the old debts. Instead it issued more and more paper money (called 'assignat') that supposedly were grounded seized lands. The result was escalating inflation. The government imposed price controls and persecuted speculators and traders in the black market. People increasingly refused to pay taxes as the annual government deficit increased from 10% of gross national product in 1789 to 64% in 1793. By 1795, after the bad harvest of 1794 and the removal of price controls, inflation had reached a level of 3500%. The assignats were withdrawn in 1796 but the replacements also fueled inflation. The inflation was finally ended by Napoleon in1803 with the franc as the new currency.

Bankruptcy was imminent everywhere and pillages, burnings, flooding, starvation; all the bad times joined to make the country desolate. The inhabitants of Pierrefaites, were obliged to search for wheat all the way to Avrecourt (10 miles N) and Forfileres.

The Church was the largest landowner in the country, and before 1789 known as the First Estate, controlled properties which provided massive revenues from its tenants. The Church also had an enormous income from the collection of tithes. Since the Church kept the registry of births, deaths, and marriages and was the only institution that provided hospitals and education in some parts of the country, it influenced all citizens.

The Assembly decreed (23 August) repressive controls on the Church and confiscated the properties of the Church for the profit of the State, set a charge to even enter the churches and dispensed with any help or solace for the poor (2 December); abolition of Christmas greetings, suppression of all religious orders (13 February 1790); sold National property (16 April); confiscated the furniture, and innumerable other properties of immigrants and clergy, regular and secular; appropriated all abbeys, priories, fabrics, pictures, chapels, etc.

This madness generated resentment and many reprisals against the administrative centers.

The decrees of 13 July and 27 November 1790 requiring all the ecclesiastic titillaters (scornfully titling them as entertainers) to swear allegiance to the Constitution (before allegiance to God under pain of imprisonment or death) bravely inspiring priests to denounce the famous Constitution as schismatic and heretical.To remove all the scruples anyone might have, the administration argued that it had royal ratification, therefore this odious act had the highest authority. They spread the hateful hoax that it did not need the approbation of the Sovereign Pontiff and that all allegiance to him must stop and all must swear this oath.

In all the departments the oath taking ceremony was fixed on 23 January 1791. After the parish mass the Municipal appeared in front of the sanctuary to receive, in front of all the faithful, from each one, the oath that demanded allegiance to the State in all things. It was forbidden to accept the Pope as our spiritual leader. Some ecclesiastics swore the oath as the formula prescribed: we called them 'the sworn'. Others refused. Most swore but safeguarded the sacred rites of the Church. These were deemed to have refused the oath. Those who refused to sign were deprived of their functions, and imprisoned in the hulks of rotting sailing ships and starved to death or immediately hung.

This question terminated, we were required to convene the electors of each district to nominate titillaters to fill the vacancies. We called these elected lay cures intrus (intruders) because they were not educated in the canonical institutes. Others took the road of emigration; others hide themselves and continue to say Holy Mass and administrate the sacraments in particular houses. But the brigades of gendarmes and the nations guards make searches, arrest the refractories, and take all the objects that are important. The fierce law of 23 April 1793 ordained that the refactories be incarcerated within a week in the capital of their department; embarked without delay, and shipped to Guyana, where they will be locked up and aged no less than sixteen years. In each village, there were suspects, that is to say, there are men who do not accept the minister of intrus and others whose citizenship was doubtful or suspected of antisocial behavior. Our government made them suffer all sorts of vexations. By order of the administrators of the districts, the members of the counsel general of the commune assisted a detachment of national guards and transport, on March and April 1793, all the suspects they have listed their domiciles are to be searched and all arms, and munitions that they find seized. They will take all the fowls, meat, mattocks, and forks of fire (needed to keep the hearth fire going) to dispose at the registry of the municipality.

Following the directions of the Directory of Haute-Marne (22 April 1793), all those persons suspected were placed under the surveillance of the authorities. They were required to present themselves in front of the municipal officers every day from ten o'clock in the morning until the seventh hour of the evening for the purpose of inscribing the charges on the register.

At Vicq, a woman named Anne Charlot, not having yet made the slightest resistance, suddenly on the 4 May, the municipality charged the commandant of the guard nationale to seize her and bring her in front of them. They put a rope around her neck, and in public menaced her by hanging her on a tree they called the Liberty tree.

At Pierrefaites the patriots (peasant revolutionaries) exultantly bound up Madam de Hurault and placed her on an ass and led her, among hundreds of boos, throughout the roads of the village. Shortly after, they incinerated, with all the family of Minette, the chief-lieutenant of the district. (These people had apparently generated long standing animosity of the peasants who, given the opportunity, extracted their revenge)The prisons were full of suspects. It was a reign of terror.

Soon the constitutionals (revolutionaries) themselves would be pursued and pressured to remove all furniture, and religious emblems from every church and with clubs they profane and mutilate statues, break the crosses, steal all the sacred vessels and sang impious chants. One bell was left at each village. The cords of the bells were sent to the arsenal of the navy.

At the middle of these changes and ruins there were the Christian schools and revolutionary schools. Many masters, in accord with the fathers and mothers of families, persevered in teaching religious assignments even during the time of the terror; M. Fayet tes Caublot at Lavernoy (1792-1803); Clement at Hortes (1793-1817); Doudey at Frettes (1770-1809); Noirrot at Velles (1786-1800); Noblot at Charmony and (Abbot) Mulson at Pierrefaites.

At Fayl-Billot the 29 pluvoice (17 February 1793) the national agent pronounced in front of the Council of the community, *"I demand that you assign a man and charge him to be sure all children are being taught only republicanism principals in every grade"*. Immediately schools were closed in refusal to teach these immoral and anti-Christian principals. During a meeting of 27 venemiaire V (14 October 1796) (after the revolution had taken a seriously different turn) the mayor suggested that since the schools had been closed since AN II (1793) and the infants had not received instructions in the commune and it was urgent that this deplorable situation cease. He proposed that reestablishment of schools in the ancient methods as soon as possible. This motion received unanimous acceptance.

1. Voir les details dans le Diocese de Langres, t, I, p. 355 , etc., IV. Et suiv.

SUPPLEMENTS FROM ABBOT MULSON AND OTHERS

In the ancient worlds of Egypt and Mesopotamia, the social structure was rooted in religioustenets. People believed their religious foundations were their god's plan for the world and rebellion against the social forms was unthinkable. Medieval men inherited that attitude and built upon it, some believing poverty was a blessing and nothing in Scripture suggested that man should rebel against that social order. The inherited monarchical system that came to exist 3000 years before did not change substantially before the middle 19th century. During these later years there was some loosening of the strictures imposed upon the peasant/surf class but their exploitation was not an invention of the Middle Ages.

An Egyptian mummy, reincarnated back into life during that time, would not have been surprised at the way peasants were living. It is estimated 90% of the population were peasants, who, incidentally because of diet, were more than five inches shorter then the aristocracy. Aristocrats comprised less than 5% of the total population, the balance being artisans and burgers.

YEARS OF PLAGUES AND EPIDEMICS	YEARS OF FAMINE	YEARS OF UNUSUAL WEATHER
1703, 1720, 1721, 1773-1774,-1775, 1776,-1780,-1781,-1784 1786, PLAGUE KILLS 120,00 IN CITY OF PARIS- MANY YEARS OF VARIOLE, GRIPPE, THYPUS, DYSENTERY,- PNEUMONIA—1880-TYPHUS KILLS 192,000 IN BRETAGNE	1700,-1710 1724,-1725 1726,-1739 1740,-1747 1750,-1751 1752,-1766 1769,-1770 1775,-1782 1787,-1789	1701-1800 —THE WHOLE CENTURY IS PLAGUED WITH EXTREME COLD -40C IN THE EARLY YEARS WITH A RISING TEMPERATURE TO +40C THE HIGHEST EVER RECORDED WHICH RUINED CROPS

OWNED BY AUTHOR

Land was owned by the aristocrats and served as the source of wealth and even today, land ownership retains its mystique as a symbol of power and prestige. Permitting the peasant class to own land would have given them an opportunity to gain power and constitute a threat to their safety and wealth.

Possibility of freedom from the yoke of the nobility and abbots was sparked by our successful rebellion against the British in 1772. Once expressed, this never-dormant desire, catalyzed by improved communications in the form of handbills and pamphlets, united the oppressed masses as never before. For the first time they dared hope that freedom and land ownership might be possible. In any case, what else could a poor peasant do but violently revolt? Where could he go to escape his fate? No matter which direction he faced, the world was in the same pitiful condition, and offered no possible succor to a moneyless uneducated stranger.

On just one night of 4 August 1789 France abolished the long-lasting remnants of the feudal order. It announced, *"The National Assembly abolishes the feudal system entirely."* Lefebvre explains: *"Without debate the Assembly enthusiastically adopted equality of taxation and redemption of all manorial rights except for those involving personal servitude — which were to be abolished without indemnification".*

Other proposals followed with the same success: the equality of legal punishment, admission of all to public office, abolition of venality in office, conversion of the tithe into payments subject to redemption, freedom of worship, prohibition of plural holding of benefices.... Privileges of provinces and towns were offered as a last sacrifice.

Ordinarily the peasants were supposed to pay for the release of seigneurial dues; these dues affected more than a fourth of the farmland in France and provided most of the income of the large landowners. The majority refused to pay and in 1793 the obligation was cancelled. Thus the peasants got their land free, and also no longer paid the tithe to the church.

As the 18th century drew to a close, two decades of poor cereal harvests, drought, cattle disease and skyrocketing bread prices had kindled unrest among peasants and the urban poor in France.

Many expressed their desperation and resentment toward a regime that imposed heavy taxes yet failed to provide relief by rioting, looting and striking. Tensions erupted into the French Revolution of 1789, which some historians have connected to the Little Ice Age.

During the 20 years prior to July 14th, 1789, waves of increased taxation, special 'corvees' (forced road work), arbitrary arrests, harsh punishment for trivial crimes (read 'Les Miserables' by Victor Hugo, for a taste of the social climate), and three successive years of extremely cold summers with unseasonable hail, late snow and inadequate rainfall had disheartened the populace.

Accurate rumors of wide spread corruption by officials of King Louis XVI, who, disregarding severe food shortages, confiscated the grain crops and gained huge profits by exportation to England.

During this period, it is estimated that people were spending from 40% to 60% of their entire budget for bread, which the bakers had contaminated with non-nutritional fillers such as sawdust, marble dust, etc. While the peasants were starving, landed gentry and the nobility ate choice foods served on silver and golden plates. This elite class, while exercising their exclusive hunting rights, destroyed the grain fields of the peasants as they galloped behind their packs of hounds.

The courts were full of starving poachers who received little mercy and were sent to prison, slave galleys, or executed. Peasants had no voting rights but were supposedly represented by a body of nobility who paid for a seat in what was called the 'Paralement.' These nobles treated their responsibilities as an easily acquired privilege, only being interested in personal enrichment. During this time, only 15,000 out of a total population of 25,000,000 had the right to vote.

Abuses toward the common people were not constrained to food, land ownership, and work. Historians estimate that the Bourbon monarch, Louis XVI, debauched as many as 6,000 girls, whose ages ranged from ten to twelve years of age. The Marquise de Pompadour, wife of the King, in order to distract the King from her own sexual affairs, was instrumental in the forcible abduction of these children from helpless parents throughout France.

The King's advisors enriched themselves through corruption, and coupled with profligate spending by Louis and The Pompadour, depleted the treasury to the point where income would not even pay interest on the debt. He and the entire nobility, totally engrossed in their own rights and prerogatives, failed to sense the dangerous thoughts and changing attitudes created by the success of the American Revolution.

The following is a sketchy outline of a very complex and terrible era for the French.

Louis XVI convened the Paralement or 'Etais generaux' on 5 May 1789 and the Constituent of the National Assembly on 17 May. Each day, his ineptitude resulted in increased loss of control to the radical elements and agitated the passion of the poor throughout Paris. Led to the breaking point, on the evening of 14 July 1789, the starving poor (National Assembly) arose in revolt and with their bare hands tore down the Bastille, a much hated prison where many had entered without ever being seen again. The starving, ragged, barefooted mob, in a livid rage, threw themselves against this stone monster, oblivious to any consequences. The first 100-odd victims shot in the process began the blood bath which eventually led, over the next four decades, 3,000,000 French men women, and children, prematurely into their graves. The massive death toll inflicted on other European and Middle East countries is not included.

That same month the inhabitants of Rougeux broke into the Abbey of Beaulieu, menaced the religious and forced them to sign a statement which ceased all pending legal action against them, forced them to forgo the right of the abbey to pasture their animals wherever they pleased, and permitted the peasants the use of Abbey property. It was a prelude to what was coming. Peasants burned many abbeys and chateau's in order to destroy records of debts and property liens with the unfortunate effect of destroying many ancient archives. (Fortunately those of Beaulieu dating after 1600 largely escaped)

The first act of the Revolution on 4 August 1789 eradicated the rights of the feudal system, eliminated the jurisdiction of the seigneurs and removed their privileges over villages and provinces. These prerogatives the Revolutionaries claimed for themselves. Soon all credit, work, and commerce ceased and a famine began to engulf the country. Failure of commerce, bankruptcy, pillages, burnings, hailstorms, and floods-all the grievous events which can overtake a country exploded in full force.

An act of 13 February 1790 mandated all funds previously paid to house and feed priests was to be paid instead to the government, and dispensed with the meager relief for the poverty stricken, begun by the government in 1745. The act of 2 December abolished religious vows, suppressed the religious orders, and seized personal properties of value, including furniture from all abbeys, chapels, bishops, priests, clergy, regular and secular,cures, etc. Teams of men searched for 'Loyalists' (the Church was staunchly loyal to the king) and wantonly destroyed many churches throughout the countryside. Miraculously, an enormous facade of a magnificent cathedral built under the reign of St. Louis IX (1226-1270), destroyed during this period, is still proudly standing in Reims.

On the 22 November 1790 the municipalities of Fayl-Billot, Poinson and of Rougeux, educated on the issue, prepared a long memorandum addressed to the National Assembly against the changes imposed on their district. (The National Assembly had made drastic changes to boundaries, the calendar, religion and social restrictions of France. It is not apparent they were in any way successful in this effort)

A decree of 13 July 1790 forbade all clergy from claiming the validity of their religious constitution and required them to state that it was schismatic and heretical. Also, included in an immediately proceeding act, was a decree that, "It is an odious noise to believe the Pope has any authority."

Vendee rebellion (Civil war in SW France)1793-1796: 100,000

Revolution and Prussia, England, Invasion of Russia, two wars with Austria (1792-1815):
KIA, Died of Wounds + Camp Disease, France Proper: 1,400,000 during the period 1792-1815, incl. 916,000 [65%] under the Empire. [Which would leave 484,000 dead (or 35%) under the Republic.]
Total war dead among all European armies: 3 million (35% or 1.05M under the Republic)

Reign of Terror: 40,000
Executed with Trial: 17,000
Executed w/o Trial: 12,000
Died in jail: "thousands"

OWNED BY AUTHOR

On 2 January 1791, after each parish mass in the departments, standing in front of the sanctuary, a member of the municipality (there were no shortages of anti-Christians in every place) demanded that all religious and parishioners swear an oath to the above decree. Those priests who refused to submit were stripped of their possessions and either slaughtered or by the ferocious act of 23 April 1793, or sent to prison on Devil's Island in French Guiana. (The islands were part of a penal colony from 1852 onwards for common-law criminals of France, who were convicted by juries rather than magistrates. The main part of the penal colony was a labor camp that stretched along the border with Dutch Guiana (present-day Suriname) This penal colony was controversial as it had a reputation for harshness and brutality. Prisoner-on-prisoner violence was common; tropical diseases were rife. Only a small minority of broken survivors returned to France to tell how horrible it was)

By 1793 the Revolution was beginning to slip into the power of the Republicans (2nd estate) and the reaction to this is known as the Terror. The sharp knife of the guillotine began its work. The heads of the King and Queen along with thousands of the nobility, fell into the basket.

In each village, a list of those suspected of sheltering priests, was compiled by spies. These suspects were then arrested, their houses ransacked, their meat, mattocks, pitch forks, casks, and implements stolen, and only excepting the aged and those under sixteen, were thrown into prison. Others, suspected of resisting, were placed under the surveillance of the authorities and, in an attempt to weaken their resolve, were required to present themselves every day, in the morning at 10 o'clock and in the evening at 7 o'clock, in front of the officers of the municipality, to register in a book. Already struggling with the effects of the widespread famine, imagine the onerous burden it was to be required to walk two round trips of several miles each day to Fayl-Billot for such a useless task and still accomplish the necessary manual labor required to survive. As it is in every age, there are neighbors and 'friends' who are willing to do the dirty work of those in power. What hate must have been felt toward them! It is interesting to consider the fate of these toadies after the Revolution failed! One woman, Anne Charlot, several times failed to sign the book at the allotted time, and in punishment, the gendarmes dragged her in front of the magistrate who tied a rope around her neck, and without a trial, hung her from the tree of 'Liberty' in the village.

In Pierrefaites, Madam Hurault was marched through all the roads of the village while the residents were forced to shout at her. She was afterwards restricted to her place for a full year. Immediately after, they burned, with all the family members, the Minot house and barn. Soon the revolutionaries formed mobs and went from one church to another, and equipped with clubs, broke the statues, windows, holy vases, crosses, and church bells. They stole the chalices, vestments, and other objects of value and turned them over to the magistrates. Even the bell ropes were confiscated and given to the Navy.

Determined to wipe out Christianity, Robespierre and his godless followers forbade the rites of religion and wrote a new calendar which eliminated Sundays. They increased the length of each week to ten days and 22 September of the year 1792 began the year one (AN I), with each month having thirty days. (The calendar is deceptively difficult to calculate and has had a number of various systems over thousands of years. The Revolutionaries found themselves with a can of worms and Napoleon put an end to this comedy. It is an interesting read and only lightly touched upon here.

After all public practice of religion was forbidden, it was determined that ceremonies for baptisms and marriages were still a social and legal necessity. In order to accommodate these requirements, these Christian rites were changed to a completely secular rote.

In Archives #3 of 'The Long Journey' are copies of a number of such ceremonies before, during and after this period. Two of these marriage ceremonies occurred during the time of the Revolution (1792-1804) and were held in the commune building of the village. The first was between JB2 and Marguerite Moulet on the 21st day of Vendemiaire of the year III (11 November 1795); the second is between JB2 and Catherine Ageron on the 4th of Brumaire in the year X (24 October 1802) God and Christ were not mentioned in any of them.

The pope recognized the futility of attempting to immediately change the regime, and on 28 May 1793 issued the following proclamation, *"When it is impossible to have recourse to the*

Catholic priest, it suffices for the marriage validity, that it be consecrated before witnesses, although without the presence of a priest." It is almost amusing how empty the newly invented rites became after God was eliminated from the ceremony. As a replacement, the bride and groom stood in the door of the Communal House and shouted to the great outdoors. "We are taking each other in marriage".

After secularization of the Church, in secret within their homes, a number of families, under great danger, held catechism classes for their children. One of those known today, was a

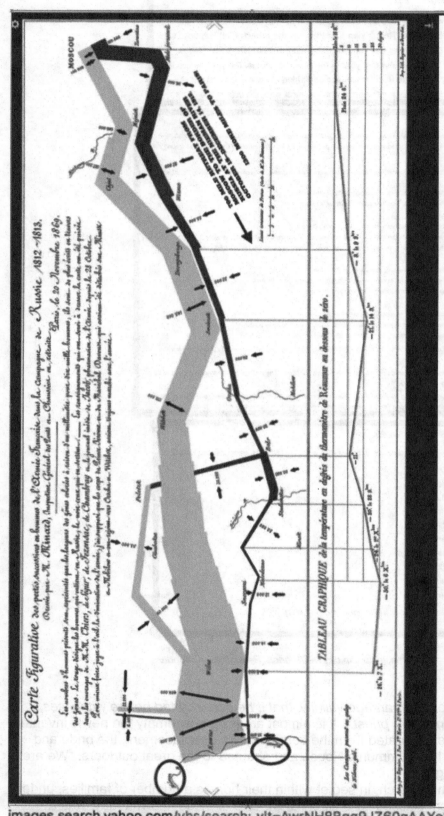

FiGURATIVE MAP of the successive losses in men of the French Army in the Russian campaign 1812-1813. Drawn by Mr. Minard, Inspector General of Bridges and Roads in retirement. Paris, 20 November 1869.

The numbers of men present are represented by the widths of the colored zones in a rate of one millimeter for ten thousand men; these are also written beside the zones. Red designates men moving into Russia, black those on retreat. — The informations used for drawing the map were taken from the works of Messrs. Thiers, de Ségur, de Fezensac, de Chambray and the unpublished diary of Jacob, pharmacist of the Army since 28 October.

In order to facilitate the judgement of the eye regarding the diminution of the army, I supposed that the troops under Prince Jérôme and under Marshal Davoust, who were sent to Minsk and Mobilow and who rejoined near Orscha and Witebsk, had always marched with the army.

Mulson at Pierrefaites, a relative of my grandmother (a Mignot and wife of my grandfather, John Baptiste Rougeux IV)

Caught up in the enthusiasm of the revolution and determined to change everything nothing was spared in the French society, including the length of the week, their names and the names of the months and lasted about a decade until 1804.

Great confusion, execution of Revolutionaries, royalty, and poor continued at a rapid pace. Hunger, war with Germany, suppression of religion, bad weather, defeat of the army, and profound fear among the populace led to the assumption of power by Napoleon in 1799 and eventual dictatorship in 1804.

Napoleon came into power and returned the calendar to its previous system. After ravaging all of Europe during the decade of his rule, Napoleon's defeat at the hands of the Russians in 1812 led to his eventual overthrow in 1814 and his sentencing to the island of Elba, just off the Italian coast.

In 1815 he escaped and returned to a tumultuous welcome of an exhausted people who wanted leadership. For 100 days he managed to reclaim the throne of France but his defeat at Waterloo signaled the attack on France by Russia, Austria, England, and the Prussians. All traditional enemies, they were anxious to extract revenge for the years of defeat suffered at his hands. Continuous battles against the allied enemies resulted in severe destruction and loss of life in the Rougeux region before France was defeated and Paris occupied. (Read 'A Tale of Two Cities' for another glimpse of bleak life in those days) He was exiled in the remote South Atlantic island of St Helena and died there in 1821 at age 51.

Following his exile severe shortage of manpower for the defeated army outside the occupied areas forced the French to conscript every able-bodied man the country, including young boys and middle aged men. Both armies combed the countryside for food and devoured critical seed grains and created wide spread famine during the following years. Multiplying all their other suffering, monstrous anger and resentment must have been felt against this godless crowd!

Adding to the misery, in 1815 and 1816, gloom, extremely low summer temperatures and incessant rainfall, extending into 1817, caused by dust particles trapped in the upper atmosphere from volcanic eruptions of Tambora, a volcanic mountain in Indonesia. This

ST HELENS ISLAND IN THE SOUTH PACIFIC

NAPLEONS LAST HOME

commons.wikimedia.org

eruption was the largest volcanic eruption in recorded history and caused global climate anomalies that included the phenomenon known as 'volcanic winter'. Coupled with the general chill of the Little Ice Age, 1816 became known as the famously frosty 'Year Without a Summer'. Crops failed and livestock died in much of the Northern Hemisphere, resulting in the worst famine of the 19th century.

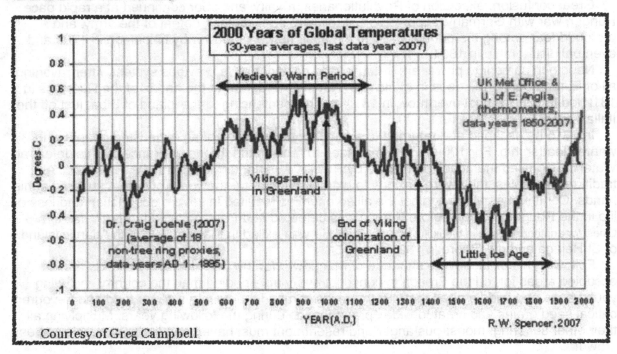

2000 Years of Global Temperatures
(30-year averages, last data year 2007)

Medieval Warm Period

UK Met Office & U. of E. Anglia (thermometers, data years 1850-2007)

Vikings arrive in Greenland

Dr. Craig Loehle (2007) (average of 18 non-tree ring proxies, data years AD 1 - 1935)

End of Viking colonization of Greenland

Little Ice Age

YEAR (A.D.)

R.W. Spencer, 2007

Courtesy of Greg Campbell

My dad said his father once told him how soldiers, forced to join the army, hated Napoleon and did all they safely could to hinder him. Following his loss at Waterloo and deposition in 1815, powerful men tricked the fickle populace into accepting Charles X, another of the corrupt Bourbons as king.

All the promises made by Charles X before his coronation were immediately discarded and the familiar forms of corruption returned in full force. In 1820, all civil liberties were suppressed, savage penalties imposed for minor infractions and the use of thousands of internal spies caused fear and constant unrest. Financial distress was rampant. Freedom of the press was abolished and on 28 July 1830 the first dead bodies of another major revolution lay on the streets of Paris. At its end, because of the machinations of the powerful, the revolutionaries succeeded only in again replacing one Bourbon king for another.

Thousands perished in a widespread cholera epidemic during 1832, reviving great fears the Black Plague was about to recommence.

June 1832 saw another brutally suppressed peasant uprising in the streets of Paris and a revolt by woolen weavers (which is what JBIII and his family did to survive) against the widespread dishonesty and corruption of the suppliers. These disturbances created widespread economic depression and undoubtably seriously impacted all forms of commerce, especially for products whose purchase could be delayed. Hunger always lurked in the daily lives of the peasants.

Undoubtedly, these events placed severe economic pressures on JBIII (John B. Rougeux, my great-grandfather) and were likely some of the major factors leading to his emigration in 1835.

Shortly after procuring their free passport and as indigents, likely free travel assistance from the French Government on March 1st, 1834, they no doubt began immediate preparations to leave. They certainly must have had correspondence with Mr. Keating in the

172

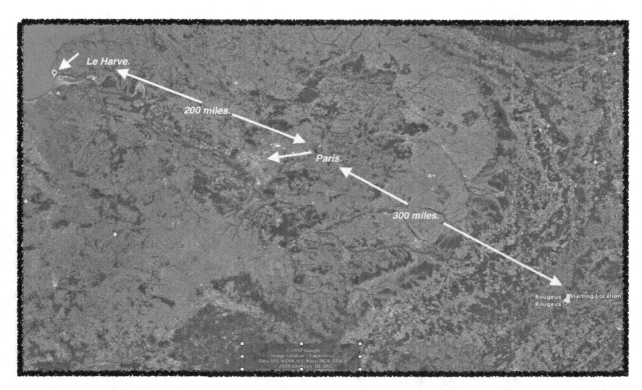

US but I have not found any extant records of how the arrangements to locate the ship and its departure schedule 500 miles away were communicated. They and others from neighboring villages planning to also make the trip undoubtably joined together. A 500 mile trip in that era was a phenomenal journey through villages and large cities such as Paris which they had never before seen would never again. A guide must have accompanied and assisted them with shelter and food as well as the right roads and streets to follow on what must have, at best, a 7-10 day trip to Le Harve. Sailing vessels had wide latitude in their schedules and at complete mercy of the winds and weather therefore a certain indefinite wait at the docks was certain to

happen. Who supplied their necessities is unknown. The next phase was normally a 3 month ordeal on the damp, moldy and endlessly rolling ship. Supplies were loaded in proportion to the number of passengers for a specific number of days, Cooking was done below decks by the passengers on the single stove available. Delays and arguments apparently often ensued if excessive time was taken at the stove.

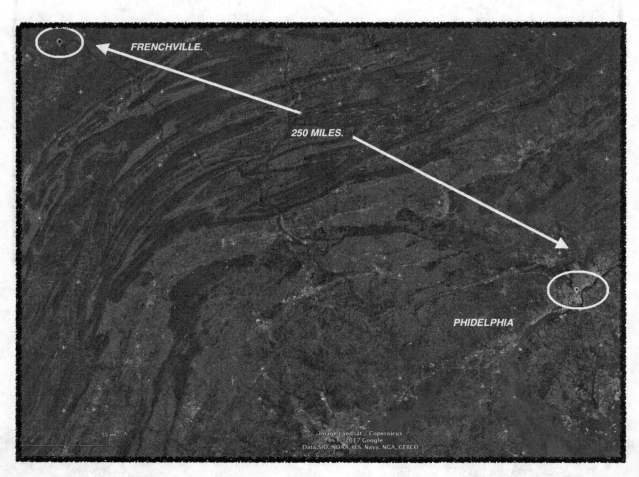

Great-Grandad had responsibility for his pregnant wife, two small daughters, his aunt and mother-in law, the last two in their 60's. Available records indicate the loss of a daughter and birth of a son probably during this voyage.Upon arrival at Philadelphia, there are indications that care was given by a religious order until they recovered from the effects of this ordeal.

Numerous verbal accounts probably confirm that they walked the final 200 miles across the fertile fields of SE Pennsylvania, then climbed the 800 foot escarpment that defines the Southern boundary of the Appalachians in this area arriving into the densely wooded mountains for the final 150 mile journey. My Dad told me he heard his grandfather related the joy they felt as they walked across the flat fertile countryside of SE Pennsylvania in the false assumption they would be owning similar land. What a cruel disappointment the thin and infertile land they owned must have dealt them—not to mention the thick growth of massive white pine trees—which would ultimately be the source of their survival and prosperity.

According to Francois Joffrain, *"From the years 1800-1820 much vineyard was planted in the south-east of Haute-Marne, including Pierrefaites. The quality of the wine was average or mediocre. a large part sold to the inhabitants of Paris and suburbs (not the middle-class but the workers). Near 1860, the vineyards reached their peak and the villages were densely populated. Near 1870, an illness (phylloxera) ruined the vineyards and brought about the decline of population of the villages. I think JB Rougeux(JB2) (b.1768) became a winemaker as many other people in that region, keeping some cows and some fields cultivated and becoming a winemaker while staying a little farmer. "*

From La Vendue until Moulin Jobart, on the facing east slopes, there was a large vineyard (perhaps 3 acres). Its possible that JB1 wasthe owner of a part."

(Abbot Mulson quotes the following from either correspondence or direct contact with an emigrant to Frenchville sometime soon after 1891.)

"In those happy days (1830's) children were numerous and our countryside overcrowded. (Its ironic how memories can neglect the civil wars, insurrections, famines, poverty—our ancestor is listed as an indigent in the passport application file at Chamont in 1834—and continuing unrest from the Revolution when homesickness is a factor). A wave of emigration carried the extra population towards America".

"In April 1832 the Mulson-Pierrot family, made up of the father, Mother and their 9 children left Pierrefaites and embarked at Le Harve, together with two other families of the neighborhood. When arrived in New York, the immigrants moved inland and stopped in a place where the Anabaptists had been unable to stay. (This was not the case for our emigrants—they contracted for 40 acres at Frenchville prior to departure and had a defined destination—see the 'Long Journey' for the full and complicated background of their adventure). They named it 'Frenchville' in memory of their native land."

"The very first beginnings were very hard indeed. They were short of everything, even the food they had to get from a distance." My Father told me his father, as a boy drive a team to Tyrone, (a two day-40 mile trip) for grocery supplies and other necessary items. (Another verbal source handed down to the present day is quoted, "We had to carry our farine (flour) on our backs". (Possibly Tyrone). "It was a vie de chien" (dogs life).

"They starved many a time whenever the overflowing rivers cut communications. They started by exploiting the forest: using only their arms they rolled or dragged the tree trunks.

Virgin white pine stumps near the farm at Frenchville Pa 1900 Grampa Rougeux cleared 300 acres of these trees and stumps all with the help of horses and a pick.

"What our compatriots missed most of all was being deprived of religious assistance. They were staunch observers of Sunday as a day of rest, compulsory in America anyway, and as they were unable to attend Mass because they were too far away from a church, they would gather in one of the rooms of their farms which was arranged an oratory. The prayers were said in common followed by psalms, hymns and songs all in connection with the day which they sang from the books of the diocese of Langres (15 miles W) that they had (with good foresight) brought with them. How happy they were when a Catholic priest came to visit them! "

"Other emigrants from our region had not been long in joining the and after 12 years, the population scattered about the territory amounted to almost 150 people. Then they built a wooden chapel and got a priest to come and celebrate services from time to time. Fifteen years later they were numerous enough to contemplate building a church. Stone is scarce in the area. Walking through the forest, someFrenchvilleman providentially came across a huge block of stone, just above the ground. They all got down to work; the rock was cut up into freestones and rubble stone with which they could build a beautiful church with a parsonage next to it. The bishop of Harrisburg sent the congregation a French priest from Auvergne (Fr. Berbigier)) who was their first minister. Subsequently they built a school for boys and one for girls. The latter was entrusted to nuns. According to the existing laws in America, immigrants are responsible for the expenses for worship and instruction."

"Crops in Frenchville are not much different from ours. The pips, stones and grafts they had brought with them or which had been sent from France, soon became trees with good yield."

"So far, vine could not be acclimatized, only the climbing one, which gives a little wine, is cultivated."

"For a long time the settlement kept its habits, customs and even the dialect from its homeland but now that the market town (Clearfield?) contains over 1500 souls, the Yankee element threatens to absorb the original population entirely. (Finally happened in 2000). Even 10 years ago, (1881) the bishop of Harrisburg, Irish by birth, imposed on the congregation a priest (Fr. Hugh Mullen) who doesn't speak our language."

No records exist on how Marguerite Ageron Rougeux supported herself, her five year old son, JB3 and three stepsons, Nicholas, Jean and Pierre, during the eight years following the death of JB2 in 1811. Her marriage, on June 19th, 1819 to Nicholas Gardel, shoemaker at Broncourt, ended her widowhood and her residence at La Gite farm where she had lived during those years.

JB3 may not have learned the shoemaking trade because on his passport application he lists himself as a weaver and probably served a term as an apprentice during his youth. It does not appear he ever learned to write. Meanwhile his older brother, Pierre followed them to Broncourt and apparently lived there his entire life in poverty as a weaver. Documents prove Nicholas immigrated to Frenchville four years prior to JB3 in 1830 and eventually relocating in Ohio where he died at an old age. Jean apparently perished at some early age.

August Term 1846

Certificate of

John. B. Rangeau

Reverse side of JB3"s Citizenship papers
Granted in the Clearfield County Court August 1846

Citizenship confirmation of JB3 September 1, 1843

BE IT REMEMBERED, That a Court of Common Pleas held at Clearfield for the county of Clearfield, in the Commonwealth of Pennsylvania, in the United States of America on the *first* day of *Septo* in the year of our Lord one thousand eight hundred and *forty* *six* *John B Rougeaux* a native of *France* exhibited a petition praying to be admitted to become a citizen of the United States, and it appearing to the said Court that he had declared on *his solemn oath* before the Prothonotary of the Court for the county of *Clearfield* on the *Seventeenth* day of *October* A. D. 18*43* that it was bona fide his intention to become a citizen of the United States, and to renounce forever all allegiance and fidelity to any foreign Prince, Potentate, State or Sovereignity whatsoever and particularly the *King of France* of whom he was at that time a *Subject* and the said *John B. Rougeaux* having on his solemn *oath* declared and also made proof thereof by competent testimony of *F. F. Conduict & Jacob Fralin* citizens of the United States, that he had resided one year and upwards within the State of Pennsylvania, and within the United States of America, upwards of five years immediately preceding his application, and it appearing to the satisfaction of the Court that during that time he had behaved as a man of good moral character; attached to the principles of the Constitution of the United States, and well disposed to the good order and happiness of the same; and having on his solemn *oath* before the said Court that he would support the Constitution of the United States, and that he did absolutely and entirely renounce and abjure all allegiance and fidelity to every foreign Prince, Potentate, State and Sovereignity whatever, and particularly to the *King of France* of whom he was before a

Thereupon the Court admitted the said *John B Rougeaux* to become a citizen of the United States, and ordered all the proceedings aforesaid to be recorded by the Prothonotary of the said Court, and which was done accordingly.

Wm C. Welch Prothonotary.

LIST OF NEW FAMILIES AT PIERREFAITES DURING THE 18TH CENTURY

3° Liste des nouvelles familles qui apparaissent à Pierrefaite pendant le XVIII° siècle

Ageron, 1731. Andriot, 1709.

Bailly, 1731. Béguinot, 1700. Blanchard, 1760. Belin (1), 1710. Blondot, 1748. Bonhomme, 1733. Bourcier (2), 1706. Branchet, 1705. Brugnon, 1771.

Cailliet, 1709. Canot, 1731. César, 1753. Chamelet, 1738. Chapeau, 1707. Chauffournier, 1721. Chaussin, 1737. Chevillot (3), 1701. Chodet, 1750. Collicy, 1751. Courtejoie, 1759. Cressot, 1712.

Daguin, 1773. Delacoue, 1730. Delatour, 1728. Dartois, 1734. Davignon, 1716. Debigu, 1733. Drouot (4), Drouhin, 1718.

Faulle, 1730. Fournoy, 1709. Febvre, 1700. Fleury, 1710. Floriot, 1718.

Galissot, 1717. Gallois, 1781. Gaudiot, 1710. Gauthier, 1738. Gennois, 1720. Gentilhomme, 1735. Gilbert, 1734. Girault, 1703. Goblet, 1730. Goublet, 1714. Grandmanche, 1721. Gruyot, 1730.

Henri, 1723. Huguenin, 1707.

Jachiet, 1723. Jacquet, 1735. Jeanninet, 1724. Jobard, 1723. Jolivet, 1720.

Létalnet, 1722. Liect, 1712. Logerot, 1781. Loiselot, 1766. Lombard, 1711. Luquet (5), 1743.

Maisonnet, 1739. Marcel, 1703. Marchal, 1731. Marichal, 1735. Martin, 1720. Mathey, 1718. Mergey, 1730. Mordin, 1764. Mojuet, 1721. Monniot, 1753. Mioguet, 1717. Moris, 1700. Morisot, 1755. Mortel, 1752. Morot, 1725.

Ouvrardot, 1731.

Paille, 1718. Péchinet, 1758. Pelleteret, 1773. Philpin, 170?. Picard, 1769. Pierre, 1759. Pignot, 1710. Pinget, 1757. Poinsot, 1737. Prudent, 1731.

Robert, 1705. Roberty, 1780. Roodot, 1733. Rosoy, 1705. Rougeux, 1712. Roussée (6), 1730. Ruffin, 1703.

Sautot, 1755. Seurre, 1718.

Thevenin, 1712.

Vallot, 1715. Vaudin, 1733. Vaulot, 1711. Varney, 1701. Viard, 1716. Viardot, 1716. Verdier, 1743. Villemin, 1792. Voinchet, 1745.

⊕ FAMILIAR NAMES AT FRENCHVILLE

(1) Jacques Belin, sergent en la justice de Pierrefaite, 1750-1778.
(2) Revers Bourcier, chaud.
(3) P. Chevillot, huissier royal en la justice de Pierrefaite, 1707-1709.
(4) S. Drouot, greffier en la justice de Pierrefaite, 1750 1-98.
(5) Claude Luquet, lieutenant en la justice de Pierrefaite, 1734.
(6) Luis de Roussée, comme de terre.

FAMILIES WHO DEPARTED PIERREFAITES 1803-1833

4° Liste des familles qui existent à Pierrefaite, de 1803 à 1833

Ageron, Andriot, Aubert.

Bastien, Bardel, Barthélemy, Belin, Bessel, Bergeret, Berquier, Blanchard, Blugeon, Doubet, Bournot, Bourcier, Brayer, Braconnier, Brenodl.

Cailliet, Carné, Cartaret, Cersoy, Chameroy, Chaussin, Charles, Champion, Chodet, Collin, Courtejoie, Coussin.

Duponsois, Dumoulin.

Faivre, Febvre.

Gardiennet, Gaudiot, Gauthier, Géault, Girod, Girault, Goblet, Grossetête, Gruyot.

Hasse, Henri, Hubert, Huot.

Igaard.

Jacquinot, Jaugey, Jeanninelle, Jobart, Jobard, Jolivet, Jourdheuil.

Labarbe, Lambert, Lamirat, Lamotte, Laprevotte, Lecoq, Lemoine, Loiselot.

Mallair, Mamnde, Marcout, Martin, Masson, Mathey, Maurice, Mercier, Mergey, Mouret, Mille, Millot, de Minette de Beaujeu, Moluet, Mordin, Moris, Morisot, Mortel, Mortel, Muleon.

Ouvrardot.

Paille, Peltrat, Pierrot, Pinget, Pioche, Plein, Ploub, Prctols.

Quentel.

Ragot, Havetet, Richard, Roberty, Roger, Rougeux, Roussel, Ruffin.

Sel.

Thirion, Tierce, Tisserand, Tripier.

Valette, Valory, Varney, Vauthrin, Villemin, Voirin, Willet (Quillet).

Total: 113 noms de famille, dont plus de 90 ont déjà disparu.

TOTAL 113 NAMES OF FAMILIES AND MORE THAN 90 HAVE ALREADY DEPARTED.

The Rougeux's left France in 1835

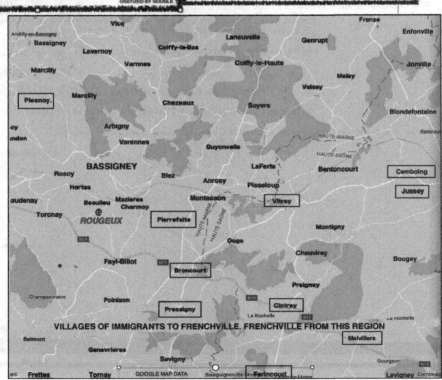

VILLAGES OF IMMIGRANTS TO FRENCHVILLE. FRENCHVILLE FROM THIS REGION

COMMUNES.	POPULATION.					RAPPORT par cent entre 1801 et 1856.
	1801.	1831.	1841.	1856.	Moyenne.	
Piépape	373	295	240	276	283	—16
Pierrefaite	585	618	620	582	601	0
Pierrefontaine	60	80	68	55	65	— 8
Pisseloup.............	278	265	236	215	248	—22
Planrupt.............	202	279	306	308	271	53
Plesnoy	384	470	458	451	440	18
Poinsenot	274	253	231	179	221	—22
Poinson-les-Fays	602	569	586	494	562	—18
Poinson-les-Grancey.....	206	250	212	183	210	—11
Poinson-les Nogent	324	406	406	401	383	25
Poiseul.............	176	234	260	230	225	30
Poissons.............	1632	1623	1595	1478	1582	— 9
Pont-la-Ville.........	368	435	467	381	412	3
Pouilly.............	608	679	641	608	632	0
Poulangy.............	681	796	780	750	751	10
Prangey.............	535	532	499	468	508	—12
Praslay..............	329	368	329	297	329	—10
Pratz	70	70	79	47	64	—32
Prauthoy............	654	676	735	690	693	6
Pressigny............	598	846	875	739	804	14
Prez-sous-Lafauche	510	590	665	650	603	28
Prez-sur-Marne	147	205	228	200	195	36
Provenchères-Marne	138	156	178	153	156	11
Provenchères-Meuse.	473	620	633	570	574	20
Puellemontier.........	548	541	533	466	522	—15
Puits-des-Mèzes (le)....	256	305	307	270	283	12
Ragecourt-sur-Blaise	112	157	140	138	136	23
Ragecourt-sur-Marne	144	151	424	485	301	236
Ranconnières	379	391	386	380	384	0
Rangecourt	321	310	289	263	295	—18
Ravenne-Fontaine	303	300	290	251	286	—17
Récourt	269	312	321	309	302	14
Renneport...........	363	295	305	280	310	—23
Reynel	492	520	590	540	535	9
Riaucourt...........	317	435	493	581	436	51
Richebourg..........	585	689	656	596	631	2
Rimaucourt..........	539	720	864	817	736	51
Rivières-le-Bois......	324	327	303	295	312	— 9
Rivières-les-Fosses	883	755	780	724	785	—18
Rizaucourt	296	350	390	353	348	19
Robert-Magnil	436	468	466	485	463	11
Rochefort...........	262	251	250	230	247	— 5
Roche-sur-Marne.......	325	384	411	407	381	25
Roche-sur-Rognon......	452	525	660	714	587	58
Rochetaillée	403	370	405	404	395	0
Rolampont...........	1134	1226	1281	1194	1208	5
Romain	525	553	538	478	523	— 9
Roécourt	301	323	336	310	312	18
Rosoy	545	624	663	643	618	18
Rouécourt	225	235	251	216	236	— 4
Rouelles	245	275	144	164	206	—35
Rougeux	358	395	481	435	416	21
Rouvre	469	535	474	435	478	— 7
Rouvroy	254	279	299	390	305	54
Rozières............	364	354	299	258	343	— 3
R....pt.............	213	380	343	348	308	64

```
ADDENDUM
IN AN ATTEMPT TO MAKE THIS HISTORY A MORE COMREHENSIVE
ACCOUNT OF OUR IMMIGRANTS' TRAVAILS AND ACCOMPLISHMENTS,
THE FOLLOWING PAGES HAVE BEEN EXCERPTED FROM 'THE LONG
JOURNEY', A HISTORY FOCUSED ON THEIR LIFE IN THE USA.
```

Pennsylvania is divided into two regions; warm fertile fields in the east and the colder Allegheny Mountains crossing the center of the state. Near Hymer, not above 50 miles from Frenchville, these mountains yield rocks containing mastodon and other fossils from the Devonian Period (400,000,000 years ago).

Originally joined in a landmass forming what is now southwestern Ireland, Africa, Europe, Australia, Antarctica, and South America, they formed part of a continent named Pangaea where Africa is now located. One of the large segments that separated from Pangaea gradually moved north and west and eventually separated into two sections. One which now forms southwestern Ireland and the other forms all the land east of the Alleghenies to the Atlantic. The eventual collision with the continent which lay in its path to the west compressed and uplifted the region forming the Allegheny Mountains. It has been postulated that these mountains are some of the oldest and may have been the highest in the world, perhaps reaching 40,000 feet but across these millions of years have eroded to their present elevations.

The Susquehanna, an Indian name probably meaning *"The Long Crooked River"*, spreads its tentacles across eastern Pennsylvania, filling its valleys with beauty and sometimes with menace and turmoil. Draining 20,000 square miles, many of its tributaries are still seldom visited even by hunters. Clearfield County is situated in the central mountainous region of Pennsylvania. The 200 mile long West Branch (of the Susquehanna River) cuts across Clearfield County from the southwest to the northeast. To the east of the river rise the great Appalachian Divide paralleling the river irregularly and draining the eastern two-thirds to the Chesapeake Bay. The other one third of the mountains on the west drains into the Mississippi River.

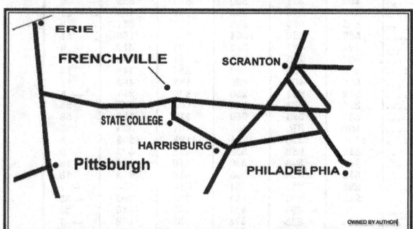

The history of Pennsylvania leads us directly to William Penn. Born in a high social position with an excellent education, he shocked his friends when he joined the Quakers, a persecuted religious sect with substantially differing life styles than that which he was accustomed. Admiral Penn, William's father, had previously loaned King Charles 16,000£ which the King was unable to repay. When Admiral Penn died, he bequeathed William vast estates in

73

England and Scotland and the accounts receivable of the King. Seeking a haven for the Quakers, William asked the King to grant him land between Lord Baltimore's province of Maryland and the Duke of York's province of New York as payment of the debt. The King agreed and the charter was signed March 4th, 1681.The charter was to include all the land between the thirty-ninth and forty-second degrees of north latitude and from the Delaware River westward for five degrees of longitude; slightly under 100,000 square miles.

Eastern Pennsylvania had been settled much earlier by Scotch, Irish, German and English peoples. Because of the 800-foot high Allegheny Front, an abrupt escarpment which passes through Altoona, State College, and up to Williamsport in a northeasterly direction, migration followed the more level country southwest along this front through Cumberland Gap to Kentucky and beyond. Nobody wanted to try to farm the infertile soil in the mountains of Clearfield County, which ranges from 1400 feet at Frenchville to more than 2100 feet further north. This geological fault had long caused the population to remain sparse in Clearfield County. *

The territory embracing Clearfield County has the distinction of having been under three different national and ecclesiastical governments: first, under the French flag and the see of Quebec from 1753 to 1758; second, under the English and the Vicariate Apostolic of London from 1758 to the Treaty of Paris in 1783; and third, under the American flag and successively under the Sees of Baltimore, Philadelphia, Pittsburgh, and Erie (after Erie was formed into a See in 1853).

Despite the isolation and difficult terrain, by 1769 early surveyors had completed their surveys of the region encompassing Clearfield County long before any settlements were made. The County contained the finest white pine forests in the world and was known as *"The Dark Land"*. It was formed in 1804 from Huntington and Lycoming counties. The county seat of Clearfield was fixed by the legislature in 1805 and, at that time, it contained 104 *"taxable inhabitants and 16 single freemen."* By 1810 Clearfield County had 875 settlers and by 1830 had grown to 4800 hundred souls. That year Clearfield consisted of the Court House, three˅ hotels, a few stores, and about a dozen houses scattered over the town site. Construction of the Catholic Church was begun soon after 1830.

The following description, almost illegible, is taken from the first known official map of Clearfield County, showing six counties and dated 1816. It is written in such glowing term's one wonders if it was used as a sales brochure to help entice the prospective immigrants.

> *DESCRIPTION: Clearfield town, which is intended for the seat of justice, contains, in addition to a brick courthouse not quite finished, 5 dwelling houses. The West Branch of the Susquehanna (borders) the West part of the town and forms its grant. Curwensville has 4 houses. Karthaus has 4 houses. Near this village (Karthaus) (which is of very recent date) iron works have been created and important improvements are progressing fostered by the care of the industrious——people. MOUNTAINS—this country contains no mountains of great magnitude but form the great range of the Allegheny and Appalachian mountains which skirt its Southern—— — ——East to West in its whole extent, numerous ridges of various sizes stretch themselves in different directions and present an appearance highly picturesque. SOIL—about ⅓ this of the county is tillable and is of various*

As a note of interest, the Pike leading from Louisville south to Bardtown, Kentucky, hundreds of miles west, in 1835 had carved limestone mile markers along its route.

descriptions, generally speaking it is——— ——— ———, excepting the ——Creek flats, which are of a rich loam sufficiently intermixed with——gravel and said to render it highly proper for cultivation of Indian corn. As far as experiments have been made,—— —— prove that much of the upland ridges, because of (good) summer rains ——— ——- ———winter——have been cultivated with considerable success. —— in experiences and when acquired it will no doubt have excellent —— ———for——considerable part of it still covered with large timber among the various types are the pine, oak, hemlock,—,maple,—,birch, with many ——————— ——— ——— MINERALS—An——bituminous coal promises (next two sentences illegible). Naphtha might be obtained——GAME—The wild elk, bear,—— —, white tailed deer, and others common to the climate abound. ——in the panther, wolves, wild turkey, black—— DIVISION—The county is divided into 6 townships. CLIMATE—The winters are very cold——and last 5 months. The summers are mild and pleasant. NAVIGATION—The West Branch of the Susquehanna River which is the line of Clearfield county, coming essentially—, is —— and at the Canoe place 17 yards wide. This stream, with proper improvement, may be made navigable to this latter place for boats at all seasons of the year. (The balance of the writing is illegible).

In the *Historical Journal*, vol. II, page 290, located in the Historical Society in Clearfield, there is an interesting story about P. A. Karthaus whose actions became pivotal to the future of the Rougeux tribe. The following is a statement by George A. Snyder, son of the governor of

"The first time I saw Peter was in the year 1812 when he was in my father's house in Harrisburg. He had recently arrived from Germany with a model of a boat having a wheel at its head connected to a lever. The ends of the lever were attached to poles whereby the boat was to be shoved against the current. It is not worthwhile to describe a more minute description of the contrivance; suffice to say it was constructed on the principle that the force of the current would rotate the wheel, which would set the lever and poles in motion to propel the boat against the current; something like mounting a chair to look over the top of ones own head. Peter built his boat

View of mountians and the Sesquehanna near Frenchville, PA

but of course discovered it would not go up stream because the current was against it and would not go downstream because the poles would not let it."

"After a few days in Harrisburg, Peter departed for Clearfield County where he purchased large tracts of land. He was rich and having discovered his lands were well supplied with coal, timber, iron ore, and some waterpower, resolved to become richer. Accordingly, by 1820 he had laid out thousands of dollars in erecting a furnace, a forge, a large mill, a coke oven, a convenient

wharf, and several large houses, all of stone. Peter manufactured iron but, behold, there was no way to export his products and his businesses failed, resulting in bankruptcy and foreclosure of his lands by Mr. John Keating (and leading to the eventual arrival of JB3!)."

Another article in the Historical Journal states:

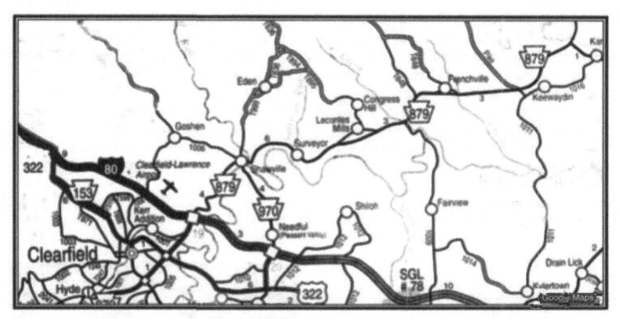

"During 1817 Karthaus and Rev. Frederick Geisenhainer erected a furnace on Moshannon Creek (located at the bottom of the mountain upon which Karthaus is built). Bog ore was brought up the river from near the head of Buttermilk Falls, four miles below Karthaus, in canoes and flat boats to supply the furnace. Hollowware, stoves, etc of the best quality was manufactured. This production was of great help to Allegheny Coal company because of the demand for coal created by the furnaces. After his bankruptcy, another company, in 1836, spent $80,000 dollars developing the furnaces but all suffered the same lack of transportation facilities and by 1840 this effort too, had failed."

The West Branch of the Sesquahanna near Frenchville 1965
OWNED BY AUTHOR

Frenchville, situated within Covington Township, is located in the northeastern corner of Clearfield county, approximately seventeen miles northeast of Clearfield, the county seat. The West Branch of the Susquehanna River passes near Frenchville as it winds its tortuous course through the mountains. As to the origin of Frenchville, nothing is certain. We must depend upon tradition, heresay, and certain undocumented folklore. One fanciful account states that the Frenchville Territory was originally purchased as an asylum for Napoleon Bonaparte. Another tale says it was secured from a failed settlement of "Anabaptists" (original name for the Baptist religion). Neither story, however, have ever been substantiated.

The following deduction, pieced together from various bits of information, seems to have the most basis of fact. Associated events tend to confirm at least some parts of the story.

When Covington Township was formed in 1815 it was already famous for its millions of white pine trees. After foreclosing on the Peter Karthaus holdings, Mr. John Keating immediately concluded that the beautiful stands of oak and white pine timber contained in his newly acquired acres were worthless unless the enormous manpower required to harvest this timber could be found. Commencing in 1827, he commissioned a man by the name of J. Schnarrs to act as agent for the sale of these lands, and sent him to the regions of Haute Marne and Haute Soane, France to entice the poverty stricken and landless peasants to emigrate to America. Traveling from village to village, he enticed a family from this village, two from another and so on. His route through the region can be traced by comparing the names of those who emigrated to their town of origin. According to *"History of French Settlers"* by Margaret Mignot, he also recruited settlers from Normandy and Picardy.

OWNED BY AUTHOR

Copied from a tintype taken about 1865

John B Rougeux III   1806-1888
Immigrant from Haute_Marne, France-1835

OWNED BY AUTHOR

Wife of JB2 who emigrated
with him in 1835

JB3 was probably able to emigrate due in part to Keatings willingness to defer payments until after he had established himself. This offer, accompanied by the reasonably confirmed story of a twelve acre bonus given for prompt acceptance of the offer, would have been powerful inducements for a favorable decision. At any rate, we definitely know the existing social conditions in France were awful, a probably embellished description of the New World and the ingrained desire for land ownership all proved irresistible to our ancestor and many others like them.

When the persuasive and untiring salesman, traveling through Haute Marne and other regions, entered their village, it was to forever change their lives. Overcoming deeply inbred resistance and suspicion of strangers, he planted a desire powerful enough to forever separate themselves from relatives, friends, native tongue, and motherland to embark upon a dangerous

79

voyage to an alien land, whose language and customs were totally foreign. It is interesting to speculate about the conversations between themselves and friends, what it took to win over those who were reluctant, the sleepless nights, and the day when, finally, ambivalence was subdued. This decision required a depth of courage difficult for us to comprehend. Nevertheless, with undoubted excitement and expectation, mixed with trepidation, JB3 applied for a passport on March 1st, 1834. The application states he, John (age 28); his wife, Marguerite Anne Morot, (age 33); his recently widowed mother, Catherine Ageron, (age 63); his aunt, Marguerite Ageron (age 66); and two infants, (unnamed on the passport but whose names were Marguerite-Melaine, age 3, and Francoise-Marguerite, age 1) wanted to emigrate to *"establish himself in the United States."* JB3 listed his occupation as a weaver. This information is all documented in the indigent passport application file #85M6 located in the archives of the Department of Ardennes-Champagne in the village of Chaumont, France. (Copy in *Appendix #3*). In April 1987, Shirley and I spent three futile hours searching through the ancient 1830-1840 string-bound pile of hand written passport applications, for this data. With great disappointment I returned the files to the clerk who spoke no English. My French was fortunately adequate to communicate with her and her quick reply to my anxious question for additional files for that period, *"Oh, yes, there are yet the indigent files,"* was music to my ears. In those dusty pages we quickly found a sheet containing the names of our ancestors, along with those of Voinchets, Renauds and others who could not afford to purchase a passport!

| #526 1st March 1834 | Rougeux, Jean Bt. His wife, Mary Morol His mother, Catherine A Ageron, His aunt, Marguerite Ageron and two infants. | 27 | Weaver | Pierrefaites Broncourt | United States of America | to establish himself |

This passport application was found at Chaumont, France in the Ardennes-Champagne Department with great difficulty by Don and Shirley Rougeux on April 25, 1987.

80

Nicolas Gardel, stepfather of JB3, and second husband to Catherine Ageron, died in 1833 at Broncourt at the time JB3 was considering his adventure. Possibly her reluctance to finish life forever separated from her only son and grandchildren, or perhaps she had no place to live at this late stage in her life, were sufficient reasons to overcome what must have been a wrenching

decision for her. She survived the trip and by the time of her death in 1850, had lived long enough to see the beginning of JB3s accomplishments in Frenchville. JB3's inability to pay for the passport application causes speculation about their capability to provision themselves for the three to five month long journey, pay their ocean passage, and have funds for survival and initial startup costs in Frenchville. Did Catherine inherit some amount from the estate of her recently deceased husband, Nicholas Gardel or did Mr. Keating advance the wherewithal for them to accomplish this enormous task? I fear this will always remain a mystery.

It is not known how they traveled over 350 miles to the nearest seaport, normally, Le Harve. It is highly probable that this determined man, accompanied by two old women, two infant children and a pregnant (with JB4- b. 6/35) wife traveled on foot and carried their possessions and food the entire distance to Le Harve. They could not have progressed more than ten miles a day-possibly less. Best estimates indicate this part of the journey would have required, at a very minimum, thirty-five days.

Sailing ships, according to the 1849 schedule shown, departed Le Harve for the four month round trip to Baltimore, departing on January 16th, May 16th, and September 24th. Assuming comparable sailing schedules in 1834 and 1835, one the following sequences probably happened.

In one case, assuming quick approval and receipt of their passports after their application on March 1st, 1834 and followed by prompt disposal of unneeded personal property, they may have been able to arrive at Le Harve in time to make their necessary travel arrangements for the

81

May 16th departure. Presuming this, they would have arrived at Philadelphia perhaps sixty days later. Allowing another month, their earliest probable arrival in Frenchville would have been August or September-far too late to make a clearing and plant a few crops, but just in time for the death of Marguerite.

A second possibility, was a departure from Le Harve in September, 1834. Such a late departure would require travel through stormy ocean waters and a cold winter walk, with arrival in Frenchville during late winter of 1834, or early in 1835. An early spring arrival would have provided adequate time to clear a small plot and plant a few spring crops, but given the thick forest, lack of draught animals and any farming equipment, it is extremely improbable that self sufficiency could be attained within a year. However, if Dad was correct, and JB3 was born during the voyage (June 1835), this scenario would be completely discounted by placing their arrival far too late in the season but in adequate time for Marguerite's death in September of that year.

It hardly matters in what season they arrived, they needed, at the very least, a year to become self sufficient; necessitating their dependence on others for this period

Commonly without adequate Vitamin C, scurvy caused the death of many seafarers. An 1780 account of a trip by a Private Flohr, a young German who volunteered to fight with the French in our War of Independence, states that; *"life on board was marked by frequent deaths, boredom, strong language, 'Godless life' and spates of feverish prayer during the frequent storms."* Flying fish and sighting of whales brought Flohr only temporary diversion from the onset of scurvy and the pain of watching *"how daily our brothers were thrown into the depths of the ocean, yet nobody was surprised since the food was bad enough to destroy us all"*. It was not until later that Vitamin C provided by lime juice, effectively solved the problem of scurvy. The British discovered this cure and is the reason they are called "limeys" to this day. Of course, scurvy did not afflict the officers because their rich table provided more than adequate amounts of vitamin "C."

Accounts of the Trappists (Cistercians), who came to Kentucky in 1849 on a sailing vessel from Le Harve, relate their construction of an oven in the steerage (bottom) of the vessel. Their willingness to share their bread and soup with eighty fortunate fellow passengers, who had not boarded as well prepared, and had soon begun to suffer ill effects, was a rare event for most of those who crossed the Atlantic. As well prepared as the Trappists were, even they, during the fifty-seven day voyage, lost one of their members to illness.

Our intrepid foreparents did not travel with such generous men and probably operated at the limits of their endurance during their long passage. It can be reasonably speculated their youngest, Francoise-Marguerite, was lost on the crossing because no records have been found of her arrival or burial at Frenchville. It is very possible, (reported by my father) that JB4 was born during the extremely difficult conditions aboard the vessel. It has been reported that after thirty to eighty-two days under sail, depending on weather conditions, they finally arrived at Philadelphia where they were met by Jack Weiskopf, an agent of Mr. Keating. Unable to speak English, it has been said the immigrants were sheltered by an order of priests called *"The French Fathers of St. Suplice"*(still active).

A search of the archives at Washington, DC, failed to uncover any Rougeux's or other passengers with common names at Frenchville who may have disembarked at any Atlantic seacoast between 1832 and 1845. In that era, passenger disembarkations lists were not faithfully

82
188

kept or may have been lost in one of the many fires which occurred in those days. Some historical documents state some Frenchville immigrants arrived in New York, which makes it seem this was an unusual item worthy of note.

The records state Irrene Plubell, who arrived in 1830 was the first settler in the region and the first to die in 1833. Nicholas Roussey, who arrived at the same time, settled on Tract #1939.

Based on the following, however, there may be earlier settlers who failed to be recorded in the official bookkeeping of the time. Some accounts say a John Smith squatted on land in Covington Township in 1775 but eventually moved westward. Another tale, found in the September 12, 1938 *Clearfield Progress*, quotes W. J. McGovern, a well know local historian, that, *The first man to die in Clearfield county was a Frenchman by the name of Tohas Auxe. In 1896, when farmers were clearing land for planting of wheat, they found on the farm of Nestor Mignot, in Covington Township, a sand stone apparently from the bed of a nearby small creek on which the French inscription: "1771, Sept. 1 to 8. Friend, goodbye. In the life eternal we hope to meet again. revoir."*

On the reverse side of the stone was: "In memory of Tohas Auxe 35 R. J."

Where the grave and headstone were found was an old Indian hunting camp along a small stream a mile back from the Susquehanna River. Tohas Auxe was a native of France and with two Frenchmen and two Indian guides was enroute West when he contracted "wood fever."

Although not named as an early settler, disembarkment records at New York indicate a Nicholas Rougeux (b. 1796) as arrived on June 4, 1830. The genealogy charts in *Appendix #7* make it fairly certain that he was a half brother to JB3. Other early arrivals were Desera Billotte, Beauseigneurs, M. Mulson, Peter Mulson, Francois Renaud, and Francois LaMotte. In 1840 there were forty families in Frenchville. In Clearfield County on October 1832, Bishop Kendrick mentions in his diary: *"there are many French families recently settled in this section of the county."*

A John Smith, apparently the first settler, squatted on land in Covington Township in 1775 but eventually moved westward. Another tale, found in the September 12, 1938 *Clearfield Progress* quotes W. J. McGovern, a well know historian, that, *The first man to die in Clearfield county was a Frenchman by the name of Tohas Auxe. In 1896, when farmers were clearing land for planting of wheat, they found on the farm of Nestor Mignot, in Covington Township, a sand stone apparently from the bed of a nearby small creek on which the French inscription: "1771, Sept. 1 to 8. Friend, goodbye. In the life eternal we hope to meet again. revoir."*

On the reverse side of the stone was: "In memory of Tohas Auxe 35 R. J."

Where the grave and headstone were found was an old Indian hunting camp along a small stream a mile back from the Susquehanna River. Tohas Auxe was a native of France and with two Frenchmen and two Indian guides was enroute West when he contracted "wood fever."

The following sixty-five names were listed as *"Original French Families"* in Margaret Billotte Mignot's, *"History of the French Settlers in Covington and Girard Townships" (1968)*:

Ageron, Barmoy, Bamat, Billotte, Bornoel, Bergy, Boloppiew, Beas, Beausigneur, Boutellier, Centillet, Coudriet, Chanet, DeLisles, Demange, Dumont, Frelin, Fontenois, Gaulin, Gorgier, Genny, Hyacinth, Hughueney, Hugard, Hugnot, Jannot, Lachets, Leigey, LaMotte, LeContes, Laird, Longin, Mulson, Mignot, Martel, Marin, Merat, Picard, Plubell, Perrot (Pero?), Rougeux, Rolliet, Roussey, Royer, Renaud, Ravinet, Renoe, Sayer, Sirgey, Risser, Triponier, Turail, Viard, Variot, Valimont, Vermeluen, Voinchet.

To this list I have added the names of settlers listed in material I found in Dad's old green trunk and the 1866 map which llists property owners and the location of their homes. Barre, Billaud, Boutellier, Francois Berthot, J. Cudry, (Coudriet?), Denis, Dormain, A. Jet, Larain, Henry Berthot, Faconnier, Nick Fontenoy, Francois, Gauliard, Greullet, Anthony Gette, A. Gorger (Gorgier?), Grossaint, Alex Hugney, J. Huegenout, H. Huegnet, August Hugney, Jennie, Nodier, John Pattio, v. Partillot, Pegignot, John Reiter, Alex Risser, D. St Clair, Simmonet, Vernot, Charles Vincent.

The following names have been linked to villages in the regions of Haute Marne and nearby Haute Soane. The chart indicates the proximity of these villages from Rougeux and their occupation, where available.

Ageron	Pierrefaites	3 miles east	
Barmoy	Broncourt	5 miles southwest	
Bergy	Cintrey	10 miles southeast	farmer
Billaud	Jussey	5 miles east	day worker
Coudriet	Malvillers	11 miles southeast	farmer
Charbonnet	Cemboin	15 miles east	farmer
Denis	Farincourt	7 miles south	shoemaker
Francois	Guyonville	7 miles northeast	farmer
Gauliard	Omory	21 miles northeast	
Greullet	Jussey	5 miles east	winemaker

84

Grossaint	Broncourt	5 miles southeast	farmer
Mulson	Pierrefaites	3 miles east	cooper
Mulson	Broncourt	5 miles southeast	wheelwright
Mignot	Cintrey	10 miles southeast	farmer
Martel	Farincourt	7 miles south	farmer
Nodier	Faincourt	7 miles southeast	farmer
Plubell	Preigney	12 miles west	winemaker
Picard	Guyonville	7 miles northeast	farmer
Plubell	Preigney	12 miles west	winemaker
Perrot	Pierrefaites	3 miles east	
Rougeux	Broncourt	5 miles southeast	weaver
Renaud	illegible		
Royer	Pierrefaites	3 miles east	farmer
Royer	Rosey	3 miles west	
Vincent	Vitrey	9 miles east	farmer
Voinchet	illegible		weaver

From Philadelphia they would have walked through Harrisburg, up the Susquehanna to Liverpool, then west to Reedsville. From Reedsville the shortest route to Frenchville was northwest to Bellefonte, then Snowshoe and Frenchville. Alternatively, from Reedville they could have taken the longer but better toll road to Tyrone, thence to Frenchville.

Another possible route was the Old Erie Turnpike from Northumberland to Philipsburg using one of the freighting companies who frequented this road, however wagon freight costs ran about $6.00 per hundred-weight; a very expensive proposition for people who lacked funds to pay for their passport.

Comments by Dad and others lead one to believe that they carried their possessions on their backs from Philadelphia. But when this thoughtlessly made comment is considered, one marvels at the immensity of the effort. Without doubt JB3's wife was either extremely pregnant or more probably with a newly born infant (JB4) and had in her care, two year old Anne-Marguerite, (assuming she survived) and four old Marguerite. Accompanying them were two women in their sixties, one of whom may have been seriously ill who died shortly after their arrival, neither likely to be capable of carrying any substantial weight. As the single major load bearer, JB3 would have been hard pressed to carry much beyond their daily necessities and spare clothing. What food and shelter did they find during their trek from Philadelphia? Where did they find shelter at night? Did they have to pay for it or did they sleep out of doors?

My father repeated tales of the encouragement felt by JB3 as they observed the beauty of the countryside as they walked westward through the gently rolling and rich countryside of the Lebanon Valley; even surpassing what they had left behind in France. However, as they entered the mountains some forty miles from Frenchville, they found the land had become thickly forested, with thin sour topsoil and a much colder climate.

Their arrival in Frenchville by 9/14/35, three months after JB3's birth, is proven by Marguerite's Ageron's tombstone, which can still be found in the Frenchville cemetery. The inscription reads in part, *"Marguerite Ageron, died in Frenchville Sept. 14, 1835,"* the privation and the rigors of the long trip apparently overwhelmed her physical reserves.

85

Even though they had lived in an agricultural economy and would have been familiar with farming in their homeland, JB3's training as a weaver would have been of little value in surviving their first years in Frenchville.

Food and shelter were their first concerns upon arrival. To shelter themselves from the snow and cold of winter, these early immigrants built log cabins hewn by broad axes, possibly made at the Karthaus Iron Works. They girdled the (removed a ring of bark from around the trunk of the tree, which soon caused it to die) of huge, closely spaced 250-year-old, trees and planted their first crops with hand tools under still standing and dying giants. Scarcity of game in these deep woods is well documented, but even if somewhat exaggerated, it is highly unlikely they had $25.00 to buy a gun, powder, and balls, and gain experience in loading firing a muzzle loader. A reasonable conclusion can be drawn; they obviously required early assistance to survive. It is very possible Mr. Keating, a fine Christian, as reported in the 1940 issue of *St. Mary's Centennial* booklet, and noted for his generosity, provided it during those early times. Nicholas, JB3's half brother and an earlier arrival, may have provided initial shelter, (see *Appendix #2)* for details about Nicholas) but as indigents, it is interesting to speculate how and where they obtained funds to purchase the original seeds, tools, axes, wagons, plows, harnesses, oxen and other livestock so vital to their survival.

As time passed, they periodically intermarried with the friendly Indians, who taught them critical lessons about what was safe to eat and preparation methods. The natives assisted our settlers to live off the land by finding wild greens, nuts, mushrooms, and fruit. They taught our settlers to wash and boil the tender roots of spring pokeberry four times to get rid of the poison and then to eat it like spinach. They taught them to gather sweet bush bark, sassafras, sweet fern, and the flowerettes from staghorn sumac and and brew them into a tea. Spring growth of dandelion and other weeds were eaten. At least twenty varieties of mushrooms were safe to eat, but a strict rule was "don't eat if not sure." Indian medicines included jewelweed to sooth cuts and bites; boneset tea for pain and arthritis; pennyroyal, wild cherry bark, and thousand hole for fevers; venison bone oil and pipe smoke for ear ache. Bear was eaten like pork and its grease used to soothe burns and a wide variety of other purposes, and when mixed with wood ashes was made into soap. Several old histories of the county mention the great number of insect pests; flies, mosquitoes, and ticks, which plagued man and beast alike.

Gradually, as tax returns prove, their tenacious efforts provided an income which enabled them to establish themselves and slowly begin a century long effort to survive and prosper.

86

SOME PERSONAL THOUGHTS

Other than the tattered clothes on their backs, our immigrants arrived at Frenchville with nothing of physical value sometime during the first half of 1835.

What they did bring was their profound Catholic Faith, their French language and a totally committed desire to improve their life free of the unjust actions of the rich few upper class who controlled every facet of their lives overlaid with murderous taxation, a hopeless future, and ancient social practices and attitudes.

Unrelenting hard work, enterprise in their planning, and unbound determination to rise from poverty was amply demonstrated by their monstrous efforts to clear the forest of massive white pine trees, remove the stumps and plant crops.

Ancient customs of closely guarded interfamily relationships with profound suspicion and mistrust of people and other villages, some of whom had a history of engaging in actual warfare that generated animosities lasting centuries—Rougeux itself having been burned to the ground after losing to a neighboring village—was profoundly inculcated into the marrow our ancestors.

Necessary for survival and a defensive reaction against the endless vicissitudes of life within the endless turmoil of society in Europe, this attitude was necessarily deeply frayed in the generations following their fresh start in the New World.

When I was a child 80 years ago, remnants of this profoundly ingrained attitude was still tightly clutched within the old ones who knew the immigrants in their youth. Most of the following generations were gradually freed of this attitude by common faith, language, survival in this vast, unforgiving, unpopulated region, common poverty, and gradual dispersal and assimilation into other cultures. However the original immigrants and most of the first generation were bound by poverty and the necessity of survival and without a close knit community this was not possible and had to be done by joining with their new neighbors and perfect strangers fortunately with a common background.

They brought song books from the Church in France and with common faith soon began to meet as a community at one of their log homes in worship without the benefit of a priest. Their faith was a powerful motivator in the formation of their community and the friendships necessary for its survival.

Researched and drawn by Guy Rougeux 1938

FIRST ST. MARY'S CHURCH—FRENCHVILLE—1840

This fusion of strangers was so strong that within five years of Great-Grandfathers arrival, by 1840, they built this log church to worship together. (This drawing is the result of a long and diligent research, consisting of many interviews, which I was priviledged to have accompanied my Father, of old survivors who had remaining recollections of this building before its destruction by fire in 1878. (A more comprehensive history can be found in "The Long Journey".)

Undoubtably, their unity in formation of this parish, with its universally French language being spoken, was vital in establishing new and entirely unprecentated for them, relationships with people of the numerous adjacent villages dotting the French countryside whom they would have never known, or even entertained a desire, to meet. Cast into the same melting pot they had little choice!

Communication with France was obviously extermely limited, however as enticing words filtered back a surge of immigrants occured during the 1840's, mostly French but with a scattering of Germans and a dribble of other nationalities, and the population continued to grow.

By the end of the Civil War it became obvious a new church was necessary, and following the archeticture of the Old Country and the fortutious discovery of a massive limestone outcrop on the ridge of a mountian two miles north, volunteers began construction. The skill of the stonemasons who carefully chiseled the hard sandstone into beautiful shaps is readily obvious to even the most casual observor. By 1870 first services were held.

In the old photo below it appears that a temporary bell housing was constructed during the interim before the steeple was constructed, however they had certainly purchased the bell by that time. I have wondered if it was the same bell depitcted in the separate bell tower shown in the drawing of the original church.

St. Mary's about 1875

By 1895 the steeple had been constructed along with an elaborate rectory, and a large well constructed school building where local children had been taught since 1890 by nuns of The Holy Humility Order.

The unity of this community was still very much in evidence during my childhood years. I think it was expressed in what was a very common manner and probably a tradition prevalent in village churches in France. With an obvious majority of French speaking members of the congregation, only 'contaminated' by periodic attendance from one or more of the mission churches located in villages located 7 miles away and populated by immigrants from various other countries, or one of the very few, like my Mother, who had been 'shanghaied' into living there, French was by far the language normally spoken by the majority of the congregation gathered on the cement pad in front of the church after every Mass.

All during the years of my childhood, as I stood at my Father's side, pressed around and about by bodies whose legs were all I could see. But I could hear. And I could understand because the only language my Father and I ever spoke, with rare exceptions until his death many years later, was French. I was not particularly interested in their conversations but between times of serious conversations about the economy, about pigs being slaughtered along the road because the farmers could not afford to feed them, this in the midst of starvation across the land, of piles of oranges having kerosene dumped on them in protest of the low prices, impending war, and other social issues plaguing the country, there were always light hearted ribbing and things said that brought out the distinctive guffaws and laughs of the various cousins and friends involved.

One, which I didn't catch until some years later, was inflicted upon Dad in the fall of 1937 after his return from his two year enlistment in the CCC camp. It seems that he had hurt his back in some man ner and was mentioning his discomfort whn he was interrupted by Lawrence Mignot, his cousin, I now this because Lawrence had an especially memorably unique way of laughing. Dad was scarcely finished before Lawrence interrupted him with a loud, (in French, of course), "It's no damn wonder". This brought an uproarious amount of loud laughing and an odd, and perhaps with a trace of embarrassment look on Dads face, totally indecipherable to me. On May 8th, the following spring much to my astonishment, my brother, Bill, was born.

Another interesting character, Lawrence's brother, Jesse, who was our mailman for many years beginning by the mid 1930's, always was ready to have a conversation, in French, and unrestricted by any time constraints, especially with Dad, but even with me, and I always enjoyed being able to be at the mailbox when he made his delivery, but more so when dad and he were able to rattle on with conversations both enjoyed as good friends.

My much older cousin, Alfred, also was willing to talk with me as a youngster and as I grew older and especially after Dads death in 1961, with fewer surviving French speaking friends, I always made it a point to spend some French speaking time with him during infrequent visits but as time passed lack of practice caused my skills to rapidly diminish and now are generally gone.

The French, spoken in isolated, rural, Central Pennsylvania, unaltered by 5 generations from the French spoken centuries ago, its isolation preserving and protecting it from the gradually evolving way of all languages over the centuries.

French in Frenchville generally ceased to be spoken sometime during the 1960's and only a small handful of old survivors can barely speak it today, and eventual casualty of the stirring of the population caused by WWII and widespread communication across the world. My own loss of the language was a direct result of relocation to rapidly expanding job opportunities during and after the war.

St. Marys of the Assumption, Frenchville, Pa. 2018

Photos by Bill Tilton

196

Photos by Bill Tilton

Photos by Bill Tilton

HISTORICAL PAINTING WITH INTERESTING LEGENDS
SURROUNDING ITS PROVANCE.
SHIPPED FROM FRANCE SOMETIME
BEFORE 1850.

ST MARY'S. 2018

Ancient stained glass windows—St Mary's

Photo by Bill Tilton

ORIGINAL ALTAR BEFORE REMODELING DURING THE 1960"S.

TAKEN CHRISTMAS 1939.

DAD DONATED THIS GOLD FILIGREED LACE

Frenchville 1965

View of Frenchville

The Sesquehanna near Frenchville   2001

Sesquehanna River near Frenchville 1967

John B Rougeux   May 26, 1913   78 yrs old

JOHN (JBIV) AND LUCILLE ROUGEUX   1916

Uncle August Rougeux May 26, 1913

Charles   Frank   Jule   Ada   Guy

Hector   Fred   John B IV   Lucille   Ed   Gust

Lawrence   Albert

Frenchville Picnic   1910

owned by author

THE JBIV 2ND GENERATION—MY FATHER IS GUY

202

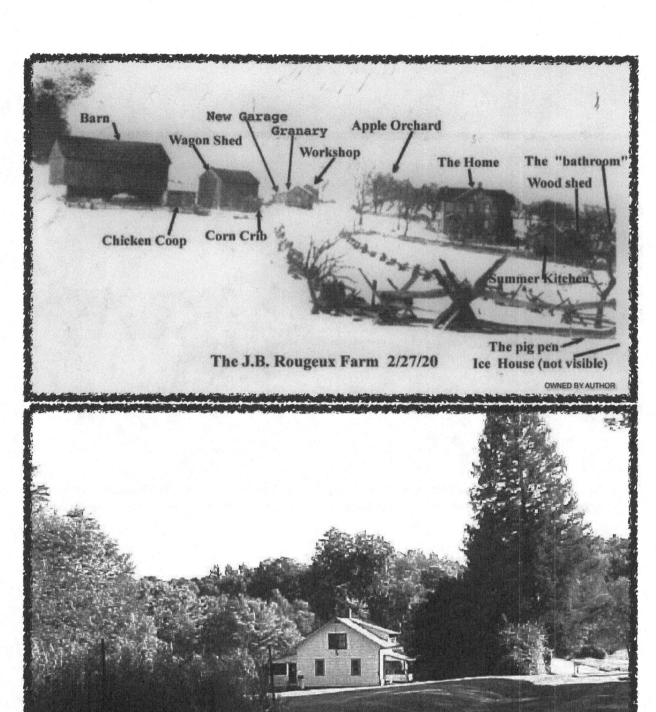

Barn

New Garage

Wagon Shed

Granary

Apple Orchard

Workshop

The Home

The "bathroom"

Wood shed

Chicken Coop

Corn Crib

Summer Kitchen

The pig pen

Ice House (not visible)

The J.B. Rougeux Farm 2/27/20

SITE OF ORIGINAL JBIII FARMHOUSE   2005

Ice house on the JB Rx farm

1920

Telegraph line to Cuz Alfords house

wood shed

ice house

Dam

"bathroom"

1920

NICHOLAS

While researching for 'The Long Journey' I found very little information about Nicholas, the half-brother of JBIII who emigrated from France and passed through New York in 1803, apart from the enclosed photo and an anecdotal account from my father who told me, "Nicholas went to Chicago about 1850 or 1860." He applied for naturalization in 1830 but no records I found confirmed his final process was ever completed.

Nicholas was the first Rougeux to arrive in Frenchville and established himself as the following tax records indicate.

1796—born of JBII and Margurite Moulet

1830—emigrated to the USA/ New York— possibly with his wife and son Nicholas, JR. (b. 6/22/1830)

1835—daughter Amelia born in Frenchville—no additional records were found for her. She may have died at a young age and may be the child in the photograph.

The following tax records were taken from the Clearfield County Courthouse records.

Nicholas Rougeux, his wife and child. About 1845.

1842---Rusey, N. 2 oxen---1 cow
1843---Rusey, N   2 oxen---2 cows $3.74
1844---1845---same as above
1846---1847---Rugsey, Nicholas 2 cows---2 oxen (note name change)
1848---Ruger, Nicholas   2 horses---2cows $5.25
1849---1850 Rushey, Nicholas   2 horses---2 cows
1851---1854 Russey, Nicholas 2 horses---3 cows
1855--- Russet, Nicholas--Name and tax owed crossed off the tax record and 2 horses and 2
        cows were transferred to Rousses (JB II). (In 1867 the name Roussey was crossed
        through and Rougeux was written above the name in the tax records.
1855---Nicholas (Sr.) disappeared from the personal property tax records in Clearfield
County and this is the last written information I was able to
        find for him. I have deduced that he (they) went to Fairfield County, Ohio. (Lancaster is
        the county seat).
1862---Mary Ann, daughter of Nicholas (Jr) and Amelia Meeker is born in   Fairfield County,
        OH. (Born out of wedlock)
        1863---May 23, 1863 Nicholas (Jr) (b. 6/22/30--age 33 at time of marriage to Amelia
        Meeker (b. 4/18/35--age 27 at their time of marriage in
        Lancaster, Ohio. Nicholas Sr., if alive, would have been 67 years of age at that time.

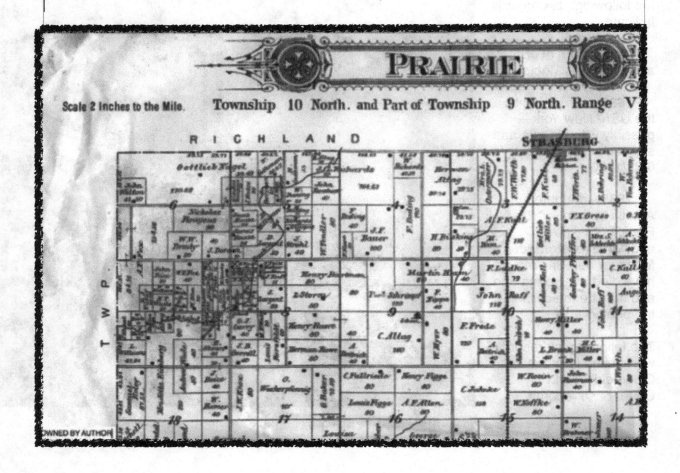

206

Union Cemetery, IL 2007
Son of the immigrant

Amelia Rougeux
2007   Union Cemetery, IL

1865---November 27--Book 2—Section 32-page34. Nicholas Rougeux(Jr) sold to the Illinois
    Central RR Co. for $300: the NW quarter of the SW quarter of the SE quarter of
    Section 6 in Twp. 10 N of Range 5 E of the 3rd principal Meridian.
1865---Nicholas Rougeux (Jr)
    Personal property tax:
    Valuation: $218.00
        State tax: 2.17
        Town: .13
        School: .53
        Civil War Tax:$3.75. (IL imposed this heavy tax to pay state war debts.)
1876---Nicholas sold to John Welton the property he purchased on January 13, 1866. (15
    acres) This property was not contiguous with their main farm.
1880---Prairie County, IL Census:
        Rugere, Nicholas   Age   53 poss. b. France but not the immigrant
            Emma (Amelia)   Age 45
            Mary Ann   Age 16
1885---Shelby County, IL----Joseph Fisher of Richland in the County of Shelby, IL, age 33 and
    Miss Mary A. Rougeux of Prairie in the county of Shelby, IL age 21 years, were
    married in the village of Stewardson, IL by a Justice of the Peace on the 28th of
    February, 1885.
        There are no birth records from 1884 to 1906 due to a fire.
1901---Amelia died June 6, 1901 and is buried in Union Cemetery, Prairie Twp. Shelby County
    IL ---located at 500 N 2325 E.
1913---Nicholas (Jr) died June 22 and is buried adjacent to Amelia.

   This sparse information about Nicholas, Sr, is somewhat disappointing but at lEast
provides some factual information of what happened to this missing half-brother of JBIII. Its
seems certain that Nicholas himself died in Fairfield County, Ohio where he owned property.
   This photograph and the birth records apparently show their approximately 15 year child,
who apparently is dressed as a female more probably is Nicholas, JR b. 1830. There are no
records of any other children of Nicholas's and the birth date of their son is fairly well
established.
   They established themselves in Frenchville until 1855 when they disappeared from the tax
records.
   In 1862 Nicholas, JR, obviously their son, had a child out of wedlock to Amelia Meeker in
Fairfield County, Ohio and they were married in 1863. May have been living in Illinois at that
time and it cannot be concluded that Nicholas Sr also was living in Ohio at that time. This
doubt is raised because in 1865 Nicholas Jr sold property to the Illinois Central RR in Shelby
County, IL, apparently having acquired it before that time. In 1876 he sold additional property
acquired in 1866.
   It appears that his lineage may ended with his daughter Mary Ann's marriage to Joseph
Fisher in 1885 because I could find no other siblings.
   The date and location of death of Nicholas Sr has not been found. Nicholas Jr died in
1913 and his wife Amelia died in 1901. I did not find the death or any descendants of Mary
Ann during my search of records in Ohio or Springfield, Illinois.
   This was a difficult search because the records were written in difficult to read and less
than easily decipherable handwriting with alternating first names listed first combined with last
names first, depending on the clerk. After spending hours scanning those old documents, it
became clear that I was fortunate to have found the above information, however there is more
to be discovered.

   Don Rougeux

MIGNOTS

In 1987 Shirley and I visited this family of Mignots we found living about 15 miles SE of Rougeux. Gisele had recollections of tales from the past about the immigrants who departed for Frenchville in 1845. She knew that after a number of years one had returned to his homeland. They were extremely sociable and told us of their days under Nazi rule. Her husband, a very young man at the time, hid in the woods over four years to escape slave labor only returning home for supplies at night. Miraculously, he survived that ordeal!

Gisele
Mignot
Bouveret
BEtoncourt-Les-Menetriers
70120 Gombeaufontaine, France

Shirley
Rougeux

200 year old farmhouse where Mignots currently live in
BEtoncourt, France·

BETONCOURT

Google Earth

BETONCOURT

Home of Mignots in France

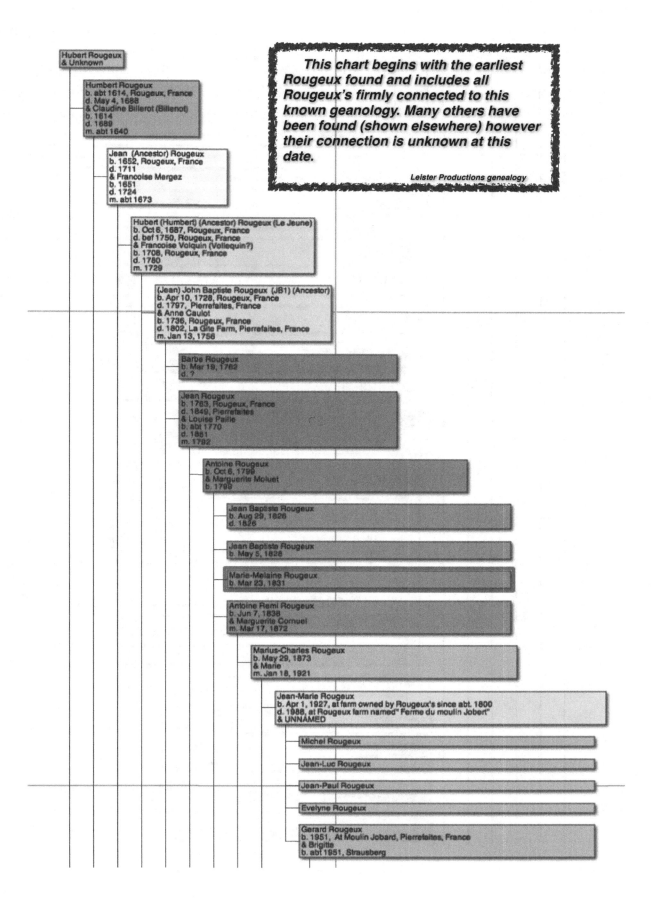

Hubert Rougeux
& Unknown

Humbert Rougeux
b. abt 1614, Rougeux, France
d. May 4, 1688
& Claudine Billerot (Billenot)
b. 1614
d. 1689
m. abt 1640

Jean (Ancestor) Rougeux
b. 1652, Rougeux, France
d. 1711
& Francoise Mergez
b. 1651
d. 1724
m. abt 1673

Hubert (Humbert) (Ancestor) Rougeux (Le Jeune)
b. Oct 6, 1687, Rougeux, France
d. bef 1750, Rougeux, France
& Francoise Volquin (Vollequin?)
b. 1708, Rougeux, France
d. 1780
m. 1729

(Jean) John Baptiste Rougeux (JB1) (Ancestor)
b. Apr 10, 1728, Rougeux, France
d. 1797, Pierrefaites, France
& Anne Caulot
b. 1736, Rougeux, France
d. 1802, La Gite Farm, Pierrefaites, France
m. Jan 13, 1756

Barbe Rougeux
b. Mar 19, 1762
d. ?

Jean Rougeux
b. 1763, Rougeux, France
d. 1849, Pierrefaites
& Louise Paille
b. abt 1770
d. 1861
m. 1792

Antoine Rougeux
b. Oct 6, 1799
& Marguerite Moluet
b. 1799

Jean Baptiste Rougeux
b. Aug 29, 1826
d. 1826

Jean Baptiste Rougeux
b. May 5, 1828

Marie-Melaine Rougeux
b. Mar 23, 1831

Antoine Remi Rougeux
b. Jun 7, 1838
& Marguerite Cornuel
m. Mar 17, 1872

Marius-Charles Rougeux
b. May 29, 1873
& Marie
m. Jan 18, 1921

Jean-Marie Rougeux
b. Apr 1, 1927, at farm owned by Rougeux's since abt. 1800
d. 1988, at Rougeux farm named" Ferme du moulin Jobert"
& UNNAMED

Michel Rougeux

Jean-Luc Rougeux

Jean-Paul Rougeux

Evelyne Rougeux

Gerard Rougeux
b. 1951, At Moulin Jobard, Pierrefaites, France
& Brigitte
b. abt 1951, Strausberg

This chart begins with the earliest
Rougeux found and includes all
Rougeux's firmly connected to this
known geanology. Many others have
been found (shown elsewhere) however
their connection is unknown at this
date.

Leister Productions genealogy

211

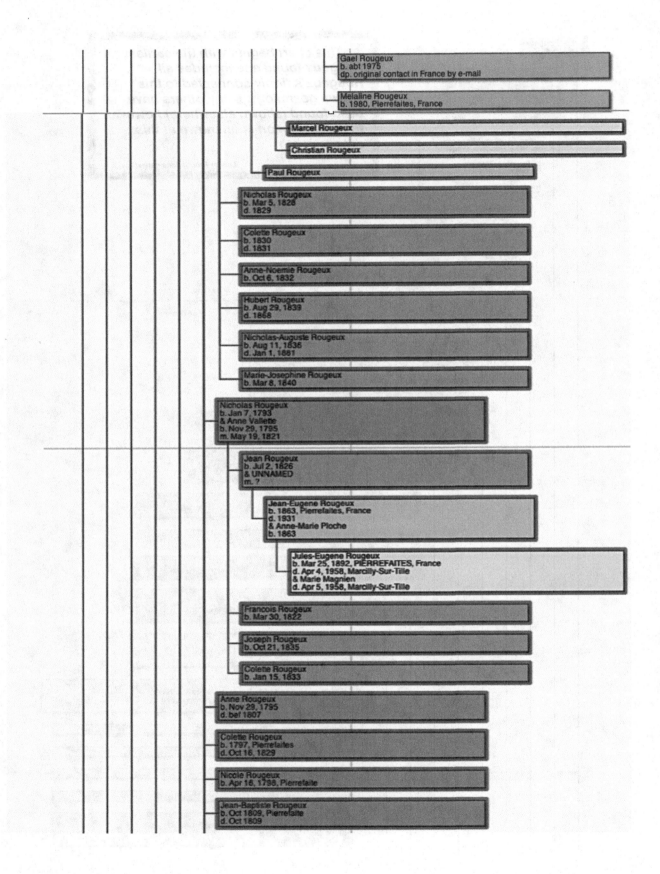

Gael Rougeux
b. abt 1975
dp. original contact in France by e-mail

Melaline Rougeux
b. 1980, Pierrefaites, France

Marcel Rougeux

Christian Rougeux

Paul Rougeux

Nicholas Rougeux
b. Mar 5, 1828
d. 1829

Colette Rougeux
b. 1830
d. 1831

Anne-Noemie Rougeux
b. Oct 6, 1832

Hubert Rougeux
b. Aug 29, 1839
d. 1868

Nicholas-Auguste Rougeux
b. Aug 11, 1836
d. Jan 1, 1881

Marie-Josephine Rougeux
b. Mar 8, 1840

Nicholas Rougeux
b. Jan 7, 1793
& Anne Vallette
b. Nov 29, 1795
m. May 19, 1821

Jean Rougeux
b. Jul 2, 1826
& UNNAMED
m. ?

Jean-Eugene Rougeux
b. 1863, Pierrefaites, France
d. 1931
& Anne-Marie Ploche
b. 1863

Jules-Eugene Rougeux
b. Mar 25, 1892, PIERREFAITES, France
d. Apr 4, 1958, Marcilly-Sur-Tille
& Marie Magnien
d. Apr 5, 1958, Marcilly-Sur-Tille

Francois Rougeux
b. Mar 30, 1822

Joseph Rougeux
b. Oct 21, 1835

Colette Rougeux
b. Jan 15, 1833

Anne Rougeux
b. Nov 29, 1795
d. bef 1807

Colette Rougeux
b. 1797, Pierrefaites
d. Oct 16, 1829

Nicole Rougeux
b. Apr 16, 1798, Pierrefaite

Jean-Baptiste Rougeux
b. Oct 1809, Pierrefaite
d. Oct 1809

212

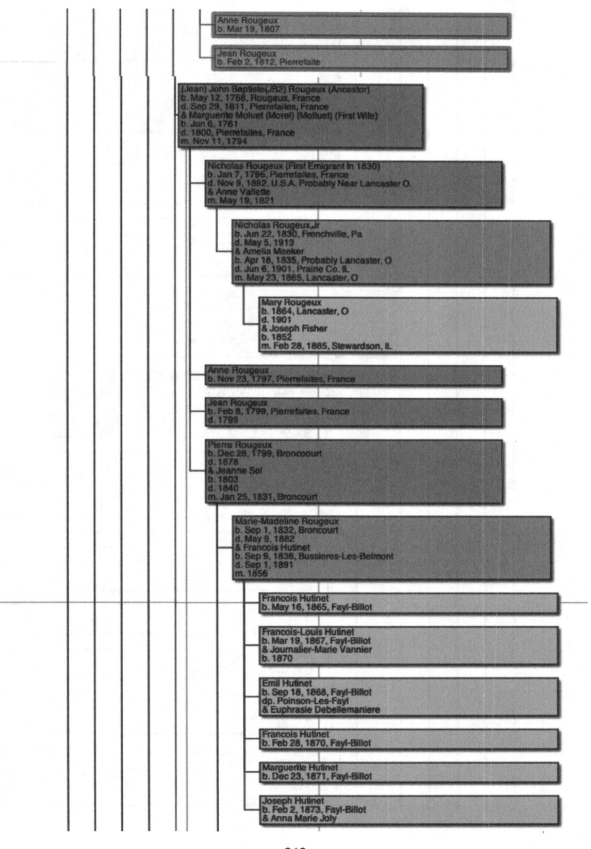

Anne Rougeux
b. Mar 19, 1807

Jean Rougeux
b. Feb 2, 1812, Pierrefaite

(Jean) John Baptiste(JB2) Rougeux (Ancestor)
b. May 12, 1768, Rougeux, France
d. Sep 29, 1811, Pierrefaites, France
& Marguerite Moluet (Morel) (Molluet) (First Wife)
b. Jun 6, 1761
d. 1800, Pierrefaites, France
m. Nov 11, 1794

Nicholas Rougeux (First Emigrant In 1830)
b. Jan 7, 1796, Pierrefaites, France
d. Nov 9, 1882, U.S.A. Probably Near Lancaster O.
& Anne Vallette
m. May 19, 1821

Nicholas Rougeux,Jr
b. Jun 22, 1830, Frenchville, Pa
d. May 5, 1913
& Amelia Meeker
b. Apr 18, 1835, Probably Lancaster, O
d. Jun 6, 1901, Prairie Co. Il.
m. May 23, 1865, Lancaster, O

Mary Rougeux
b. 1864, Lancaster, O
d. 1901
& Joseph Fisher
b. 1852
m. Feb 28, 1885, Stewardson, IL

Anne Rougeux
b. Nov 23, 1797, Pierrefaites, France

Jean Rougeux
b. Feb 8, 1799, Pierrefaites, France
d. 1799

Pierre Rougeux
b. Dec 28, 1799, Broncoourt
d. 1878
& Jeanne Sol
b. 1803
d. 1840
m. Jan 25, 1831, Broncourt

Marie-Madeline Rougeux
b. Sep 1, 1832, Broncourt
d. May 9, 1882
& Francois Hutinet
b. Sep 9, 1836, Bussieres-Les-Belmont
d. Sep 1, 1891
m. 1856

Francois Hutinet
b. May 16, 1865, Fayl-Billot

Francois-Louis Hutinet
b. Mar 19, 1867, Fayl-Billot
& Journalier-Marie Vannier
b. 1870

Emil Hutinet
b. Sep 18, 1868, Fayl-Billot
dp. Poinson-Les-Fayl
& Euphrasie Debellemaniere

Francois Hutinet
b. Feb 28, 1870, Fayl-Billot

Marguerite Hutinet
b. Dec 23, 1871, Fayl-Billot

Joseph Hutinet
b. Feb 2, 1873, Fayl-Billot
& Anna Marie Joly

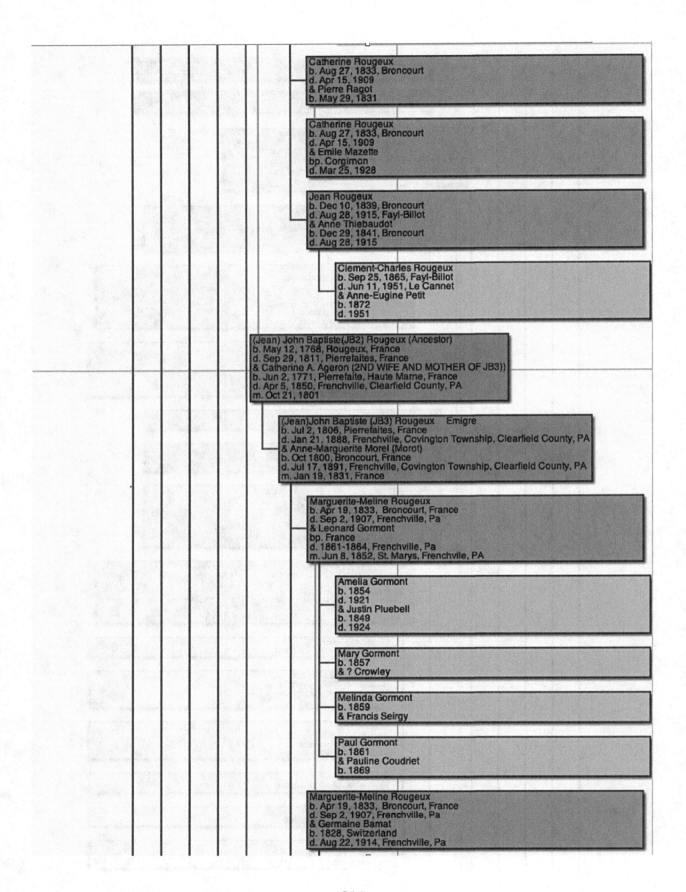

Catherine Rougeux
b. Aug 27, 1833, Broncourt
d. Apr 15, 1909
& Pierre Ragot
b. May 29, 1831

Catherine Rougeux
b. Aug 27, 1833, Broncourt
d. Apr 15, 1909
& Emile Mazette
bp. Corgirnon
d. Mar 25, 1928

Jean Rougeux
b. Dec 10, 1839, Broncourt
d. Aug 28, 1915, Fayl-Billot
& Anne Thiebaudot
b. Dec 29, 1841, Broncourt
d. Aug 28, 1915

Clement-Charles Rougeux
b. Sep 25, 1865, Fayl-Billot
d. Jun 11, 1951, Le Cannet
& Anne-Eugine Petit
b. 1872
d. 1951

(Jean) John Baptiste(JB2) Rougeux (Ancestor)
b. May 12, 1768, Rougeux, France
d. Sep 29, 1811, Pierrefaites, France
& Catherine A. Ageron (2ND WIFE AND MOTHER OF JB3))
b. Jun 2, 1771, Pierrefaite, Haute Marne, France
d. Apr 5, 1850, Frenchville, Clearfield County, PA
m. Oct 21, 1801

(Jean)John Baptiste (JB3) Rougeux   Emigre
b. Jul 2, 1806, Pierrefaites, France
d. Jan 21, 1888, Frenchville, Covington Township, Clearfield County, PA
& Anne-Marguerite Morel (Morot)
b. Oct 1800, Broncourt, France
d. Jul 17, 1891, Frenchville, Covington Township, Clearfield County, PA
m. Jan 19, 1831, France

Marguerite-Meline Rougeux
b. Apr 19, 1833, Broncourt, France
d. Sep 2, 1907, Frenchville, Pa
& Leonard Gormont
bp. France
d. 1861-1864, Frenchville, Pa
m. Jun 8, 1852, St. Marys, Frenchvile, PA

Amelia Gormont
b. 1854
d. 1921
& Justin Pluebell
b. 1849
d. 1924

Mary Gormont
b. 1857
& ? Crowley

Melinda Gormont
b. 1859
& Francis Seirgy

Paul Gormont
b. 1861
& Pauline Coudriet
b. 1869

Marguerite-Meline Rougeux
b. Apr 19, 1833, Broncourt, France
d. Sep 2, 1907, Frenchville, Pa
& Germaine Bamat
b. 1828, Switzerland
d. Aug 22, 1914, Frenchville, Pa

214

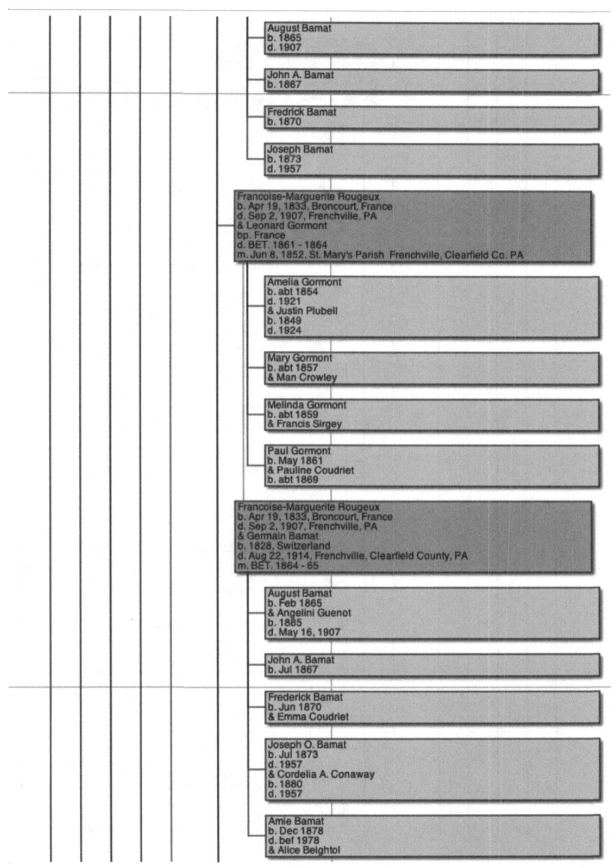

August Bamat
b. 1865
d. 1907

John A. Bamat
b. 1867

Fredrick Bamat
b. 1870

Joseph Bamat
b. 1873
d. 1957

Francoise-Marguerite Rougeux
b. Apr 19, 1833, Broncourt, France
d. Sep 2, 1907, Frenchville, PA
& Leonard Gormont
bp. France
d. BET. 1861 - 1864
m. Jun 8, 1852, St. Mary's Parish Frenchville, Clearfield Co. PA

Amelia Gormont
b. abt 1854
d. 1921
& Justin Plubell
b. 1849
d. 1924

Mary Gormont
b. abt 1857
& Man Crowley

Melinda Gormont
b. abt 1859
& Francis Sirgey

Paul Gormont
b. May 1861
& Pauline Coudriet
b. abt 1869

Francoise-Marguerite Rougeux
b. Apr 19, 1833, Broncourt, France
d. Sep 2, 1907, Frenchville, PA
& Germain Bamat
b. 1828, Switzerland
d. Aug 22, 1914, Frenchville, Clearfield County, PA
m. BET. 1864 - 65

August Bamat
b. Feb 1865
& Angelini Guenot
b. 1885
d. May 16, 1907

John A. Bamat
b. Jul 1867

Frederick Bamat
b. Jun 1870
& Emma Coudriet

Joseph O. Bamat
b. Jul 1873
d. 1957
& Cordelia A. Conaway
b. 1880
d. 1957

Amie Bamat
b. Dec 1878
d. bef 1978
& Alice Beightol

John Baptiste (JB4) Rougeux
b. Jun 30, 1835, on the high seas or Frenchville, PA, USA
d. 1927, Frenchville, Pa, USA
& Lucille Mignot
b. 1847, Frenchville, Covington Township, Clearfield County, PA
d. Dec 14, 1922, Frenchville, Clearfield County, PA
m. May 17, 1865, St. Mary's Parish Frenchville, Clearfield Co. PA

Ferdinand A. Rougeux
b. Apr 2, 1866, Clearfield Co, PA
d. Jun 24, 1916, gangrene of hemmoroids
& Alice M. Viard
b. Mar 19, 1871, Frenchville, Clearfield County, PA
d. Nov 4, 1965, Frenchville, Clearfield County, PA
m. May 22, 1895, Frenchville, Clearfield Co., PA

Edward O. Rougeux
b. 1867, Clearfield Co, PA
d. Jan 1960
& Sadie Mignot
b. 1870
d. 1940

Gustave J. Rougeux
b. Mar 12, 1869, Clearfield Co, PA
d. Mar 30, 1918, crippling arthitritis
& Ida Jane Picard
b. May 18, 1883
d. Nov 21, 1979, Clearfield, PA
m. May 12, 1903

Hector L. Rougeux
b. 1871, Clearfield Co, PA
d. Jun 6, 1959
& Elva Coudriet
b. 1886, Frenchvile, Pa
d. 1964
m. Jun 20, 1905, Frenchville, Clearfield County, PA

Charles E. Rougeux
b. Feb 9, 1873, Frenchville, PA
d. Sep 13, 1878, Frenchville, PA   diptheria

Ada Rougeux
b. 1875, Clearfield Co, PA
d. Jan 1941
& John Hoover
d. 1943
m. Aug 15, 1899

Francois (Frank) A. Rougeux
b. 1879, Clearfield Co, PA
d. Feb 6, 1942, cancer of brain
& Nora Stienkeckner
d. bef 1964
m. May 19, 1915

Jules E. Rougeux
b. Jan 1, 1880, Clearfield Co, PA
d. Jun 4, 1947

Belle M. Rougeux
b. Mar 16, 1881, Frenchville, Clearfield County, PA
d. Jul 30, 1964, Akron, Summit County, Ohio
& Rudolph Guderjahn
b. May 5, 1891, Akron, Summit County, Ohio
d. Nov 13, 1959, Akron, Summit County, Ohio

Charles Joseph Rougeux
b. Mar 24, 1884, Frenchville, Clearfield County, PA
d. Oct 3, 1974, Frenchville, Clearfield County, PA
& Anna Matilda Guenot
b. Oct 14, 1886
d. Feb 1979
m. Jun 14, 1911

216

Guy J. Rougeux
b. Sep 13, 1886, Frenchville, Clearfield County, PA
d. Jun 2, 1961, Louisville, KY   brain cancer
& Mildred Beamer
b. 1903
d. Aug 1968
m. 1928

Helen E. Rougeux
b. 1887, Frenchville, Clearfield County, Pennsylvania USA
d. Nov 13, 1932, Goldenrod, Florida mushroom poisoning
& Otto Cline

Albert J. Rougeux
b. 1889, Frenchville, Clearfield County, PA
d. Jan 8, 1918, flu epidemic of 1918
& Mary Emily Michaels
b. 1895, Biglar, PA
d. Apr 1985, Curwensville, PA
m. Oct 22, 1913, Frenchville, Clearfield Co., PA

Lawrence Paul Rougeux
b. Sep 27, 1892, Frenchville, Clearfield County, PA
d. Mar 16, 1990, Winter Park, Florida
& Bessie Eunice Coudriet
b. Mar 9, 1896, Driftwood, PA
d. Aug 17, 1985, Winter Park, Florida
m. May 12, 1915, Frenchville, Clearfield Co., PA

Emil Rougeux
b. Sep 1837, Frenchville, Covington Township, Clearfield County, PA
d. 1920, PA, USA
& Mary Barr
b. 1845
d. 1934, PA, USA
m. Jun 28, 1864, St. Mary's Assumption, Frenchville PA

Edmund Rougeux
b. Apr 20, 1865
d. Sep 10, 1867

John E. Rougeux
b. 1867
d. bef 1987
& Ellen Coudriet
d. bef 1987
m. May 19, 1896

August E. Rougeux
b. 1869, Frenchville, Clearfield County, PA
d. aft 1950
& Rose Frances Berthot
b. 1873, Frenchville, Clearfield County, PA
d. Mar 26, 1950, Frenchville, Clearfield County, PA
m. May 15, 1895, Frenchville, Clearfield Co., PA

Elizabeth Rougeux
b. 1871
d. aft 1967
& Alphonse F. Coudriet
b. 1867
d. bef 1967
m. May 12, 1891, Frenchville, Clearfield County, PA

Amie Rougeux
b. 1873, Frenchville, Clearfield, PA.
d. 1928, Frenchville, Clearfield, PA.
& Cora Jannot
b. 1880, Frenchville, Clearfield, PA.
d. Apr 27, 1917, Frenchville, Clearfield, PA.
m. Dec 4, 1900, Frenchville, Clearfield Co., PA

Raymond Rougeux
b. abt 1875, Frenchville, Clearfield County, PA
& Alma B.

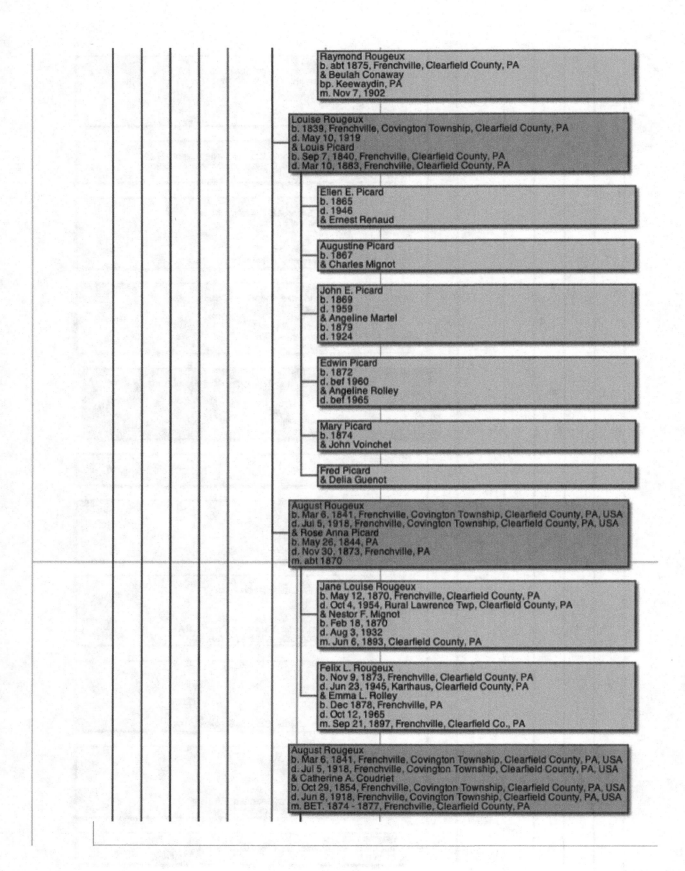

Raymond Rougeux
b. abt 1875, Frenchville, Clearfield County, PA
& Beulah Conaway
bp. Keewaydin, PA
m. Nov 7, 1902

Louise Rougeux
b. 1839, Frenchville, Covington Township, Clearfield County, PA
d. May 10, 1919
& Louis Picard
b. Sep 7, 1840, Frenchville, Clearfield County, PA
d. Mar 10, 1883, Frenchville, Clearfield County, PA

Ellen E. Picard
b. 1865
d. 1946
& Ernest Renaud

Augustine Picard
b. 1867
& Charles Mignot

John E. Picard
b. 1869
d. 1959
& Angeline Martel
b. 1879
d. 1924

Edwin Picard
b. 1872
d. bef 1960
& Angeline Rolley
d. bef 1965

Mary Picard
b. 1874
& John Voinchet

Fred Picard
& Delia Guenot

August Rougeux
b. Mar 6, 1841, Frenchville, Covington Township, Clearfield County, PA, USA
d. Jul 5, 1918, Frenchville, Covington Township, Clearfield County, PA, USA
& Rose Anna Picard
b. May 26, 1844, PA
d. Nov 30, 1873, Frenchville, PA
m. abt 1870

Jane Louise Rougeux
b. May 12, 1870, Frenchville, Clearfield County, PA
d. Oct 4, 1954, Rural Lawrence Twp, Clearfield County, PA
& Nestor F. Mignot
b. Feb 18, 1870
d. Aug 3, 1932
m. Jun 6, 1893, Clearfield County, PA

Felix L. Rougeux
b. Nov 9, 1873, Frenchville, Clearfield County, PA
d. Jun 23, 1945, Karthaus, Clearfield County, PA
& Emma L. Rolley
b. Dec 1878, Frenchville, PA
d. Oct 12, 1965
m. Sep 21, 1897, Frenchville, Clearfield Co., PA

August Rougeux
b. Mar 6, 1841, Frenchville, Covington Township, Clearfield County, PA, USA
d. Jul 5, 1918, Frenchville, Covington Township, Clearfield County, PA, USA
& Catherine A. Coudriet
b. Oct 29, 1854, Frenchville, Covington Township, Clearfield County, PA, USA
d. Jun 8, 1918, Frenchville, Covington Township, Clearfield County, PA, USA
m. BET. 1874 - 1877, Frenchville, Clearfield County, PA

Clara M. Rougeux
b. Aug 12, 1877, Frenchville, PA
d. Dec 4, 1967, Williamsville, NY
& Edward P. Shade
b. May 20, 1875
d. Apr 4, 1950, Clearfield, Clearfield County, PA
m. May 1, 1901, St. Francis Church, Clearfield County, PA

Basil Octave Rougeux
b. Nov 1, 1878, Frenchville, Covington Township, Clearfield County, PA
d. Nov 24, 1953, Clearfield, Clearfield County, PA
& Rose Mary Plubell
b. Oct 17, 1880, Frenchville, Clearfield County, PA
d. Apr 19, 1964, Clearfield County, PA
m. Sep 20, 1904, Frenchville, Clearfield Co., PA

Clement Louis Rougeux
b. Jan 25, 1880, Frenchville, Covington Township, Clearfield County, PA
d. bef 1980
& Elizabeth Holton
b. Aug 19, 1884
d. Jul 1969
m. Oct 11, 1911, Grampian, PA

Blanche Amelia Rougeux
b. Jun 21, 1882, Frenchville, Covington Township, Clearfield County, PA
d. Jul 10, 1963, Curwensville, Clearfield County, PA
& Vincent DiPalma
b. 1882, Curwensville, PA
d. bef 1963
m. Sep 19, 1911, Frenchville, Clearfield Co., PA

Marie (May?) Helen Rougeux
b. Jun 21, 1882, Frenchville, Covington Township, Clearfield County, PA
d. Jan 13, 1961, Rural Bellaria Twp, Clearfield County, PA
& Charles Herman Fontenoy
b. Oct 16, 1879
d. Nov 27, 1964, Clearfield, PA
m. Jun 20, 1906, Frenchville, Clearfield County, PA

Edgar G. Rougeux
b. May 4, 1884, Frenchville, Covington Township, Clearfield County, PA
d. Aug 18, 1946, Frenchville, Covington Township, Clearfield County, PA

Peter A. Rouge(a)ux
b. Aug 11, 1886, Frenchville, PA
d. Dec 29, 1940, Niagara Falls, New York, USA
& Louise M. Conway
b. Nov 27, 1887
d. Oct 1969
m. May 11, 1910, Clearfield County, PA

Mary Ann Rose Rougeux
b. Mar 25, 1887, Frenchville, Covington Township, Clearfield County, PA
d. Sep 22, 1980, Mc Kees Rocks, Allegheny Co., PA
& John Daly
b. May 4, 1883, Scotland
d. Jan 15, 1932, Mc Kees Rocks, Allegheny Co., PA
m. Mar 3, 1908, Frenchville, Clearfield Co., PA

Mary Ann Rose Rougeux
b. Mar 25, 1887, Frenchville, Covington Township, Clearfield County, PA
d. Sep 22, 1980, Mc Kees Rocks, Allegheny Co., PA
& John Blackburn
b. Nov 14, 1898, Lynchburg, Virginia
d. Nov 1976, Mc Kees Rocks, Allegheny Co., PA
m. Jun 1944, Mc Kees Rocks, Allegheny Co., PA

Maurice Fredrick Rougeux
b. Sep 24, 1888, Frenchville, Clearfield County, Pennsylvania USA
d. Sep 15, 1953, Niagara Falls, New York USA
& Marguerite Agnes Thompson
b. May 1, 1896, Niagara Falls, New York USA
d. Jun 22, 1995, Niagara Falls, New York USA
m. Oct 10, 1917, 7 AM at St.Mary's Parish, Niagara Falls, NY

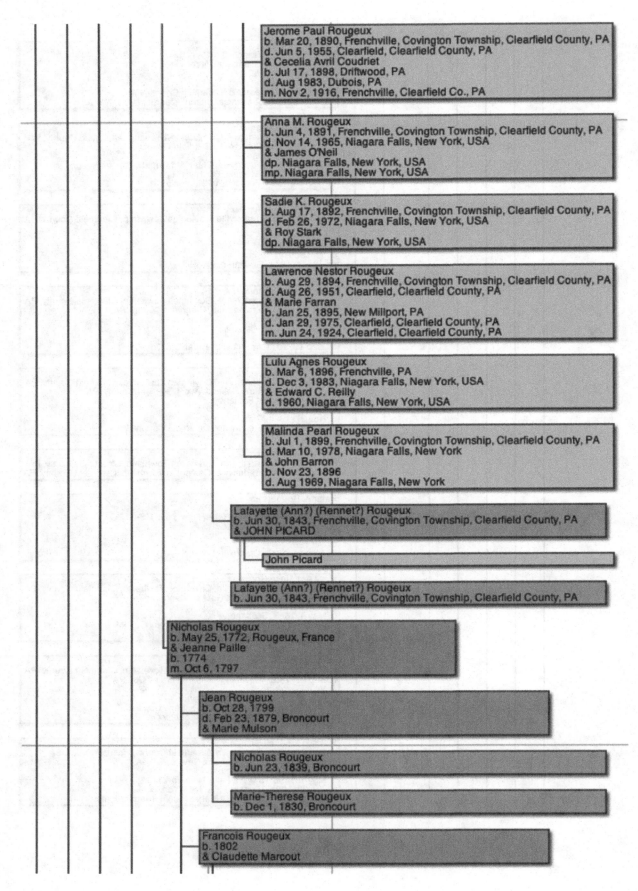

Jerome Paul Rougeux
b. Mar 20, 1890, Frenchville, Covington Township, Clearfield County, PA
d. Jun 5, 1955, Clearfield, Clearfield County, PA
& Cecelia Avril Coudriet
b. Jul 17, 1898, Driftwood, PA
d. Aug 1983, Dubois, PA
m. Nov 2, 1916, Frenchville, Clearfield Co., PA

Anna M. Rougeux
b. Jun 4, 1891, Frenchville, Covington Township, Clearfield County, PA
d. Nov 14, 1965, Niagara Falls, New York, USA
& James O'Neil
dp. Niagara Falls, New York, USA
mp. Niagara Falls, New York, USA

Sadie K. Rougeux
b. Aug 17, 1892, Frenchville, Covington Township, Clearfield County, PA
d. Feb 26, 1972, Niagara Falls, New York, USA
& Roy Stark
dp. Niagara Falls, New York, USA

Lawrence Nestor Rougeux
b. Aug 29, 1894, Frenchville, Covington Township, Clearfield County, PA
d. Aug 26, 1951, Clearfield, Clearfield County, PA
& Marie Farran
b. Jan 25, 1895, New Millport, PA
d. Jan 29, 1975, Clearfield, Clearfield County, PA
m. Jun 24, 1924, Clearfield, Clearfield County, PA

Lulu Agnes Rougeux
b. Mar 6, 1896, Frenchville, PA
d. Dec 3, 1983, Niagara Falls, New York, USA
& Edward C. Reilly
d. 1960, Niagara Falls, New York, USA

Malinda Pearl Rougeux
b. Jul 1, 1899, Frenchville, Covington Township, Clearfield County, PA
d. Mar 10, 1978, Niagara Falls, New York
& John Barron
b. Nov 23, 1896
d. Aug 1969, Niagara Falls, New York

Lafayette (Ann?) (Rennet?) Rougeux
b. Jun 30, 1843, Frenchville, Covington Township, Clearfield County, PA
& JOHN PICARD

John Picard

Lafayette (Ann?) (Rennet?) Rougeux
b. Jun 30, 1843, Frenchville, Covington Township, Clearfield County, PA

Nicholas Rougeux
b. May 25, 1772, Rougeux, France
& Jeanne Paille
b. 1774
m. Oct 6, 1797

Jean Rougeux
b. Oct 28, 1799
d. Feb 23, 1879, Broncourt
& Marie Mulson

Nicholas Rougeux
b. Jun 23, 1839, Broncourt

Marie-Therese Rougeux
b. Dec 1, 1830, Broncourt

Francois Rougeux
b. 1802
& Claudette Marcout

220

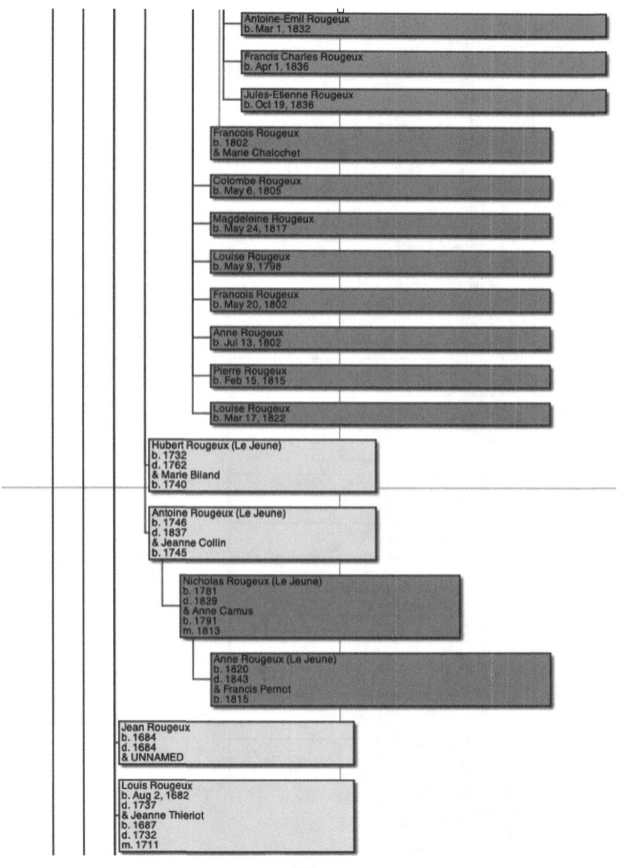

Antoine-Emil Rougeux
b. Mar 1, 1832

Francis Charles Rougeux
b. Apr 1, 1836

Jules-Etienne Rougeux
b. Oct 19, 1836

Francois Rougeux
b. 1802
& Marie Chalochet

Colombe Rougeux
b. May 6, 1805

Magdeleine Rougeux
b. May 24, 1817

Louise Rougeux
b. May 9, 1798

Francois Rougeux
b. May 20, 1802

Anne Rougeux
b. Jul 13, 1802

Pierre Rougeux
b. Feb 15, 1815

Louise Rougeux
b. Mar 17, 1822

Hubert Rougeux (Le Jeune)
b. 1732
d. 1762
& Marie Biland
b. 1740

Antoine Rougeux (Le Jeune)
b. 1746
d. 1837
& Jeanne Collin
b. 1745

Nicholas Rougeux (Le Jeune)
b. 1781
d. 1829
& Anne Camus
b. 1791
m. 1813

Anne Rougeux (Le Jeune)
b. 1820
d. 1843
& Francis Pernot
b. 1815

Jean Rougeux
b. 1684
d. 1684
& UNNAMED

Louis Rougeux
b. Aug 2, 1682
d. 1737
& Jeanne Thieriot
b. 1687
d. 1732
m. 1711

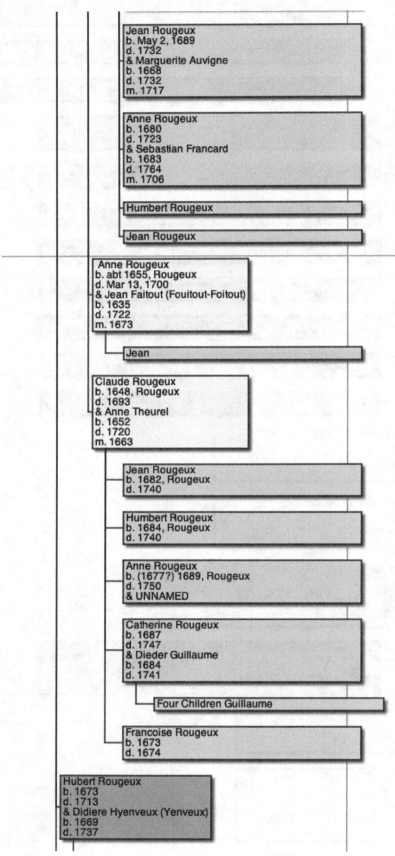

Jean Rougeux
b. May 2, 1689
d. 1732
& Marguerite Auvigne
b. 1668
d. 1732
m. 1717

Anne Rougeux
b. 1680
d. 1723
& Sebastian Francard
b. 1683
d. 1764
m. 1706

Humbert Rougeux

Jean Rougeux

Anne Rougeux
b. abt 1655, Rougeux
d. Mar 13, 1700
& Jean Faitout (Fouitout-Foitout)
b. 1635
d. 1722
m. 1673

Jean

Claude Rougeux
b. 1648, Rougeux
d. 1693
& Anne Theurel
b. 1652
d. 1720
m. 1663

Jean Rougeux
b. 1682, Rougeux
d. 1740

Humbert Rougeux
b. 1684, Rougeux
d. 1740

Anne Rougeux
b. (1677?) 1689, Rougeux
d. 1750
& UNNAMED

Catherine Rougeux
b. 1687
d. 1747
& Dieder Guillaume
b. 1684
d. 1741

Four Children Guillaume

Francoise Rougeux
b. 1673
d. 1674

Hubert Rougeux
b. 1673
d. 1713
& Didiere Hyenveux (Yenveux)
b. 1669
d. 1737

222

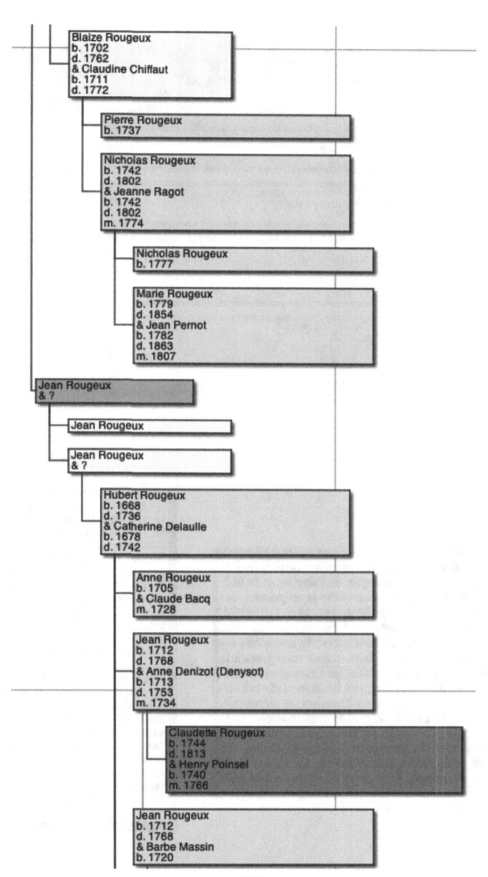

Blaize Rougeux
b. 1702
d. 1762
& Claudine Chiffaut
b. 1711
d. 1772

Pierre Rougeux
b. 1737

Nicholas Rougeux
b. 1742
d. 1802
& Jeanne Ragot
b. 1742
d. 1802
m. 1774

Nicholas Rougeux
b. 1777

Marie Rougeux
b. 1779
d. 1854
& Jean Pernot
b. 1782
d. 1863
m. 1807

Jean Rougeux
& ?

Jean Rougeux

Jean Rougeux
& ?

Hubert Rougeux
b. 1668
d. 1736
& Catherine Delaulle
b. 1678
d. 1742

Anne Rougeux
b. 1705
& Claude Bacq
m. 1728

Jean Rougeux
b. 1712
d. 1768
& Anne Denizot (Denysot)
b. 1713
d. 1753
m. 1734

Claudette Rougeux
b. 1744
d. 1813
& Henry Poinsel
b. 1740
m. 1766

Jean Rougeux
b. 1712
d. 1768
& Barbe Massin
b. 1720

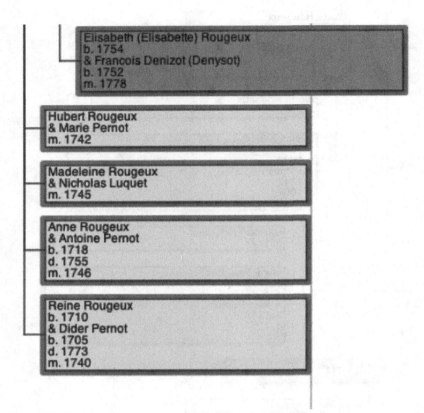

Elisabeth (Elisabette) Rougeux
b. 1754
& Francois Denizot (Denysot)
b. 1752
m. 1778

Hubert Rougeux
& Marie Pernot
m. 1742

Madeleine Rougeux
& Nicholas Luquet
m. 1745

Anne Rougeux
& Antoine Pernot
b. 1718
d. 1755
m. 1746

Reine Rougeux
b. 1710
& Dider Pernot
b. 1705
d. 1773
m. 1740

Rougeux, *Rogiolum, Rubeolus,* faisait partie de la généralité de Champagne, de l'élection et du bailliage de Langres. Au XIIIᵉ siècle la seigneurie appartenait à l'abbaye de Bèze, qui, vers l'an 1255, vendit la dîme de Rougeux à l'abbaye de Beaulieu. Peu après cette seigneurie passa, du moins en partie, aux chevaliers de Malte et leur resta jusqu'à la Révolution. Ils partageaient les dîmes avec les religieux de Beaulieu. Rougeux faisait partie de la commanderie d'Arbigny-sous-Varennes et dépendait, comme Arbigny, de la grande commanderie de la Romagne. Ce village fut plusieurs fois pillé et ravagé durant les guerres de la Franche-Comté. En 1636, cinquante habitants environ furent massacrés par les ennemis, et la partie du village qui est bâtie

ROUGEUX, ROGIOLUM, RUBEOLUS. MADE PART OF THE GENERAL AREA OF CHAMPAGNE MADE OF THE CHOICE AND BAILWICK OF LANGRES. DURING THE 13TH CENTURY THE SEIGNIOR APPROPRIATED THE ABBY OF BIEZ, WHO, NEAR THE YEAR 1255 SOLD THE TITHES OF ROUGEUX TO THE ABBY OF BEAULIEU. AFTER THAT SEIGNEUR DIED THE MONKS PARTNERED WITH THE CHEVALIERS OF MALTA AND THEIR SUCCESSORS, LASTING UNTIL THE REVOLUTION. THEY DIVIDED THE TITHES WITH THE RELIGIOUS OF BEAULIEU. ROUGEUX MADE A PARTNERSHIP WITH THE COMMANDER OF ARBIGNY-UNDER-VARENNES AND DEPENDANT, LIKE ARBIGNY, ON THE GRAND COMMANDER OF THE ROMAGE. THIS VILLAGE (ROUGEUX) WAS PILLAGED AND RAVAGED MANY TIMES DURING THE WAR OF THE FRANCHE-COMPTE. IN 1636,FIFTY INHABITANTS WERE MASSACRED BY THE ENEMIES. AND THE PART OF THE VILLAGE CONSTRUCTED (ON THE SIDE OF THE HILL WAS BURNED) (FROM ANOTHER SOURCE).

OWNED BY AUTHOR

224

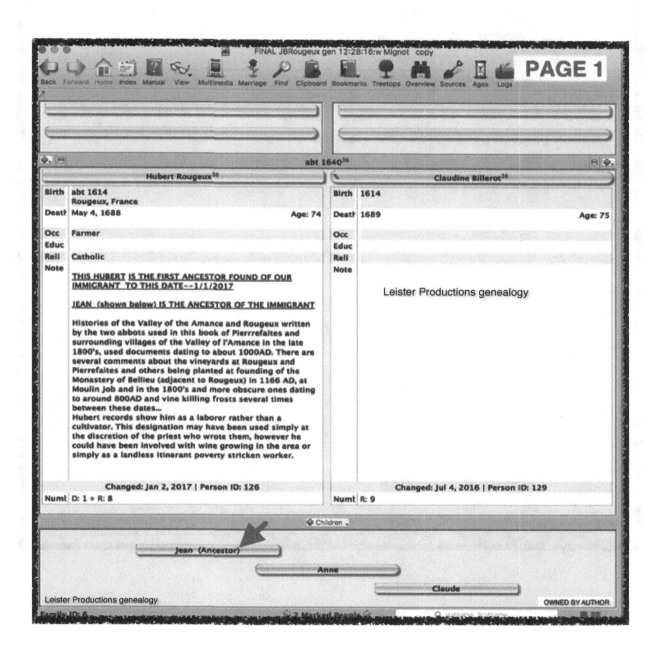

FINAL JBRougeux gen 12:28:16:w Mignot copy

Back Forward Home Index Manual View Multimedia Marriage Find Clipboard Bookmarks Treetops Overview Sources Ages Logs

PAGE 1

abt 1640[36]

Hubert Rougeux[36]

Birth	abt 1614
	Rougeux, France
Death	May 4, 1688 Age: 74
Occ	Farmer
Educ	
Reli	Catholic
Note	

THIS HUBERT IS THE FIRST ANCESTOR FOUND OF OUR IMMIGRANT TO THIS DATE--1/1/2017

JEAN (shown below) IS THE ANCESTOR OF THE IMMIGRANT

Histories of the Valley of the Amance and Rougeux written by the two abbots used in this book of Pierrrefaites and surrounding villages of the Valley of l'Amance in the late 1800's, used documents dating to about 1000AD. There are several comments about the vineyards at Rougeux and Pierrefaites and others being planted at founding of the Monastery of Bellieu (adjacent to Rougeux) in 1166 AD, at Moulin Job and in the 1800's and more obscure ones dating to around 800AD and vine killing frosts several times between these dates...

Hubert records show him as a laborer rather than a cultivator. This designation may have been used simply at the discretion of the priest who wrote them, however he could have been involved with wine growing in the area or simply as a landless itinerant poverty stricken worker.

Changed: Jan 2, 2017 | Person ID: 126

Numt D: 1 • R: 8

Claudine Billerot[36]

Birth	1614
Death	1689 Age: 75
Occ	
Educ	
Reli	
Note	

Leister Productions genealogy

Changed: Jul 4, 2016 | Person ID: 129

Numt R: 9

Children

Jean (Ancestor)

Anne

Claude

Leister Productions genealogy

OWNED BY AUTHOR

Family ID 6   2 Marked People

225

FINAL JBRougeux gen 12:28:16:w Mignot copy

Back   Forward   Home   Index   Manual   View   Multimedia   Marriage   Find   Clipboard   Bookmarks   Treetops   Overview   Sources   Ages   Logs

Hubert Rougeux	Jean Mergez
abt 1614 – May 4, 1688	
Claudine Billerot	Nicole Logerot
1614 – 1689	

abt 1673

Jean (Ancestor) Rougeux[36]		Francoise Mergez[36]	
Birth	abt 1642 Rougeux, France	Birth	1651
Death	abt 1711 Age: 69	Death	1724 Age: 73
Occ	FARMER OR LABORER OR VINEGROWER PROBABLY AT ROUGE[	Occ	
Educ		Educ	
Reli	Catholic	Reli	
Note		Note	

Changed: Jan 2, 2017	Person ID: 31	Changed: Dec 31, 2016	Person ID: 130
Numt D: 2 • R: 4	Numt R: 5

Children

Hubert (Humbert) (Ancestor)	Louis
Jean	Jean

Leister Productions genealogy

Family ID: 5   2 Marked People   remove firstna

Find a person.

Back Forward Home Index Manual View Multimedia Marriage Find Clipboard Bookmarks Treetops Overview Sources Ages Logs

Jean (Ancestor) Rougeux	Ehenne Volquin
abt 1642 – abt 1711	
Francoise Mergez	Marguerite Auvigne
1651 – 1724	

1729[36]

Hubert (Humbert) (Ancestor) Rougeux (Le Jeune)[36]		Francoise Volquin (Vollequin?)[36]	
Birth	Oct 6, 1695	Birth	1708
	Rougeux, France		Rougeux, France
Death	bef 1750 Age: 54	Death	1780 Age: 72
	Rougeux, France		
Occ	Laborer At Rougeux	Occ	
Educ		Educ	
Reli	Catholic	Reli	Catholic
Note		Note	
Changed: Dec 27, 2016	Person ID: 144		Changed: Jul 4, 2016	Person ID: 19	
Numt	D: 5 ● R: 2	Numt	R: 3

Children

(Jean) John Baptiste

Leister Productions genealogy

Family ID: 4   2 Marked People   lastname, firstname

PAGE 4

Back Forward Home Index Manual View Multimedia Marriage Find Clipboard Bookmarks Treetops Overview Sources Ages Logs

| Hubert (Humbert) (Ancestor) Rougeux (Le Jeune) |
| Oct 6, 1695 – bef 1750 |
| Francoise Volquin (Vollequin?) |
| 1708 – 1780 |

| Simon Caulot Caulot |
| Francoise Garnier |

Jan 13, 1756[36]

	(Jean) John Baptiste Rougeux (JB1) (Ancestor)[36]
Birth	Apr 10, 1728 Rougeux, France[36]
Death	1797 Age: 68 Pierrefaites, France
Occ	Farmer (And Possibly Vine Grower At La Gite Farm)
Educ	
Reli	Catholic
Note	(JEAN) JOHN BAPTISTE (JB2) IS THE ANCESTOR OF THE IMMIGRANT Lived and was a laborer at Rougeux at the time of his wedding. Could sign his name. He died sometime after the wedding of JB2, his son, ie., after 11/11/1794 and older than 63 John B. (JBI) was 24 years of age at his wedding He is the grandfather of the emigre. His 2nd son, Jean (1763–1799), was a farmer at La Gite, and had 7 children. We can only speculate when Jean moved there or if it was in the time of JB1. His brother, Barbe may had deceased by that time. Witnesses at the wedding: Hubert Rougeux--unknown brother to JB1. Jean Rougeux, 1st cousin to JB1 and laborer at Montresson, a five minute walk to the Moulin Jobard ruins. This Jean was apparently a resident there. Hobert Maitre --skilled laborer at Rougeux. For some reason, this was a civil rather than a church wedding. There is confusion about his birth date in the records. If he was born in 1728 vs 1732 then he was
	Changed: Dec 31, 2016	Person ID: 5
Numb	D: 14 • R: 1

	Anne Caulot[36]
Birth	1736 Rougeux, France[36]
Death	1802 Age: 66 La Gite Farm, Pierrefaites, France
Occ	
Educ	
Reli	Catholic
Note	could not sign her name She lost the use of her reason.
	Changed: Dec 31, 2016	Person ID: 20
Numb	

⬇ Children ⬇

| Barbe |
| Jean |

| (Jean) John Baptiste(JB2) ⬍ |
| Nicholas |

Leister Productions genealogy

OWNED BY AUTHOR

Family ID: 3   ⚲ 2 Marked People ⚲   Q lastname, firstname

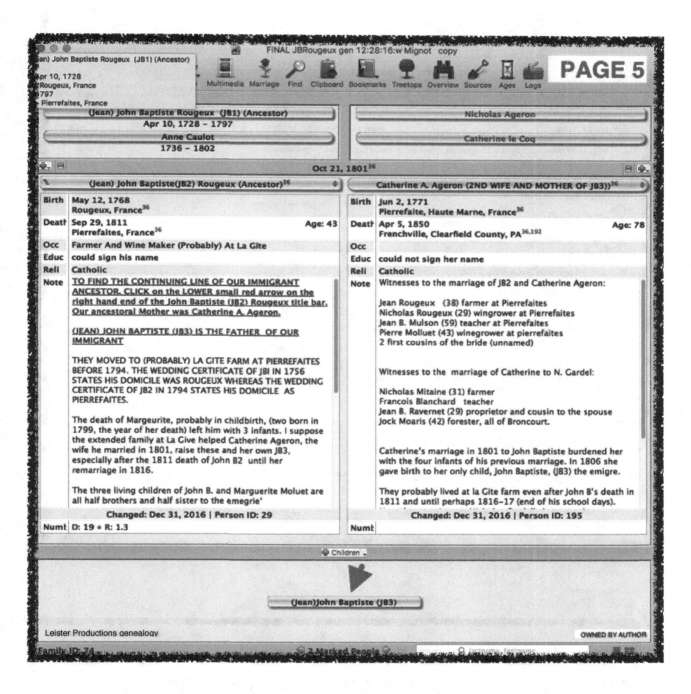

FINAL JBRougeux gen 12:28:16:w Mignot copy

Multimedia Marriage Find Clipboard Bookmarks Treetops Overview Sources Ages Logs

(Jean) John Baptiste Rougeux (JB1) (Ancestor)
Apr 10, 1728
Rougeux, France
1797
Pierrefaites, France

(Jean) John Baptiste Rougeux (JB1) (Ancestor)	Nicholas Ageron
Apr 10, 1728 – 1797	
Anne Caulot	Catherine le Coq
1736 – 1802	

Oct 21, 1801[36]

(Jean) John Baptiste(JB2) Rougeux (Ancestor)[36]	Catherine A. Ageron (2ND WIFE AND MOTHER OF JB3))[36]
Birth May 12, 1768 Rougeux, France[36]	**Birth** Jun 2, 1771 Pierrefaite, Haute Marne, France[36]
Death Sep 29, 1811 Age: 43 Pierrefaites, France[36]	**Death** Apr 5, 1850 Age: 78 Frenchville, Clearfield County, PA[36,192]
Occ Farmer And Wine Maker (Probably) At La Gite	**Occ**
Educ could sign his name	**Educ** could not sign her name
Reli Catholic	**Reli** Catholic
Note TO FIND THE CONTINUING LINE OF OUR IMMIGRANT ANCESTOR, CLICK on the LOWER small red arrow on the right hand end of the John Baptiste (JB2) Rougeux title bar. Our ancestoral Mother was Catherine A. Ageron. (JEAN) JOHN BAPTISTE (JB3) IS THE FATHER OF OUR IMMIGRANT THEY MOVED TO (PROBABLY) LA GITE FARM AT PIERREFAITES BEFORE 1794. THE WEDDING CERTIFICATE OF JB1 IN 1756 STATES HIS DOMICILE WAS ROUGEUX WHEREAS THE WEDDING CERTIFICATE OF JB2 IN 1794 STATES HIS DOMICILE AS PIERREFAITES. The death of Margeurite, probably in childbirth, (two born in 1799, the year of her death) left him with 3 infants. I suppose the extended family at La Give helped Catherine Ageron, the wife he married in 1801, raise these and her own JB3, especially after the 1811 death of John B2 until her remarriage in 1816. The three living children of John B. and Marguerite Moluet are all half brothers and half sister to the emegrie'	**Note** Witnesses to the marriage of JB2 and Catherine Ageron: Jean Rougeux (38) farmer at Pierrefaites Nicholas Rougeux (29) wingrower at Pierrefaites Jean B. Mulson (59) teacher at Pierrefaites Pierre Molluet (43) winegrower at pierrefaites 2 first cousins of the bride (unnamed) Witnesses to the marriage of Catherine to N. Gardel: Nicholas Mitaine (31) farmer Francois Blanchard teacher Jean B. Ravernet (29) proprietor and cousin to the spouse Jock Moaris (42) forester, all of Broncourt. Catherine's marriage in 1801 to John Baptiste burdened her with the four infants of his previous marriage. In 1806 she gave birth to her only child, John Baptiste, (JB3) the emigre. They probably lived at la Gite farm even after John B's death in 1811 and until perhaps 1816-17 (end of his school days).
**Changed: Dec 31, 2016	Person ID: 29**	**Changed: Dec 31, 2016	Person ID: 195**
Numb D: 19 + R: 1.3	**Numb**

Children

(Jean)John Baptiste (JB3)

Leister Productions genealogy   OWNED BY AUTHOR

Family ID: 74   2 Marked People   lastname, firstname

229

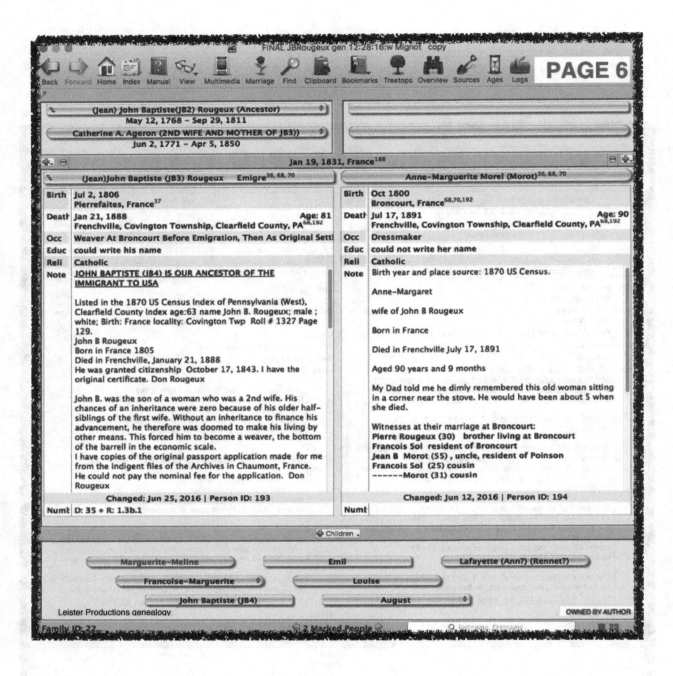

(Jean) John Baptiste(JB2) Rougeux (Ancestor)
May 12, 1768 – Sep 29, 1811
Catherine A. Ageron (2ND WIFE AND MOTHER OF JB3))
Jun 2, 1771 – Apr 5, 1850

Jan 19, 1831, France[188]

(Jean)John Baptiste (JB3) Rougeux   Emigre[36, 68, 70]

Birth	Jul 2, 1806 Pierrefaites, France[37]
Death	Jan 21, 1888 Age: 81 Frenchville, Covington Township, Clearfield County, PA[68,192]
Occ	Weaver At Broncourt Before Emigration, Then As Original Settl
Educ	could write his name
Reli	Catholic
Note	JOHN BAPTISTE (JB4) IS OUR ANCESTOR OF THE IMMIGRANT TO USA Listed in the 1870 US Census Index of Pennsylvania (West), Clearfield County Index age:63 name John B. Rougeux; male ; white; Birth: France locality: Covington Twp Roll # 1327 Page 129. John B Rougeux Born in France 1805 Died in Frenchville, January 21, 1888 He was granted citizenship October 17, 1843. I have the original certificate. Don Rougeux John B. was the son of a woman who was a 2nd wife. His chances of an inheritance were zero because of his older half- siblings of the first wife. Without an inheritance to finance his advancement, he therefore was doomed to make his living by other means. This forced him to become a weaver, the bottom of the barrell in the economic scale. I have copies of the original passport application made for me from the indigent files of the Archives in Chaumont, France. He could not pay the nominal fee for the application. Don Rougeux

Changed: Jun 25, 2016 | Person ID: 193

Numt D: 35 ∗ R: 1.3b.1

Anne-Marguerite Morel (Morot)[36, 68, 70]

Birth	Oct 1800 Broncourt, France[68,70,192]
Death	Jul 17, 1891 Age: 90 Frenchville, Covington Township, Clearfield County, PA[68,192]
Occ	Dressmaker
Educ	could not write her name
Reli	Catholic
Note	Birth year and place source: 1870 US Census. Anne-Margaret wife of John B Rougeux Born in France Died in Frenchville July 17, 1891 Aged 90 years and 9 months My Dad told me he dimly remembered this old woman sitting in a corner near the stove. He would have been about 5 when she died. Witnesses at their marriage at Broncourt: Pierre Rougeux (30) brother living at Broncourt Francois Sol resident of Broncourt Jean B Morot (55) , uncle, resident of Poinson Francois Sol (25) cousin ------Morot (31) cousin

Changed: Jun 12, 2016 | Person ID: 194

Numt

⊕ Children ⌄

Marguerite-Meline   Emil   Lafayette (Ann?) (Rennet?)

Francoise-Marguerite   Louise

John Baptiste (JB4)   August

Leister Productions genealogy   OWNED BY AUTHOR

Family ID: 22   ⊕ 2 Marked People ⊕

X

THE NAMES ON THE FOLLOWING LISTS, BUT NOT THEIR CONNECTIONS TO OUR ANCIENT ANCESTORS, WERE FOUND AT THIS TIME (1/1/17)

Date : 24/11/1705
Husband Name : SANTOT
Husband First Name : pierre
Age of Husband : 27
Husband's Father Name SANTOT :

Husband's Father Name françois :

Husband's Mother HUMBLOT Name :
Husband's Mother First jeanne Name :
Wife Name : ROBELET
Wife First Name : barbe
Wife's Father Last ROBELET Name :
Wife's Father First gilles Name :
Wife's Mother Name : ROUGEUX
Wife's Mother First françoise Name :

Date : 19/01/1706
Husband Name : ROBELET
Husband First Name : etienne
Age of Husband : 22
Husband's Father Name ROBELET :

Husband's Father Name gilles :

Husband's Mother ROUGEUX Name :
Husband's Mother First françoise Name :
Wife Name : FOUREAU
Wife First Name : françoise
Age of Wife : 22
Wife's Father Last FOUREAU Name :
Wife's Father First christophe Name :
Wife's Mother Name : BRISON
Wife's Mother First barbe Name :

Date : 09/11/1676
Husband Name : TROCHON
Husband First Name : charles
Husband's Former CHAMPOROL Spouse Last Name :
Husband's Former marguerite Spouse First Name :
Husband Place of Birth st Michel Polaud

Wife Name : HUMBLOT
Wife First Name : remonde
Wife's Father Last HUMBLOT Name :
Wife's Father First guillaume Name :
Wife's Mother Name : ROUGEUX
Wife's Mother First elisabeth Name :

Date : 26/02/1711
Husband Name : FREROT
Husband First Name : claude
Age of Husband : 21
Husband's Father Name FREROt :

Husband's Father Name pierre :

Husband's Mother FOU__AULT Name :
Husband's Mother First +noël Name :
Wife Name : BARTHELEMY
Wife First Name : claire
Age of Wife : 22
Wife's Father Last BARTHELEMY Name :
Wife's Father First pierre Name :
Wife's Mother Name : ROUGEUX
Wife's Mother First +barbe Name :

Date : 31/01/1719
Husband Name : ROBELET
Husband First Name : gilles
Age of Husband : 27
Husband's Father Name ROBELET :

Husband's Father Name +gilles :

Husband's Mother ROUGEUX Name :
Husband's Mother First françoise Name :
Wife Name : CHEVRESSON
Wife First Name : marguerite
Age of Wife : 34
Wife's Father Last CHEVRESSON Name :
Wife's Mother Name : SILVESTRE
Wife's Mother First marir Name :

Date : 04/02/1681
Husband Name : HUMBLOT
Husband First Name : sébastien
Age of Husband : 24
Husband's Father Name HUMBLOT :

Husband's Father Name guillaume :

Husband's Mother ROUGEUX Name :
Husband's Mother First elisabeth Name :
Wife Name : ROYER
Wife First Name : françoise
Age of Wife : 22
Wife's Father Last ROYER Name :
Wife's Father First nicolas Name :
Wife's Mother Name : GIRAUT
Wife's Mother First marguerite Name :

Date : 07/11/1719
Husband Name : HUMBLOT
Husband First Name : gilles
Age of Husband : 21
Husband's Father Name HUMBLOT :

Husband's Father Name didier :

Husband's Mother VACHEROT Name :
Husband's Mother First marthe Name :
Wife Name : BARTHELEMY
Wife First Name : nicole
Age of Wife : 29
Wife's Father Last BARTHELEMY Name :
Wife's Father First pierre Name :
Wife's Mother Name : ROUGEUX
Wife's Mother First +barbe Name :

Date : 22/02/1724
Husband Name : ROBELET
Husband First Name : antoine
Age of Husband : 28
Husband's Father Name ROBELET :

Husband's Father Name +gilles :

Husband's Mother ROUGEUX Name :
Husband's Mother First françoise Name :
Wife Name : HUMBLOT
Wife First Name : nicole
Age of Wife : 27
Wife's Father Last HUMBLOT Name :
Wife's Father First didier Name :
Wife's Mother Name : VACHEROT
Wife's Mother First marthe Name :

Date : 22/05/1684
Husband Name : ROUGEUX
Husband First Name : claude
Age of Husband : 26
Husband's Father Name ROUGEUX :

Husband's Father Name jacques :

Husband's Mother CHAIGNET Name :
Husband's Mother First etiennette Name :
Wife Name : VEILLEMIN
Wife First Name : françoise
Age of Wife : 23
Wife's Father Last VEILLEMIN Name :
Wife's Father First +françois Name :
Wife's Mother Name : GUILLAUME
Wife's Mother First nicole Name :

Date : 31/01/1690
Husband Name : HUMBLOT
Husband First Name : antoine
Age of Husband : 22
Husband's Father Name : HUMBLOT
Husband's Father Name : guillaume
Husband's Mother Name : ROUGEUX
Husband's Mother First Name : elisabeth
Wife Name : DETOURBET
Wife First Name : simone
Age of Wife : 22
Wife's Father Last Name : DETOURBET
Wife's Father First Name : agnus
Wife's Mother Name : NOIRET
Wife's Mother First Name : simone

Date : 27/11/1691
Husband Name : HUMBLOT
Husband First Name : jean
Age of Husband : 20
Husband's Father Name : HUMBLOT
Husband's Father Name : guillaume
Husband's Mother Name : ROUGEUX
Husband's Mother First Name : elisabeth
Wife Name : TARTARIN
Wife First Name : claire
Wife's Father Last Name : TARTARIN
Wife's Father First Name : gilles
Wife's Mother Name : FLICHE
Wife's Mother First Name : jeanne

Date : 21/11/1677
Husband Name : BARTHELEMY
Husband First Name : pierre
Age of Husband : 20
Husband's Father Name : BARTHELEMY
Husband's Father Name : jacques
Husband's Mother Name : ROYER
Husband's Mother First Name : didiere
Wife Name : ROUGEUX
Wife First Name : barbe
Age of Wife : 21
Wife's Father Last Name : ROUGEUX
Wife's Father First Name : jacques
Wife's Mother Name : CHAIGNET
Wife's Mother First Name : etiennette

Date : 24/01/1695
Husband Name : HUMBLOT
Husband First Name : elyot
Husband's Father Name : HUMBLOT
Husband's Father Name : guillaume
Husband's Mother Name : ROUGEUX
Husband's Mother First Name : elisabeth
Wife Name : GUIDEL
Wife First Name : claire
Age of Wife : 24
Wife's Father Last Name : GUIDEL
Wife's Father First Name : simon
Wife's Mother Name : LANDREY
Wife's Mother First Name : françoise

Date : 10/03/1699
Husband Name : MATHEY
Husband First Name : nicolas
Age of Husband : 22
Husband's Father Name : MATHEY
Husband's Father Name : +vincent
Husband's Mother Name : COUCHU
Husband's Mother First Name : jeanne
Wife Name : BARTHELEMY
Wife First Name : françoise
Age of Wife : 18
Wife's Father Last Name : BARTHELEMY
Wife's Father First Name : pierre
Wife's Mother Name : ROUGEUX
Wife's Mother First Name : barbe

Date : 19/01/1683
Husband Name : ROBELET
Husband First Name : gilles
Age of Husband : 22
Husband's Father Name : ROBELET
Husband's Father Name : +claude
Husband's Mother First Name : +marguerite
Wife Name : ROUGEUX
Wife First Name : françoise
Age of Wife : 22
Wife's Father Last Name : ROUGEUX
Wife's Father First Name : jacques
Wife's Mother Name : CHAIGNET
Wife's Mother First Name : etiennette

Date : 21/02/1702
Husband Name : ROUGEUX
Husband First Name : elyot
Age of Husband : 26
Husband's Father Name : ROUGEUX
Husband's Father Name : +elyot
Husband's Mother Name : SANTOT
Husband's Mother First Name : catherine
Wife Name : FROUSSARD
Wife First Name : françoise
Age of Wife : 27
Wife's Father Last Name : FROUSSARD
Wife's Father First Name : +françois
Wife's Mother Name : PERINET
Wife's Mother First Name : claude
Wife Place of Birth : Chailley

Date : 09/02/1705
Husband Name : BARTHELEMY
Husband First Name : jacques
Age of Husband : 23
Husband's Father Name : BARTHELEMY
Husband's Father Name : pierre
Husband's Mother Name : ROUGEUX
Husband's Mother First Name : barbe
Wife Name : REMOND
Wife First Name : barbe
Wife's Father Last Name : REMOND
Wife's Father First Name : etienne
Wife's Mother Name : DALLET
Wife's Mother First Name : simone

Date : 10/02/1688
Husband Name : HUMBLOT
Husband First Name : françois
Husband's Father Name : HUMBLOT
Husband's Father Name : guillaume
Husband's Mother Name : ROUGEUX
Husband's Mother First Name : elisabeth
Wife Name : GUIDEL
Wife First Name : jeanne
Wife's Father Last Name : GUIDEL
Wife's Father First Name : nicolas
Wife's Mother Name : DEGALISSE
Wife's Mother First Name : simone
Wife Place of Birth : Brenne

Date : 31/01/1741

Husband Last Name : LEBRUN
Husband First Name : gilles
Age of Husband : 22
Father's Name of Spouse : LEBRUN
Husband's Father Name : jean
Husband's Mother Name : ROYER
Husband's Mother First Name : anne
Wife Last Name : MATHEY
Wife First Name : claire
Age of Wife : 20
Wife's Father Last Name : MATHEY
Wife's Father First Name : +simon
Mother's Name of Spouse : ROUGEUX
Wife's Mother First Name : didiere

Date : 31/01/1741

Husband Last Name : MATHEY
Husband First Name : brice
Age of Husband : 24
ather's Name of Spouse : MATHEY
Husband's Father Name : +simon
Husband's Mother Name : ROUGEUX
nd's Mother First Name : +didiere
Wife Last Name : CHAIGNET
Wife First Name : genevieve
Wife's Father Last Name : CHAIGNET
ife's Father First Name : jean
ther's Name of Spouse : GUERIN
Ife's Mother First Name : huguette

Date : 03/02/1728

Husband Name : BARTHELEMY
Husband First Name : pierre
Age of Husband : 27
Husband's Father Name : BARTHELEMY
:
Husband's Father Name : pierre
:
Husband's Mother Name : ROUGEUX
Name :
Husband's Mother First : barbe
Name :
Wife Name : CLERC
Wife First Name : anne
Age of Wife : 32
Wife's Father Last : CLERC
Name :
Wife's Father First : simon
Name :
Wife's Mother Name : MICHELET
Wife's Mother First : barbe
Name :

Date : 08/02/1757

Husband Last Name : LAPOPIN
Husband First Name : pierre
Age of Husband : 29
Wife Last Name : MATHEY
Wife First Name : jeanne
Age of Wife : 26
Wife's Father Last Name : MATHEY
Wife's Father First Name : +simon
Mother's Name of Spouse : ROUGEUX
Wife's Mother First Name : didiere

Date : 01/01/1727

Husband Name : LEHEU
Husband First Name : nicolas
Age of Husband : 28
Husband's Father Name : LEHEU
:
Husband's Father Name : +toussain
:
Husband's Mother : HEARD
Name :
Husband's Mother First : +catherine
Name :
Husband Place of Birth : st Martin
Wife Name : BARTHELEMY
Wife First Name : reine
Wife's Father Last : BARTHELEMY
Name :
Wife's Father First : pierre
Name :
Wife's Mother Name : ROUGEUX
Wife's Mother First : +barbe
Name :

233

1. Agathe ROUGEUX - International Genealogical Index
Gender: F Christening: 12 Oct 1725 Aigremont, Haute-Marne, France

2. Agathe ROUGEUX - International Genealogical Index
Gender: F Christening: 20 Jan 1747 Aigremont, Haute-Marne, France

3. Agathe ROUGEUX - International Genealogical Index
Gender: F Christening: 3 Jan 1753 Aigremont, Haute-Marne, France

4. Agathe ROUGEUX - International Genealogical Index
Gender: F Christening: 11 Jan 1788 Aigremont, Haute-Marne, France

5. Anne ROUGEUX - International Genealogical Index
Gender: F Christening: 8 Jun 1728 Aigremont, Haute-Marne, France

6. Anne ROUGEUX - International Genealogical Index
Gender: F Christening: 13 Jul 1758 Aigremont, Haute-Marne, France

7. Anne ROUGEUX - International Genealogical Index
Gender: F Christening: 26 Sep 1744 Aigremont, Haute-Marne, France

8. Anne ROUGEUX - International Genealogical Index
Gender: F Christening: 1 Apr 1717 Aigremont, Haute-Marne, France

9. Anne ROUGEUX - International Genealogical Index
Gender: F Christening: 9 Nov 1768 Aigremont, Haute-Marne, France

10. Anne ROUGEUX - International Genealogical Index
Gender: F Marriage: 25 Oct 1727 Aigremont, Haute-Marne, France

11. Antoine ROUGEUX - International Genealogical Index
Gender: M Christening: 17 Jun 1723 Aigremont, Haute-Marne, France

12. Antoine ROUGEUX - International Genealogical Index
Gender: M Christening: 17 Nov 1739 Aigremont, Haute-Marne, France

13. Antoine ROUGEUX - International Genealogical Index
Gender: M Christening: 12 Sep 1752 Aigremont, Haute-Marne, France

14. Antoine ROUGEUX - International Genealogical Index
Gender: M Christening: 18 Oct 1746 Aigremont, Haute-Marne, France

16. Antoine ROUGEUX - International Genealogical Index
Gender: M Marriage: 26 Jan 1717 Aigremont, Haute-Marne, France

17. Antoine ROUGEUX - International Genealogical Index
Gender: M Marriage: 22 Nov 1746 Aigremont, Haute-Marne, France

18. Antoine ROUGEUX - International Genealogical Index
Gender: M Marriage: 21 Feb 1751 Aigremont, Haute-Marne, France

19. Benigne ROUGEUX - International Genealogical Index
Gender: F Christening: 22 Jan 1744 Aigremont, Haute-Marne, France

20. Catherine ROUGEUX - International Genealogical Index
Gender: F Christening: 18 May 1719 Aigremont, Haute-Marne, France

21. Cecile ROUGEUX - International Genealogical Index
Gender: F Christening: 24 Nov 1755 Aigremont, Haute-Marne, France

22. Cecille ROUGEUX - International Genealogical Index
Gender: F Christening: 24 Jun 1729 Aigremont, Haute-Marne, France

23. Cecile ROUGEUX - International Genealogical Index
Gender: F Marriage: 14 Nov 1768 Aigremont, Haute-Marne, France

24. Claude ROUGEUX - International Genealogical Index
Gender: M Christening: 4 Dec 1761 Aigremont, Haute-Marne, France

25. Coecile ROUGEUX - International Genealogical Index
Gender: F Christening: 22 Dec 1751 Aigremont, Haute-Marne, France

26. Francois ROUGEUX - International Genealogical Index
Gender: M Christening: 6 Dec 1735 Aigremont, Haute-Marne, France

27. Francois ROUGEUX - International Genealogical Index
Gender: M Christening: 18 Mar 1750 Aigremont, Haute-Marne, France

28. Francois ROUGEUX - International Genealogical Index
Gender: M Christening: 20 Oct 1756 Aigremont, Haute-Marne, France

29. Francois ROUGEUX - International Genealogical Index
Gender: M Christening: 26 Nov 1760 Aigremont, Haute-Marne, France

30. Francois ROUGEUX - International Genealogical Index
Gender: M Christening: 19 Mar 1751 Aigremont, Haute-Marne, France

42. Jean Baptiste ROUGEUX - International Genealogical Index
Gender: M Christening: 10 Feb 1791 Aigremont, Haute-Marne, France

43. Jean Francois ROUGEUX - International Genealogical Index
Gender: M Christening: 14 Sep 1756 Aigremont, Haute-Marne, France

44. Jean ROUGEUX - International Genealogical Index
Gender: M Christening: 29 Dec 1765 Aigremont, Haute-Marne, France

45. Jean Baptiste ROUGEUX - International Genealogical Index
Gender: M Christening: 16 Feb 1771 Aigremont, Haute-Marne, France

46. Jean Baptiste ROUGEUX - International Genealogical Index
Gender: M Christening: 13 Jun 1769 Aigremont, Haute-Marne, France

47. Jean ROUGEUX - International Genealogical Index
Gender: M Marriage: 25 Nov 1698 Aigremont, Haute-Marne, France

48. Louis ROUGEUX - International Genealogical Index
Gender: M Christening: 3 Mar 1754 Aigremont, Haute-Marne, France

49. Louie ROUGEUX - International Genealogical Index
Gender: M Christening: 8 Sep 1688 Aigremont, Haute-Marne, France

50. Louis Nicolas ROUGEUX - International Genealogical Index
Gender: M Christening: 2 Nov 1786 Aigremont, Haute-Marne, France

51. Margueritte ROUGEUX - International Genealogical Index
Gender: F Christening: 16 Feb 1795 Aigremont, Haute-Marne, France

60. Michel ROUGEUX - International Genealogical Index
Gender: M Christening: 15 Mar 1716 Aigremont, Haute-Marne, France

61. Nicolas ROUGEUX - International Genealogical Index
Gender: M Christening: 19 Feb 1763 Aigremont, Haute-Marne, France

62. Nicolas ROUGEUX - International Genealogical Index
Gender: M Christening: 21 Aug 1705 Aigremont, Haute-Marne, France

63. Nicolas ROUGEUX - International Genealogical Index
Gender: M Christening: 29 Jul 1725 Aigremont, Haute-Marne, France

64. Nicolas ROUGEUX - International Genealogical Index
Gender: M Christening: 2 Oct 1703 Aigremont, Haute-Marne, France

66. Philippe ROUGEUX - International Genealogical Index
Gender: M Christening: 10 May 1716 Aigremont, Haute-Marne, France

67. Philippe ROUGEUX - International Genealogical Index
Gender: M Christening: 17 May 1724 Aigremont, Haute-Marne, France

68. Pierre ROUGEUX - International Genealogical Index
Gender: M Christening: 21 Feb 1718 Aigremont, Haute-Marne, France

69. Pierre ROUGEUX - International Genealogical Index
Gender: M Christening: 6 Sep 1759 Aigremont, Haute-Marne, France

70. Pierre ROUGEUX - International Genealogical Index
Gender: M Christening: 12 Mar 1789 Aigremont, Haute-Marne, France

71. Pierre ROUGEUX - International Genealogical Index
Gender: M Marriage: 6 Feb 1786 Aigremont, Haute-Marne, France

72. Simon ROUGEUX - International Genealogical Index
Gender: M Christening: 15 Jul 1760 Aigremont, Haute-Marne, France

73. Therese ROUGEUX - International Genealogical Index
Gender: F Christening: 8 May 1754 Aigremont, Haute-Marne, France

74. Therese ROUGEUX - International Genealogical Index
Gender: F Christening: 17 Jan 1719 Aigremont, Haute-Marne, France

75. Therese ROUGEUX - International Genealogical Index
Gender: F Christening: 28 Sep 1721 Aigremont, Haute-Marne, France

76. Therese ROUGEUX - International Genealogical Index
Gender: F Marriage: 12 Jan 1740 Aigremont, Haute-Marne, France

AIGREMONT IS 22 MILES NORTH OF ROUGEUX.
ST GERMINE-EN-LAVE IN A SECTION OF PARIS

ROUGEUX, commune of the section of Fays-Billot, at 56 kilometers *(about 33 miles east)* from Chaumont, hanging on the edge of a mountian of 354 meters *(1161 feet)* of altitude and at the base of this runs a stream, an affluent to the right bank of the river Amance.

ROUGEUX, commune du canton de Fays-Billot, à 56 kilomètres de Chaumont, sur le penchant d'une montagne qui a 354 mètres d'altitude et au pied de laquelle coule un ruisseau, affluent de l'Amance, rive droite. Pop. 435 hab. Le territoire, qui est traversé par la route impériale n° 19, a 641 hectares d'étendue. On y exploite des carrières de grès pour la construction. Ecart : la ferme du *Haut-Chemin*. Il y a dans cette commune, qui ne possède pas de bois, un bureau de bienfaisance. L'église, dédiée à la Vierge en son assomption, a un desservant. — En 1789, cette église, du doyenné de Pierrefaite dans l'évêché de Langres, était succursale de celle de Hortes. Pour le temporel, les habitants, qui étaient champenois, dépendaient de l'élection et du bailliage de Langres. La seigneurie appartenait à l'ordre de Malte et dépendait de la Romagne. Le seigneur commandeur était en même temps décimateur; mais il partageait les dîmes avec l'abbaye de Beaulieu. Au XIIIe siècle, cette seigneurie appartenait encore à l'abbaye de Bèze, comme le prouve une transaction de 1269, entre les moines et le maieur. C'est probablement peu de temps après qu'elle a été cédée aux chevaliers. Il existait à Rougeux une forteresse qui fut démantelée en 1611, lorsque les seigneurs du pays de Langres, à la tête des milices bourgeoises, la reprirent sur les Lorrains qui s'en étaient emparés dans leurs excursions sur le territoire français.

Population 435 inhabitants. The territory, which is travassed by the imperial route N 19 degrees, has 642 hectares *(1561 acres)* in area. There are exploited sandstone mines used for construction. At a distance: the farm of Haute-Chemin. There are in this commune, that does not possess any woodland, an organizaton of charity. *(Does he mean the lack of woodlands, and its necessity for supplying fuel, create the need for charity?)* The church, dedicated th the Assumption of the Blessed Virgin Mary, has a person who dispenses benefices. — In 1789, this church, of the parish of Pierrefaite, under the Bishop of Langres, was assisted by the church of Hortes. For the spiritual, the inhabitants, who were undecided *(perhaps about the incursions of the Lutherians)* depended upon the election and the bailwick of Langres. The seigneur appointed the Order of Malta as a dependant of the Romagne. The seigneur commander was, at the same time, decimater; *(translation does not make sense however an alternative has not been found even in my 1800 edition.) (dispenser would be more apropriate)* but he divides the tithes with the Abby of Beaulieu. During the 13th century this same seigneur *(position, not individual)* once again appropriated the Abby of Beze, using as proof of his right the transaction of 1269 between the monks and the mayor. Its probable during later times that it was ceeded to the chavaliers *(Order of Malta).*

There existed at Rougeux a fortress, dismantled in 1644 when the seigneurs of the province of Langres were the head of the militia of the bourgoises, they repented *(does this mean surrendered?)* over the Lorrians who were seizing power during their excursions on the territory of the French.

chart #3

MARIAGE de JEAN-BAPTISTE ROUGEUX et CATHERINE AGERON

(26 octobre 1801)

" Le 4 brumaire de l'an 10 de la République Française . Acte de mariage de Jean-Baptiste ROUGEUX , veuf de la défunte Marguerite Molluet sa 1ère épouse , âgé de 33 ans et 5 mois , né à Rougeux , département de la Haute-Marne , le 12 mai 1768 , profession de vigneron , demeurant à Pierrefaites , département de la Haute-Marne , fils du défunt Jean Rougeux demeurant à Pierrefaites , département de la Haute-Marne et de Anne Collot demeurant à Pierrefaites , département de la Haute-Marne , ayant perdu l' usage de la raison ; et Catherine AGERON âgée de 30 ans et 5 mois née à Pierrefaites , département de la Haute-Marne , le 2 juin 1771 , demeurant Pierrefaites , département de la Haute-Marne , fille de Nicolas Ageron demeurant à Pierrefaites , département de la Haute-Marne , et de la défunte Catherine le Coq demeurant à Pierrefaites , département de la Haute-Marne , les publications et les actes préliminaires sont extraits des registres des publica--tions de mariage faits à leur domicile en présence des père et mère vivant , les affiches et publications ayant été faites au terme de la loi , le tout en forme ; de tous ces actes , il a été donné lecture par moi , officier public , au terme de la loi , les 2 époux présents ont déclarés se prendre en mariage , l'un Catherine AGERON pour son épouse ; l'autre Jean-Baptiste ROUGEUX pour son époux ; en présence de Jean Rougeux demeurant à Pierrefaites , département de la Haute-Marne âgé de 38 ans profession de cultivateur , de Nicolas Rougeux demeurant à Pierrefaites , département de la Haute-Marne , profession de vigneron , âgé de 29 ans , de Jean Baptiste Mulson demeurant à Pierrefaites , département de la Haute-Marne , âgé de 59 ans profession d'instituteur , et de Pierre Mollaet demeurant à Pierrefaites , département de la Haute-Marne , âgé de 43 ans profes--sion de vigneron ; les 2 premiers témoins frères du futur époux , les 2 autres cousins-germains de la future épouse ; après quoi moi Gabriel Peinget adjoint au maire de la commune de Pierrefaites , faisant fonction d'officier public de l'état civil , ai prononcé qu'au nom de la loi les 2 époux sont unis par le mariage . Les époux et témoins ont signés avec moi , exceptées Anne Collot qui a déclaré ne savoir signer et Catherine Ageron qui a déclaré ne savoir signer . Approuvé et fait à la maison commune le jour , mois et ...." ← five words illegible

Signatures :   J.B. ROUGEUX   AGERON   MULSON

    J. ROUGEUX   N. ROUGEUX   P. MOLUET

    G. PEINGET
        (adjoint)

Sometime between 1756 and 1794, JB1 (John Baptiste I, our immigrants) relocated his family from Rougeux to the large and imposing 'La Gite' farm near Pierrefaite. (The location of his domicile in Rougeux is not known) He probably relocated there as a live-in laborer because there are no documentation nor obvious possibility of being able to accumulate, and certainly not inherit, the substantial sum needed to purchase the very large home and out buildings on that farm, let alone its associated prime farmland or the adjacent farm of 'La Vendure'. This opportunity came as a result of the high mortality resulting form the plagues sweeping the country.

The nearby 'Moulin Jobard' farm with its large home and extensive farmland where descendants and cousins of our line also eventually lived also falls into this line of probability.

These large and elaborate, for the period, homes and farms are typical of the manorial residences of the seigneuries and local rulers of those ancient times 300 plus years ago.

The Revolution and decapitation of the King led to upheaval of the rights of the gentry and distribution of land the opportunity to accumulate property apparently led to their ability to acquire ownership of these three prime farms.

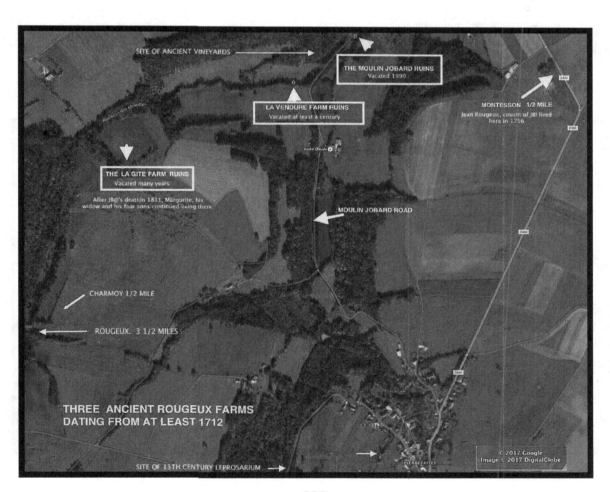

RUINS OF LA GITE

© 2017 Google

Image © 2017 DigitalGlobe

THOMAS ROUGEUX

FRANÇOIS JOFFRAIN

LA GITE, 2016

LA GITE 2016   THOMAS ROUGEUX

THOMAS ROUGEUX

239

LA GITE 2016

THOMAS ROUGEUX

LA GITE

THOMAS ROUGEUX

LA GITE   THOMAS ROUGEUX

241

RUINS OF MOULIN JOBARD FARM 2016

(CURRENTLY BEING REHABILITED 2017)

Old Rougeux home on Moulin Jobard Road.

Owned by author~

Radiused stone soffets indicate upper class.

300 year old house abandoned in 1990 after approximately
200 years of occupancy by Rougeux's

Being rehabilated in 2017 by new owners.

Moulin Jobard 2016.

ROUGEUX HOUSE ON MOULIN JORBARD

THOMAS ROUGEUX

THREE FARMS WERE OWNED BY ROUGEUX'S
SINCE AT LEAST 1764 (ACCORDING TO AVAILABLE
DOCUMENTS). MOULIN JOBARD (THIS ONE) WAS
OCCUPIED BY ROUGEUX'S UNTIL 1990.

APPROXIMATELY 3 ACRES OF GRAPES WERE
GROWN ON THESE SLOPES BY ROUGEUX'S.
THE OTHER TWO FARMS WERE FURTHER
UP MOULIN JOBARD ROAD.

THOMAS ROUGEUX

LOOKING NORTH ON MOULIN JOBARD ROAD FROM THE HOUSE

TOM ROUGEUX 2016

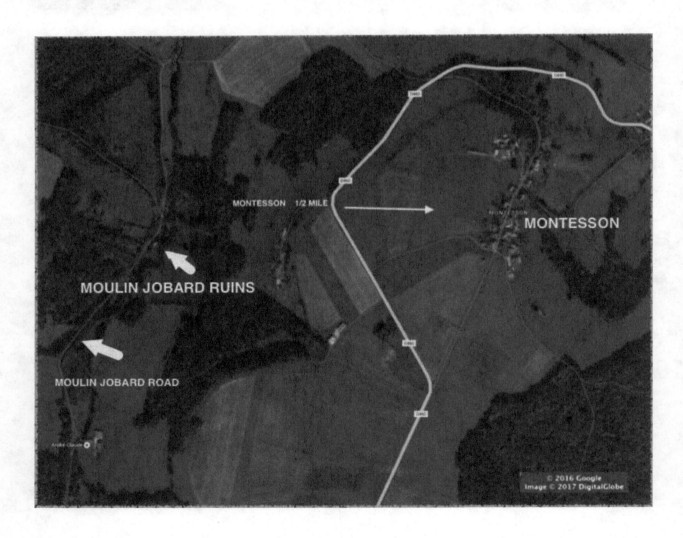

MONTESSON 1/2 MILE

MONTESSON

MOULIN JOBARD RUINS

MOULIN JOBARD ROAD

© 2016 Google
Image © 2017 DigitalGlobe

THE NAME OF THE ROUGEUX WHO FARMED AT LA VENDURE IS UNKNOWN HOWEVER IT IS PROBABLE ONE OF THE SONS OF JB1 WAS THE OCCUPANT AT THAT TIME.

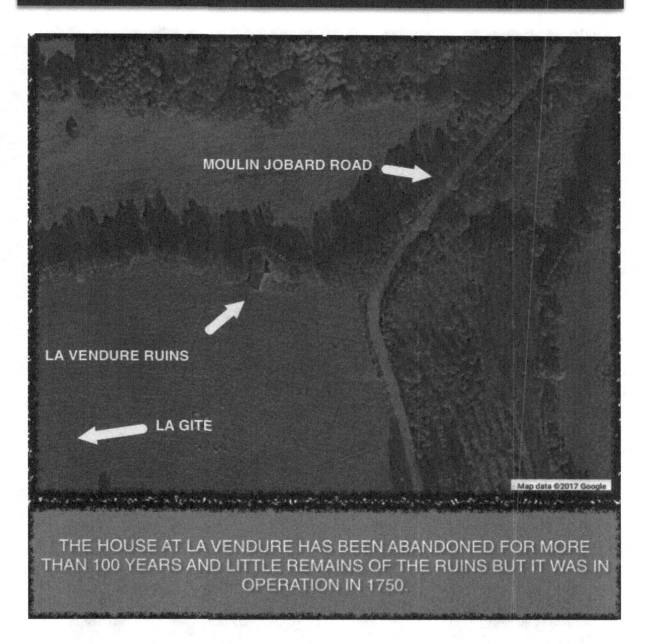

MOULIN JOBARD ROAD

LA VENDURE RUINS

LA GITE

Map data ©2017 Google

THE HOUSE AT LA VENDURE HAS BEEN ABANDONED FOR MORE THAN 100 YEARS AND LITTLE REMAINS OF THE RUINS BUT IT WAS IN OPERATION IN 1750.

1977 View of Rougeux
OWNED BY AUTHOR

Rougeux 1977
OWNED BY AUTHOR

ROUGEUX. 2016.   THOMAS ROUGEUX

ROUGEUX   1979

OWNED BY AUTHOR

Rougeux 1977

ROUGEUX

OWNED BY AUTHOR

ALTAR INSIDE THE CHURCH AT ROUGEUX

COURTESY OF RON MILLER. 2016

THOMAS ROUGEUX

ROUGEUX 2016

MRS MARCHAEL'S HOME 1980

THOMAS ROUGEUX

SS troopers billeted here during WWII

MME Marechal's house

MY RENTAL

SHIRLEY IN CAR

4/20/84

OWNED BY AUTHOR

Rougeux

250

THOMAS ROUGEUX

ROUGEUX 2016

1914-1918

45
D 313
ROUGEUX

OWNED BY AUTHOR

4/87

251

Shirely & Mrs Marechal

The Marechal home

Mrs Marechal

Rougeux 1979

PORCH ROOF HAS BEEN
CHANGED

THOMAS ROUGEUX   ROUGEUX 2016

Madam Marechals house   hotel

church

1987   20 4 87

OWNED BY AUTHOR

253

Rougeux 1977

THOMAS ROUGEUX

ROUGEUX 2016

Shirley   1979

front door of mayor's house   1977

Cemetary 2016

THOMAS ROUGEUX

THOMAS ROUGEUX   ROUGEUX 2016

256

ROUGEUX 2016

OMAS ROUGE

Mayors house nd barn   1977

OWNED BY AUTHOR

257

Winter fuel   Main St Rouguex   1977

Sign at Dijon train station commerating millions of Frenchmen who passed through this station on their way to Hitler's death camps. It doesn't mention at least half that number were Jews collected by Frenchmen working for the Germans.

Dijon is only 40 miles south of Rougeux.

PASSANT...

DE 1940 A 1944 POUR AVOIR VOULU DEFENDRE LEUR LIBERTE ET LA TIENNE AUSSI DES MILLIERS DE FRANCAISES ET DE FRANCAIS SORTIS DE LA PRISON DE DIJON FURENT EMBARQUES SUR LES QUAIS DE CETTE GARE A DESTINATION DES CAMPS DE LA MORT HITLERIENS PLUS DE LA MOITIE NE SONT JAMAIS REVENUS

SOUVIENS TOI!

Dear Friends

I hope your sense of appreciation, as has mine, been greatly deepened for the old ones who led the way from generation to generation and of the suffering they endured. It is obvious from the impressive churches, laboriously and voluntarily constructed in every small village many times in sight of each other, that endlessly experienced adversity in countless centuries failed to quench their faith in God. Their blood and tears were fertilizer for the faith of future generations.

It has been a blessing to me and I have immensely enjoyed doing it.

I am deeply grateful to those individuals who have graciously agreed to permit me to use their material. Google's wonderful 'Google Earth' permitted me unlimited use of a large number of the photos in the book. But of course, without the inestimable help of Francois Joffrain none of the basic information would have been available and darkness would continue to surround knowledge of our ancient homeland in this tiny, rustic corner of France.

Bob Tilton, Tom Rougeux, Ron Miller and others also granted immediate use of their work. "Reunion", Leister Productions' great genealogy software was used in the displays in this book.

Searching for and finding about 1500 widely scattered relatives in this country would not have been possible without the tireless efforts of Joanne Rougeux Nadovich and Delores Rougeux Sykes.

Don Rougeux
Louisville, KY
12/15/17

Printed in the United States
By Bookmasters